CONTENTS

RED HOT CHILI PEPPERS

By the Way

The Biography

Dave Thompson

This edition first published in 2004 by
Virgin Books Ltd
Thames Wharf Studios
Rainville Road
London
W6 9HA

First published in Great Britain in 1993 by Virgin Publishing Ltd

A catalogue record for this book is available from the British Library.

ISBN 0 7535 0970 9

Typeset by TW Typesetting, Plymouth, Devon
Printed and bound in Great Britain by Bookmarque Ltd

PREFACE

Much has changed in the decade since this book was first published, back in 1993. Bands that, back then, seemed more than ready for the long haul have faded and died; artists that we predicted would be with us forever instead lie forgotten; and trends that then seemed life-changing have been revealed as less than ephemeral. Some things, however, have not changed, including the reasons that I wrote this book in the first place.

In 1993, it is true, the Red Hot Chili Peppers were still regarded as relative newcomers to the higher plateaux of commercial fame; less than four years had passed since their first hit album, and memories of the years before that, during which the group was just one among so many other underground alternative bands, were still fresh. In 2003, the Red Hot Chili Peppers are rightly ranked among the biggest and best-loved groups on the planet, with a fan base for whom those early days of history are simply so much ancient history.

But the friendships that bound the band together in the first place remain as vital today as they ever were in the early days, and it is that friendship that lies at the heart of this book, as much today as it did ten years ago; as much, in fact, as it did twenty years ago, when Anthony Kiedis and Michael 'Flea' Balzary first embarked upon the musical journey that has been the Red Hot Chili Peppers' career to date.

As for the book itself: this edition thoroughly revises the original 1993 publication, slicing away (hopefully) the naive omissions and glaring errors that marked the earlier version, clarifying a number of vagaries and incorporating a wealth of new information – including several passages whose absence from the original edition now strikes me as unforgivable.

In addition, the story of the band has been completely updated, to follow the Red Hot Chili Peppers' career from the release (coincidentally, but somehow appropriately) of their first 'best of' compilation, *What Hits!*, to that of their latest, November 2003's *Greatest Hits*. In-between times, the convolutions of both the band's line-up and their commercial fortunes spread out across ten additional years of history and, while the physical act of updating this book has been nothing but a pleasure, tracing that journey across the band's entire career was not, necessarily, a wholly joyful task.

More than any other band of their generation, the Red Hot Chili Peppers have been assailed by so much tragedy, confusion, disruption and disturbance that, were one to publish their story as a work of fiction, it would barely seem believable – which sounds like a dreadful cliché, but is nonetheless true for all of that.

The fact that these catastrophes have only made the group stronger sounds awfully glib as well, but it, too, is undeniable; as Anthony Kiedis himself once remarked, 'you never get sick for no reason', and the Red Hot Chili Peppers' greatest strength may well be their ability to seek out those reasons, and do something about them.

In the life of a band, longevity is very much the most difficult aspiration of them all and, though it has certainly not been easy, the Red Hot Chili Peppers have achieved that; an accomplishment which, in turn, means that even if they were to pack it all in tomorrow, still they would have reached a chronological milestone that precious few other groups, of their generation or any other, have even glimpsed.

And, to think, it all began as a joke.

ACKNOWLEDGEMENTS

Thanks to my agent, Sherrill Chidiac, and Stuart Slater at Virgin Books, for bringing this revised and updated edition to fruition; photographer Alison Braun and self-proclaimed 'scenester' Baptist Thor, whose personal recollections of Los Angeles punk brought much of the flavour to the early chapters of this book; Jack Irons, Alain Johannes and Natasha Schneider, for their insights into the Peppers' formative years; Robert Cherry, Joe Banks and Jason Pettigrew, editors at *Alternative Press* magazine, whose journalistic noses unearthed information I might otherwise have missed; Amy Hanson, for fearless fact-checking; Lisa Ridley, for sharing her Lollapalooza with me; Jo-Ann Greene, for her interview with Martin Atkins; Kris Ferraro, for patience far beyond the call of duty; and to everybody at Virgin Books.

Thanks, also, to everyone who, for reasons of their own, spoke only on condition of anonymity, in 1993 and across the decade since then. Their recollections, and the factual wrongs that they righted, made all the difference. And, finally, to: Anchorite Man, Andrew & Esther, Bateerz and family, Blind Pew, Kevin Coral, Barb East, Ella, Gaye & Tim, the Gremlins who live in the furnace, K-Mart (not the store), Jane & Nathan & Jessica, Geoff Monmouth, Nutkin, the Schecklers Three, Snarleyyowl the Cat Fiend, Sprocket, all the Thompsons and Neville Viking. And finally, to Tony Secunda and Mark 'Rooster' Williams, both of whom brought so much to the first edition of this book, a decade ago.

I would also like to acknowledge the many magazines, articles and websites that I consulted during my research. These include the All Music Guide (allmusic.com), *Alternative Press*, *BAM*, *Billboard*, *Goldmine*, *Guitar Player*, *Guitar World*, *Hits*, *Ice*, *Interview*, *Kerrang!*, the *Los Angeles Times*, *Melody Maker*, *Mojo*, *Musician*, *Musicmakers*, the *New Musical Express*, *Paper*, *People*, *Powerline*, *Pulse*, *Q*, *Record Collector*, Redhotchilipeppers.com, *Rip*, Rock'sBackPages.com, *Rolling Stone*, *Select*, *Spin*, *Variety* and *Vibe*.

Of especial value were the following articles: 'The Red Hot Chili Peppers Will Pose Nude in Public . . .' by Danny Weizmann (*LA Weekly*, 1984); 'What's Red Hot and Chili?' by Glenn O'Brien (*Spin*, 1984); 'Big Brother Meets Twisted Sister' by David Zueehino (*Rolling Stone*, November 1985); 'Fee-Fi-Fo-Funk!' by Jason Pettigrew

(*Alternative Press*, November 1989); 'Physical Graffiti' by Dean Kuipers (*Spin*, February 1990); 'The Red Hot Chili Peppers' by Simon Reynolds (*Observer*, 1991); 'The Red Hot Chili Peppers' by David Fricke (*Rolling Stone*, 25 June 1992); 'Whole Lotta Love' by Anthony Kiedis (*Details for Men*, July 1992); 'Stand by Me (And My Friends)' by Steve Roeser (*Goldmine*, 7 August 1992); 'New Kid in the Sock' by Alan DiPerna (*Guitar World*, November 1992); 'The Censorship Thing' by Gil Griffin (*Billboard*, 28 November 1992); 'Red Hot Chili Peppers' by Eric Gladstone (*Alternative Press*, 1997); 'Red Hot Chili Peppers' by David Fricke (*Rolling Stone*, 7 April 1999); 'Interview with John Frusciante' by Ian Fortnam (*Kerrang!*, March 2001); 'Red Hot & New' by David Wild (*Rolling Stone*, 8 July 2002).

1. YOU NEVER HAD TO LISTEN TO JOE WALSH

Fairfax was the original rock'n'roll high school, coming to terms with its future before it even knew what that future held. Jerry Leiber, a wisecracking Jewish kid fresh in from New York City, armed with the walk and the talk that would one day give the world 'Hound Dog' and Elvis and 'Yakety Yak', called it his for six years.

Then came Phil Spector, another New Yorker, another Jew, another swaggering rocker before rock began to roll. But only in his heart. Insanely shy, spotty and slouching, Spector grasped the American dream by the horns and was still stuffing cotton in the gore holes. Like Leiber, Spector grew up on black R&B; unlike Leiber, he had neither the time nor the courage to walk the corridors of self-confident affluence that were his generation's postwar birthright. Not until he was seventeen did he flower, overcoming a personal past that was simply too painful to contemplate further. In 1957 he won the school talent contest; by 1958 he was on nationwide TV.

There was Shel Talmy, broad, brash and, in his own way, even crazier than Phil. Like Spector, he would one day revolutionise the way people made music. For now, he was content to revolutionise the way they listened to it, interrupting his studies and everybody else's to savagely denounce whatever the early morning DJ had offended his ears with that day.

Every so often the teenage Herb Alpert would rocket through the corridor, scurrying on to another class, not yet dreaming of the day when his Tijuana Brass Band would compete with Spector at the top of the charts. Jan Berry and Dean Torrance who, in two or three years, would lose their surnames and start surfing instead, were a couple of grades further down.

Fairfax nurtured them all, edged them on through their schoolwork, but never pulled the plugs on ambition. In 1958, the Third Year of Our Lord Elvis, Fairfax alumni spent nine weeks at the top of the American charts. By the mid-1960s, it was the most successful pop music academy in the country.

But things have changed since the days when the owlish Spector hauled his books down Melrose Avenue and trundled unwillingly towards the school gates, or the teenage Jan and Dean would dream of taking Dead Man's Curve. Fairfax has changed, Hollywood has changed and, most of all, Los Angeles has changed.

For motorists exiting the Hollywood Freeway at night, Los Angeles really is the city of tiny lights that Frank Zappa immortalised in song. It stretches forever, much further than you can see by day, when the smog settles comfortably back into place and, sometimes, you're lucky if you can make out the next block. The heat of the day still hangs heavy over West Hollywood and, if the passing traffic stops long enough, you can almost feel yourself vibrating with the air conditioners that hum in every apartment. But the streets are alive anyway, and you can't help thinking, if New York is the city that never sleeps, then Hollywood doesn't even doze.

Connect with any one of the major junctions that tear frenziedly up towards Beverly Hills, and you're not in a car any longer, driving through one of the largest metropolises in the world. Now you're in a twisted, tortured Disneyland, where everything's for sale and what isn't is free. Queues form for whatever reason they can: to get into clubs or get over the road, or just for the sake of forming, as though only by bunching together is humankind safe from itself.

Slow down and, if the cops don't grab you for kerb crawling, every other face looks familiar. In Hollywood, Hollywood is the biggest employer in town and if someone wasn't an extra in a movie last week, chances are they'll be one tomorrow. In-between times, they're just marking time, waiting tables or helping out in a store, selling art or selling their bodies, anything to keep heart and soul together while they await their chance to rewrite history. In Hollywood, even dreams form orderly queues.

Thirty years ago, though, it was very different. A small town on the fringes of a great big city, Tinseltown, trash town, trashcan, was a bored suburban nightmare still coming down from its last fix of the sixties. Along Hollywood Boulevard, the stars' stars twinkled amid the polystyrene and paper, springing to life only when the busloads of tourists poured out to lay their hands on Marilyn, Bela or Clark. A few drag queens swam past, this one Betty Grable, that one Rita Hayworth. The tourists whirled and clicked their Instamatics, one more freak for the folks back home, then they'd board the bus again, happily gibbering as Boredom City sped by and the first movie star mansions roared into view.

A few blocks further south, resembling nothing so much as a downtrodden department store, Fairfax High stretched upwards from a predominantly Jewish, lower-middle-class neighbourhood, pockmarked by the decaying relics of an Old World culture: delicatessens and tailors, a sheet-metal shop, and a few mouldering thrift stores where you could buy a complete new wardrobe for less than $10 and the school kids played truant behind stacks of worn books. Passing peace-and-lovers, drifting in from the mortgages and families down the block, stopped by to rummage through clothes and flick idly through the worn-out record racks. Flips, the lonely herald of what would, one day, become an empire, stood like an outpost of slowly shifting fashions.

Every so often, a wooden facade newer than the rest remembered the earthquake that rattled through town on 9 February 1971, killing 65 people in the San Fernando Valley and all but levelling the old art deco Fairfax High School. For the young and bored and Hollywood bred, that was the best excitement to happen in years and the streets were screaming their outrage. You could hear it outside Vinyl Fetish, where collectors and cornballs gathered to swap stories about coloured wax and factory-sealed promos. You could hear it outside the handful of clubs that still kept their doors open: the Palace, the Roxy and the Troubadour. And you could hear it outside the discos, ricocheting off the walls as Fleetwood Mac and Peter Frampton, Linda Ronstadt and the Eagles sang their turgid mantras to Cally-for-nye-aye, and it didn't matter how fucked the rest of the world was. In the City of Angels, everything's swell. The streets were screaming, but no one over twenty-one was listening. Hollywood might never have been two cities. But it had always been two cultures.

Get off the Boulevards and the view grew even grimmer. Every foothill, every flat, was pocked with blistered paint and weather-worn wood, a washed-out, colour-flecked sprawl of cheapo apartments, parking-lot art for a city that would never have enough roads. Fringed by choking palm trees, a shanty town in paradise, Hollywood thought it could sustain itself on its image alone. Now, even the letters on the hill that spelled out its hallowed name were cracking. One day, the joke went, someone would breeze into town in search of immortality and find it beneath a giant, shattered 'O'. The one that rolled down the hill and spattered their brains on the pavement.

Then the earth moved again. Punk rock came to Los Angeles in late 1976. It moved in slowly, cautiously, as though unsure of how it would be received. The city itself knew damned well it was dying but, to the world outside, it was still hunky-dory. The very idea of punk taking root in utopia was absurd, as absurd as Ozzy Osbourne playing Buckingham Palace, or the President blowing sax on TV.

But Rodney Bingenheimer saw the gap, the Ramones started to fill it and, by the time the Damned hit town in May 1977, all they needed to do was stamp the earth back down. With every fresh footfall, the ground shook some more. As the junk culture upon which LA had fed for so long began extending its tentacles into the quietest neighbourhoods, so a junk society was created to accommodate it. Asked why West Hollywood has so many fast-food joints, a street artist simply replied, 'You are what you eat.' And why was Hollywood suddenly bursting at the seams with disaffected youth? 'You don't always like what you become.'

The synthesis, not only within the narrow confines of Fairfax High School, but everywhere kids gathered, for fair means or foul, was music. It was always music. Fads had always come and gone and a straight line drawn from the class of '53 to that of '77 was going to carve through a hell of a lot of people.

But there was something markedly different and decidedly nasty about this new one. Imported, like so much other trash, from Britain, punk rock took even the slapdash values of previous generations and ripped them all to shreds. It bred a new, swaggering dissidence and encouraged the sense of bitter arrogance that forever smouldered just beneath the laid-back facade of the California lifestyle. It took a generation whose demented diffidence was the product of years of careful in-breeding and gave them something to fight for, to live for. All they needed to do was grasp it with both hands.

The rage of earlier generations was always channelled into something constructive: ban the bomb, stop the war, legalise dope. Punk rock came to destroy. Privilege, the cultural (if not the social) watchword that hung over those past manifestations of teenage disaffection, counted for little in these new circles. As the smouldering winter of 1976 exploded into the white heat of the New Year, it was as if Los Angeles as a whole, tired of forever being the butt of countless Seals & Croft jokes, had finally risen in rebellion.

You could see it in the eyes of the kids who stalked the streets, the line of white-faced, grotesquely apparelled punk rockers who turned out every day to transform the seedy Boulevards into Day-Glo shock-headed freak shows. Rebellion, hatred, destruction.

To the hippies who cruised past in their campers, there was nothing to relate it to whatsoever. The only home-grown points of reference were Bomp Records' retail outlet, with its regular influx of imported British 45s and the pictures of London punks pinned on its walls; and, if you flicked the dial around far enough, Rodney on the ROQ.

Wired and wiry, with a finger on every pulse in pop, DJ Rodney Bingenheimer's Pasadena-based punk radio show aired a constant barrage of 'new' music, from New York, London, Australia and France. When the earliest LA punk bands cut their first singles, Bingenheimer played them as well, and he didn't even care if they were any good or not. Just as long as they had the bit in their teeth and the fire in their eyes and whipped up the inferno of noise that would burn the Hotel California to the ground. Towards the end of 1977, a couple of LA punks showed up in London, checking out bands at one of the city's dingiest dives. 'I could never figure out what you guys had to rebel against,' one remarked in scorn-dripping earnest. 'You never had to listen to Joe Walsh.'

Punk, wrote journalist Pleasant Gehman, was ATTITUDE. 'The style didn't matter. Everyone . . . wanted to look like monsters. Not ugly, but really crazy.' Before they even left the house, Gehman and Darby Crash, vocalist with the band the Germs, would spatter themselves with everything they could that made a colour. 'Ketchup, piccalilli steak sauce, spray paint, motor oil. We'd dump it onto the shirts and hang them out to dry, then write stories on them.'

According to legend, Crash was so nervous before the Germs' first gig, opening for the Weirdos at the Orpheum in the spring of '77, that he smothered his body in red liquorice whips. While the band played the only two songs that it knew over and over till the plugs were pulled, Crash simply stood there and melted. But the noise that the band made that night was to have far-reaching consequences, not only across the infant LA punk scene, but even further afield. Just ten years old when the Germs self-destructed, an aspiring New York guitarist named John Frusciante later reflected, 'The Germs . . . made me realise that being good at the guitar wasn't something you had to work at. As long as you put the right kind of energy and feeling into your playing, that was what mattered.'

Punks were outcasts from the start. In July 1977, punk rock was banned from the Starwood after the Weirdos played an Independence Day party and cremated the American flag. Other venues, chastened by the violence and disorder that accompanied more and more shows, grew leery about rebooking punk bands. The Troubadour, throughout the 1970s the most prestigious joint in town (Elton John played his record-breaking American debut there), dipped a tentative toe into the swirling waters, then withdrew it the moment the Bags' audience started overturning the tables. The next night the club's waitresses ganged up on management and handed over a petition: Either the punks go or we do. The punks went.

Only the Masque, a vacant basement beneath the Hollywood Center at Cherokee and Hollywood, stayed open. Brendan Mullen, half-Irish, half-Scot, found the place when he fell down its stairs and thought it would make a useful rehearsal studio. He slid unconsciously into running a club, charging at the door only when he counted the kids who dropped by to watch the punk bands at practice.

It was here that the Spastics were chased off the stage when the audience turned the fire hoses on them. It was here where carelessly lost longhairs had their tresses set ablaze; it was here where the scene 'zine *Slash* swore you'd find 'the pit's pyjamas'. And it was here that the violent subculture that lay beneath the surface of the Los Angeles punk scene was first spotted bubbling through the cracks in the pavement and the police started trying to clean up the mess. By mid-1978, when the LAPD finally padlocked the Masque's paint-scarred doors, punk rock was dead and the only thing left was its grey zombie ghost, popping out by day to scare Sunset sightseers, then returning to the underground to feed on its own decay.

On St Patrick's Day, 17 March 1979, the police descended upon the Elks Lodge to break up a show by the Alleycats, the Go-Gos and the Plugz. At first, people thought they'd just dropped by for a look around; decked out in full riot-squad drag, the lawmen walked in, walked out and everyone breathed a huge sigh of relief. The cops even closed the doors behind them, but only so they would have something to kick in a few minutes later, when they charged back in and began beating unarmed kids with their clubs.

A fully fledged riot broke out and it set a precedent. In the past, when the cops wanted to taste punk blood, they'd go for the kids a few at a time, skulking around street corners waiting for parties to start getting boisterous, or for a club to discharge too loudly into the street. Otherwise, they didn't give a damn about a crowd of weird-looking kids drinking, dancing and listening to brain-damaging music.

Following the St Patrick's Day Massacre, however, the destructive undertow that, by early 1980, threatened to sweep LA punk into the ocean was set in motion, stamping punk gigs with an only partially self-inflicted reputation for violence. It was inevitable, nevertheless, that in reacting to the increasingly vicious scenes being played out around them, the new wave of bands should take punk's already shattered self-belief and carve their own flesh with the shards.

From the Fleetwood, a club over on Huntington Beach, came the first manifestations of the Slam, a dance so crude that the ambulances started turning up before the first injuries were even reported. They seldom went away disappointed. For the bands serenading the carnage, all they could do was play and keep playing, and hope that nobody noticed them up there.

Slam dancing spread. Early in the new decade, the LA Times ran its infamous THE SLAM story, highlighting the violent new dance which was sweeping the city and giving fresh life and bitter outrage to every middle-aged, middle-class neurosis punk rock ever bred. Less responsible media followed gratefully in its wake. Punk became synonymous with crime, its adherents with criminals. Why should a society look to itself in its search for solutions to the problems that hurt, when there was an entire culture beyond it just begging to be the scapegoat?

In Huntington Beach, the police department started referring to bands as gangs and their fans as gang members, as if there were not already enough gangs roaming the City of Angels. With over 400 gangs already known to claim the allegiance of some 50,000 kids, lawmen and counsellors trained in the ways of the Crips and the Bloods – two of the urban sprawl's most notorious street gangs – suddenly found themselves coming to terms with the Circle Jerks and the Blades.

Unsolved murders were laid at punk's door; in a hysterical tabloid press, beach punk killers became a catchphrase for psychopaths; there were Nazi surf punk psychos under every palm tree; and every halfwit suburban subhuman in the region was drawn to the scene. Faced with a phenomenon it could not hope to understand, the media, at last, knew what it had to do. Destroy the mutant child.

Naked aggression fired punk rock in the first place and detonated the last truly street-level explosion in rock'n'roll history. Now that same naked aggression was being used against it and not only in LA. Everywhere that youth gathered in protest, be it the anti-fascist rallies that sent London lurching into a summer of street fighting, or a handful of kids hurling insults at Grateful Dead fans in San Francisco, the confrontations that inevitably ensued were invariably punk versus policeman, the forces of law and order a thin blue line against the rising tide of multi-hued anarchy.

Fifteen years earlier, in the mid-1960s, society divided over the length of the Beatles' hair. Now it fought over the colour. Against this backdrop of unreasoning, unreasonable hatred, punk rock made its final shuddering transformation. In Britain, bound to a burgeoning trend in right-wing extremism, it was called Oi! In America, where punk and mainstream politics never truly came together, it was hardcore, the final liberation of emotion from the music. Once the severance was complete, the two forces could, and did, lead one another into utterly untapped territory.

Punk came to destroy all that had gone before it. Hardcore came to give rock'n'roll a new basis upon which to build. But it was during the period in between, the cultural vacuum in which the past was taboo and the future unforgiving, that the seeds of change were truly sown. It was during this time that people could finally reach out of the narrow confines into which rock'n'roll squeezed itself, and grasp hold of salvation from elsewhere. 'Hardcore,' explained Barry Henssler, vocalist with early 1990s Ann Arbor metal-punx Big Chief, 'came to scrape off the Styxs and the Speedwagons and the remnant punk bullshit. Only when that was done could people get on with something different.'

Eighteen-year-old Anthony Kiedis, careening wildly through his final year at Fairfax, was one of the handful of kids blessed with the vision to see what that something different might eventually lead to.

'Hardcore had such an emotionally potent impact on the connection between the heart and soul and gut,' he later said. 'I remember thinking, if music can make me this sexually excited, this emotionally excited, this physically compelled to thrust my body back and forth across the floor, wouldn't that be a wonderful thing to make other people feel with your own music?'

Like so many other kids in Los Angeles, Anthony Kiedis was not a native Californian. He was born on 1 November 1962, in Grand Rapids, Michigan, a city whose greatest contribution to rock'n'roll was hosting a few early Grand Funk Railroad gigs when Mark Farner and company first thundered out of nearby Flint.

Grand Rapids is home to the largest Dutch population in the United States (Kiedis, however, is a Lithuanian name) and the place names around it echo that heritage. Take I-196 west of town and Zeeland and Holland both flash past, names that are strangely at peace with the Native American words other communities have retained, the likes of Saugatuck and Muskegon. In the melting pot of America's Midwest, old and new worlds seldom collided so gracefully. The city itself was once the furniture-building capital of the United States. In the decades following World War Two, however, the century-old industry first diversified, then declined. By the end of the 1970s, it had all but collapsed.

Kiedis's parents split up while he was still a child, and he remained living with his mother, Margaret. His father stayed in touch though, and throughout the bitter Michigan winters, when the mercury drained below freezing and even the highways seized up, Kiedis would think longingly of his dad living it up in LA, sunning himself by the pool with a girl on each arm and a party every night.

A small-time actor who went by the typically self-mythologising name of Blackie Dammett, the elder Kiedis never raised himself above passing roles of a villainous nature. With a hard face sandwiching a handlebar moustache, his skull topped with a luxurious floss of ebony hair that cascaded down to the middle of his back, Blackie drifted in and out of television as if it were a nightclub.

His letters and phone calls to Kiedis bustled with news of roles he was aiming for, parts he lost and, just occasionally, triumphantly, those he won. And, though his screen time was minimal, he would dominate the picture nevertheless and Kiedis would run howling to school the next morning: 'Did you see my pop on the TV last night?'

Of course, Blackie lived in Hollywood and that just added to the magic. He balanced himself upon seven-inch heels, propped on a pair of rainbow silver platform boots that hugged his legs to the thigh. He spoke with defiant self-confidence and, to Kiedis, possessed a character to match. Always in search of a good time, always sure he would get one, he was, enthused Kiedis, 'usually up to illegal things. He was your basic semi-subversive underground hooligan playboy womaniser type of character. But he was an outlaw in the beautiful sense of the word.' Even from halfway across the country, 'he definitely had a strong influence upon me'.

Around the time of his eleventh birthday, in 1973, Kiedis finally left his mother behind in Grand Rapids and moved out to Hollywood to live with Blackie. Though she could scarcely approve of his lifestyle, neither could Kiedis's mother continue to justify keeping father and son apart. They were peas in a pod, but Blackie would see that his young son got by. He sorted out schooling, he would maintain order. And besides, the only thing Michigan offered Kiedis was the chance to make angel wings in the snow.

There was no snow in Los Angeles, but there were plenty of angels. Blackie remained true to his word. He did make sure Kiedis went to school, he did curb him if he got too wild. But how wild, Kiedis wondered, was too wild? Every night, it seemed, the small apartment father and son shared would play host to an endless stream of 'fights, drugs and lots of guys and girls getting crazy'. Life was essentially 'anarchy on a plate'. Blackie, Kiedis once remarked, 'had a constant turnover of girlfriends. He had this insatiable desire to meet all of the beautiful girls in the world.'

So, as he grew older, did the fast-maturing Kiedis. It was the greatest thing in the world, he reminisced, 'to have all these beautiful women come into my house and not be uptight about me hanging out with them'. Later, as he moved into his teens, he boasted that they were similarly happy for him to have sex with them. 'You can believe my friends were rather impressed with my situation.'

Neither did Blackie care too much about a tightly regimented curriculum for his son. At nights they would hit the town together, dressed to the nines in matching pinstripe suits, and they got the red-carpet treatment in all the clubs.

From their table, father and son would nod to Blackie's friends and acquaintances, the renegade arsehole high rollers who orbited Keith Moon or outdrank Alice Cooper. John Lennon and Harry Nilsson, out on the town for the longest lost weekend in history, passed close enough to touch. David Bowie drifted through with a circus of freaks and retainers. Blackie seemingly knew them all. Conversation was wired, wild and weaving. Deals were struck and, when they soured, so were chins. Sitting wide-eyed but increasingly less innocent, Kiedis watched as the Hollywood Babylon blazed triumphantly around him. In his heart, he blazed with it.

'Los Angeles is a part of me,' he reflected thirty years later. 'This is where I got turned on to the magic of life and music and sex and drugs and movies and all the friends that I'll be with for the rest of my life. These are the streets that I walk up and down and where I wrote my lyrics. It's where I got stabbed, it's where everything happened to me. So it's part of who I am, and I don't look at it as inhospitable because it never was. It's the greatest place in the world.'

Kiedis was twelve, he said, when he lost his virginity. At eighteen, the red-haired Kimberley Smith was nothing less than 'a fully developed goddess' to her escort, particularly as the effects of one-quarter of a Quaalude buzzed through his system. It didn't even matter that Blackie was fucking her as well. Somehow it just brought the two of them closer together, a shared experience between father and son, like playing with trains or going to sports.

She treated him like 'a prince. Never before had I felt my mind, body and spirit come together in an erotic effort that transcended the bullshit and suffering of life,' Kiedis wrote in an essay for *Details for Men* magazine. 'The possibilities, combinations and innuendos seemed infinite and, at the age of twelve, so did life.'

But, as he admitted in that same candid article, 'having a semi-maniacal womaniser for a father had its disadvantages'. Blackie's womanising desensitised Kiedis towards 'wanting to attain true love with a single partner. With my not necessarily unwarranted sense of self-confidence [the greatest, perhaps, of Blackie's gifts to his child], I was constantly attempting to unite with a woman.'

Blackie aside, the only other reasonably stable influence in Kiedis's teenage life was the pop singer Sonny Bono. A close friend of Blackie's, Bono was still bitterly, and often publicly, coming to terms with the acrimonious break-up of his own marriage to the siren-like singer Cher. According to Kiedis, Bono was to become a surrogate father to him, often stepping into the little breaches in the boy's emotional development which Blackie was too preoccupied, or too careless, to fill himself. Kiedis remembered affectionately, 'We took a liking to each other and he used to take me on different trips that my father might not have been able to afford.'

In September 1977, Kiedis began his career at Fairfax High School. It was an unwilling debut; with the exception of English, for which he thanked his seventh-grade teacher Jill Vernon, the boy had long since decided that school could teach him nothing that he could not learn elsewhere. The companionship that high school offered too, appeared limp compared to the wider, wilder life Blackie taught him to expect. Despite his protests, however, he attended and did so with such regularity that, when he was absent, people noticed.

For a long time, Kiedis's closest and, some say, only friend was a boy named Tony Sherr. Both wild, both sassy, both apparently old beyond their tender fifteen years, the two Tonys appeared inseparable. So when another boy, Michael Balzary, took it in his head to administer a sound thrashing to Sherr, his first concern was to make sure that Kiedis was nowhere in sight.

His luck didn't hold. Holding the hapless Sherr in a one-armed headlock, pummelling him with his free fist, Balzary didn't even see his victim's friend until Kiedis was already upon him. Kiedis didn't mince words. Balzary remembered, 'He told me to let go of Tony or he'd knock my block off. He looked pretty mean, so I let go.' More than that, 'I figured I better get on his good side. He looked so weird, because he had this short little flat-top. He looked like a lunatic.'

It was a logical conclusion to draw. Kiedis's unconventional home life might have excited a lot of admiration, but it also inspired a rabid jealousy among his classmates, particularly when Kiedis came into school in the morning, with his fuck-by-suck accounts of his latest carnal encounter. The fact that he had the credentials to back up much of his storytelling only increased his contemporaries' envy. Early the previous year, 1976, Kiedis won out over any number of aspiring teenage child stars and landed the role of Sylvester Stallone's son in the *Rocky* star's new movie, *F.I.S.T.* The story of Johnny Kovak, the head of the Federate Inter-State Truckers Union (F.I.S.T.) drifted around the Hollywood script market for several years before Stallone got involved. And, despite the star's high profile, it was regarded as a loser even before Stallone – a man not generally noted for his wide-ranging vocabulary – announced that he would be rewriting Joe Eszterhas's original script.

Eszterhas responded with the wrath of a parent who had just been forced to turn his only child over to an irresponsible nanny. And, as the war of words heated up on the set and in the pages of the Hollywood press and as Stallone's own attempts to defend himself were interpreted as spoiled-brat arrogance, the seven-month shoot became an experience that its cast and creators still dislike discussing.

Working under his recently assumed stage name of Cole Dammett (Cole of course being close enough in intent to Blackie to reinforce his allegiance to his father), Kiedis's part was not substantial. In fact, few film guides even mention the scruffy kid who drifts around Kovak's home, and Alain Johannes, another of Kiedis's tenth-grade contemporaries, doesn't even recall hearing about the movie until Kiedis started discussing it in interviews half a decade later.

'Anthony was an actor,' he said. 'But he was an actor in the school play.' In fact, Kiedis's prominence among the Fairfax thespians was to continue until his senior year, when he was voted the school's best actor. And, among those circles in which Kiedis's accomplishments were known, even a limited debut in a despised movie established him as a boy who was going somewhere. The only question was, exactly where was that going to be?

Kiedis himself wasn't too sure. The things he found most inspirational were Woody Allen, punk rock, naked women and, as he put it, 'experiencing life on a physical level, diving off high things into water'. Even acting scraped in behind those pursuits. He certainly had no intention of getting involved in music. Too many of his father's friends, he insisted, were 'these really amazing musicians. The thought of trying to compete with them on their own level had very little allure.'

Instead, while he waited for his role in *F.I.S.T.* to start paying dividends, he concentrated on establishing his reputation in other ways, by becoming the wildest, craziest kid in the school. And, in Michael Balzary, the boy whose fists made such an impression upon Tony Sherr, he found the perfect partner-in-crime.

2. WE MADE AN AWFUL NOISE

Anthony Kiedis and Michael Balzary arrived in the world sixteen days and some 20,000 miles apart. Balzary was born in Melbourne, Australia, on 16 October 1962. He arrived in the United States five years later; like Kiedis, Balzary's parents divorced while he was still a toddler and, when his mother remarried in 1967, Balzary and his older sister, Karen, accompanied her and her new husband, jazz bassist Walter Urban Jr, to New York City. The family moved again, to Los Angeles, when Balzary was eleven and, as time passed, the boy's Australian citizenship was cancelled. It would be thirty years more before he reclaimed it but, in 2003, he was able to tell the Australian *Daily Telegraph*, 'after years of bureaucratic red tape, lawyers, forms, money and nightmares, I am an Australian citizen. I know where I was born, I am proud to be Australian and I consider myself Australian.'

No less than Blackie's influence on Kiedis, Urban's impact on the young Balzary was profound. The boy was raised in an environment where jazz and classical music ruled. Regularly at weekends, Urban would invite his musician friends over to the house and, while their mother prepared a barbecue, Michael and Karen would be treated to lengthy jam sessions. Just being around so much talent, for Balzary, 'gave me the most ecstatic, euphoric, wonderful feeling. I was, like, seven years old when that started happening, and I would roll around the floor in laughter. I would get the greatest feeling I'd ever had listening to them, just being amazed by the whole mystery of how the hell that could happen.'

He told the *LA Times*, 'It was the one discipline that I had when I was a kid – definitely the most *stable* part of my life. I loved going to music class; I had, I guess, kind of an emotionally tumultuous upbringing, and [music] and playing basketball were the two things that were really good and happy for me.'

What Kiedis was experiencing through his first juvenile taste of sex, Balzary was savouring through music. 'I've never been studious as far as learning things or knowing about theory or compositions by other musicians and stuff, but I've always taken pretty easily to just kind of jumping in on a groove. I just love playing music. It's the greatest universal, spiritual thing people can have in the world.'

The first instrument to catch his ear was drums, but at the age of nine, Balzary picked up the trumpet. By the time the family packed up and relocated to Los Angeles in 1973, Balzary was proficient enough to enter his father's jam sessions and was introduced to Dominic Caliechio, founder of the last surviving trumpet manufacturer whose instruments were still made by hand. A photographer was there to record the presentation and, afterwards, when a biography of Caliechio was published, that photograph was included in it, a smiling child prodigy cradling his trumpet, with Caliechio standing beaming beside him.

On another occasion, Balzary's mother, Patricia, took him backstage at a Dizzy Gillespie concert and introduced the boy to possibly the greatest jazz trumpeter who ever lived. For the young Balzary, 'It was the most exciting fucking thing in my life.' Dizzy put an arm around his speechless young admirer 'and held me real tight for like fifteen minutes, right until he went onstage'.

Balzary's love for the trumpet followed him into his first-ever band, formed with a handful of schoolfriends. They rehearsed once, at the Balzary house, but gave up when the only piece they found they could play was Henry Mancini's 'Theme from the Pink Panther'.

Perhaps more than any other part of his upbringing, it was this love of jazz that brought home to Balzary just how different he was from the other kids he knew. In an era when such metallic mastodons as Led Zeppelin, Deep Purple and Black Sabbath, and the introspective acoustics of James Taylor, were the undisputed rulers of rock'n'roll, when even modern jazz was only just being rediscovered by erstwhile rock critics disillusioned by the sickening thuds with which the 1960s finally hit the carpet, Balzary was listening to Miles Davis and Ornette Coleman, and passing personal judgements on the music that eclipsed any his elders read about in *Rolling Stone* and the *Voice*.

He played with both the school orchestra and, on several occasions, the Los Angeles Junior Philharmonic and, at a time when the 'hip' kids piled down to Rodney Bingenheimer's English Disco at 7561 Sunset, to dance to the hit imported sounds of Mud, Sweet and T-Rex, Balzary would be alone in his bedroom practising his trumpet. Later, when punk hit the Hollywood streets, Balzary moved even further away from the crowd. The closest he ever came to the rock'n'roll mainstream was when his sister Karen succeeded in turning him on to Joni Mitchell.

Sensing in the Canadian songstress's delicate sensitivity the streams of musical awareness that would later coalesce on Mitchell's 1979 tribute to jazzman Charles Mingus (the *Mingus* album), Balzary revelled in discovering for himself the intricacies of Mitchell's decade-long career. But rock'n'roll continued to leave him cold. To the kids who passed him by in school, he was a hopeless case. One of his Junior High School colleagues remembered Balzary as 'a quiet kid, something of a favourite with the teachers. Because of his trumpet playing, they had a lot of respect for him.' Of course, that set Balzary even further apart.

His first day at Bancroft Junior High, on Highland and Willoughby, set the pace for Balzary's next few years at school. A runty eleven-year-old with an accent – part Australian, part New York and part indescribable slang – that immediately marked him as a target for cruel attentions, he was 'the new kid,' he admitted, 'and I was really scared'.

Sitting in class that morning, he noticed the other sixth graders passing around a piece of paper, studying it, glancing quickly in Balzary's direction, then bursting out laughing. It took an eternity for the note to pass around, but finally it reached him. 'It was this picture of this ugly, retarded monster thing with snot dripping out of his nose.' Balzary's name was printed beneath it.

The author of the outrage was Jack Irons.

Irons was an apparent rarity in his own circle, a native Californian whose family had lived in Los Angeles ever since Irons's grandparents left their native Jerusalem when their son, Jack's father, was three years old.

As he moved effortlessly through elementary school with deceptively soft-spoken ebullience, Irons's biggest childhood concern was to prove to his parents that he was responsible enough to be given a drum kit. The instrument fascinated him, but Mr and Mrs Irons were less than confident. The annals of parenthood are littered with the shattered eardrums of indulgent families who thought junior needed something to bang on.

But, even at eleven, Irons was convinced that his future lay in percussion. When the radio played, he followed the drum lines, driving his parents and his younger sister Sharon crazy by emulating them with silverware on the table, or on the back of a chair or anything else that lay in reach. And, when he got together with another classmate, Hillel Slovak, all they could talk about was music; hearing it, playing it and, ultimately, living it.

Like Kiedis and Balzary, Slovak was an outsider, born thirteen years earlier on 13 April 1962, among the historic hills of Haifa, Israel. He had few memories of the city that could not be confused with childhood recollections of Los Angeles; he was no older than five when his parents scooped Slovak and his brother James from the increasingly beleaguered Jewish state and brought them to America, first to New York's Bronx and then to LA, where the sun was just as warm and the palm trees just as green.

From the hub of the old world to the centre of the new, the tanned, blond Slovak could have spent his entire life on the California beach and, if he overheard his parents discussing the war that shook his homeland shortly after the family resettled in the United States, it was as though it were more than a world away; it was an entire lifetime away.

Slovak stood out in a crowd, regardless. He was, insisted Anthony Kiedis, a 'kind of funny-looking kid, real skinny with long hair and big lips'. But he shared with Irons something that the other kids did not, something that bound them even closer than their shared Jewishness. A lot of the kids at school liked Kiss, the posturing glam rockers whose phenomenal success upset every prediction for the course of rock's third decade. Irons and Slovak, however, worshipped the band.

Since their emergence out of New York City in the summer of 1973, Kiss – Gene Simmons, Paul Stanley, Peter Criss and Ace Frehley – had rewritten every page in America's rock'n'roll rule book. No one knew what the group's members really looked like: they never appeared before their public in anything less than full performance drag – disfiguring face paint, towering heels, pro-football padding, the lot.

The guitarist fired skyrockets from his guitar, the bassist breathed fire, the drummer levitated and, all the while, flash bombs like atom bombs would detonate across the stage and clouds of dry ice would choke the first fifteen rows. Their manager, Bill Aucoin, figured it cost $10,000 a week simply to keep the band on the road. But they sold a million with every record and there was barely a critic in the country that would even stay in the same room as them.

Perhaps producer Bob Ezrin related the story that best sums up Kiss. He'd already worked with Alice Cooper and Lou Reed, so he knew what glam rock was all about – and, when he first saw Kiss, he knew what they were all about as well. But, one day, his curiosity was aroused during a conversation with a Detroit high schooler.

'Kiss? Oh, man, they're great. The kids at school love them. The only problem is, their records are so shitty. But we buy them anyway, simply because they look good.' That was Kiss's secret. And it was a secret that Jack Irons and Hillel Slovak were in on from the start.

Irons and Slovak had known one another since they were ten, but it was Slovak's thirteenth birthday party, in 1975, that finally brought them together. Slovak's parents told him he could invite a certain number of friends to the house and, passing over a couple of boys who apparently packed far greater claims on his friendship than Irons, Slovak issued Irons with an invitation. Among the birthday boy's presents was his very first guitar, a gift from his Uncle Aron. As Irons watched him unwrap it, he caught his first glimpse, too, of the pair's future together.

By 1977, when they, too, entered Fairfax High School, Irons and Slovak's camaraderie was legendary, all the more so after they decided to take their love of Kiss to its logical extreme and form their own mini-Kiss.

Like members everywhere of the Kiss Army fan club, they pooled their resources and purchased theatrical greasepaint by the bucket-load. But not from the $1.99 advertisements that appeared alongside the X-Ray Spex and Amazing Sea Monkeys in the Marvel comics of the day, where your dollars barely purchased enough to cover an eye. They shopped with the real make-up merchants in town.

'They put together a Kiss mime act,' remembered classmate Alain Johannes. 'Hillel would be Paul Stanley, Jack was Gene Simmons. They built their own Kiss costumes, Jack got some frothing blood capsules which he would spit out, and they'd put on these shows in class, where they mimed to the records. They used to stay up all night doing their make-up before each show.'

When Kiss played in Los Angeles one time, the pair spent several days hanging out in front of the band's hotel, hoping that one of the group would poke his head out of a window. 'They really were dedicated,' Johannes enthused; the mime act simply developed from that dedication.

'We were just fans,' countered Irons. 'Of course we had to emulate them!'

One morning before Irons and Slovak's latest performance, Johannes was sitting in class watching as Irons made his way up to the front of the room. Irons had recently added a new accessory to his costume, a codpiece, complete with realistic rivets. It looked, said Johannes, 'really armour-like and, for some reason, I decided to give it a bit of a test'. As Irons drew level with his seat, Johannes reached out and whacked the codpiece, 'just to see how strong it was. It turned out to not be very strong at all.'

After the performance, Johannes approached the still smarting Irons. Irons turned to his partner and made the necessary introduction. 'This is the cunt who just punched me in the balls.'

'Our friendship,' said Johannes, 'just kind of built from there.'

Born in Chile in 1962, Alain Johannes lived in Switzerland and Mexico before his family finally settled in Los Angeles in the late summer of 1974. His parents were entertainers, travelling in an extended family group within which every member had his or her own speciality. One uncle, Johannes remembered, was forever trying to break into television, spending his time conceiving pilots for shows involving 'some very strange Spanish versions of typical English humour'.

The constant moves from house to house and country to country were as unpredictable as they were exciting. 'Sometimes a better gig came up; other times, the debts got too big. Either way, we would have to move.'

Although Johannes's parents were adamant that their son would not follow in their showbiz footsteps, to the extent of mapping out a career in architecture for him, they did little to discourage him from picking up the guitar. By the time Johannes was thirteen, he was already a power in Fairfax's musical hierarchy, hanging out with older players and forever flitting in and out of the little bands that flourished among his circle of friends.

Slovak and Irons, on the other hand, were scarcely off the starting blocks. Irons's parents had finally given in to his years of pleading for a drum kit and the two friends were now taking formal lessons, Slovak in a neighbourhood guitar workshop, Irons next door in a drum class. At the time of their meeting with Johannes, neither had more than a year's worth of practice behind him and Slovak, at least, remained painfully insecure about his abilities.

To Slovak, learning guitar before discovering Jimi Hendrix was like writing a novel, then discovering Charles Dickens. Lying in his bedroom in the dark, it seemed to Slovak that Hendrix's music was incredibly sweet, unbelievably accomplished, but raw and crude also. Even though he knew the instruments on the Hendrix recordings and recognised their sounds, Slovak could not get over how they changed, twisting, turning and, as he'd seen on television, burning until they seemed to be one, an impossible meshing that was accomplished against all odds.

Looking over at his own guitar, Slovak shook his head sadly. Everybody said his guitar playing was coming along well and Irons was certainly impressed. But Jimi Hendrix was even younger than Slovak when he first set eyes on a guitar, younger again when he first picked it up and learned, from plucking its strings and caressing its body, to bring it to shuddering, aural orgasm, a scream of pleasure and pain that ripped from the amplifiers and infected everyone in earshot.

Slovak wondered how Hendrix felt the first time he learned he could make a guitar come. Jimi's first guitar cost him $5 back in 1955. He'd mastered ukulele first, an instrument that howled for music-hall comedians to come strumming and thumping across the stages of imagination; played it upside down because left-handed instruments weren't very common back then. It was good practice as well. When Jimi's first left-handed guitar was stolen at a club in Seattle, the fifteen-year-old simply borrowed someone else's right-handed instrument and didn't even need to restring it. Slovak tried playing his guitar from the top. It just didn't sound right.

Hendrix, though, never sounded anything but right. Even towards the end, when his critics said he was becoming self-indulgent and his friends described him as lost, when he plugged in and burned, he was like Johnny B Goode, playing guitar as if he were ringing a bell. He didn't even have to be in the mood to play. At Woodstock, the rain, mud and hunger left him itching to leave. He was supposed to have played late Sunday night, but would wind up waking the sun at six the following morning. Cold, damp and tired, all Hendrix wanted to do was get home. Instead, he stole the festival and the cameras couldn't lie. Once he was playing, he was into it.

That was the devotion Slovak wanted to feel. When he picked up his instrument, he needed to merge with it, as though he and it were one and coaxing out its magic would become as easy as scratching his foot or biting a nail.

Right now, all it did was give him blisters.

Looking at the painted buffoons sitting beside him, Johannes sensed none of this insecurity. He comprehended only that there was more to Slovak and Irons than a few haphazard ideas and a need to dress up. 'I felt really good about them. We started to jam together and, sometime around the end of 1977, we put together our first group.' He and Slovak shared guitar duties, Irons took the drum seat and another friend, Tom Strasman, came in on bass. They called themselves Chain Reaction.

Irons and Slovak brought their repertoire of Kiss songs, Johannes and Strasman introduced Queen, Led Zeppelin (a bruising version of 'Rock and Roll') and what Irons remembered as 'some more progress- ive stuff'. The group had little time for punk rock. 'I was a late bloomer to the whole concept of punk,' Irons insisted. 'I wasn't a rebel when

I was a teenager; I was kinda happy, so I don't think I actually understood what the music meant, as opposed to what it sounded like. A lot of the time I'd listen and it was too crazy. I didn't understand that there was a reason for that craziness.'

Chain Reaction's showpiece was a sprawling epic that Irons described as 'a sort of version of Queen's "Ogre Battle" ', an incredibly accomplished piece of music that strained the group's limited powers of interpretation to their utmost. Even before the individual members' voices broke, they struggled to reach the high notes that Freddie Mercury attained so effortlessly. Once the group felt confident enough to start writing and playing their own material, 'Ogre Battle' was among the first songs to be dropped from the repertoire.

Chain Reaction debuted before a crowd of friends in the school gymnasium one lunchtime shortly before Christmas 1977. It was a difficult show. Irons and Slovak were terrified. It was one thing to turn out in face paint and Kiss drag and mime to their favourite records, quite another to stand there, alone in front of the school and make their own music.

Self-deprecatingly, Irons recalled, 'Alain was already a very accomplished player, a lot more developed musically than we were. I still don't know why he stuck it out with us.' But the show passed off 'really well' and, when Johannes asked if the others were ready to do it again, their faces alone told the story.

Shortly after that first show, the group's name changed to Anthem; later, upon discovering another, better-known band with the same name, it became Anthym. Every day after school the four would troop to Irons's house to rehearse. 'His parents were very gracious to put up with it,' Alain Johannes said with a laugh. 'We made an awful noise.'

By 1979, Anthym's live circuit was expanding beyond Fairfax's confines to include various other schools in the area. In addition, Irons was also playing in the 26-member school orchestra. It was the members' penultimate year at school, but rather than slow down their extracurricular activities, Johannes, Irons and Slovak talked only of increasing them. For Tom Strasman, however, that was enough. His heart was already set on becoming a lawyer and, with graduation little more than a year away, he was painfully aware that Anthym was slowly eroding his grade-point average.

'Suddenly we needed a bass player,' said Johannes, 'and we thought it would be really good to take somebody who didn't play and mould them to our own style.' The group's next scheduled show, an inter-school battle of the bands, was still three months away, 'so we picked the only other person we knew who had both the musical ability and the kind of attitude we were looking for'. That person was Michael Balzary.

In the years since he first started hanging out with Anthony Kiedis, Balzary had undergone a profound change. For Kiedis, the life he led was just another part of experiencing life to the fullest. For Balzary, it was more therapeutic, the final shaking off of a childhood innocence perpetuated into his teenage years by an almost crippling shyness. 'I was just scared of people,' he confessed. 'The whole concept of asking girls out on dates completely terrified me.'

But the withdrawn little boy whose greatest thrill ever was meeting Dizzy Gillespie, and who later recalled painfully that other kids in school called him 'fag', was long gone. Now Anthony Kiedis was his guiding light and Balzary, his hair newly, boldly shaved away, is adamant that if Kiedis didn't come to school, he'd be lost. 'I'd pretend to get something out of my locker, walk around, go back to my locker.' All day long.

Almost two decades later, the Flea reflected on these formative days. 'I was just thinking . . . what a huge influence Anthony Kiedis has been on me.' He told *Guitar World*, 'when we were in high school, I remember going out to the movies or something and me having this outfit – these brown corduroy pants and brown top – that I thought was really suave and cool. And I said to Anthony, "Hey, like my new shirt?" And he said, "That's OK. But anybody could wear that. The thing is to wear something that no one else would wear and be totally different." I started wearing all these oddball clothes. And that totally affected the way I looked at music. I felt, "I just wanna play music like no one else would play it." Anthony's feeling like that – just to do your thing and not be like anyone else, and delve into your concept of art and your own individual emotions – was a really big influence on me. And affected my music profoundly.' Michael Balzary was dead. In his place stood Mike B the Flea.

The name resulted from a trip into the mountains with another friend, Keith Barry. He, too, was a juvenile jazz freak, an accomplished viola player who played alongside Jack Irons (and, occasionally, Balzary himself) in the school band, and who fell in love with Coltrane, Parker and Coleman after reading their names in the sleeve notes of an album belonging to his father's girlfriend.

One day, he, Balzary and Kiedis embarked upon what Barry recalled as a 'ski trip where we were going to be real hoodlums. We were going to ski recklessly, and we thought it would be a lark to not refer to each other by our real names.' Kiedis became the Swan, Balzary became the

Flea, Barry the Tree. 'In retrospect,' Barry told the *LA Times*, 'I think Flea and I have always had this quality of being diametrically opposed in so many ways, we had always been so tight and yet we had always been very, very different. You know, like, Flea: very capricious; me: very *not* capricious. And if you think of it that way, the nicknames really fit.'

Scraping together the coach fare, the trio headed to Mammoth Mountain in the Sierra Nevada, one of California's prime resorts, and spent a riotous 48 hours skiing by day and, at night, crashing in the laundry room of a mercifully convenient apartment block, feeding quarters into the clothes dryer in a bid to keep warm. 'We hiked into the woods and the mountains for ten days,' Flea remembered. 'Jumping into a river, standing on top of a mountain, one I've just climbed, being one with the earth, is the most profound feeling you can have, the greatest moments of happiness.'

On another occasion, Kiedis returned to visit his mother in Michigan for a time, then called Flea out to join him. Recalling how he undertook the journey by Greyhound bus, with only an increasingly sticky copy of *Penthouse* for company, Flea told visitors to the Red Hot Chili Peppers' website, 'we spent a lot of time jumping off a bridge into a river and sneaking around drinking beer and smoking weed with the locals, we drove his parents' car into a ditch, and went inner-tubing in the river. We had a great time and we picked berries and I played trumpet in a cornfield.'

Every morning, Fairfax buzzed with the activities of the crew-cut Kiedis and his shaven-headed compatriot. Like the time they decided to scale a giant billboard and celebrate its conquest by unzipping their pants and waving their cocks at the onlookers gathered below.

Walking home, they would climb the walls of people's homes and, with bloodcurdling screams and yells, hurl themselves off the roof into the swimming pools below. Even if they were careful, it was a dangerous pastime; it was so easy to misjudge a dive and end up sprawling on the hard concrete below. Fired with bravado and adrenaline, Kiedis and Flea were seldom careful. 'One time,' Kiedis remembered, 'I got a little overzealous and overshot one and broke my back. Another friend ran away, but Flea stayed, dealt with the cop and made sure I got to the hospital.' Alain Johannes confirmed his story. Two weeks later, he marvelled, 'Anthony was walking around as though nothing had happened, with just a little support thing.'

Johannes also recollected Kiedis's first car. The vehicle itself was nothing spectacular; what set it apart from every other car on the road was that it had no brakes. 'If Anthony had to go out anywhere, he'd just drive from here to there without stopping for anything, red lights included. The amazing thing is, he never actually hit anything.'

'Anthony and Flea used to get themselves into terrible trouble,' Johannes concluded, regarding their teenage antics. 'They really did have little angels looking out for them.'

Although they were frequently together in the classroom, there was precious little common ground between the musicianly Irons, Slovak and Alain Johannes, and the tearaway Swan and Flea. It took someone else to bring them together; someone whose own interests, let alone instincts, surely begged him to leave well enough alone. His name was Don Platt, and he was one of the social studies teachers.

'Actually, he was my favourite teacher, the best I ever had,' enthused Johannes. 'It was just a matter of whether you were in with him or not. He was the sort who threw the book away and just talked.'

Kiedis was the first to feel the lash of the balding Mr Platt's tongue. Flea and Slovak followed. The teacher was armed with a very dry sense of humour and had no compunction whatsoever about putting people down. When the trio was in class, Platt's favourite target was Charles Bukowski, the bucolic Bohemian poet whose work they were just beginning to discover and whose books accompanied Kiedis everywhere, including the classroom. And, whereas most of Platt's barbs were aimed, said Johannes, at getting some kid's gander up so he'd become interested in the class, this particular war swiftly assumed a very different complexion. The two parties truly loathed one another.

Finally Kiedis had had enough. The school play was just a few days away and, shortly after the announcement was placed in large clip-on letters on the marquee outside the gymnasium, Kiedis and Flea made their way precariously up the side of the building and set about rearranging the words. The following morning, Johannes remembered, Fairfax High School, and a portion of Melrose besides, awoke to learn DON PLATT SUCKS ANUS. Kiedis did not attend another social studies class.

Flea's initiation into Anthym was slow, but exhaustive. With Johannes and Slovak his more than willing tutors, by the time the battle of the bands came around, Mike B was at least proficient enough to power the group into a very respectable runners-up position. 'Whatever the reasons were for us not winning,' Johannes explained, 'they had nothing to do with Flea.'

With Flea on board, Anthym also commenced their slow drift away from straight-ahead hard rock'n'roll. Out went the last surviving semi-metal numbers; in their place, Johannes and Slovak, Anthym's

principal songwriters, started introducing increasingly more complicated time signatures.

The style of bass playing Flea was eventually to develop, the heavily
jazz-funk-tinged 'slap and pop' method he has since made his own,
was hijacked from countless other bass players of the era and he
admitted that, when he first picked up the instrument, it seemed
natural to ape what was, after all, a highly visual routine for an
otherwise traditionally non-visual role in the band.

But it swiftly became apparent that his style was considerably more
advanced, even in its most formative stages, than the average high-
school bass player's. Flea was blessed with a natural funkiness, a sense
and style of delivery derived from his childhood diet of jazz, which
tied even the simplest song up in knots and only slowly let it unwind.
What made him even more formidable was the fact that he had taken
just one formal bass lesson, walking out when the teacher presented
him with the Eagles' 'Take It Easy'. 'I just wasn't into it. I decided to
figure things out on my own.'

In the spring of 1980, before its members graduated from high
school, Anthym itself climbed one further step up the ladder, onto the
Hollywood club circuit. The word was out that Anthym was always
ready to play and the group was rewarded with ever more frequent
support slots, opening for better-known bands at the Troubadour, the
Starwood and the Whiskey. Often it was a frustrating experience.
Because of the group's age, nervous club owners would insist that the
band members awaited showtime in their dressing room. 'But we were
also gloating,' related Johannes, 'because we were so much younger
than the other bands who were there.'

The highlight of any given week came when Anthym was booked
to headline the regular Young Nights at the Starwood. Every high-
school kid in Hollywood would descend to roar on their friends and,
according to Johannes, 'we did manage to create quite the little
following. We could play the Troubadour and pack it, then go back
to school on Monday and feel like we were stars. And of course, our
grades started to plummet because we got all cocky about it.'

The group's youth did not always work in its favour. One night that
spring, Anthym appeared alongside the fast-rising Oingo Boingo at the
Orange County Fair. Although it was scarcely an audience the group
encouraged, Oingo Boingo was regarded as minor royalty in LA's
neo-Nazi circle, a high-octane octet that laced its whacked-out punk
adrenaline with exuberant silliness. Anthym was little more than
another petty irritant standing between the crowd and its heroes.

The group completed its set and even had the cheek to thank the audience for its attention, but the hail of bottles and glasses that descended around them as they played left no one in any doubt as to the crowd's true feelings. By the time the four high-school kids left the stage, Johannes, at least, was nursing the spots where some projectiles had struck him in the face.

Of all Anthym's followers, few were more vocal in their appreciation than Anthony Kiedis. He was dating a girl from school, Haya Handel, and they were inseparable. But the beautiful brunette, a member of the school gymnastics team and, during this final year at Fairfax, the senior class president, never tore Kiedis from the bosom of his friends, nor the insanity of their behaviour. Even from halfway across a crowded hall, his voice was unmistakable, a very loud and very fake stoned Latino drawl that he lifted lock, stock and smokin' barrel from one of the surprise movie hits of the last year – Cheech and Chong's *Up in Smoke*.

Richard Marin, the Mexican-American son of a California policeman and Chinese-Canadian Thomas Chong, who a decade earlier led a band that included a teenage unknown named Jimi Hendrix, had spent the past seven years performing as two terminally doped up pot-heads, forever in search of the perfect joint. The duo's records, five of them by the time of *Up in Smoke* (including three that only narrowly missed topping the charts), obsessed on the subject. Their movie debut drove that obsession to the breaking point.

Kiedis's love for the duo's whacked-out comedy routines was calculated to draw the most adverse reaction from the Fairfax teaching staff, which only encouraged the behaviour to spread, not only in Kiedis's vocabulary, but throughout that of his friends' as well. Not altogether unsurprisingly, the craziness started in Mr Platt's social studies classes, but now the delinquent conspirators, 'Los Faces', as they dubbed themselves, lurked at the back of every class, cackling out their own crazed version of the stoned immaculate. Perhaps it was simply inevitable that, having learned for themselves how much fun it can be to sound like dope fiends, Slovak and Kiedis should want to try feeling like one as well.

'When Hillel and I were kids,' Kiedis recalled years later, 'we . . . were heavy-duty drug experimenters. We took LSD, we did cocaine, we did heroin, smoked a lot of pot and did a lot of alcohols and different combinations of barbiturates. But it was all in good fun; we weren't slaves to the drugs.'

Not then, anyway. They were barely eighteen, they were in Hollywood, most of them were in a band. Life stretched out ahead of them like a wide-open highway. There were no speed cops to slow them, no turnings to confuse them. With one foot on the gas and one hand sliding up a California girl's thigh, the road looked like it would go on forever.

3. I DON'T WANNA BE A SIDEMAN

Flea had never been to a punk rock show. Of course he knew what punk represented; he had been exposed to it on record and, thanks to K-ROQ, radio alike. But he had yet to experience it in the flesh. That summer of 1980, his amigos among Los Faces decided it was time to complete his musical re-education.

Black Flag were playing at the Starwood and, however much of a national impact the dynamic X were now threatening to make, the uncompromising dynamism of Black Flag promised that they would soon make one of their own.

The band had just recruited a new lead singer, D.C. punks State of Alert's incendiary Henry Rollins, and, in his hands, a group of friends who started out two years earlier as little more than another carbon-copy Sex Pistols commenced its sub-metallic lurch towards its ultimate musical destiny, a grinding hardcore barrage that would eventually alienate even the last vestiges of the band's original punk following.

'I just thought it was disgusting,' Flea swore later. 'People were getting the shit kicked out of them for having long hair and people were being carried away in ambulances, a bloody, violent thing. It really made me sick and scared. Punk rock was awful.' Despite the circles in which he now moved, maybe Flea was still his stepfather's son at heart.

Slovak and Kiedis, however, dived headlong into Los Angeles' turbulent punk mainstream, sensing in its chaotic rhythms and near-absolute timelessness the total physical liberation that no other form of music was ever able to offer them. But their friends appeared blind to the fierce, burning light.

Irons admitted that it wasn't until he reached his early twenties, 'by which time I was a much more accomplished musician', that he gained respect and love for the music whose spirit, he proudly remarks, he still carries with him today. Johannes, too, was 'a late developer. I was heavily into jazz at this point; I kind of grew into punk. I really didn't know much about it. There was a whole group of kids who were into that stuff a lot more than we were; we were still into Led Zeppelin, Stevie Wonder and so on.'

But Flea wasn't simply willing to learn about it; he wanted to feel it sear his impressionable soul.

'What punk rock was about to me,' he explained a decade later, 'was never having to say you're sorry.' Six months after Black Flag so abruptly punctured his punk virginity, Flea was at the Germs' last-ever show, at the Starwood on 3 December 1980. He was thrown out, he boasted, 'about one second' after the band blasted into the opening 'Circle One'.

Four days after that show, singer Darby Crash scratched out a suicide note to a member of his band, slammed close to $400 worth of heroin into a body that had already been pushed to the limit, then spread himself out on the floor in the shape of a cross and died. It was the ultimate rock'n'roll death – heartless and senseless but, best of all, painless.

Long before he contributed a delightful solo version of the band's 'Media Blitz' to the 1996 tribute A Small Circle of Friends, Flea was enthusing 'I love the Germs'. And the same feeling consumed – and still consumes – his fellow Los Faces. When an animated Anthony Kiedis drove a car through the video for 'Californication', the licence plate read, simply, GERMS. When he leaped out of a speeding taxi in the 'By the Way' promo, to escape the maniacal driver who had just kidnapped him, the book he left behind on the back seat was the Germs' biography, Lexicon Devils. And, when that same cab driver reappeared onstage at the end of the 'Universally Speaking' video, it was to return that same book to its owner. Kiedis, too, agrees with Flea's insistence that '[the Germs] were one of the best rock bands ever'.

Los Faces graduated from Fairfax High in July 1980. Their school yearbook shows three smirking youths, Kiedis looking considerably younger than his years as he gazes out from beneath his almost Beatle-esque fringe, resplendent in black blazer and red tie; Irons appearing more dishevelled, his naturally fly-away hair apparently caught in a wind machine; and Slovak is simply the ultimate high-school vagabond, his tie knotted tightly beneath his Adam's apple, but provocatively bare-chested beneath his blazer. Flea, revelling in his continued sense of rebellion, didn't even have his photograph taken.

Los Faces were neither to be missed nor, particularly, remembered following their departure from Fairfax. To the teaching staff, they were just another teenage clique, no more or less undisciplined and obnoxious than any other; to younger kids, they were role models only inasmuch as they did things few other people ever dared to do. The only time anybody expected to hear their names again was if they got arrested.

Falling out of Fairfax, Flea and Slovak alone made up their minds to try making careers out of music. Irons and Johannes, as much to please their parents as anything else, enrolled at Northridge College before moving on to a Valley college, and Kiedis followed suit. During his last years at Fairfax, he discovered writing 'with the help of my father and certain exceptional English teachers'. In September 1980, he took his place in the freshman class at UCLA.

Times had changed since UCLA was at the forefront of radical student politics. Attendance no longer conferred some kind of free-spirited longhair respectability upon all who walked across campus. Jim Morrison no longer spray-painted his tribal-sexual consciousness across campus; the students no longer posed with their placards and a floral tribute for the National Guard.

Life there was easy for a political-science major, but even the handful of classes he had to attend got in Kiedis's way. His best work, he knew, came outside the classroom, when he wrote poetry for fun, and that was still the only possible reason he could see for doing anything. When Flea approached him about getting somehow in-volved with Anthym, Kiedis immediately agreed. 'I had so much fun writing and my friends were having so much fun playing music, that eventually our paths crossed.' Anything that developed out of such a union, he insisted, 'was an accident'.

With one already highly accomplished songwriter, Alain Johannes, in the band, and a second, Slovak, moving up in the fast lane, Kiedis stepped first into the role of the band's MC, appearing onstage at the start of their set simply to bawl out jokes and chat with the audience. Such a display came easy to him. A natural extrovert, he swiftly developed a repertoire of asides that he continues to draw from today.

Only at the end of his performance, as the group itself prepared to take the stage, Flea remembered, did Kiedis fall back upon a rehearsed script: 'Cal Worthington calls them the hottest rockers in LA. Their parents call them crazy and the girls call them all the time. But I call them like I see them and, I call them . . . ANTHYM!' Then the lights would blaze, the band would kick into their opening number and Kiedis would leap out to join Haya, herself flashing the smile that the Fairfax Yearbook preserves as the nicest at the school, and begin crazy-dancing into anything that stood in his way.

In 1981, after one year at UCLA, 19-year-old Kiedis bowed out of academia. Just like high school, he found it a stultifying experience, a succession of useless theories that had nothing to do with the real world. The only true learning experience, he later wrote, was life itself.

If you couldn't learn what you needed from life, then it probably wasn't worth learning in the first place.

To keep body and soul together, without any notion of making his career in the field, he took a job at a small film company in Hollywood. Sharing an apartment with Flea and the Tree, he operated on autopilot, working for the pay-cheque which, in turn, afforded him the licence to continue 'punk-rocking my way through the insidiously twisted streets of Hollywood'.

He had parted from Haya by now, after almost three years. Now most mornings found him awakening with a different face alongside him and revelling in a crash course in intense 'low-brow gluttony' that was not always sexually successful, but was nothing to complain about, either. 'My sex life was rocking and I was happy.'

He was also still suffering from childhood wanderlust. One weekend he persuaded Flea that the pair of them needed a haircut and a holiday – in that order. Mohawks, the rooster-like haircuts that left the entire head shaven save for one violent geyser of coloured hair from forehead to neck, had just exploded across the face of punk fashion, courtesy of the new generation of British Oi! bands – skinhead speed gangsters whose music was no more debased than California's hardcore, but was laced with a political vision with which LA simply couldn't compete.

If punk was the conflict between the old order and the new, such bands as ChronGen, Anti-Pasti and the Exploited were sending postcards back from the front line. Their hairstyles alone were offensive weapons. The circled letter A that stood for 'Anarchy' on their leather jackets, the stud-and-bullet bracelets and belts, and the sheer aural assault of their music simply made sure that the barrage hit its target.

Resplendent in their new hairstyles, Kiedis and Flea hopped the first northbound train and were just getting comfortable when the conductor came through. Ticketless and, apparently, penniless, they were thrown off the train at the next stop; 'San Jose or Santa Barbara,' Flea recollected. 'Someplace weird.'

Rather than return to the railroad and risk a repeat performance, it struck them as easier just to hitchhike the remainder of the journey until, according to Flea, they were eventually picked up by a transvestite, the perfect start to what was shaping up to be an 'insane weekend of sleeping on people's porches covered in newspapers, being woken by cops prodding us with sticks and doing a lot of unmentionably weird things'.

Faced with a gruelling return journey, Kiedis and Flea decided to give the trains another go. A freight train full of beets appeared to be heading in the right direction, so they jumped aboard, buried themselves in vegetables and were just congratulating themselves on a smooth journey home when the train stopped. It had travelled less than five miles and the pair were now sitting in the goods yard of a beet factory in the heart of an industrial wasteland.

Back on the highway, dripping beet juice, their shaven scalps still itching infuriatingly and slowly despairing of anybody ever stopping to allow such monstrous visions into their precious car, the two finally flagged down a ride back to LA. The driver, glad for such distinctive company on the 400-mile journey down Interstate 5, was a big Mexican with LOS VENOS A CHICOS tattooed on his neck. It was an hour or so into the ride before he revealed that he was a fugitive from the law and not until they reached LA that he told his passengers that they could keep the car. 'I stole it!' he proclaimed, laughing as he pulled up and jumped out.

Flea drove the car for another block, then he and Kiedis got out. 'I got scared, so we abandoned it.' But the weekend still had one further trick to play. When Flea reported in the next day at the animal hospital where he worked as a receptionist, he was told he was fired. His vivid Mohawk was one transgression too many.

Johannes and Irons, meanwhile, followed Kiedis's lead and bowed out of college. The Johannes family's dream of Alain becoming an architect was forgotten; instead, he concentrated on letting the world know that Anthym, too, was now capable of standing on its own two feet. But not, he insisted, as Anthym. The name packed too many connotations, not least of all being the kind of cheese-ball nom-de-wimp that the burgeoning tide of local heavy metal bands were now lining up to grab.

'We didn't think it was fitting the music we were playing anymore,' explained Irons. 'Basically we just outgrew it.'

Certainly Anthym had developed into something some leagues away from the high-school hijinks that they were getting away with before. The group always relied heavily on odd metres and tempos within its songs, but now the band members found their tastes drifting towards pure rock improvisation, heavily indebted to Captain Beefheart but in tune, also, with what Johannes described as 'the downtown underground scene'.

Undercurrents of mutant funk had long been swirling through punk's still seething underbelly; the word had forever been out about the Gang of 4, Public Image Ltd and the inappropriately named Pop Group, British bands that were taking the accepted laws of pure rock'n'roll and tearing them to shreds. The media had already sated itself on Old Wave and New. Now these bands arrived to herald the onset of the No Wave.

For all its later descent into cliché and uniformity, the British punk rock movement was always a remarkably egalitarian beast. Performers like Elvis Costello, Sting and Bob Geldof, in modern times so broadly spread across the mainstream musical landscape, all fell as unquestioningly beneath punk's banner as the artists whose names remain locked within that primitive world of safety pins, spit and a barrage of noise: Sid Vicious, Johnny Rotten, Rat Scabies.

There were no barriers. Reggae bands slipped as comfortably into the punk ethic as guitar groups; jazzman Don Cherry gigged with the noise auteur Slits; and the electronic minimalism of Germany's Kraftwerk encouraged young punks everywhere to invest in synthesisers. And no sooner had John Lydon walked out of the Sex Pistols in January 1978, than he was scheming a new band more in tune with his private musical preferences. Public Image Ltd would never give themselves wholly over to any single style, but the ménage in which their best music was made, equal parts funk, dub, jam and jagged experimentation, was unequivocally touched by each all the same, ascending to the rarefied ranks of those post-punk bands who were truly transcending even their own original visions of disrupting the musical status quo.

The yowling defiance of 'Public Image', the band's debut (late 1978) single; the apocalyptic 'Death Disco'; the unyielding 'Fodderstompf'; all were naked slabs of industrial funk, seismic bass lines which carved primeval grooves into the dancefloor. *Metal Box*, the group's devastating second album, not only revolutionised what would shortly become tagged industrial music, it also brought about a complete reappraisal of how rock'n'roll could be packaged. True to its title, *Metal Box* was released in an aluminium case. Now, whether through cosmic symbiosis or simply copycat fervour, it suddenly emerged that Lydon and his bandmates were not the only post-punk pioneers thinking along those lines.

Self-appointed punk historian Jon Savage later quipped 'the name "James Brown" was whispered', but in truth it was being shouted, from the northern city of Leeds, where agit-punk art students Gang of 4 were to be found driving out their own brittle, grooving fractures; from the western port of Bristol, where the Pop Group formed around

vocalist Mark Stewart's insistence that 'punk [had become] a new kind
of orthodoxy, and we wanted to experiment'; and in the new, hip
clubs around London, where Light Of The World were fusing a ragged
approximation of 'classic' funk with the electronic disciplines of the
synthesiser scene.

Stewart continued, 'from the word go, I wanted to play funk, really,
really heavy funk. I also wanted a funk producer, but [we couldn't get
one] so we got in the best English reggae producer, Dennis Bovell.'
Following in PiL's footsteps (and, before them, early 70s pioneers
Cymande), the ensuing hybrid cut its funk basics with dub techniques. Uniquely, however, the Pop Group then used that basis as a
launching pad for further wild experimentation, and two albums
which would inform producers as far apart as Bill Laswell and Adrian
Sherwood, and musicians as disparate as Al Jourgensen and Afrika
Bambaataa.

'We couldn't play,' Stewart admitted. 'We were sixteen-year-old
kids, friends from the youth club, mates from school, coming out of
punk. We could only play three chords, and we were trying to play
funk. Editors from the New Musical Express kept coming to the
concerts and saying we were like Captain Beefheart. But we never
heard of Captain Beefheart! The only reason why we sounded like that
is we couldn't play. In fact, it was quite unlistenable, but amid what
was going on at the time, it broke a lot of barriers.'

The first time the Pop Group played London – the first few times,
in fact – the audience was so appalled that the band performed
beneath a barrage of cans and abuse. Only slowly did they attract a
following which even pretended to enjoy their music (it was a mark
of true avant-garde individuality to profess to be a fan); and even more
slowly dawned the realisation that, beneath the cacophony, there
really was something worthy going down. Indeed, it took the
emergence of the considerably more conventional Gang of 4 as critical
darlings in early 1979, to allow many ears to focus on the Pop Group's
convolutions, an event which the Pop Group themselves facilitated by
inviting the Gang to open one of their London shows.

If the Pop Group emerged as one of the first genuinely innovative
funk bands in British musical history, the Gang of 4 proved one of the
most respected. Gang of 4 guitarist Andy Gill, reflecting on the band
for their 100 Flowers Bloom box set, explained, 'what is special about
the Gang of 4 is that they're funky. Most [other] bands weren't.'
Politically outspoken, musically accessible and commercially successful, Gang of 4 combined the post-punk fascination for kinetic tension

with an inherently earthy danceability – angular and stuttering across their *Entertainment* debut album, deep, dark and deliberate across their *Solid Gold* sophomore set.

Spouting a revolutionary rhetoric that, during the first years of Margaret Thatcher's right-wing Conservative regime, was perhaps even more convincing than the ultrapolitical Clash's middle-class terror tactics, the Gang of 4 was simultaneously brittle and brutal. In conversation, the band members tangled the names of the political left with those of their own musical heroes: George Clinton and James Brown and the new wave of uncompromisingly underground British bands that sprung up alongside them: the Slits, the Raincoats, Blurt . . .

Over the course of five albums and a slew of startling mini-hit singles ('Damaged Goods', 'At Home, He's a Tourist' and 'Man in Uniform'), Gang of 4 walked a precariously deranged tightrope across the semi-detached minefields of pure punk and raging funk, a fusion that, as Britain schizophrenically raced towards military confrontation with her old ally Argentina, and political union with her traditional European enemies, sounded the clarion call for Armageddon.

These were the sounds that burned into the artists who would no longer be called Anthym. Slovak's short, biting guitar solos were being complemented by Flea's trumpet routines. Jeans and shaggy hair gave way to tuxedos and vampire cuts. Songs extended into bottomless jams, with only a pounding rhythm to hold them down.

It took a few nights of brainstorming to get there, but finally a suitable new name for the band emerged from the fog: What Is This. 'Somehow,' Johannes believed, 'it seemed to fit.' It also summed up the reaction of people who caught the group live and puzzled over the curious amalgam of solid punk, scapegoat jazz and rough'n'ready funk with which the group was assaulting their ears. What Is This . . . what is this?

There were no boundaries. 'It was still hard rock,' Johannes insisted, 'but it was very quirky hard rock. It was all adrenaline and testosterone.'

Kiedis, although he remained nothing more than an enthusiastic observer of the group's sudden lurch into the outer limits of musical fusion, applauded What Is This's change of direction. He might even have taken some responsibility for it.

Nightclubbing fearlessly, Kiedis was coming into contact with considerably more than the willing flesh he set out in search of. Eschewing the traditional punk clubs, he was moving deeper into Hollywood's soul, hitting unknown basement clubs where the music had little in common with the testosterone-driven energies of white rock'n'roll. Funk music, he knew, was the ideal soundtrack for coupling. Now he was discovering that hip hop was the supreme aphrodisiac.

It was Kiedis who brought Grandmaster Flash into What Is This's life; Kiedis, too, who turned up one day raving about Defunkt, a heartstopping funk band whose dream of wresting funk rock from the hands of late-seventies shamans like Earth, Wind and Fire was a closely guarded secret. Without Kiedis even being conscious of the fact, his fast-shifting musical tastes were burning holes through What Is This's own perceptions and performances. In his own words, tinted of course by hindsight, he 'gave them some . . . colour'.

The colour that Kiedis was anticipating, that was to eventually reshape both his and What Is This's entire lives, was the rap movement then stirring in the metropolitan centres of America's East Coast.

The indigenous scenes nurtured within its urban sprawls notwithstanding, rap was the closest America ever came to creating a true punk ethic. Like punk in Britain, with which it coincided both in timing and attitude, rap was forged, not forced into life, a guerrilla war against the anaemic excesses of the corporate giants that swamped the black dance scene as greedily as they swallowed white rock. With the Bee Gees on one side and John Travolta on the other, disco had become a pejorative term, a bland boogie-bop for white kids from the suburbs. It had nothing to do with the culture that created it and nothing to give to the people who truly needed it.

When the worm started turning, it did so underground. Just like the first Sex Pistols and Damned shows, rap started in the shadows, at house parties where the DJs were only as good as their last show. If they dropped the beat for a moment, misjudged a mood or flunked a feeling, they were as close to death as they would be on their knees in a gutter with a bayonet in their backs. The trick was not to pretend you weren't scared, because that was only human. The trick was never to let your guard down.

The DJs took to working in pairs – not for protection, although when reloading their van in the street late at night that may not have been a bad idea, but so they could work off one another. While one spun records, the other would launch into his rhythmic mantra, supplementing, even sublimating, the music beneath his own intoxicating rap.

Scientifically dissected, rap's antecedents were both obvious and plentiful: the motormouth speedjocks of the rock'n'roll era, the dissident street poetry of the Last Poets and the Watts Prophets, the Rastafarian toasters of Jamaican reggae, the speedfreak poets of punk's ranting subculture. The audiences that turned out to dance, however, weren't into science.

Eddie Cheeba, a Bronx Community College kid working out with Easy Gee, packed a rap that swung to the bass line (and the bass line alone) of Parliament's 'Flashlight'. 'Cheeba Cheeba,' he chanted, 'chee-chee-chee-Cheeba'. Of course it was primitive, but it was lethal as well, a combination of beat and Beat that cut through the dancers like a caseload of cattle prods.

The focal point for the scene was the Palm Room of the Dip, the seedy twelve-floor Hotel Diplomat, which totters just around the corner from New York's Times Square and which opened its doors to rap in late 1977. Russell Simmons, the club's promoter, picked the venue deliberately; it crouched just two doors away from Xenon, a ritzy disco nightclub that was so exclusive that even its regular clientele, grovellingly adhering to the stringent dress code, could not be guaranteed entry.

Admission alone to Xenon cost $15 a head – as much as a bed for the night at the neighbouring Dip. Seldom before had two such diverse cultures come into such close proximity with each other and it was only inevitable that, as word of the Dip dances spread through the bowels of New York, the street outside should grow as crowded as the dance floor within. The Xenon crowd started looking for new ways to get into their bouncer-fortified haven. If they passed by the Dip, chances were they'd get rolled.

Life was not much safer for the Dip's own staff. Simmons and his DJs spent most of every evening hiding out in the hotel's bullet-proof box offices, emerging only when it was time to perform. Fists, knives and guns flourished on the Dip's spacious dance floor and ambulances and police cars swiftly added to the mêlée on the pavement outside.

Eddie Cheeba and Kool DJ Kurt, the future Kurtis Blow, were the Dip's first attractions. But, as word of their prowess spread, so the streets exploded with new ringmasters: DJ Hollywood, whose 'hibby the hibbity hip hip hop' rap would one day be abbreviated to describe an entire musical genre; DJ Run – Kurtis Blow's thirteen-year-old brother and, later, one-third of Run DMC; and the greatest of them all, Grandmaster Flash and the Furious Five.

Flash himself was a DJ, grandmaster of perhaps the two most crucial elements in the entire rap scene, scratching and cutting. Cutting was an art that DJs had been perfecting since before time began, segueing two records together so smartly that they didn't miss a beat. Scratching was something else entirely. With two records playing at once, the Grandmaster could cut effortlessly from one to the other, inserting everything from short blasts of noise to entire musical passages into one long, solid collage of sound.

Flash's finest routine was one in which he'd introduce two other DJs and, together, they'd prowl around the stage in a circle, pausing only when one of them reached the turntable and, without dropping the tempo, cut to another record. Around and around they went, each new disc spinning only for as long as it took each DJ to complete his full circuit and, if their routine was almost callously choreographed, it was also spellbinding. By the time Flash wheeled out the Furious Five rap team, or their genius soloist Melle Mel, even the fighting had stopped.

From spinning records to making them, the primal rappers and their disc jockey cohorts blew the disco scene out of the water. Seedy New York hotels gave way to clubs and even concert halls. By 1978, amateur tape recordings of the top rappers were the only true soundtrack to New York's urban city life, blasting out from the first generation of affordable ghettoblaster tape machines. By mid-1979, DJ rappers the Cold Crush Brothers, the Funky 4+1 and Afrika Bambaataa were regularly releasing live tapes of their performances. Eazy AD of the Cold Crush Brothers claims sales of over 500,000 tapes long before any rap *records* were ever released.

When the disco-funk veterans of the Fatback Band recruited a rapper/MC of their own, Tim Washington, aka King Tim III, the original intention was simply to bring a new dimension to their live shows. It was the response of audiences which prompted them to combine one of King Tim's raps over a track called 'Catch The Beat', retitle it 'King Tim III' and, much against the better instincts of their record label, place it on the B-side of their next single, 'You're My Candy Sweet'.

But nobody could have predicted what happened next. New York DJs completely ignored 'Candy Sweet' and, instead, slammed all six minutes of 'King Tim III' into constant rotation. Rap had hit the record racks.

The release, just one week later, of the Sugarhill Gang's similarly themed union with 'We Got The Funk' hitmakers Positive Force, 'Rapper's Delight', stole some of Fatback's thunder. But while history recalled the latter as the first rap record to make the pop Top 40, 'King Tim III' was the first, by a matter of seven days, to make the R&B

chart. By the end of the year, Kurtis Blow became the first rap star to sign a major recording deal, with Mercury Records. And, by 1980, kids all over the country were dancing to their own home-grown rappers.

But only black kids. Almost only, anyway. Rap was first and foremost ghetto music, made for the crumbling stoops of urban America's poorest neighbourhoods, from which it roared out in a cocktail of sound: part baby screaming, part mama yelling and, as time passed, part the sound of disaffection, the roar of flames and the dying screams of the old fat rich.

Cast into the powder keg that was LA, rap was as potent as a book of burning matches. It would be another decade before the city finally exploded, a three-day firestorm ignited by an all-white jury's exculpation of the four white cops who beat the black Rodney King. But it was fired by the fury that built up over a lifetime of injustice, a mute fury that rap finally gave voice to. Another decade, too, would pass before rapper Ice-T was forced to publicly place art behind artifice and withdraw the 'Cop Killer' track from his *Body Count* album; and finally confirm the conspiratorial constraints that so many past black artists considered themselves bound by.

The scene, however, was set long before that, in the minds of a bunch of Hollywood kids hanging out on the farthest fringes of the LA punk ethic. For them, the transition from punk to funk to a hip hop-themed hybrid of both was as natural and, in many ways as innocent, as it was for the first generation of British punks to fall under the spell of Jamaican reggae. Even though the sentiments were yet to fall precisely into place, more than punk, more than Oi!, even more than the brutal skull-smashing nausea of hardcore, rap was the ultimate rebel yell. And What Is This wanted to rebel.

But rebel against what? Alain Johannes, Michael Balzary, Hillel Slovak, Jack Irons and Anthony Kiedis hailed from comfortable, if somewhat unconventional, backgrounds. They were young and white and, although Balzary still held his Australian citizenship, they were American. In the land of opportunity, the career consultant posters bellowed, you needed only reach out and you could grab yourself a slice of the dream; and looking around them, the five knew that was true.

Everywhere, the white light of economic optimism was blazing, from the eyes of California's own former Governor, President Ronald Reagan, to those of the humblest factory worker or waitress. Television bristled with the lives of the rich and famous, the top-rated shows of the new decade were the opulent grandiosity of a new generation of soaps, the *Dallas*'s and *Dynasty*'s that led a pampered generation into the halls of power and privilege.

Even rock'n'roll was now firmly in the hands of corporate sponsors. The biggest tour of 1981 was the Rolling Stones, 50 million dollars' worth of White House lawn parties and a song that became the anthem for the smug self-assurance of the 1980s. 'If you start me up,' it threatened, 'I'll never stop.'

London street punks the Clash were co-headlining the USA Festival, a mad Yuppie Woodstock where even the mud stank of money. Billy Idol, once the sneering snotnose bombshell who fronted Generation X, was camping it up with disco-sheen and sharing a manager with Kiss. And, on 1 August 1981, the very last vestiges of power slipped from the hands of the people when twenty-four-hour Music Television arrived to change the way they listened to music, simply by providing a new way to watch it. Reality had taken a vacation; the American dream had taken its place.

The minimum wage was increased. Stock-exchange trading soared to unknown highs. On the day of President Reagan's inauguration, Iran released the 52 American hostages it had held since the dawn of the Islamic revolution 444 days before. If anybody needed proof that, at long last, America had placed the wintry impotence of the seventies behind her, their release was it. Now it didn't matter what else the 70-year-old former actor did: in the eyes of America, Ronald Reagan would forever remain the Freedom President. For five white kids, with that freedom stretching out before them, it was almost churlish to complain and dishonest to disown their heritage.

But living in LA, that heritage appeared somehow hollow. Living in LA, you come to recognise the ghosts that haunt the BRAIN-TO-LET glaze in the eyes of every runaway who ever swapped blow-jobs for bucks in the front seat of a truck. They litter the streets like disposable cigarette lighters, a human mosaic of shattered dreams and broken illusions; and every one looks dead. A few, though, still have a drop of gas left inside and enough of a flint to crack a sick spark. Before you know it, they're at your throat, last month's wine swilling last year's halitosis, bumming a cigarette, begging for cash, holding a .44 in your gut and demanding everything you've got or they'll blow your fucking guts all the way across town.

Stepping over their corpses and those of their victims, kicking spent ammunition aside like so many discarded old Coke cans, What Is This passed through their nightmare dreamscape with only one aim in life:

to survive. To tighten their belts and prepare themselves for the sociological firestorm they knew was just around the corner. It just wasn't always easy to find the right way of doing all that.

'We've dealt with a lot of underground shit, hanging out with the local weirdoes.' Flea still speaks with the cynicism he once felt. 'At the same time, we were driving out to the beach, going backpacking in the Sierras.' That kind of living, such a savage, mindless dichotomy – you could only find it if you lived in Los Angeles. And only Los Angeles could enjoy it.

'Life is full of beauty and ugliness and love and hate.' Kiedis, anxious not to tie himself to any adaptable political creed, long ago abandoned any dreams of changing the world. 'You just have to accept it all, because to ignore it would be closed-minded. I try not to wear blinkers, [but] I choose to aim for the happy side.'

His aim, all his life, has been unfaltering. But the happy side he chose, the ever-escalating continuation of the chemical experiments that whiled away dull school days, did not deaden the pain or sweep away the confusion. It simply made him more aware that he was blotting it out. It is not difficult to score in LA. Everyone knows someone whom they can tap for something and even the specialised fancies that fade in and out are there for the taking if you know where to go.

Kiedis and Slovak were generally content with what was readily available. They did not have a drug problem, for to call it that would suggest that they were aware of something being wrong. And right now, nothing was wrong. For them, getting high came as natural as breathing, eating or taking a shit. So did the actual mechanics of scoring: the long trips uptown to meet the guy who might have the right stuff; the hanging around in sections of town that even the psychos steered clear of; and the constant paranoia every time a cop looked twice when they walked around holding.

They were never loyal to any one drug, or at least not in the self-mythologising sense in which some junkies can happily ram a needle full of horseshit into their veins while they put down their buddy for his brainful of dogs'. Anything went – smack, acid, coke. Each produced a different high; each, then, had its own purpose. Some nights and many mornings, too, they couldn't even remember what they'd done or how they'd spent their time afterwards.

The low-brow gluttony in which Kiedis painlessly revelled was collapsing even on its own skewed sense of morality, until nothing was too demeaning; everything was an experience worth having. It was only a matter of time before his constant quest for new experiences brought him into contact with the seething underbelly of LA's black culture.

Introducing What Is This to Defunkt and Flash, and sharing with Slovak the drugs they both wanted, was only the tip of Kiedis's iceberg of influence. Although he had neither asked for, nor officially been given, anything more than an equal role in the fraternity that surrounded the group, Kiedis did more than add colour to their proceedings. He offered them an identity as well.

Partying while What Is This practised, Kiedis embroiled himself completely in the rap culture. It gave him, he said, 'the notion that I could do something musical without being Marvin Gaye'. The crowning moment for Kiedis, as it was for so many of the other kids who were standing outside looking in, came with Grandmaster Flash's 'The Message'.

Although it has been described as such, 'The Message' was not the first record to tap rap's potential for socio-political commentary. It was, however, the first such offering to breach the US charts, in October 1982, and to do so in a fashion that completely belied its lowly peak of No. 62. Suddenly rap was exploding across the pop mainstream, alerting and becoming accessible to an audience far wider than the discos and nightclubs ever played host to, opening up to artists and audiences alike the chance to experience to the hilt one another's culture.

At last, traditional white pop had a new challenge to meet, one that spoke to its people as firmly and as rousingly as any of rock'n'roll's most incandescent leaders. No less than Presley or Dylan, the Rolling Stones or the Sex Pistols, rap communicated not the frustrations and anger of youth, for that is a cliché that no street music could ever fulfil, but those of an entire people.

The facade of 'equal opportunities' and 'racial harmony', the emotional placebos with which successive American governments satisfied the civil rights viper that writhed within the country's breast, was finally being stripped away. Still disadvantaged, still discriminated against, still the victims of supremacist taunting and institutionalised abuse, America's black population was scarcely more integrated into society than little green men from Mars.

Unemployment, homelessness, poverty, hopelessness, these were the roles Uncle Sam reserved for his blacks and, for every Clarence Thomas or Colin Powell, effortlessly scaling the judicial ladder until they came to rest in the galleries of government, there were thousands of others for whom Powell and his ilk were, at best, the ones who slipped through the net, at worst the ones who sold out their birthright in their haste to escape. Either way, they didn't belong.

Rap spoke of these frustrations and the music industry reacted in the only way it knew how: by accepting the medium, but utterly rejecting the message. Adam Ant, the post-punk glam rocker whose entire career so far was one long, expensive video, and Blondie, wholesome pop masquerading as platinum sex, struck out first. Adam's 'Ant Rap' in December 1981 was pale, derivative, pathetic and, to those who understood, as close to rap as the Supremes were to soul. The difference was that at least the Supremes had a few good songs.

Blondie's effort was no more convincing. In 1979, 'Heart of Glass' effortlessly, almost accidentally, established the New York garage band as a disco power to be reckoned with. But it sold to the same people as the Rolling Stones' 'Miss You' and Rod Stewart's 'Do Ya Think I'm Sexy', the high-gloss Xenon crowd, for whom mirror balls were the height of sophisticated chic and John Travolta really was a cool dancer.

'Rapture', in January 1981, possessed none of its predecessors' innocence. Far from establishing itself within the genre, Blondie were now coldly, callously and, above all, uncomprehendingly trying to turn the procedure inside out and to establish the genre within themselves. When 'Rapture' climbed to No. 1, it was not on the strength of its assumed authenticity; it was through the support of the people who read of rap as an undefined movement and who believed that, in 'Rapture', they had discovered its essence. They were not the same people who would be buying the Grandmaster's 'Message', but they might be the same people who made stars out of Hammer and Vanilla Ice.

For Anthony Kiedis, the contradictions embodied within the white mainstream's acceptance of rap only furthered his own need to become involved. But, if he played any of the games that other aspiring rappers played, D-I-Y scratching in his bedroom after dark, or allowing his poetry to adapt itself into the stream of lyrical consciousness that rap now embodied, he showed little, if any, of his work to his friends. Rather, he just longingly spoke of the principles and continued their musical education.

Within the ranks of What Is This, Flea, too, was feeling the need to expand his horizons. He had already dipped a tentative toe into wider waters, albeit more for the experience than any perceived satisfaction, when he spent a few nights playing congas for a cut-rate disco band, running through polished performances of Rick Dees and Linda Ronstadt numbers. 'It was a very kooky experience.'

Similarly, if not equally, short-lived was his and Slovak's involvement with New York saxophonist James White. A former member of Lydia Lunch's ferocious Teenaged Jesus and the Jerks, Milwaukee-born White freely mingled jazz, funk and post-punk imagery, keeping his own musical identities only partially separated by operating under a variety of incestuously commingled pseudonyms.

James Chance, the Contortions and the Blacks not only maintained a constant stream of provocative new releases throughout the early 1980s, but the bands that White assembled behind him also proved the jumping-off point for a number of other acts – the Bush Tetras, Defunkt (which was originally White's own horn section) and Jody Harris among them. Now, having sewn up the New York No Wave scene, White was in the process of creating a West Coast version of the already near-legendary Blacks. Auditions were held and Flea and Slovak both went along, as much out of curiosity as anything else. They recognised in White a kindred spirit, a compliment that White obviously returned. Alongside Joe Berardi of the Fibonaccis, both were offered roles in the new group but, after a handful of jams and a gig or two at best, they quit. White offered advancement but not creativity, and Flea and Slovak needed both.

4. THE MIRACULOUSLY MAJESTIC MASTERS OF MAYHEM

The James White interlude at an end, Slovak returned to What Is This; Flea continued his search for new musical experiences. And, sometime during the summer of 1981, gently riding on a tab of acid, he found what he was looking for. He quit What Is This immediately after.

Fear were one of the last wave of LA punk bands to still be playing a music that was recognisably rooted in the genre's most basic instincts. Led by the skinny obstreperousness of part-time actor Lee Ving, whose confrontational attitudes towards homosexuality turned even the punk culture's semi-enlightened attitudes to so much scorched earth, Fear's policy of alienate first, entertain later, erupted into bloodletting more times than anyone could remember.

When the Masque's old operator, Brendan Mullen, opened Club Lingerie on West Sunset, Fear were among the first bands to play, appearing as the Valley Gay Men's Violin Quartet, confident that the audience they pulled would self-destruct once it heard Ving in full homophobic flight.

At the Starwood, it was a Fear fan who caused the venue's subsequent banning of punk acts when, in midshow, he stabbed a bouncer. At the Stardust Ballroom, a club that opened back in the 1930s to accommodate a new dance called the foxtrot and was now struggling to contain the slam, bassist Derf Scratch was almost killed by a giant skinhead. Other bands encouraged violence; Fear appeared to breed it.

Even amid the breakneck competition for gigs in LA, however, Fear established themselves immediately. For a short time in 1978, their 'I Love Living in the City' attracted the same compulsive fascination in LA as Jonathan Richman's 'Roadrunner' did in Boston or the Clash's 'London Calling' in the network of British ex-pats. A Halloween 1981 appearance on NBC television's *Saturday Night Live* cemented Fear's reputation even further. The band played its two scheduled songs, then returned to LA to dismiss their whole experience in song: 'New York's Alright If You Like Saxophones'.

When the brilliant but erratic Penelope Spheeris made her cult movie debut with *The Decline of Western Civilization*, an LA punk-scene documentary filmed throughout the winter of 1979 (but only given a general release in 1981), it was Fear who closed the action, ahead even of the iconoclastic Germs and the fast-breaking X.

'I wish you wouldn't bite so hard when I come,' Ving tells one heckler before presenting shocked cinemagoers with a three-song showcase that remains filth-encrusted, even after the excesses of the other bands in the movie have obliterated the most docile viewer's reservations. Fear might not have been a great punk band but, in terms of shock horror verbals, Lee Ving was a great punk.

Watching the band in action at the Club Lingerie that summer evening, Flea felt an excitement that What Is This hadn't fulfilled in a long time. 'They were really tight, fast and aggressive. They blew my mind.' When he heard, about a week later, that Derf Scratch was on the verge of leaving, Flea felt no qualms about recommending himself as replacement. Fear, faced with a tight calendar of upcoming shows, were glad to accept.

From the start, it was obvious that Flea's style of playing, the heavy pounding he dealt out to his instrument during even the quietest numbers, was incompatible with Fear's. But nobody would admit that a mistake had been made, least of all Flea himself. If Lee Ving, the band's principal songwriter, thought he could make a mindless rocker out of a bassist who was otherwise spiralling towards jazz-funk fusion, so Flea, wittingly or otherwise, was working towards the day when Fear would themselves get a little funkier. The results, unrecorded but still remembered with an admixture of wonder and worry by the band's following, were uncompromising to say the least.

'Fear was the first band I was in that made any money and that people came to see,' Flea recollected. He admitted that he did cave in to their demand that he use a pick for the first time in his life and that he play only down strokes, but he has also acknowledged that he even found a way around those limitations. If Fear was going to mess with his playing, he decided, he was going to fuck with their heads.

'Fear were your original white dopes on punk,' resolved writer Jo-Ann Greene. 'Their problem was, they really didn't know what they were doing. Sometimes you'd stumble across them and they'd be playing this real cool bluesy number, then suddenly Philo (guitarist Cramer) would hit the sickest chord you'd ever heard and they'd just disintegrate, start screaming PUNK ROCK! at the top of their voices.

'Then another time, there they'd be, the hippest jazz band on the planet, really getting into a groove and Spit (Stix) would suddenly kick his kit as hard as he could and off they'd go again. PUNK ROCK!'

Flea just added to the confusion. Two decades later, he confided, 'I was a crazy kid and they were older and more mature than me. I was never really comfortable in that band, never could really be myself, but it was a great learning experience.' Indeed it was. Forever jumping, forever hopping, living up to his nickname with a bloody-minded vengeance, it did not matter how maniacal the rest of Fear could appear, Flea was worse. His bandmates' attempts to curb his excesses only provoked him to further heights, and raised his reputation even higher. Soon, word of his uncompromising stance had even reached the ears of Public Image Ltd's John Lydon. And what a combination that could have been.

By 1982, however, PIL were struggling somewhat. Lydon himself had lost – or discarded – almost every trace of the suss punk iconoclast he once was. Still snotty, still snarling, still capable of alternating between the most mild-mannered bloke in the world and the biggest shit on two legs, he had nevertheless taken the PIL joke too far, changing the punchline so often that even he didn't know when to laugh anymore.

Certainly his bandmates were tiring of his tantrums. Bassist John (Jah Wobble) Wardle quit shortly before the band's fourth album, 1981's *Flowers of Romance*. Lydon promptly turned around and recorded the album without a bass. 'There's more than enough strings on a guitar,' he laconically explained. 'Who wants to pay some other cunt to play more?'

With a Far Eastern tour now looming, however, the LA-based Lydon evidently recanted. Drummer Martin Atkins recalled, 'We were in Pasadena, auditioning bass players and Flea came along. He was stunning, he just blew all the other bass players away.' Atkins and Flea jammed together for half an hour and 'the faster and more intricate I played,' said Atkins, 'the more he was just totally on top of it. It was stunning.'

There was no doubt in Atkins's mind that Flea was the man for the job but, when they spoke the next day, Flea demurred. 'To be honest, I don't want to join PIL. I just came down to jam with Martin.'

'I guess I was one of his favourite drummers at the time,' Atkins recalled, laughing, but he wasn't going to give up on such a promising acolyte. 'I'm going, "You can't fucking do that. You have to join, you have to come to Japan and Australia with us." '

Flea asked if he could have some time to think about it and, according to Atkins, 'he disappeared into the mountains for a few weeks, just to sit and think. But when he came back, his answer remained the same.' (Flea and Atkins would eventually record together

– in 1994, the bassist was among the guests on *Notes from the Underground*, the latest album by Atkins's current band, Pigface.)

'Yeah, they asked me to play in PIL,' Flea recalled some years later. And for a brief moment, he admitted, he considered it. Then he decided, 'Fuck that, I'm not going to be a sideman to someone else. Look at what would have happened if I would have done that. I would have gotten fired and replaced by Bill Laswell.'

'If I make films that are on the heavy side,' director Penelope Spheeris once remarked, 'it's because that's what I've been dealt.'

Her father was a circus strongman; he was murdered when Penelope was seven, defending a black man from an attack in Alabama. The remainder of what passed for childhood was spent watching as her mother married and divorced seven times more.

Shortly before she enrolled at UCLA, Spheeris started living with cameraman Robert Schoeller, father of her daughter Anna. He died in 1974 at the age of 29 and Penelope was sent reeling headfirst into a nervous breakdown. She was still recovering when she met director Albert Brooks four years later.

Spheeris started her university career studying behavioural psychology; she switched to filmmaking when she learned 'that I could express myself that way'. By the late 1970s, she was working on *Saturday Night Live*, producing a series of short films. When Brooks offered her production duties on his forthcoming *Real Life* feature, she jumped at it.

Real Life opened to critical and commercial acclaim in 1979 and, suddenly, Spheeris found herself faced with a simple choice: 'I had to decide if I was going to make mainstream pictures or say goodbye to the money and all the influential films and do the weird stuff.'

She chose the weird stuff. A document of the Los Angeles punk scene, *The Decline of Western Civilization* was made on a budget of $125,000 (its follow-up, the video rental-oriented *Part Two*, cost $1 million) and immediately established Spheeris's punk credentials. Like the similarly intentioned movies that documented the London and New York punk scenes of 1976–77, Ivan Kral's *Blank Generation* and Wolfgang Büld's *Punk in London*, *Decline* showcased the bands and their fans alone.

There was no room for directorial interference and no need for it, either. Black Flag, the Circle Jerks, X and Claude Bessy's Catholic Guilt between them made every point that needed to be made; and any that they left behind, Fear picked up on, Lee Ving burning his presence into every eyeball that encountered him.

Even the Germs, caught at the tail end of their slowly shattering career, played with the panache of an alleyful of cut-throats, the same alleyful, no doubt, whom Spheeris's cameras caught on the dance floor with increasing regularity. Had Darby Crash not died in December 1980, Spheeris might never have returned to punk rock; *Decline* said everything there was to say. But his demise put a whole different complexion upon the proceedings. In the eyes of a frightened, fragmented punk culture, he was a martyr, both to the violence he inflicted upon himself and that which was afflicting the punk crowd in general. 'Most of the trouble that took place at punk gigs,' affirmed photographer Alison Braun, 'came from outside the punk community. The bouncers reacting to what they'd read, the police to what they'd heard, it was almost always outsiders.'

But whereas other scenes, once touched by violence, strove to shake it off, LA punk embraced it. When that bouncer was stabbed at a Fear show, the gig rose so high in punk mythology that soon, recalled Braun, 'everyone was saying they were there, that they had seen – or not seen – the stabbing'. The scene was sick, it was selfish and, for Spheeris, it held a fascination she simply had to exorcise. When, in late 1982, she began working on her next movie, *Suburbia*, the stabbing of a bouncer became an integral part of the story.

Suburbia – a cross between Suburb and Utopia – is the archetypal middle-class district, row upon row of normal-looking houses in which normal-looking families go about their normal-looking lives. But are they normal? Behind one door, a viciously alcoholic mother throws abuse and bottles at her teenage son. Behind another, a fat slob father rapes his own daughter, then beats her if she complains. Behind a third, a girl fights to forget the night she was savagely stripped naked at a Vandals gig. With nowhere else to turn, these teenagers converge upon one vacant house and live there together.

Rejected by their families, the outlandish-looking crowd swiftly discovers that society at large, too, despises them. Isolated harassments turn increasingly violent, a sequence of events whose senselessness is compounded by the townfolks' ritual culling of another group of rejects, the wild dogs who live on a nearby patch of waste ground, and who provide moving-target practice for any gun-toting 'citizen' who fancies it – a disgusting fixture of local life that the Red Hot Chili Peppers themselves would later savage with the condemnatory 'True Men Don't Kill Coyotes'. Here, though the analogy itself was heavy-handed, it remained valid nevertheless.

Auditions for *Suburbia* took place in a disused storefront in a ritzy

Sunset Strip mall; it was a strangely ostentatious choice in an area littered with crash pads and punk hangouts, but Spheeris selected perhaps the one place where the punks would not blend in. By the same token, in an area where the true punk experience was there for the taking, the movie punks' home was 'decorated' by professional Hollywood set designers, whose own idea of anarchic graffiti remained some miles removed from its naked spray-gun reality.

Casting the movie, Spheeris aimed for a balance between 'genuine' actors and genuine punks: her own daughter, Anna, took one part; a well-known local, a one-legged punk named Andre, another. Caught midway between these two extremes was the character of Razzle, played by Mike B the Flea. 'He was given a rat to carry around with him,' recalled Alison Braun scornfully. 'How "punk"!'

Braun dropped out of the race for parts in *Suburbia* when she learned that she was to be cast as the girl who loses her clothes during the movie's opening sequence. She remained available for walk-on parts, however, and laughed at her 'big moment on screen' when she is glimpsed during a crowd scene at a TSOL show. 'The concert footage was probably the only genuine part of the movie,' she remembered. It was shot at a disused (and now demolished) theatre on Sunset, being run under the auspices of a local religious cult bent on 'saving' punks. The club was called God's and closed down, one rumour insisted, when far from saving any punks, one of the club's organisers actually joined them.

God's failed for the same reasons as *Suburbia*. The rebellion Spheeris caught shimmering just beneath the surface throughout *The Decline of Western Civilization* was now being dragged into the daylight with the subtlety of a pig bite; the symbolism embodied in the wild dogs was forgotten and even the optimism with which Spheeris and producer Roger Corman evidently viewed punk itself was lost, as *Suburbia* lurched visibly from examining a cult to exploiting it, as victim became aggressor and, even in mourning, the punks were outraged.

For Flea, the commercial failure of *Suburbia* was little more than he expected. The filming over, and with his continued allegiance to Fear having been proven by their two subliminal appearances in the movie (a glimpse of their name carefully daubed onto one wall, a concert poster tacked onto another), he threw himself immediately into another pet project. He and Kiedis were just starting their best joke yet. He was curious to see where it ended.

Ever since singer Gary Allen quit the LA punk band Neighborhood Voices, he had been formulating a costumed cabaret lip-sync routine, which he would be presenting at the Rhythm Lounge in April 1983. Knowing Kiedis only as the kind of wild man who was prepared to do anything for a laugh, Allen asked him to put together some kind of freaky one-off stage show, which would preface Allen's own routine.

Of course, Kiedis agreed, but it wasn't until he and Flea were sitting around one day listening to Defunkt, while Flea played and slowly began to distort one of that band's bass riffs, that he worked out exactly what he wanted to do.

'I've got a rap that will go perfectly with that,' Kiedis told him, as Flea completed his mutant meanderings. 'I wrote it after the gig last week.' He'd seen Grandmaster Flash and the Furious Five and had been scribbling things down ever since. While Flea repeated the bass line, Kiedis grabbed a piece of paper and began reciting. A rapid-fire tour of the city's most sordid secrets, it was called 'Out in LA'.

None of the people filing into the Rhythm Lounge that night in the spring of 1983 knew exactly what to expect from the evening's entertainment. Gary Allen himself promised only a night of weirdness, but even he had no idea what Kiedis and Flea had up their sleeves.

He knew that Irons and Slovak had been co-opted from What Is This for the show, but beyond that he hoped only that they hadn't burned out their creative glands thinking up their name for the night ... although Tony Flow and the Miraculously Majestic Masters of Mayhem looked so good on the advertising posters that they probably could have just left it there. With a name like that, who cared about the performance?

At any rate, the Majestic Masters turned in a performance of such power, such strength, such absolute, unbelievable brevity that some people were still calling for more when Gary Allen came onstage.

'I had a funky bass line,' Flea said with a shrug, 'and Anthony had a poem.' They stoked up with enough acid to keep them buzzing for the two or three minutes it took for everyone to plug in, blast through their number and get off again without laughing too hard. It didn't matter that they didn't rehearse before the show; it didn't even matter whether or not people liked what they were doing. In many ways, the Miraculously Majestic Masters of Mayhem were hoping that they wouldn't.

Instead, 'people went crazy for it. There was a cosmic gelling and we exploded.' Kiedis was incredulous. The Masters of Mayhem had scarcely left the stage when the manager of the Rhythm Lounge asked them back for a repeat performance. If they had a few more songs, then maybe they could even headline.

There were only a couple of hundred witnesses to the Masters of Mayhem's performance, perhaps even fewer than that. People in the toilets missed it completely. So did people around the box office and anyone still outside checking in their coats and bags. It was they who started the stampede for the next show, then, after they emerged onto the dance floor to find the entire lounge on its feet in stunned delirium. 'You . . . just . . . missed . . . the best fucking show of all time!'

'We did our first gig as a joke,' Flea shrugged. 'The next time we played, there were lines around the block.'

The Masters of Mayhem vanished from view sometime between their first proper rehearsal and the appearance of the posters advertising their return. It was a great name, but it was also a little glib. The band wanted a name that perhaps suggested something a little more substantial, a little less bound to the novelty world. Walking in the Hollywood Hills, Kiedis stumbled upon it, glowing, he insisted, from 'a psychedelic bush that had band names on it'. The Red Hot Chili Peppers simply sounded too good to pass up, even if it did have a slightly second-hand air to it: a decade earlier, Chilli Willie and the Red Hot Peppers were a major draw on London's pub circuit; now, their nomenclatural descendants were to cause a similar stir in LA.

'The next show we did, we had two songs,' Jack Irons said with a laugh, ' "Out in LA" and "Get Up and Jump". It wasn't like we were trying to fool people; they wanted to see us play and we only had two songs, so that's all we could give them.' By the time of their third show, however, 'Green Heaven' entered the Red Hot Chili Peppers' repertoire, together with the first of the trademark cover versions that have distinguished the group ever since.

'We learned a load of campfire songs, which we performed a cappella,' Irons continued. 'They went down really well, because everybody else knew them as well. Gigs turned into these enormous singsongs!' After a mere handful of shows, the Red Hot Chili Peppers had learned diversification and, though it was necessity that first demanded that they slide effortlessly from sandblasted funk to echoing rap and into a straight-faced rendition of 'She'll Be Coming Round the Mountain', still they were perfecting a skill that many more established acts might never embrace. 'Within a matter of two or three months,' said Flea, 'we were the hottest band in LA.'

'I never thought, "Hey, I've got a great idea! Let's take punk rock and funk and put them together and make a song!" ' Flea is adamant on this point. 'It was just elements of all the things that I loved. It was what I liked, what I listened to and what I was able to play. It was never really conscious. When I picked up my bass and started wailing by myself, that was the kind of shit I played. I liked playing funk, but the natural me was very aggressive. I liked that feeling of beating the shit out of the bass, but doing it in a funky way.' And now, he averred, 'We're the granddaddy groove gooses and we drink our smooth juices and we're the slidenest, glidenest, movinest, groovinest, hippinest, hoppinest, rockinest, jamminest, slamminest. We're on a mission.'

Those first months passed by quickly, in a blur of opportunity. By day, the Red Hot Chili Peppers passed the time in whatever way they could think of that would guarantee something new to talk about at night; before evening drew them out onto the streets, to explore Hollywood's ever-exploding nightlife.

Madame Wong's was a favourite hang-out, all the more so after a band called Fishbone took up residence there, to prove that even the Red Hot Chili Peppers' sonic hybrid could be enlarged upon. Formed at Junior High in the San Fernando Valley by saxophonist Angelo Moore, bassist Norwood Fisher, trumpeters Walter Kibby II and Chris Dowd, guitarist Kendall Jones and Fisher's drummer brother Phillip, Fishbone drew their inspiration from any place they wished. Ska and jazz, rock and reggae, P-Funk and punk, all took their position in the Fishbone stew, and did so with a flourish that the watching Red Hot Chili Peppers were unable to resist.

A lasting friendship was born, one that was soon to be found spreading itself over every club stage in town and outward from there. When the Israeli-born promoter Lyor Cohen opened a new nightclub, the Mix, in the shell of the Stardust Ballroom, he admitted that he wasn't sure whether the out-of-town headliners Run DMC would be enough to pack the place. So he called in the Circle Jerks, Social Distortion and Fear to give added weight to the bill, and, to kick everything off, Fishbone and the Red Hot Chili Peppers.

He was right to be concerned. Run DMC were playing another three shows in LA that same night and each one overran. By the time the New York rap trio reached the Mix, the doors were closed and the audience had gone home. The Red Hot Chili Peppers, as comfortably intimate with the 3,500-strong crowd as they normally were with one quarter of that number, had already exhausted them before the rest of the show even started. When Flea reappeared with Fear, the roar of recognition drowned even that welcome; and, when Circle Jerks brought the night to a close, calls for the Red Hot Chili Peppers could still be heard.

Lyor Cohen was certainly impressed. Over the next few months, he was to book the group into the Mix on several more occasions and, by the time Run DMC returned to the club on 16 June 1984, the Red Hot Chili Peppers had risen to third on the bill, behind Run DMC and the Dickies, but ahead of Fishbone, Cathedral of Tears and the Cambridge Apostles. A year after that, with Run DMC now national celebrities and chart-toppers to boot, the Red Hot Chili Peppers were literally breathing down their necks onstage in both LA and San Francisco.

Throughout the autumn of 1983, the Red Hot Chili Peppers were also hosting a residency at the Cathay de Grand. Dividing their time between What Is This and the Red Hot Chili Peppers, Slovak and Irons never worked so hard, or so often, in their lives. Both bands were perched on the verge of taking off, although whether the popularity of one was influencing the other, none could say. The pair saw the same kids at both bands' shows and, though the Red Hot Chili Peppers' style was certainly far more abandoned, What Is This lost no time in keeping pace on the dance floor.

Nevertheless, Irons recalled that 'there were definitely some bizarre feelings starting to grow between the two groups, because the Red Hot Chili Peppers were taking off a lot quicker. What Is This's appeal was a lot more of a struggle to get across and that, in itself, became a little conflict.' But not, he hastens to add, between the band members themselves. The one time the two groups were booked to appear side by side, at Brendan Mullen's Club Lingerie in September 1983, the six musicians spent the evening getting deliciously drunk together, then turned in the shows of their lives.

Indeed, the only real tensions appeared to have been between Slovak and Hans Reunscheussel, the Hamburg-born bassist who joined What Is This when Flea went off to join Fear. 'The band had never worked off negative chemistry before,' said Johannes, 'and things had usually gone pretty smoothly. But Hans and Hillel didn't get on at all well.'

For Reunscheussel, Slovak's carefree moonlighting with a rival group eventually became too much to stomach. He quit after no more than three months with What Is This and was replaced by the infinitely more buoyant Chris Hutchinson.

Simultaneously, however, Johannes admitted, he was as aware as Reunscheussel of the pitfalls embodied in What Is This's arrangement with the Red Hot Chili Peppers. He conceded that 'they were getting the bigger gigs and the most attention' and, acknowledging that Slovak was certainly hankering for the same slice of What Is This's limelight as he was granted in the Red Hot Chili Peppers, he added, 'I found myself holding back a lot more than I normally would. I allowed him to be the guitar player.'

Few people who knew Slovak as a teen describe him as a natural extrovert. 'He had a lot of ideas,' remembered one former friend, 'but he preferred to let them speak through his playing and his art.' Many of the Red Hot Chili Peppers' earliest shows, she continued, were advertised with handbills designed by Slovak, while his apartment was slowly stacking up with his paintings. 'But, as the Peppers began to take off, he certainly became a lot louder personality-wise.' Both in and out of the group, Slovak became more demanding.

'He was becoming more concerned with what he could do in terms of fashion,' said Johannes. 'Not clothing, but the alternative underground lifestyle.' Without passing on to Kiedis and Flea either the credit or the blame for what, in retrospect, was Slovak's slow decline, Johannes cannot disguise the knowledge that it was with the birth of the Red Hot Chili Peppers that it began.

From the start, the Red Hot Chili Peppers were tapped into a whole different concept of performing, the abandoned mania that they themselves would describe with the title of their second album: *Freaky Styley*. It wasn't the people in the group that changed Slovak; it was the very nature of the group itself.

But neither Kiedis nor Flea was ready to resist Slovak's absorption into archetypal rock'n'roll culture, because they themselves were already living it. Flea cheerfully admitted that, as an awkward teen, he believed that being in a band was the best way to land chicks. The reality of the situation exceeded even his wildest dreams.

The Red Hot Chili Peppers' own appeal, said Kiedis, was simple. 'We were so twisted. We wore clashing clothes and were basically outcasts. We used to have a huge geek following.'

Bound not only through friendship, but also through the shared passions that circulated through their tight group of friends, the Red Hot Chili Peppers were creating for themselves a safe haven in the eye of a storm. Around them, relationships both pure and impure, permanent and transitory, seethed in a constant turmoil. Even a quick visit to the rooms that they called home reflected that.

Individually and collectively, home for the band members was, in fact, any one of a succession of memorably sordid apartments. Kiedis spent some time in what Flea called 'some kind of weird office space upstairs at Hollywood Boulevard and Cherokee'; there was a spell up on Wilton, which ended when Flea burned down the kitchen; and another in Hollywood, where their inability to pay the rent one month prompted the landlady to remove the front door and lay bare Pepperland to every passer-by who cared to look in.

At every one, the scenario was the same. At any hour of the day or night, bodies, sleeping or screwing, lay underfoot. Drugs, used and abused, were on constant show. The air was thick with sweat, smoke and alcohol. Any sense of order that pervaded the apartment, the occasional bursts of housekeeping when someone picked up the strewn clothes and records or rinsed any plates in the sink, passed through unnoticed.

It was chaos, but it was also the nature of the group. Personally and musically, the Red Hot Chili Peppers offered something no other band on the circuit, What Is This included, could match. They represented an instinctive coming together of music, mayhem and, above all, attitude. When they took the stage, they didn't care what people thought of them; rather, they encouraged opprobrium and deliberately courted censure. Offstage, the same principles guided them no less unerringly. They lived with 'soul'.

'There are only two categories in music: soulful and non-soulful,' Flea affirmed. 'Anything that has human emotion and spirit and is played with heart and sincerity is really happening. We can see the beauty in Eric Dolphe, the Ramones and everything in between. We love anything that has a groove that makes you want to live. If you have an open mind, you can see the beauty in all kinds of music.'

As the future opened up to them, both as a band and as in-demand session players, each of the Red Hot Chili Peppers would confirm their broad musical tastes in the most blatant manner that they could – individually and collectively, members of the band have since appeared on tributes to acts as far afield as the Germs, the Ramones and John Lennon, while their taste in cover versions has taken them from frenetic takes on Stevie Wonder, Hank Williams and Elton John, to the positively beautiful rendition of Joy Division's 'Love Will Tear Us Apart', with which Flea and Jimmy Scott dignified an otherwise unpalatable slab of easy listening rock, 1998's *Lounge-a-palooza* compilation.

Open-mindedness, however, was not something the Red Hot Chili Peppers could always be certain of finding. For their first-ever out-of-town show, the group landed a priceless three-day residency in the exclusive skiing resort of Aspen, Colorado.

A literal playground of the rich, where lift tickets alone are a symbol of luxurious wealth, Aspen boasted among its residents, writer Hunter

S Thompson and actor Don Johnson. Fiercely elitist, ferociously exclusive, Aspen regards the tourists who flock from down-market to visit its slopes with condescension at best, loathing at worst. The Red Hot Chili Peppers, booked to cater to just such an audience, were no exception. As the group trooped offstage after their first performance, they were told to take their 'black music' back to Hollywood. According to Flea, 'We left and will never play there again.'

Bringing together the disparate strands of music that offered them the greatest emotional satisfaction, layering ideas and influences other people would have sworn would never hold, then nailing it all into place beneath Kiedis's mile-a-minute verbosity, the Red Hot Chili Peppers laid no claim to originality.

In conversation, the band members happily admitted that their ideas were nothing new in themselves; and, far from hiding behind fits of tight-lipped artistic pique, they responded gleefully, even gratefully, to fans or journalists who publicly isolated a particular debt. To understand their music, the Red Hot Chili Peppers believed, was to understand them. To appreciate what they were trying to do was the first step towards loving it.

'We don't steal,' Flea said, 'we feel.' Even with the sheer size of the band's following going into overdrive, the principle of the Red Hot Chili Peppers remained the same. 'It was all a matter,' as Kiedis puts it, 'of us being friends and what a fine idea it would be to have four close friends as bearers of the zany new funk we had in our minds and our bodies.'

'It was really fun,' Flea continued. 'We started to play more shows and write more songs. Then all of a sudden people were starting to take us seriously, and lawyers [were] trying to get us record contracts and shit.'

While the Red Hot Chili Peppers themselves honour only the LA underground with 'discovering' them, Mark 'Rooster' Richardson could take at least part of the credit for bringing the band to the attention of the outside world. Before his tragically early death from cancer in 2002, before, too, he became one of the sonic architects who helped shape the alternative landscape of the 1990s from his Triclops Studio base in Atlanta, Georgia, Rooster was one of those people who instinctively gravitated to the centre of the next musical upheaval.

Based in New York during the mid-1970s, he witnessed the rise of the first wave of American punk bands, the Television–Patti Smith– Ramones axis. A year later, in 1976, he was in London, shell-shocked and shattered as the Sex Pistols, the Clash and, best of all, the Adverts took even the naive roar of the American bands to new heights of paranoid petulance. Now he was in LA, waiting to see what his instincts had sought out this time.

'I heard about the Red Hot Chili Peppers from a director friend of mine,' Rooster recalled. 'He had done some television work with Anthony's father and he said I should go and check this band out.' A few nights later, Rooster found himself in 'this strange bar in LA, not at all the sort of place you'd expect to find a band like the Red Hot Chili Peppers playing'. In fact, it turned out that the venue had rarely, if ever, staged live music before, 'so the Red Hot Chili Peppers took everybody by surprise'.

They were simply wild, he recollected, playing as though their lives depended on it, but appearing not to give a damn either way. While Flea and Jack Irons laid down an apocalyptic barrage of sound and Slovak's guitar bellowed like a dying buffalo, Kiedis flew around the stage like a madman, his three-inch Mohawk flopping from side to side as he twisted his skinny frame into ever more bizarre contortions. If his vocals, an anguished half-howl, half-roar, harangued the audience's ears, his body literally battered their eyes.

Most of all, though, the Red Hot Chili Peppers exuded sex: hot, sweaty, unbridled energy that found its outlet in an endless, ear-piercing fuck. Rooster wasn't the only person in the club who felt it. Every eye in the joint was locked on to the band, roving hungrily as though pre-selecting a target among the four 21-year-olds who were pounding out that insatiable noise. Kiedis later tried to describe the sensations he knew the Red Hot Chili Peppers excited. 'Sex is a very big part of [our] music. It's one of the more predominant emotions we deal with. It's the whole feeling you get in your crotch when you hear this kind of music.' It was the Red Hot Chili Peppers' ability to re-create that feeling, until every nerve ending screamed out for relief, that ensured they stood out in the crowd. That and their uniqueness.

Since its heyday during the mid-1970s, funk, the pounding rhythms that built from repetition into a mesmerising grind, had very much lost its way as a musical force. Just as the music industry was now looking to embrace, and simultaneously emasculate, rap for a wider white audience, so the initial explosion of black funk bands swiftly and sadly slipped into a state approaching self-parody.

Even George Clinton, whose Parliafunkadelicament Thang mothership of bands and soloists had once driven the music to impossible heights of grandeur, quickly found himself being courted by the rock'n'roll glossies and winning the heart of the pop establishment.

Clinton himself fought desperately to remain true to his own ambitions but, from without, the pressure to come up with another Top 30 smash, like Parliament's 'Flashlight' or Funkadelic's 'One Nation Under a Groove', was immense. By the end of the 1970s, the man who once revolutionised funk had lost himself.

Earth, Wind and Fire followed Clinton into the realms of spectacular showmanship, but for them, too, an arsenal of exploding amplifiers and levitating drummers was no compensation for the band's gradual drift from musical intensity to platinum-shifting idiocy. By the early 1980s, funk was the softly pumping horns that British bands like Lynx and the truly horrible Level 42 grafted on to their facile pop, the scarcely danceable convolutions that James Chance and the Pop Group pumped from their lofty art empires, or the off-centre soundings of Fishbone, operating so far to the left of the genre that they were still appearing on reggae compilations long after the local media acknowledged the group's true musical intentions.

To find any band pounding out tight, authentic funk in 1983, then, was surprising. To find a white band doing it was even more so. And to find them doing it in Los Angeles, a city that remained almost traditionally divisive in its separation of its black and white musical cultures, was little short of miraculous.

'Los Angeles is not like New York,' confirmed writer Roy Trakin in *Musician* magazine in 1989. 'Blacks and whites don't mingle all that much in LA's largely segregated neighbourhoods, so the Red Hot Chili Peppers' collision of punk and funk makes them an anomaly here.'

Undisciplined without ever growing sloppy; apparently unable, but, in reality, simply unwilling, to prevent the entire show from sliding into inexorable chaos, clinging on to their personal vision as though it were the last raft off the *Titanic*, the Red Hot Chili Peppers bedazzled Rooster. He could not believe what he was seeing and, later, when he heard that tonight was one of the group's more restrained nights, he determined to become involved with them.

5. HARDCORE, BONE-CRUNCHING MAYHEM SEX THINGS FROM HEAVEN

Jimi Hendrix flickered across the stage, an Afro-headed blur of crimson velvet, brown skin and flames, coaxed from the corpse of his Fender in a ritual that was half showman, half shaman.

The Monterey Pop Festival in June 1967 was not the first time Hendrix burned his guitar. He did it in England as well, when the Jimi Hendrix Experience toured with the Walker Brothers in April and, according to Mitch Mitchell, his drummer, he would never do it again.

But people remembered it. At Monterey the immolation was caught on film and that short sequence of footage is possibly the best known of Hendrix's entire celluloid career. He was the 'wild man of pop' who pushed the Rolling Stones from the headlines, the savage Mau Mau warrior whom the English press held up in terror and from whom parents recoiled aghast. A sibilant hissing from the radio at night, 'foxy lady, I'm coming . . . to GETCHA!', and suddenly last year's headlines were so much scrap paper. Who cared if their daughter married a Rolling Stone? At least marriage was respectable. What Hendrix threatened was far worse.

Yet the burning was a spur-of-the-moment thing, conjured up by Hendrix's press agent to wring a few extra headlines from the following day's papers. The star was closing his set with 'Fire'; Keith Altham simply thought 'it would be great if Jimi could start one'. A roadie rushed out for a can of lighter fluid and, in the darkness at the back of the stage, manager Chas Chandler prepared the guitar while the star ad-libbed at the front.

Hendrix's first match went out. So did the next and the next. For a moment it looked as though the gag would fall flat. While the rhythm section rolled on and the stage lights dimmed, Hendrix knelt, striking lights, then let them fall to the ground. Suddenly one caught. Hendrix leaped back and flames shot four feet into the air. The entire stage appeared to burn, as the fire reflected from every surface. The audience screamed as one; the theatre management blazed with a fury of their own. And Hendrix's reputation was made.

It was only later that Hendrix realised that, so high was his star, so loud the applause, it didn't matter if he didn't play a correct note all night. All he had to do was flick his Zippo or bend his Fender and everything would be all right. Later still, after the guitarist's death in September 1970, Mitch Mitchell mourned the loss of Hendrix's artistry, as he became trapped in a world of expectations and imagery.

'What about his music, man?'

That first night at the Astoria, such concerns were far from anyone's mind.

The summer of 1983 burned on and the Red Hot Chili Peppers won a reputation for playing anytime, anyplace, and dragging a large crowd behind them. Club owners fell over one another to book them, but the band, managing itself with more aplomb than many professional organisations, was selective. Venues where they had been mistreated as patrons were out. So were shows that clashed with Irons and Slovak's schedule with What Is This. And so were ones they simply didn't fancy. But when a booking came through from the Kit Kat Club, there was not a single dissenting voice.

The Kit Kat was a strip joint, renowned not only for the beauties who worked there, but also for its one tantalising house rule. There was not a strand of pubic hair to be seen, and that despite all the girls appearing resplendent in the most tightly strung G-strings. But the Kit Kat was unusual in other ways, too. As the groups played, the girls would fan out around them and dance, a crazy re-enactment of a demented *Shindig*, that pinnacle of 60s pop Americana, where leggy ladies gyrated on podiums even higher than the bands', clearly absorbing far more of the audience's attention than the guests themselves could ever hope to.

So it was at the Kit Kat. For the first time in their career, the Red Hot Chili Peppers left the stage knowing how it felt to be upstaged. They pulled every trick in the book and, though they themselves knew how the audience felt, still it felt strange to be blown off the stage by a dozen bare breasts. How could they possibly top what they'd already done?

Then Kiedis had an idea. 'Remember the socks?'

Back in his days at UCLA, Kiedis told *Rolling Stone*, he had been frantically trying to escape the attentions of a girl who wouldn't take no for an answer. 'I really wasn't into her, but she would send me these cards with fold-out cocks, with the yardstick on it.' Little gifts like that made even her usual unsubtle overtures resemble the height of decorum.

Kiedis did his best to ignore her but, when the girl turned up unannounced at his apartment one day, he finally cracked. Disappear-

ing into his bedroom while she hung around waiting, he re-emerged
stark naked, except for a tube sock obscuring, and suspended from,
his genitalia. 'Not just over the cock, either. Over the cock and balls.'

The gag ('and it was a great gag') caught on. When Slovak and Flea
moved in with him and friends dropped by to hang out, smoke pot
and drink beer, sooner or later Los Faces would put socks 'on their
dicks and run around'. 'It was kids living together,' said Flea, 'just
having fun.'

Standing in the dressing room of the Kit Kat, with the club's
manager demanding they return to the stage for an encore, the socks
suddenly seemed a great idea again. Ripping off their clothes, the four
Red Hot Chili Peppers affixed their sweat socks over their members,
then opened the dressing room door. 'We were levitating with nervous
energy,' roared Kiedis. 'I could not find my feet on stage, and
somebody filmed it. I don't know if the film still exists, but we saw it
and we just had this look in our eyes like we were from outer space.'

'That was one of the fucking funniest moments I've ever had!' Irons
continued. 'It was so funny I started to pee in my sock. We were
laughing so hard! But it was that simple, it was us trying to upstage
the strippers who were dancing in their G-strings next to us.'

The trick worked, as well. Undisturbed by the dancers, unmolested
by the stunned audience, the Red Hot Chili Peppers blasted through
their final number, then quit the stage. When they returned to the
dressing room, the club manager was waiting for them, screaming and
hysterical. 'No pubes! I told you guys, no pubes!' The song that
debuted the cocks in socks, a moment of supreme high-spiritedness
that was not only to dominate, but dictate the Red Hot Chili Peppers'
future, was Jimi Hendrix's 'Fire'.

There was another band on the bill that night, a similarly
non-musical musical outfit called Roid Rogers and the Whirling Butt
Cherries. The troupe played no more than three concerts, this
particular evening included, but for drummer Cliff Martinez the night
was to leave an indelible impression. Roid Rogers and co's stagewear
comprised little more than diapers and jockstraps, and Martinez
recalled, 'maybe [the Chili Peppers] were trying to upstage us. They
came out in the sock thing. And that was the first time they did the
sock thing. And it was a huge hit. I just remember everybody trying
to grab Anthony's sock. It was a show-stopper.'

Though he missed the cocks-in-socks routine, Rooster knew
instinctively that any band who could develop so uncompromising a
stage act, yet retain their musical integrity, was marked out for

something special. Within days of meeting them, he arranged to accompany the Red Hot Chili Peppers into Bijou Studios to begin work on a demo tape, the first of several the band recorded during these first months together – Fear drummer Spit Stix handled another.

Confirming a stray thought that Flea has occasionally let slip over the years, Jack Irons agreed that 'there was a point that the Red Hot Chili Peppers thought the demo tapes definitely had something which the later records didn't. We were all fun and young, no real drug problems had developed, it was a very clean period.'

For their first session, recorded shortly before Rooster appeared on the scene, the band took five songs into the studio with them: 'Out in LA', 'Get Up and Jump', 'Green Heaven', 'Sex Rap' and 'Baby Appeal', all of which they would carry with them to their first album, plus a handful of the a cappella campfire singalongs. The idea behind the tape was not to prove what great songwriters the Red Hot Chili Peppers were, nor even how many original songs they already boasted. The concern was to bring into a stuffy record company A&R department a taste of the sheer anarchic excitement the group was capable of generating.

Rooster, whose interest in the Red Hot Chili Peppers had by now gone into overdrive, immediately started shopping the tape around the LA-based record companies. He also paired the band up with a long-time friend of his, MCA promo man Lindy Goetz, and there was only a hint of regret in his voice as he recalled how Goetz promptly became the group's manager; Rooster could not tell whether he harboured similar ambitions for himself. For now, it was sufficient simply to be involved with this fabulous band and to be standing alongside them as the record company and publishing offers began piling up.

After entertaining visitors from half a dozen different companies and being rejected outright by just one of them, Arista, the Red Hot Chili Peppers signed a seven-album contract with EMI America's Enigma subsidiary in November 1983, and celebrated by tracking down label A&R man Jamie Cohen and screaming the Sex Pistols' 'EMI' at him. Cohen, according to Flea, responded with 'a tolerant grin and a handshake, and it really [started] dawning on me that we were gonna make a record. It was kind of shocking.'

The group had been in existence for six months.

A division of Capitol Records, EMI America was in the money. A year earlier, David Bowie had released his first new album in three years and his debut for the label, the all-conquering *Let's Dance*. Other labels, Bowie's own former home RCA included, had written it off before it was even completed. Pairing Bowie with Chic maestro Nile Rodgers was not just a commercial absurdity; according to Bowie's own constantly proven powers of musical prophecy, it was rock'n'roll suicide. Instead, *Let's Dance* became one of the year's biggest hits, not only restoring credibility to its maker's own long-derailed career, but breathing fresh blood into conventional white dance music, too.

As the EMI executives studied the Red Hot Chili Peppers' résumé, replayed the demo tape and discussed their own independent analyses, it wasn't difficult to believe that lightning had struck twice. In the current pop climate, there was no reason on earth why the Red Hot Chili Peppers' convoluted mutant dance should not follow in Bowie's baggy-suited footsteps.

Hindsight always plays cruel tricks on one, particularly when one's career is at stake. The EMI American deal, however, remains redolent with might-have-beens, not only because it was not necessarily the best of the offers the Red Hot Chili Peppers received, but also because, in signing it, Kiedis and Flea also signed away the unity that hitherto bound the group together.

The repercussions of the decisions made at this time were to haunt the group for years to come.

The Red Hot Chili Peppers were conceived as a part-time band, something for Slovak and Irons to do during What Is This's occasional hiatuses, and to allow Flea some musical relaxation in between his now-frustrating appearances with Fear. Only Kiedis had no other consuming passion to occupy his time; and yet, his unquestioned role as the group's lyricist notwithstanding, he had never previously considered the Red Hot Chili Peppers as anything other than a group effort. It was not that he was unable to function without his three closest friends alongside him; it was that he did not want to.

Flea agreed with him. When it finally became apparent that EMI America really was serious about signing the group, a hilarious circumstance that the Red Hot Chili Peppers themselves still had difficulty taking seriously, he quit Fear. 'I just said "Fuck it" and quit.'

'Although he was their bass player,' remembered Alison Braun, 'nobody ever thought of Flea as a permanent member of Fear, particularly after the Peppers got going. It was always more like he was guesting with them.' The remainder of Fear were certainly dismissive about their former bass player's contributions, prompting Flea in later years to describe his decision as 'kind of mutual; they didn't want me. They rejected me.' And, for his own part, 'the Red Hot Chili Peppers were much closer to my heart'.

For Irons and Slovak, however, the situation was considerably more perplexing. Although the Red Hot Chili Peppers were consuming more and more of the duo's free time, What Is This, too, had been attracting its fair share of media attention. Even as the Red Hot Chili Peppers prepared to sign with EMI, the similarly prestigious MCA was moving in on What Is This.

The chances of two bands sharing two musicians, receiving two simultaneous record company offers, are minuscule, even if – as several onlookers have suggested – one company stepped in only to spoil the second's dealings, after it was thwarted in its quest for the other band. Although the Red Hot Chili Peppers were by far the better-known of the two groups, still their debt to What Is This was clear, as Alain Johannes explained: 'The Red Hot Chili Peppers did take a big chunk of the What Is This vibe and approach, especially in the beginning. A lot of the funky side of the group.' The gamble the two bands' suitors were taking was which side of the fence would Irons and Slovak choose to come down upon? Because they did have to choose. Even within the incestuous circles of LA rock'n'roll, neither friends nor advisers could think of a situation similar to that in which Slovak and Irons now found themselves. Even the most frequently cited example of Rod Stewart and the Faces – who, twenty years previous, signed separate band and solo deals (with Warner Brothers and Mercury respectively) – did not truly connect; Stewart's solo work was seen by many people as simply a continuation of the Faces' and, in the early years at least, the continued existence of one was wholly dependent upon the health of the other. It was the Faces' tireless live work that paved the way for Stewart's solo breakthrough; it was the success of Rod on his own that sustained the Faces' concert momentum.

In this instance, the conflict of interests was evident to all. It was just that Slovak and Irons did not see it that way, 'They wanted to remain involved with both bands,' recalled Alain Johannes, 'and I think Flea and Anthony would have been happy with that arrangement as well. But it would never have worked out and I told them so. And so they chose What Is This.'

According to Irons, the decision to stay with What Is This was almost wholly sentimental. 'We'd been with this group, as Anthym and What Is This, ever since Junior High. So we figured that when we had the chance to actually make a record, after all these years together, that was who we should do it with.' It wasn't an easy choice to make but, once made, they stuck with it.

Kiedis took the news badly. 'I was emotionally devastated. I was so happy to finally be in a band and to be strutting my stuff around town and for my friends to fall out like that, I thought we were over.' He admitted he went home and cried.

Flea was more stoic, even resigned, to the twosome's resolution. 'Jack and Hillel had been playing for at least six years. So what were they supposed to do: Go with the joke band that got a deal after six months? Or with the band they dedicated themselves to for six years? They went with What Is This, which is completely understandable.'

Aware of the upheavals now shaking their nest egg, if not quite certain about their long-term significance, EMI America offered the Red Hot Chili Peppers only a few months in which to regroup. The group was expected in the studio bright and early in the new year to begin work on its debut album.

Hurriedly auditioning friends and various local musicians, Flea and Kiedis finally pulled in LA session guitarist Jack Sherman and, still reeling from all he witnessed at the Kit Kat, drummer Cliff Martinez. Both were competent musicians (until its dissolution, Martinez was also a key member of Lydia Lunch's 13.13); both adhered to a credo that was close to their new bandmates' hearts ... 'Captain Beefheart has the best quote about playing music and it means a lot to me,' Martinez told Spin in 1984. 'He always said, "Hit it to hell in the breadbasket and finger-fuck the devil." I think what he meant was, always play every note like it was going to be your last.' Neither, however, was a Red Hot Chili Pepper. The onus not only of performance, but of being seen to perform, fell squarely now upon Kiedis and Flea.

It is ironic that the Red Hot Chili Peppers should begin work on their first album at half strength. Although their name was still all but unknown outside of Los Angeles, within their own community the results of the band's first studio sojourn were awaited with an impatience that bordered upon pure mania.

Writing in the LA Weekly, Danny (Shredder) Weizman laid out his own hopes and dreams for the group. 'The Chili Peppers are the (Fasten Your Seatbelts) ... NEXT BIG THING, whether your smarmy li'l too-hip patootie wants to accept the given and give up this anti-cool bit or not. No matter. Eventually you will succumb to their absolute majesty, their muscle-funky insight, their Rap-A-Long Cassidy brilliance. They are the IT-boys of the omnilocal scene, image and sonics soulfully rockin', down to a chili-pepper-colored "T". Funky is about the most oblique description of the airtight jerky sound-splash mayhem they deliver. If they're the white-funk joke-band that they're being hyped and hipped as, then it's the most solid white-hot funk and the most deadly serious barrel-of-monkeys joke I've heard for two, maybe three [millennia].'

Privately, however, Kiedis and Flea counselled forbearance. Looking back on the entire experience, Flea mourned, 'Our natural, spontaneous thing wasn't there. If we'd had that original line-up, I think . . . we would have gotten the real thing, hardcore, down on record. We were so explosive at that time and it's not an explosive record.'

But it should have been, because EMI America was pulling out all the sonic stops to make things happen, even pairing the Red Hot Chili Peppers with a dream-come-true in the form of their record's producer, all the way from the Gang of 4, guitarist Andy Gill. In commercial terms, too, the union promised dividends. The Gang of 4 split just as they teetered on the brink of a major American breakthrough, around the same time that the Red Hot Chili Peppers signed with EMI America. Couple one band's motive with the other's motivation, and the rewards would surely come streaming in.

A meeting between Gill and the Red Hot Chili Peppers was swiftly set up and, as he prepared for their first encounter, Flea was well aware that the potential of a collision between the Gang of 4 and the Red Hot Chili Peppers, one armed with the graffiti of revolution and the other with a frenetic litany of LA's lives and loves, seemed magical.

Kiedis, too, was ecstatic. A refresher course in the Gang of 4's work reintroduced him to a repertoire that certainly pointed in the same direction as the Red Hot Chili Peppers themselves were now heading, while Flea remembered the nights he spent listening to the Gang of 4's first two albums, *Entertainment* and *Solid Gold*, following the convoluted thunder of David Allen's bass riffs. Eight years later, during the Lollapalooza'92 tour, he even told Allen that everything he knew about bass playing he learned from those same albums.

'I love the Gang of 4, their first two records were hugely influential records. They are one of the finest bands that England has ever produced and, consciously or subconsciously, they have influenced a lot of things that we write.' Indeed, almost twenty years later, the spirit of the Gang of 4 continued to overhang the Red Hot Chili Peppers, as DJ Steve Lamacq pointed out when he compared 'Throw Away Your TV', a highlight of the group's *By the Way* album of 2002, to the old masters. 'That would be a great compliment,' Flea admitted.

At the time, too, 'we thought Andy would be perfect for us, because [those] albums were so fantastic,' Flea raved. Gill, his ambition of moving into production work having been fulfilled so much sooner than he expected, was equally enthralled. But such raging enthusiasm proved cruelly short-lived. 'Maybe he was just too English for us,' Flea said later, a clumsy acknowledgement that, while Gill certainly understood the Red Hot Chili Peppers' music from a technical and theoretical point of view, the cold sterility of such terms in no way prepared him for the emotional thunder that the group, even in its present, debilitated state, was capable of delivering.

Even more damaging, to the Red Hot Chili Peppers, at least, was Gill's offhand dismissal of his work with the Gang of 4. 'He said he didn't know what he was doing with those records,' Flea complained. '[Which was] disheartening, because those are great records.' If his best work was created by accident, Flea and Kiedis reasoned privately, what was going to happen now that Gill thought he knew what he was doing?

The Red Hot Chili Peppers' own naiveté, too, worked against them. Less than six months had elapsed since they first set foot in a studio with Rooster, to record demo tapes that demanded no more from the band than they were prepared to give. Now Kiedis and Flea found themselves cloistered with three complete strangers, and expected to take on the world. A handful of live shows had done little to acquaint them with Martinez and Sherman; Gill had his own circle of friends in LA and showed little interest in hitting the town with his clients.

Only Gill's engineer, Dave Jerden, appeared to be on their side. He came to the sessions fresh from working with What Is This on their vinyl debut, a five-track EP that Johannes, Irons and Slovak had no hesitation in proclaiming the greatest record they ever heard. It was they who recommended Jerden to the Red Hot Chili Peppers and they who dropped by the sessions to lend encouragement when times got rough.

But, even in the presence of their friends, there was no sense of unity in the studio for Flea and Kiedis, no suggestion that one might develop and, as the sessions dragged on, no way that Flea and Kiedis could articulate to Gill that what they were hearing in playback was somehow wrong. 'We knew what we wanted,' Flea later confessed. 'We wanted a raw fucking rocking album.' But, instead of trying to work with Gill, pinpointing the mistakes he made as he experimented with sounds and levels, it seemed easier just to walk into the control room and tell him, 'That sucks.'

'We should have been asking, "Can't we try something?" but we didn't know. He was a very uptight Englishman on top of it, so that mix didn't work very well. To this day . . .' Flea admitted four years later, '. . . I really regret our inability to deal with Andy.'

Only one enduring, and perhaps endearing, memory survives from the recording of that first album. As another unsatisfactory take was completed, Kiedis and Flea decided to visit the bathroom. 'We're just going to take a shit, Andy.'

Gill shot back, 'Yeah. Don't trouble me by bringing it back, right?'

'So Flea and I went and took the shit out of the toilet,' recalled Kiedis, 'brought it back in a pizza box and we gave it to Andy. And all he could say was, "Typical".' A variation on this story has them returning with the turd unwrapped and still dripping, and simply placing it on the control desk in front of Gill. His response was apparently unchanged.

The Red Hot Chili Peppers' studio brief was simply to make a record. Gill's was to make a hit record. 'He thought it was necessary to use rhythm machines as our drums,' complained Kiedis later, 'because that was what was getting on the radio at the time. He took it that we had to do whatever it took to conform to the sound of the radio.'

It was a misapprehension the Red Hot Chili Peppers could never have fulfilled. Exuberant, inexperienced, borne along by instinct rather than some callous notion of what may or may not sell, the Red Hot Chili Peppers both embraced and endorsed a music that, in its emotional purity, owed nothing to the increasingly synthesised sounds that the precociously three-year-old MTV was now pumping into the mainstream American rock consciousness.

Rock'n'roll's struggle to rebuild itself after the devastation of punk rock was still in its infancy. It was the fight to reinvent itself that instead was under way. Like the punks of half a decade earlier, Kiedis and Flea saw their music as a release, an extension of their own bodies that had been given sudden permission to explode and to keep exploding. They had no need for the high-tech gimmickry that the imported sensations of Frankie Goes to Hollywood, the Thompson Twins and Duran Duran were bringing into Day-Glo prominence and they had no heart for it either.

But, if they weren't exactly old-fashioned, such views were out of fashion. The punk-fired belief that not only was it unnecessary to be able to play your instruments, you didn't even need instruments, spawned a musical movement that demanded style over substance, presentation over performance. And, though the mechanics of song-writing remained unchanged, the method of presenting those songs to the public had.

As a companion to the increasingly facile synthipop music now coming to dominate the British and (in the form of a much-touted 'second' British Invasion) US airwaves, the impact of MTV was inestimable. No longer was music the principal product of the rock'n'roll industry. Suddenly video introduced a whole new set of criteria to the commercial potential of new bands and records alike. A bad video could irreparably hamstring a career; a great one could boost it far beyond the customary plateaux of success.

In many ways, this revolution worked in the Red Hot Chili Peppers' favour. A riot of colour and movement, blistering the eyeballs with their bodies, the band was a visual feast. But would the banquet translate to television? Even more importantly, could it be removed from the group's natural in-concert environment and be condensed into the three or four minutes that, even after such protracted conceits as Michael Jackson's 'Thriller' and David Bowie's 'Blue Jean' pushed the limits of the genre into orbit, were still the accepted length of a successful video? The minimal airplay that would be granted, upon release, to the frenetic 'True Men Don't Kill Coyotes' video suggests not. Painted white savages writhing in one another's arms was not the sort of image MTV wished to project.

Yet, if sound was taking second place to sight in the marketplace, still certain guidelines had been set, among them an ever-burgeoning aversion to 'organic' sounds. Britain's Spandau Ballet, whose own earliest musical flirtations centred on funk basics that were markedly similar to (if somewhat more polite than) those the Red Hot Chili Peppers now flaunted, created perhaps the most successful synthesis of art and artifice, hacking out a string of calculatedly stunning singles from their grasp of the new pop technology.

Fired by the same synthesis, the likes of Way of the West, ABC and Lynx took pop's fascination with funk to increasingly diluted extremes; by the time Frankie Goes to Hollywood erupted out of producer Trevor Horn's fervid imagination in 1983, adding socio-sexual innuendo to the already thickening brew, the ground rules of seething rhythms, soft mantras and looping, synthesised drums were set in remorseless stone.

A ruthless doctrine of ideas over ideology was installed. No matter how committed to its cause a band was, its own musical productivity was of secondary interest at best. It was what was done with that productivity, in terms of recording techniques, that counted. Where Andy Gill failed as the Red Hot Chili Peppers' producer was in assuming that this procedure could translate not only to another country, but to another culture. The punk-funk-rap fusion the Red Hot Chili Peppers espoused was unique. To appreciate it, a producer needed to have lived it as fully as the band itself. Andy Gill did not have that advantage.

Day after day, he laboured to turn in an album that offered nothing more than his own interpretation of what modern music demanded. The end result was a record that, at the time, satisfied nobody.

'That was our first record and our whole thing was being punk rock about the funk,' Flea reasoned afterwards. 'We weren't about to compromise our sound, which was based on organic bass and drums. It was a seriously different point of view that we had about going into things.'

The squabbling would go on late into the night. To Gill, the Red Hot Chili Peppers were inexperienced brats whom he needed to mould into commercial shape; to Kiedis and Flea, Gill was uptight, overbearing and had no idea what the Red Hot Chili Peppers were really all about.

Nowhere is this more apparent than on the Red Hot Chili Peppers' signature number, 'Out in LA'. The song that started it all for them was a punch-drunk mouthful of speeding rap, behind which the band thundered towards a convulsive apocalypse. The song's importance to Kiedis and Flea can never be underestimated; for years to come, it was to open their live sets, a maniacal statement of intent that would set the stage for all that was to come.

In Gill's hands, however, 'Out in LA' was no more substantial than those other, throwaway raps by which the sessions were dominated. Even the howl of defiant guitar with which Jack Sherman opened the number sounded muted, while the robotic precision of the drums stood in violent opposition to the maniacal thunder Flea patiently fought to wring from his bass. The entire experience was over in less than two minutes.

Live, the ragged 'Police Helicopter', observing and condemning the intrusive spy in the sky that the LAPD was employing with ever-increasing, ever more irritating, regularity, and 'You Always Sing', Kiedis's stumbling, incoherently raging attack on conventional thought and speech, were detonations of sound and imagery, heartbeats that start-crash-stop amid the unimaginable heat of the stage show. On vinyl, they became barely noticeable sound bites, one clocking in at little more than a minute, the other an utterly inconsequential eleven seconds. Live, the Red Hot Chili Peppers blazed with what Kiedis called the 'tension, aggression and frustration' of growing up in

Hollywood, regurgitating in their music 'the people, the traffic, the lights, the movies, the ocean, the police helicopters landing on your eyeballs'. In the studio, they simply scraped sparks.

Only occasionally, and even then by accident, did the proceedings gel. 'True Men Don't Kill Coyotes', dealing with the *Suburbia*-style just-for-kicks culling of the wild dogs in the Hollywood Hills, ripped out of the speakers with an identical 'dripping . . . passion' as the beasts in the song, while deep in the mix, Sherman's guitar screamed with animal pain. Plaudits could be aimed, too, at 'Grand Pappy Do Plenty', the band's ode to Tomata Duplenty, the former lead vocalist for LA punk band The Screamers, and a fellow resident of the apartment building where Flea and Kiedis lived.

But, while the obvious success of those numbers should have influenced the direction in which the rest of the record went, the very opposite emerged from the tapes. Flea insisted that, right up until the final mix, the 'hard-edged funk' that the Red Hot Chili Peppers heard in their heads was still vying for supremacy with the 'namby-pamby pop-funk' that Gill was apparently trying to foist upon them. But still 'we ended up with a record in between'.

At the same time, however, Flea magnanimously admitted that the group itself was not yet ready to create the record it wanted to hear. 'We didn't have a groove at the time,' he reasoned. 'We had Cliff and Jack and I don't think that configuration was capable of creating a [powerful] groove.'

This delegation of responsibility for their debut record's shortcomings was not necessarily uncalled for. With just a couple of months in which to acquaint themselves not only with the Red Hot Chili Peppers' vision, but with the Red Hot Chili Peppers themselves, Martinez and Sherman's enthusiasm for the recordings was matched only by their uncertainty. As Kiedis was to say years later, when once again the group was seeking both a guitarist and a drummer, simply trying to explain to a stranger what the Red Hot Chili Peppers were all about was difficult enough. Ensuring that person understood was even harder.

'What we originally set out to do was to be complete and utter perpetrators of hardcore, bone-crunching mayhem sex things from heaven. To try and describe that to another musician and have it mean something is nearly impossible unless you've grown up with that person.

'It was crazy, but when you get a guy in the band you've got to be prepared to embrace him emotionally for years and years. Very much like being in love and being married. And you have to be willing to accept and tolerate and compromise sometimes.' With Jack Sherman in particular, that level of commitment simply wasn't possible.

Neither did the album's problems end with the strife within both the band and the recording studio. EMI America, too, had its own agenda for the Red Hot Chili Peppers, based first on the principle that, for a first album, a new band needed more than anything to establish its name in the marketplace. Kiedis's choice of album title, *True Men Don't Kill Coyotes*, was discarded in favour of the simple *The Red Hot Chili Peppers*.

And still, *The Red Hot Chili Peppers* was not the typical 1984 album release. Sleeve designer Gary Panter's job was to recapture in caricature the mayhem that the group itself represented in life; he presented a horrific vision of the group as multicoloured monsters, tongues lolling lasciviously, eyes bloodshot and bulging, scarcely recognisable gap-toothed fiends erupting from a background of wild streaks and smears. Even Flea's newly acquired Jimi Hendrix tattoo boasted three boggling eyes. Reality impinged upon Panter's Dantesque vision only in the positioning of Martinez and Sherman. They were placed well at the back, two barely formed outlines in the shadow of the principal players.

What hope, however, did *The Red Hot Chili Peppers* have in the open marketplace? Still unknown outside of their native California, the group that was formed as a casual joke just one year earlier was now competing on open ground with the monsters of both mainstream and the newly formulated 'alternative' marketplace.

It was a year that began with number ones for Yes and Michael Jackson and ended with similar successes for Hall and Oates and Prince; in which Texan long-beards ZZ Top topped *Saturday Night Live*'s mock Presidential election with almost twice the votes reaped by real-life candidate Jesse Jackson; and in which reality finally took rock'n'roll by the throat when it conjured up the Band Aid/USA for Africa charities – a year such as that had no place for the Red Hot Chili Peppers. *The Red Hot Chili Peppers* was released in August 1984. By September, it had already been forgotten.

So the group toured. Record sales and radio play, they knew, were not going to come to them, a group whose own self-awareness was rooted in the belief that only on stage were the Chili Peppers truly Red Hot. Lindy Goetz drew up the game plan upon which every career initially depends: play hard and wide until you've established your strongholds, then build upon them until they start to connect. In

October, with a triumphant showing at Fenders International Grand Ballroom in Long Beach behind them, the Red Hot Chili Peppers set out on their first headlining tour of the United States, concentrating on the West Coast and the major Midwestern cities.

It was a fraught period. Crammed into their tiny touring bus, there was little room for ego, even less for enmity. But to Flea and Kiedis and, to a lesser degree, Cliff Martinez, Jack Sherman was fast becoming a problem with which they could no longer deal.

He was not, the others complained, a natural freak; had not grown up with both feet planted firmly on the wrong side of the authoritarian fence. He felt reservations that they did not; he was, one accomplice recalled, 'too responsible for the others. Flea and Kiedis talked about living through their music; Jack lived for it.'

In concert, even at those moments of wild abandon when the Red Hot Chili Peppers flocked to the stage in their proudly flapping socks, he seemed studious; in the studio, impatient. When the group wanted to party, Sherman wanted to sleep. And, however little common ground the others shared with their guitarist at the start of the tour, by the time they returned to LA, there was less. Without elaboration, Jack Irons said simply, 'They just didn't like him.' Excluded from conversations, harassed even over the day-to-day maintenance of his guitar, the time he took to change a string or retune between numbers, targeted with increasing regularity as the butt of Kiedis's bitter humour, by the new year, Sherman was out of the group.

There were no hard feelings, at least at first. In 1989, Sherman was among the friends invited along to Ocean Sound Studios to add some backing vocals to two of the songs that would appear on the group's *Mother's Milk* album, 'Good Time Boys' and 'Higher Ground'. In late 1992, however, it was reported that Jack Sherman was taking legal action against the group, seeking both unpaid royalties and damages for his dismissal. It was a claim that the Red Hot Chili Peppers themselves regarded as ridiculous. In terms of earnings, at least, Sherman was treated no differently than any other member of the group. Indeed, at the time Sherman joined the band, two band partnership agreements were drawn up; one relating to publishing, the other to all other services, including royalties earned from record sales. At the time those agreements were entered into, it was agreed that all band members would be treated equally, regardless of whether or not they remained with the group.

The publishing agreement, established through the Red Hot Chili Peppers' own Moebetoblame Music company, indicates precisely how even-handed this arrangement was. All eleven songs on *The Red Hot Chili Peppers* were credited jointly to the group as a whole, according to Kiedis's conviction that songwriting royalties should be split equally between everyone in the band, even though he, as the sole lyricist, certainly contributed more than 25 per cent to each song. Regardless of his actual contribution, then, the pace at which *The Red Hot Chili Peppers* (in common with the rest of the band's back catalogue) had sold in the years since *Mother's Milk*, surely offered Sherman ample recompense for his time in (and out!) of the group.

So far as recompense for his dismissal goes, the question that remained to be asked was, would the Red Hot Chili Peppers have made it with Jack Sherman still in the group? It took the success of *Mother's Milk*, five years later, to start the group's back catalogue moving, but it was the experiences of those years that created that record. With Sherman in place, those experiences could never have occurred. Even before a Superior Court judge threw out Sherman's claims, on 22 March 1994, citing the statute of limitations, Jack Irons was one of many who dismissed Sherman's complaints out of hand. 'The Red Hot Chili Peppers worked hard and I only credit Anthony and Flea for that. They've gone through a lot of hardship; it's not like they had overnight success. Jack Sherman made one record with them and that was it.'

A number of incidents contributed to Sherman's downfall, including several over which he had no control. One such came during this first tour when the band's van, skidding as it passed over an icy bridge, suddenly went hurtling out into the oncoming traffic, to slide sideways between two oncoming trucks. It was a miracle that the vehicle passed through unscathed but, as they surveyed one another's pale faces, Flea and Kiedis realised simultaneously how close they had come to death, and how important it was to be surrounded by friends at all times. No sooner was Jack Sherman out of the door than Flea and Kiedis were wooing Hillel Slovak back into the pack.

6. IF I HAD A SON LIKE THAT, I'D SHOOT HIM

It was impossible to say who got into Jimi Hendrix first, so utterly was his presence assimilated into What Is This. As the group's lead guitarist, of course, Slovak had the greatest opportunities to pay homage and the repertoire of Hendrix songs he built up in his bedroom, from the raging 'Fire' to the gentle 'Castles Made of Sand', and on to the signature riff of 'Third Stone from the Sun', made itself heard not only in rehearsal, but in his songwriting as well.

As What Is This prepared for their first recording session, he sliced through his repertoire for the songs that best represented his art: 'I Am a House', driving on a jerking rhythm from which guitar discords ran breakneck into sharp, controlled bursts of noise, and the epic instrumental 'Squeezed', from which he wrung savage liquid lyricism from the strings. It was a shame, he reflected, that the five-track EP would not have room for 'Stuck', jerking Talking Heads quirkiness laced with bellowing snorts of electrified rage. That would have to wait for the album and, in the meantime, he would polish it some more.

More than any lesson Slovak learned, from Hendrix or anybody else, was the importance of remaining true to himself. The history of rock is littered with guitarists who shattered their past and destroyed their own future when the spirit of some idol touched them too heavily and they replaced admiration with stark imitation.

But, if Slovak felt himself straying too close to the master, even if the lines he played were the greatest he had ever torn from his heart, he would retrace his footsteps. Like Hendrix, enamoured with Cream but willing only to flaunt his obsession if he could make it his own, Slovak experimented, with sounds, with chords, with notes. The heart of Hendrix's 'Voodoo Chile (Slight Return)' was Cream's 'Sunshine of Your Love' played backwards and, in practice, Slovak made similar gestures, only to abandon them in disgust. That, too, was simply following in Hendrix's footsteps. And Slovak's feet were too big to tread comfortably in them.

Since the two factions had unwillingly gone their separate ways in November 1983, What Is This trailed some way behind the Red Hot Chili Peppers, both in terms of media interest and public acceptance.

Even so, insisted Jack Irons, 'We were feeling pretty good. We released our first record, the *Squeezed* EP, and it wasn't a case of us walking around saying it was the best thing that ever happened, people were telling us that it was.'

Five tracks long, a showcase for both Alain Johannes's songwriting (he took three of the five credits, Slovak the other two) and Slovak's vagrant guitar, *Squeezed* was everything the Red Hot Chili Peppers weren't, a portrait of a band at the height of its powers. *Trouser Press* magazine described it as 'wild, muscular rock-funk with a demented outlook . . . a fearsome rhythm behemoth' over which were layered 'offbeat songs, unnervingly mental vocals and psycho guitar kicks. A gut'n'butt shaking experience you won't soon forget'; and when, in later years, that description was appended with reference to 'a passing resemblance to the Red Hot Chili Peppers', the sentiment was wholly guided by hindsight. In September 1984, the Red Hot Chili Peppers could only aspire towards the heights *Squeezed* attained.

Bolstered by the near-universal acclaim being meted out to *Squeezed*, and the way college radio stations had taken it to the heart of their playlists, MCA hastily commissioned a video to accompany the most idiosyncratic of the five tracks, Johannes's fractured 'Mind My Have Still I'.

Directed by Wayne Isham, whose later work with Billy Joel and Motley Crüe was to establish him among the top directors in the business, both the shoot and the ensuing video were dominated by Slovak. 'Hillel was really into video,' remembered Irons. 'He saw its possibilities and he really wanted to get involved in every aspect of it, far more than the rest of us. That video session was the highlight of What Is This in terms of real feeling and real bandsmanship.'

MCA also gave the group the go-ahead to begin preparing their first album, suggesting also that the band's already heightened profile would be boosted even further if they recruited a name producer: Todd Rundgren, fresh from a doomed but dynamic collaboration with the Lords of the New Church. Like the Red Hot Chili Peppers' link with Andy Gill, on paper, it was an inspired coupling. At a time when the portentous overkill of Trevor Horn was still regarded as a recipe for success, the wall-of-sound bombast in which Rundgren specialised made even Horn's greatest overtures sound feeble.

From the moment they met, however, Rundgren and Alain Johannes did not get along and, as the recording of *What Is This* progressed, the friction within their own relationship automatically communicated itself both to the other band members and to the album itself.

The crowning moment came when Johannes, Irons and Chris Hutchinson, sick of struggling through another unproductive session, announced to Rundgren that they were going to loosen themselves up by playing a 'fun' cover of the Spinners' 'I'll Be Around'. Rundgren nodded his assent and set the tapes rolling.

The following day, a posse of MCA bigwigs was due at the studio to discover for itself how work on the album was progressing.

'You're not going to play them 'I'll Be Around' are you?' Johannes asked Rundgren.

The producer shook his head. 'No. That's just between us.' What Is This never did find out how 'I'll Be Around' came to be at the start of the tape. 'But there it was,' said Johannes, 'the first thing the MCA guys heard. They flipped and weren't interested in anything else we were doing. They geared their entire promotional campaign around this one inconsequential and totally unrepresentative song.' 'I'll Be Around' went on to become a minor hit single during the summer of 1985, peaking at No. 62 in August. Before that could become a concern for the band, however, they first had to adjust themselves to Slovak's departure in January.

'I knew in my head that it was inevitable Hillel would go off with the others eventually,' reflected Irons. 'He and I both loved the Red Hot Chili Peppers; it was just that I had managed to erase them from my mind a little bit better than he had. He enjoyed that funky kind of thing; the album sessions suggested that What Is This was developing into a very different kind of band. We'd been together a long time. He just wanted the chance to do something else.'

Johannes agreed. 'Hillel was happy in What Is This, but I think he wanted to broaden his outlook a little. Plus, I think Flea and Anthony always wanted to get both him and Jack back. They were getting very good crowds, but there was a feeling that Jack Sherman was holding them back a little, in terms of just how abandoned they could be. They were very volatile live, but they could have been even more so. Hillel brought that other dimension into play.'

Simultaneously, however, Irons admitted that he did feel just a little sense of relief when Slovak finally left. Although Slovak himself was convinced that nobody knew of his increasing reliance on drugs, it was in fact an open secret that the guitarist's use had finally moved beyond the early experimental phase.

Yet he could not see it, preferring to indulge himself in the vitriolic denials that would ultimately lead to his downfall. To see Slovak taking his addiction into the Red Hot Chili Peppers, wherein Kiedis made little secret of his own dependencies, left Irons feeling so helpless that the only response he could muster was a simple 'out of sight, out of mind'.

Even before Kiedis and Slovak first started playing with drugs during their late teens, Irons was 'the guy who represented the anti-force in the whole drug thing'. He acknowledged that for both of his friends, 'Trying to talk to me about drugs, or drug problems, was a very painful thing to do. I was so against the whole thing that nobody even wanted to hear my shit.'

Alain Johannes, too, remembered how his relationship with Slovak began to change, even before the guitarist quit What Is This. They were moving in different circles, but while Johannes', inspired by his relationship with his girlfriend, Latvian-born Natasha Schneider, were growing ever wider, Slovak's were contracting, a concentric orbit that could end only in absolute isolation.

'We started to part ways a little bit,' Johannes mourns. 'Hillel got into the whole Hollywood underground scene; he was reading William Burroughs and all that kind of stuff and really beginning to identify with the Underground Suffering Artist on Drugs thing. And, of course, the Hollywood scene was very heroin-oriented. It was the accepted thing to experiment with drugs and that kind of scene just drew Hillel right in. So we stopped hanging out together at that point.'

Kiedis credits Flea with never having 'lost it to drugs. He had his experimental phase, realised he couldn't handle it and then he put them away.' But for Slovak and himself, every new experience simply called for another. Without ever confessing to personal feelings of inadequacy or insecurity, Kiedis confessed that, as much as Slovak, he 'needed that extra comfort' that drugs provided. It was only much later that he realised how deceptive that extra comfort was, and only when it was too late to do anything about it.

With Slovak in the ranks, the Red Hot Chili Peppers embarked upon the next phase of their development with renewed enthusiasm and rejuvenated abandon. The painful experience of their debut album was behind them; so were the nights of unfulfilled mock mayhem that scarred their first American tour. Slovak shared the Red Hot Chili Peppers' lifestyle, but more than that, he shared what they wanted to get out of that lifestyle. In every sense of the words.

'The more time passed,' Kiedis admitted, 'the more Hillel and I began to isolate, individually. As kids, we considered these mind-expanding situations [as a way to] view life in a different way. Then, eventually, time passes and you either become an addict or you don't. We did.'

By Christmas 1984, their first eighteen months of working together in a band had done more than open Kiedis and Flea's eyes to the world outside of Los Angeles. Their musical horizons, too, broadened far beyond the confines that originally inspired them to play. The greatest of all their discoveries was the granddaddy of American funk, George Clinton.

For Flea, the impact of hearing for the first time the earliest Funkadelic albums was nothing short of a revelation. He speaks with the fervour of a true acolyte of *America Eats Its Young*, released in 1973, 'but there's so much great stuff that most people have never heard, albums like *Hardcore Jollies* (1978) and *Let's Take It to the Stage* (1975). *One Nation Under a Groove* (1978) is an incredible record, but that was their first hit album and it was more slick and produced. The earlier Funkadelic stuff was balls-out rockin'.

'They just did the music they wanted to do and it didn't fit into any category. They were heavier metal than Black Sabbath ever was. When I first started playing in this band, I had never heard of Funkadelic. But I think what we're doing is very similar, except that they came out of the acid/hippy thing and we came out of the punk rock thing. Rock, funk, whatever you want to call it, they were one of the greatest bands.' He described Funkadelic guitarist Eddie Hazel, whose ten-minute guitar solo during 'Maggot Brain' alone established his credentials as a visionary, as being 'right up there with Jimi Hendrix'. (Hazel died of complications arising from liver failure, shortly before Christmas 1992.)

When the time came to select a producer for their upcoming second album, there was simply no question of who the Red Hot Chili Peppers wanted to work with. 'George Clinton is amazing,' Kiedis raved. 'He's the ultimate hardcore funk creator in the world, ever. James Brown is the king of his field, but he was more pure funk. If anybody ever wanted to ask you what was the greatest funk-metal ever, it would be Parliament–Funkadelic. Their music is so great that I don't think people are even capable of understanding how great it is.'

Born in 1940 in Kannapolis, North Carolina, the future Dr Funkenstein was fifteen when he formed the first incarnation of the Parliaments. A simple doo-wop band that lurched through a decade or more of disappointments, the Parliaments might have been forgotten forever had Clinton not finally decided to move the group in a direction that had hitherto remained untapped among America's black musicians, a blistered hybrid of hard rock and frenetic dance, laden not only with a ferocious rhythm, but a harsh revolutionary message as well.

While Motown was still pushing the slick sounds of the Supremes and the Miracles, and fearfully resisting attempts to push their output into a more 'aware' arena, the Parliaments established themselves at the forefront of the new rebel consciousness that was hitherto the exclusive property of privileged white America. But, if Jefferson Airplane recommended lining the motherfuckers up against the wall, the Parliaments knew exactly which wall it should be: the one that surrounded the studios out of which gushed the whiter-than-white image with which black American music was to be saddled until well into the disco era of the late 1970s.

Clinton's decision to remain in Detroit even after Motown dropped the Parliaments only heightened people's awareness of just how reactionary his vision was. Even before Berry Gordy's legal department informed him that Motown now owned the Parliaments' very name, Clinton was toying with a new concept, one that would encapsulate precisely the music he was creating. In 1969, he settled upon Funkadelic, 'a combination of funk and psychedelia which is going to blow Motown away'.

This basic premise, sensational during the dying days of hippy, exploded into outright outrage as Clinton set about capitalising upon rock'n'roll's own post-psychedelic legacy. Adopting the proto-metallic density of Black Sabbath, Led Zeppelin and Blue Cheer, and augmenting that with the visual extravagances of Britain's glam rock explosion, by the time *The Mothership Connection* went platinum in 1976, Funkadelic was the flagship for a host of Clinton-powered bands.

A reborn Parliament, Bootsy's Rubber Band and the Brides of Funkenstein between them developed into the Satanic antitheses of everything Motown and the even smoother sounds leaking insidiously from Thom Bell's Philadelphia Sound machine ever represented. 'I knew that the Temptations and Gladys Knight and the Pips had . . . the choreography, the outfits and the tight routines,' Clinton explained. 'So we decided to go to the other side and be the bad boys of the whole thing.' The shows he staged were glittering riots of sex and shock rock. No costume was too outrageous or extravagant, no pose too extreme or explicit. The mothership hovered over America like a painted, thrusting whore and everybody was welcome aboard.

The bubble burst during the late 1970s. Contractual and creative wrangling left Clinton in artistic limbo. His own sense of purpose, too, was becoming hopelessly clouded by his bands' success. Far from opening up to his vision, Clinton's audience was closing in on it, until seven near-consecutive Top 30 albums, three major hit singles and an international reputation to rival any black (and many white) artists became both constrictive and restrictive. Clinton disappeared from the public eye. By the time the Red Hot Chili Peppers caught up with him in 1985, Clinton was still hauling himself out of the abyss.

Clinton was among the drug lifestyle's most vociferous opponents. But, if the Red Hot Chili Peppers suffered any adverse reaction from Clinton once he became aware of the extent of Kiedis and Slovak's own drug use, their admiration for the man far outweighed any discomfort they may have felt.

'One thing George Clinton told me about playing funk I'll never forget is, "You have to take it all the way home",' said Flea. As *Freaky Styley*, the second Red Hot Chili Peppers' album, slowly took shape through the spring of 1985, that doctrine became the band's creed. The Red Hot Chili Peppers came to Clinton with all the raw material, but it remained unmoulded. Clinton shaped them and, in so doing, he shaped their musical destiny, too.

Flea and Lindy Goetz flew to Detroit for the first meeting with Clinton, hooking up with him at a small downtown motel. 'I was mighty nervous to meet him, but no one ever made me feel more comfortable, more quickly,' Flea reminisced. Still clad in their LA leather jackets, while the rest of Detroit piled into winter furs, the pair joined Clinton at an Aretha Franklin show and, by the time they returned to California, the deal was on.

The original plan was for the band to stay with Clinton at his home, a farm set deep within the wide-open spaces around Detroit, while they demoed their material at a small studio owned by one of the funkmeister's friends, recalled by Flea as 'some heavy kind of cat named Navarro'. Such seclusion offered an idyllic life, far removed from the hassles of recording in Los Angeles. Most days, Kiedis and Clinton would pack their fishing rods and head out to the well-stocked pond behind the farm buildings; one evening, Clinton even persuaded the singer to join him there early the following morning to catch the household's breakfast.

But that scheme went awry, said Flea . . . 'I think maybe [Anthony] crashed [Clinton's] snowmobile or something, and we were generally just kind of out of control.' Clinton relocated the band to an apartment block in Bloomfield Hills, overlooking a golf course.

The band were back at Clinton's own United Sound Studio for the actual recording and, if the quartet were on their best behaviour while they were working, night-time was a different matter entirely.

Thanking Clinton for his latest offer of another laid-back evening, the Red Hot Chili Peppers would instead make their way into Detroit and dive into the city's nightlife.

Their exploits made no headlines. For the most part, the Red Hot Chili Peppers were simply one unknown band who spent their spare time heckling other unknown bands. But one Detroit club-goer remembered the night the group invaded Lili's 21 and managed to upset almost every beer in the house before they were escorted off the premises. Playing bass for an unmemorable bar band, he claims he came close to swatting the shaven-headed Flea with his instrument after the Red Hot Chili Pepper yelled one 'You're useless, man' too many.

'Those guys were just out of control. When other bands dropped in from out of town, the only thing they wanted to do was get up and jam. But the Peppers, thinking they were a big deal because they were from LA, because they were recording out in the sticks with George Clinton. Who was George Clinton in 1985, man? And who were the Red Hot Chili Peppers? It was a has-been hippy working with a bunch of never-will punks and they behaved like they owned the city.'

Another time, Flea recalled, 'we went to a rock club and a band was playing, but when they went offstage, before they could return for their encore, we ran up and grabbed their shit and started rockin'. That was fun.' It was also the night, he said, laughing, that 'Hillel became "The Skinny Sweaty Man in the Green Suit", when he was rocking the dance floor like a crazy freak'.

The Red Hot Chili Peppers' reputation for raising hell stuck like a leech. According to Kiedis, the group's first show in his native Grand Rapids was greeted with a local newspaper headline that roared, HOMETOWN BOY MAKES GOOD. The day after the show, the paper's music correspondent admitted, 'If I had a son like that, I'd shoot him.' Kiedis's only response? 'My mom loves the socks.'

These occasional outbursts of outrageous energy served as both a valuable and a damaging outlet for the Red Hot Chili Peppers' natural exuberance. The mellow lifestyle Clinton lived, so different from his musical persona, dominated the *Freaky Styley* sessions. Gone was the rapid-fire hammering that relegated so much of *The Red Hot Chili Peppers* to the status of funk-for-funk's-sake filler; *Freaky Styley* was as developed and mature an album as the Red Hot Chili Peppers were capable of making, drawn not from their influences, but from their vision of how those influences could be made to work for them. More than anything, George Clinton, in the guise of Kiedis's 'very warm, lovable teddy bear of a funkateer', gave the Red Hot Chili Peppers the gift of musical foresight.

Clinton thrived on good-natured bullying. Midway through one take, Flea was mortified when Clinton's voice suddenly ripped through his headphones, demanding that he put more muscle into his playing. The bassist admitted that if anybody else had done that to him, 'I'd be screaming, "Shut the fuck up! I'm trying to play!" But [George] could get away with it.' Besides, when Clinton chose to deliver a compliment, 'it was the greatest sounding thing I ever heard'. So great that they actually left one of his interjections in the final mix of the album, 'bleeding through all distorted and crazy sounding, somewhere in the middle of "Hollywood" '.

'He's just a bottomless pit of funky creativity who I have a great deal of respect for,' Kiedis raved. 'I'm so fortunate to have had that experience of making a record with him. It's something that I'll never forget and I'll always cherish it just as a blessing. It was a blessing to be able to hang out with him and to learn from him and to be a part of his whole feeling there.'

Perhaps the greatest key to the Red Hot Chili Peppers' development, both within the sphere of Clinton's influence and in the wider context of their own experiences, was the two cover versions included on *Freaky Styley*: Sly Stone's 'If You Want Me to Stay' and New Orleans funk outfit the Meters' 'Africa', retitled 'Hollywood' and modified accordingly. (A second Meters' connection, a song entitled 'Jungle Man', simply borrowed one of that band's titles. 'I swear I'd never heard their song when we recorded [ours],' Flea pleaded.)

Dallas-born Sylvester 'Stone' Stewart remains among the most crucial black performers of the rock'n'roll era, a man who fused jazz, soul and blues into the cohesive whole that would see Stone, no less than George Clinton, forge a radical bridge between the psychedelic musings of late sixties white consciousness and the firmer convictions of the Black Power movement. A triumphant appearance at the Woodstock Festival in 1969 lent further momentum to Stone's personal profile and, by the dawn of the new decade, Sly and his band, the Family Stone, were set to become *the* crossover band of the early 1970s.

Stone, however, was unpredictable, his drug intake prodigious. British journalist Roy Carr described him as 'the prototype 20th Century Schizoid man', and mused on the days 'when Sly Stone and Sylvester Stewart were two entirely different personalities sharing the same host body'. Around such condemnations, the concert grapevine hummed with tales of Stone's legendary unreliability. Not only did he appear incapable of making it to a show on time, at times he appeared to go out of his way to avoid it. 'I'm just popping over to London to do some shopping,' he told a promoter in the Dutch city of Rotterdam, moments before he was due on stage. 'Tell the kids to wait.'

Musically, however, Stone let nobody down. *There's a Riot Going On*, from 1972 and *Fresh*, the following year, remain among the yardsticks by which all subsequent funk rock excursions were to be measured. That his star crashed and burned shortly after, plummeting earthward even as George Clinton's rocketed up, seemed almost incomprehensible; indeed, it was little more than cruel irony that demanded 'If You Want Me to Stay' should become his last Top 20 chart hit.

Covering 'If You Want Me to Stay' was Kiedis's idea. He had loved the song ever since his junior high-school days, when a team-mate sang it during flag football huddles. But the Red Hot Chili Peppers' rendition was to be considerably more than a simple rehash of a great old song. It was their opportunity to measure themselves against the master, tackling a number that, perhaps more than any other in Stone's catalogue, epitomised all that he accomplished during his period of greatest success.

George Clinton acknowledged that fact when he himself stepped in front of the microphone to sing the song over the Red Hot Chili Peppers' own backing track. It was an inestimable thrill for the band – twenty years later, Flea was still swooning 'Me in the same room with the great mythological hero Dr Funkenstein, him singing with our band, fuck I was in heaven'; and, if you want to talk about putting pressure on somebody, it presented Kiedis with what many singers would have considered a barely assailable target, as he set about replacing Clinton's guide vocal with his own. But he pulled it off and, when 'If You Want Me to Stay' became the most widely applauded track on *Freaky Styley*, it not only vindicated the group's decision to cover the song, it also confirmed their status as the harbingers of the next generation of great funkateers.

Stone's significance to the Red Hot Chili Peppers went beyond the undeniable impact of his music, however. Kiedis explained, 'Sly Stone is a perfect example of someone who had a very powerful message in his music that he didn't necessarily live by himself' – proof, Kiedis reasoned, that one does not necessarily have to practise what one preaches. Just because you've screwed up your own life, he insisted, it doesn't follow that you must encourage everyone else to screw up theirs. He seldom admitted that another three years would elapse before the Red Hot Chili Peppers would be in a position to put that philosophy to good use.

Freaky Styley remains the Red Hot Chili Peppers' most blatantly lustful album, its heart the uncompromising barrage of songs whose very titles – 'Sex Rap', 'Lovin' and Touching' and the brutal 'Black-eyed Blonde' (complete with the infamous 'She'll clean your clock' lyric) – suggested a somewhat less than wholesome interest in sex. Even more provocative was 'Catholic School Girls Rule', a frenzied take on one of the Red Hot Chili Peppers' more stereotypical fetishes and the subject of what remains the band's most characteristic (and, prior to its release on the *Positive Mental Octopus* collection, unseen) video. Under director Dick Rude's brilliant eye, Kiedis plays a sultry ghetto Jesus, dragging his cross behind him while he cruises a schoolroomful of decidedly un-Catholic nubiles. (Rude would work again with the band, directing 2003's 'Universally Speaking' video.)

Ironically, the one song that could have at least proved the band had feelings outside of sex, 'Millionaires Against Hunger', was omitted from the record. Six months earlier, in December 1984, Irish musician Bob Geldof launched Band Aid, an all-star musical charity designed to raise money for the victims of the Ethiopian famine. Similar projects followed in the United States and elsewhere, as the British 'Do They Know It's Christmas' and America's 'We Are the World' set new records for singles sales. But the Red Hot Chili Peppers spoke aloud the thoughts that many other people kept to themselves: namely, if so many wealthy personalities were so concerned about the Ethiopian famine, why did they not simply dip into their own personal fortunes?

Alert to the cynicism that apparently pervaded so much of the ostensibly selfless organisation, the Red Hot Chili Peppers recorded 'Millionaires Against Hunger' during the summer of 1985, possibly even on the very day of the Live Aid Benefit concerts that brought to a glittering climax the first, most public, phase of Band Aid's existence. But was there a place for such sentiments in the marketplace? EMI thought not and 'Millionaires Against Hunger' was left to languish in the can for another five years, until it surfaced on the B-side of the *Taste the Pain* EP in 1990.

Nevertheless, *Freaky Styley* remained an astonishing album. Glenn O'Brien, in *Interview* magazine, was among the first national journalists to pick up on exactly what the Red Hot Chili Peppers had accomplished, describing the group ('and I don't know how George [Clinton] would feel about this') as 'the absolute Funk Rock matrix . . . what Funkadelic is supposed to be'. Music this 'hard, relentless [and] entertaining . . . will be danced to throughout the 1,000 year Funk Reich. The Red Hots are as hard-edged as the Stooges, are funkier white boys than KC & The Sunshine Band and, philosophically speaking, they are the nose-cone.' *Freaky Styley*, he concluded, 'is the first record of the rest of your life'.

Rolling Stone made a similar attempt to place the Red Hot Chili Peppers within what was fast becoming their cultural niche. 'After nearly two decades of racial division,' Ira Robbins wrote, 'popular music is in the midst of an overdue and exciting effort to integrate itself.' And, while the Red Hot Chili Peppers' 'quasi-orthodox hard Funk might appear to be an imitation of "black" music for a white audience . . . [the band members themselves are] actually irreverent, punky rockers with a jones for rhythm and blues vernacular (lyrical and musical) and a commitment to humour, variety and unbridled stylistic independence.'

What reviewer Robbins did not point out, a fact that the Red Hot Chili Peppers themselves seemed unaware of until much later, was that, on vinyl, the Red Hot Chili Peppers remained a startlingly different group than the one that functioned so perfectly onstage. George Clinton never caught the group live, never had a chance to sample first-hand the sheer physical and sexual power of the Red Hot Chili Peppers when they were firing on all cylinders. That failure, while not translating directly to *Freaky Styley*, nevertheless broadened the gulf that divided the group from its true potential.

Some years later, Flea hit that particular nail squarely on the head. 'You can be in a studio and do a back flip and all that is going to happen is that it will sound like you missed a few notes on your instrument. If you do the same thing live, it will stir the crowd into an orgasmic frenzy.'

This pursuit for 'orgasmic frenzy' was not restricted to stage and song, either: in 1989, scandal erupted when a Virginia court found Kiedis guilty of indecent exposure and sexual battery following a backstage incident. What remains unanswered is whether such behaviour was a flagrant abuse of the group's position, or merely a vagrant abuse. At least until *Mother's Milk* finally rescued them from relative obscurity, the Red Hot Chili Peppers' greatest successes were on the so-called fraternity circuit, the collegiate world of student-room high-spiritedness wherein the pursuit of 'fun' is elevated to ritualistic proportions, redolent with both homophobic and homoerotic themes.

The physical and emotional bonding of four healthy young males onstage, the obvious delight the band members took both in their own and in one another's bodies, their savage exhibitionism and the stark sexuality of their songs bestowed upon them the reputation for almost mythical lustfulness. For four 22-year-olds, to be perceived as irresistible sex machines conveyed both honour and responsibility. It became imperative that, having garnered this status, the Red Hot Chili Peppers lived up to it, whether that meant vanishing into the night with as many willing young bodies as could reasonably be accommodated, or simply ensuring that every lady who passed them by was aware of the oppressive libidos that were there for the taking.

The cocks-in-socks routine added to the group's notoriety. Despite being used sparingly (in May 1992, Lindy Goetz estimated that it appeared at no more than 15 per cent of the Red Hot Chili Peppers' shows, and it would vanish altogether for a time in the mid-1990s), the appearance of the band butt-naked bar their tubular G-strings was nevertheless one of the best-known tricks in the industry. Even *People* magazine described the Red Hot Chili Peppers as 'the hyperactive [band] . . . who gained fame on the Los Angeles club circuit for . . . singing "Do You Know the Way to San Jose" naked'; and, when footage of the routine was included on the *Positive Mental Octopus* video collection in 1988, it dwarfed even the 'Catholic School Girls Rule' video in terms of media impact.

The combination of sex, drugs and rock'n'roll that the Red Hot Chili Peppers now represented is one of the late twentieth century's most overused clichés, but it is one that can seldom be taken for granted. As much as success must be earned, so must true notoriety. The Rolling Stones may have been portrayed as the Lucifer-driven antithesis to everything the considerably more cuddly Beatles represented when they first appeared, but it was five years more before the group's reputation was truly cemented into place by the attentions of Britain's legal establishment.

The drug-crazed pyromaniac Jimi Hendrix, the devilish executioner Alice Cooper, the spitting, swearing anti-Christ Johnny Rotten, all won their colours on the tabloid battlefield. The Red Hot Chili Peppers, however, were turning the process upon its head, launching their assault with their reputation, among their fans at least, already in place.

In the wider world, however, few people had heard of them and fewer still cared. Even as *Freaky Styley* clocked up the column inches, the Red Hot Chili Peppers remained an underground obscurity and it was within that obscurity that their notoriety flowered. Without commercial respectability to cast its watchful eye upon them, the Red Hot Chili Peppers could party with abandon.

Penning his sexual autobiography for *Details for Men* magazine in 1992, Kiedis bragged that, travelling on tour in a blue Chevy van, he would 'sample the local delicacies of the land'. Only his approach, he said, raised him above the level of every other horny young musician. 'We had no pompous pretensions of "You should fuck me because I'm in a rock'n'roll band." It was more like: "You're here, I'm here . . . let's make each other happy right now".' In those halcyon days of pre-AIDS awareness, he added, 'Nobody thought about slipping it on before slipping it in.'

Brenda (not her real name) is a willowy brunette whose family moved to Seattle from LA while she was still in her early teens. When the Red Hot Chili Peppers played the first of two nights at the local Astor Park in May 1986, she went along simply because they were from LA 'and one of my friends told me about the socks thing. It sounded like it could be fun.'

Backstage security was a joke, 'which I think is how the group preferred it'. Echoing Kiedis's own words, she remembered, 'None of the band had that "big rock star" attitude which a lot of others carry around. You met them like you'd meet any young, horny, good-looking guy and, whether they were about to go onstage or had just come off it, they were just the same.

'Hillel was the only one who seemed at all standoffish, I think because he was into a different scene. But Ant and Flea were up for anything.' To this day, she believes that the girl 'screaming . . . "fuck me, Anthony" ' in 'Party on Your Pussy' is her. 'I knew the hotel they were staying at,' she said with a laugh, 'and I probably got carried away a bit. But there again, so did he.'

'My brain was in a state of cosmic blossom,' Kiedis wrote.

The previous winter's venture across the Midwest aside, the Red Hot Chili Peppers had hitherto played mainly in Southern California, making only occasional forays into the wider world. Of the group's earliest shows, the best remembered are those, ironically, at which they were paired with other bands; the handful of supports they played with X in San Diego and Irvine in September 1985 following the September release of *Freaky Styley*, or the single show in which the support band included another Fairfax High graduate, Slash. But even his Guns N' Roses, taking the first tentative steps on the road that would eventually establish them as the decade's last pretenders to the Rolling Stones' throne of rock'n'roll excess, were no match for the Red Hot Chili Peppers. 'Our live performances [at that time] were pretty much in a class by themselves,' Flea enthused. 'A whirlwind of spontaneous anarchy, locked in with a cosmic hardcore soul groove.'

It was with this whirlwind at its raging peak, with the positive aftermath of *Freaky Styley* a welcome inclusion in the group's press package, that Lindy Goetz began punching the Red Hot Chili Peppers into the national circuit. A brace of shows with Run DMC in San Francisco and Hollywood in September 1985 was followed by a headline outing in the group's own right, which kept the Red Hot Chili Peppers on the road almost constantly from October through March 1986.

Not all the gigs were successful. Sold-out performances in Richmond and Washington, DC, a stronghold of Pepperdom ever since the band gloriously upstaged English Beat refugees General Public at the Ontario Theater the previous December, were balanced by the half-empty clubs that greeted them in Minneapolis and Buffalo. For the Red Hot Chili Peppers, however, even the smallest audience represented a party and even the coldest crowd an excuse for a knees-up.

One night, Flea suggested introducing a little culture to the proceedings and offered to teach the rest of the group Miles Davis's 'Jeanne Pierre'. It is difficult to say what surprised the band's fans the most, the classic jazz that the group played so well, or their hastily extemporised lyric for the piece, a chorus of 'We've got the biggest cocks, we've got the biggest cocks.' The frat kids loved it either way.

In October 1985, the Red Hot Chili Peppers made their debut in Pittsburgh at the Decade. After they completed the show, Kiedis was still in the mood to perform. For some reason, his travelling effects included an eighty-pound bag of popcorn and a hatchet, and tonight he felt it was time the pair was introduced.

Dismembering the bag was easy. So was distributing its contents among an audience that swiftly got into the spirit of the moment. Within minutes the club was awash in popcorn and, with the rest of the group now in a similar party mood, Flea reminisced, 'We stayed up there and did a two-hour comedy act.'

Afterwards the band's long-suffering road manager, Ben, told them they would never be able to tour again if they did shows like that. To the Red Hot Chili Peppers, shows like that were the only reason they toured in the first place. And, if the United States didn't care for the chaos, they'd simply find somewhere else that would.

Perhaps the biggest potential market for the Red Hot Chili Peppers was Europe. With its shorter distances and broader tastes, and an understanding of rock'n'roll that the American market could scarcely aspire to, the continent beckoned the Red Hot Chili Peppers long before even Lindy Goetz, the eternal optimist, dreamed of taking the group there.

EMI certainly didn't encourage his thoughts in that direction. Neither of the band's albums was released abroad; Europe's sole point of reference was a single of 'Hollywood', quietly issued in a handful of territories, and Flea's fleeting appearance in Michael J Fox's newly released *Back to the Future, Part 2* blockbuster. It was easy to miss the evil Charles J Needles, but to those viewers who cared, he at least put a public face on one of the group.

That summer of 1985, the band made their first trip overseas, a fleeting visit that took in a festival and a television date with George Clinton in Germany and a one-off performance at London's Dingwalls – where Clinton's failure to turn up for the show left them opening, instead, for Muddy Waters's piano player. There, the *New Musical Express*'s Simon Witter pronounced, 'not only were they out of place, they were complete dickheads, with a dumb line in incomprehensible jokes about their friends. But, as obnoxious as they seemed, the music was awesome, the fiercest musical combustion I've heard this year. I expected wimpy white funk and got a hair-raising hardcore storm. No matter how fast the bobbing torsos hurtle around the stage, their outrageously tight spontaneity never lets up.'

Neither did the band's taste for outrage. The evening's audience was decidedly uncertain about the band's merits, but they were rewarded with two encores regardless . . . followed by a third and then, despite the utterly undemanding silence of the rapidly emptying room, a fourth, a manic '*Freaky Styley*' performed in full cocks-on-socks splendour.

Fresh significance was added to the outing when it was revealed that the shows would also be Cliff Martinez's final gig with the Red Hot Chili Peppers. When next the Red Hot Chili Peppers convened, for a short tour of Florida in April 1986, Jack Irons would be back behind the kit.

Opting not to replace Slovak ('I just started to play louder,' explained Johannes), What Is This released their self-titled debut album in August 1985 on the heels of 'I Get Around'. It was a bizarre sensation, knowing that the audiences who would be lured into earshot on this, the group's first full American tour, were coming along on the strength of one song; more bizarre still to know that 'I Get Around' bore little resemblance to the rest of What Is This's repertoire. One moment of madness during an awkward recording session literally kicked the chair out from under their feet.

Reconvening in the studio, the tour at an end, What Is This began preparing for their second album in October 1985. Their brush with the harsh realities of success had done little for What Is This's internal confidence, however. Jack Irons in particular was feeling unhappy. He missed Slovak; but, more than that, he missed the guitarist's input, musical and personal. Johannes's girlfriend, Schneider, had now been fully incorporated into the group and, Irons diplomatically remembered, 'I could feel that my part in the band was lessening. I never really liked the direction in which we were moving; things had changed.'

The mood persisted throughout the album sessions. Irons himself may already have been considering jumping ship when 'completely out of the blue, Flea called and said, "Do you want to rejoin the Peppers?".' Irons was hesitant. 'I didn't say anything. It was something I had to think about very seriously, so I left it on hold for a little while. But finally I decided to do it.'

He completed his drum tracks; then in January 1986, with Johannes and Schneider planning to take a two-month break from recording, he quit What Is This.

Irons's recruitment did more than return the Red Hot Chili Peppers to full strength. For the first time in two years, it also returned the group to its ideal strength. But Irons represented more than the final bonding of the Red Hot Chili Peppers' Old Pals Club. It also drew the battle lines along which the band's battle for self-preservation would be fought.

7. 90 PER CENT OF POP MUSIC IS SHIT

In that it paired Run DMC with the hard rock warhorse Aerosmith, the New York rap trio's 'Walk This Way' single was the ultimate cross-over hit, tearing out of one world to embed itself in another and bearing all the hallmarks of both bands' heritage. But, not until it crashed into the US Top Five did people begin overlooking the traditional rock'n'roll half of the equation; only when Run DMC's *Raising Hell* album roared to multi-platinum status did they accept that finally rap was making its mark. And only after they made stars of the white rapping Beastie Boys did people start sizing up the bands who now trailed in their wake.

The masterminds behind both Run DMC and the Beasties were a pair of New Yorkers, Russell Simmons and Rick Rubin; one, the organiser of those long-gone dances at the Dip, the other a hardcore punk fan who suffered silently through five years of rock'n'roll's increasing senility before deciding to do something about it. When the pair joined forces in 1984, their dream was simple: to discover what would happen if their two musical preferences could somehow be combined.

They started at the lowest level they could. It was no use scouring the music press or the charts for what they wanted; in their eyes, the music industry had long since been drained of the vitality and urgency that was once its lifeblood. What they sought was something, anything, that the record labels didn't want, the radio stations wouldn't play. Within three years, Rubin was boasting that the record company he and Simmons formed was releasing 'the worst records' ever, records that were like 'roller coasters and dark rooms, places you've never been before'.

The name of the label was Def Jam, New York street slang for 'the definitive sound', or just a great noise. And its roster of artists was certainly that. Run DMC and the Beastie Boys were musical outcasts, purveyors of a racket that was less a musical experience and more a cultural catastrophe, with Rubin the demented genius producer who cooked everything into one long, screaming totality. Building a tour around the label's biggest stars, Run and the Beasties, LL Cool J and Whodini, was Rubin's way of throwing that totality into America's face. Calling the package Raising Hell left no one in any doubt of all that it portended.

On 28 June 1986, in Pittsburgh, kids leaving the auditorium went on an after-show rampage through the city centre. A week later, eight thousand rap fans apparently fought their way through Cincinnati; ten days after that, the *New York Daily News* charged that pedestrians were robbed and manhandled by rap concert-goers running amok. One month later, Raising Hell hit LA.

The show's organizers had already admitted that the 17 August show was a likely trouble spot. Even without the tour's already sullied reputation, the Long Beach Arena itself boasted a lengthy history of violent incidents. Over 100 security guards, almost half of whom were armed, were stationed throughout the auditorium. The police pledged to maintain a high profile. Nothing short of a full-scale gang war, they bragged, could disrupt the evening's proceedings. There was no way of knowing that was what they'd get.

In a scenario that set a chilling precedent for the rioting that was to char vast sections of Los Angeles six years later, it was three and a half hours before the police reinforcements finally descended upon the arena, to be confronted by the dying embers of the worst unrest in rock'n'roll history. Six deaths, four arrests and 41 hospital cases in no way reflected the enormity of the devastation, as upward of 500 gang members decided to gate-crash the proceedings.

The backlash was as immediate as it was predictable. Even as the Raising Hell tour continued on its shell-shocked way, a horror-stricken establishment began to raise the barriers. In Providence, Rhode Island, the scheduled concert was cancelled on the express orders of the local licensing board. Even the potential wrath of several thousand disappointed teenagers was preferable to what the *Washington Post* described as 'a pop music plague'.

In Britain, the rappers' imminent visit was described by the normally stoical *Melody Maker* as 'a package that [has already] rampaged across America to audiences of warring ghetto gangs'. And, back in Washington, DC, a group of bloodthirsty housewife vigilantes acting under the banner of the Parents' Music Resource Center loaded their metaphorical shotguns and levelled their sights on rap.

The Red Hot Chili Peppers watched the progress of the Raising Hell tour with mixed feelings.

There was a sense of uncontrollable excitement, the vicarious feelings of rebellion that any act of blatant defiance is capable of whipping to a frenzy. There was envy. While the Red Hot Chili

Peppers readied themselves for a night at San Francisco's 350-person-capacity Barbary Coast in September 1986, the Beastie Boys were appearing before ten times that number at London's Hammersmith Odeon. Seven months earlier, the two bands had been sharing the bill at the Chicago Hilton.

But most of all, there was a sense of accomplishment, real or imagined. 'The Beastie Boys are white, they rap,' Kiedis said. 'I'm white, I rap. By them having success, it makes it more plausible for us.'

Only to those people standing in the eye of the Red Hot Chili Peppers' storm were such apparently unimpeachable sentiments overshadowed by doubt. The group's reputation was now out of control, and their lives spiralled with it.

Until Jack Irons's return brought some welcome reinforcements, Flea was fighting a losing battle against Kiedis and Slovak's growing addictions. Any drugs he may have tried in the past were, for the most part, of the recreational variety – pot and the occasional tab of acid. He had, he admitted to the New Musical Express in 1994, dabbled in harder substances. 'Ya know, I'm no angel. I've done plenty of heroin in my life. I've done loads of drugs. [But] I don't want to come across as a drug-crazed monster. Even when I was doing them, I was against them.' And as he found himself alone in the face of his bandmates' more hardcore predilections, he knew that he was unable to stand against the tide of self-destruction that was threatening to sweep the Red Hot Chili Peppers into the abyss. 'A lot of people do heroin and they really like the way it feels. But because of the very evil nature of the drug, it takes over your life and . . . it's terrible.'

Neither were the 'hired help', people like Cliff Martinez or Lindy Goetz, able to assist him. If Kiedis and Slovak were ever going to exorcise their closest demons, they needed their closest friends around them. For Flea, Irons's return didn't merely slot into place the last piece of the band's jigsaw of friendship. It also offered him some breathing space.

Even as he made up his mind to accept Flea's invitation to return, however, Irons had no doubts of what he would find when he did. Throughout his tenure with What Is This, whenever the two groups' work schedules permitted, he joined the Red Hot Chili Peppers on crazy backpacking trips through the California wilderness, vacations that, even in the good-natured spirit of Los Faces, stripped everyone of their secrets. 'It was all out in the open,' he grieved. 'It was very difficult for me to deal with.' He would persevere, he told himself, for their sakes.

'Hillel was a wild partier. Before he got carried away with the drugs, he was a lot of fun,' lamented Kiedis. Unfortunately, similar things were being said about Kiedis himself, as he, too, discovered that getting 'carried away with – and, ultimately, by – drugs' was the almost inevitable finale to the Red Hot Chili Peppers' flirtations with LA's most potent subculture. And, though he was more aware of what was happening to him, Kiedis was no more willing to extract himself from the vicious circle of fixing up and coming down than Slovak.

Occasionally, the pair did succeed in coming out of the tunnel, but only so they could rush back in immediately. 'We would both clean up and then we would both start using again.' Why? Because it was fun, it was something to do, it was a relief from the pressures and the boredom of life in any other form. During one of these brief and, in hindsight, half-hearted, moments, Kiedis enrolled in Alcoholics Anonymous, then asked Slovak to come along to one of the meetings. Slovak laughed. 'Why? I'm not an alcoholic.'

The pair did their dealing on the streets, making their purchases from what Kiedis referred to as 'fairly unscrupulous characters involved with miniature unscrupulous Mafioso drug rings'. For Kiedis, that meant associating with the suitably connected gang members who gathered, he said, beneath a certain bridge in downtown LA – the same bridge that, in later years, would be immortalised in one of the Red Hot Chili Peppers' best-known songs.

It was a closed society into which he was entering, an almost cabalistic world of violence, distrust and death within which dealing – whether in drugs, arms, or sex – was often the only way to make a living. Certainly it represented a way of life that Kiedis had little business intruding upon. The gang member who made him swear never to visit the bridge on his own was at equal pains to convince his colleagues that Kiedis was 'family'; was, in fact, affianced to the gangster's sister. The problem was, Kiedis already possessed one family, in the Red Hot Chili Peppers. And it was beginning to suffer.

Slovak fed his habit in private, seemingly convinced that, by refusing to acknowledge it, no one would ever know it existed. Kiedis was considerably less subtle. Los Faces were his friends; he had nothing to hide from them and, even in the face of Irons and Flea's undisguised disgust, he would occasionally make deals in full view of his bandmates. 'Barry', a small-time dealer who gave up selling when he left LA, remembered, 'the Peppers had a reputation for partying really wild. When they came through town, every town, it was as if every scuzzball on the street knew about it and would make certain he was backstage.'

For all his problems, Kiedis at least remained reasonably controlled. Maybe it was because his need for the group was as strong as his need for the drug; maybe, simply, heroin affected him in a different manner to the way it affected Slovak; the fact remained, had the Red Hot Chili Peppers been carrying just one user, things might have been easier. But, as Kiedis later admitted, with fully one half of the group borne along by the dragon, 'it just slowed everything down'. The cocktail that was an integral part of the Red Hot Chili Peppers' own chemistry was crushing the band. Bickering erupted into battles. The group was in absolute disarray. Irons remembered, 'the whole process was grinding to a halt'.

The band's workload did not lighten the situation. 'I rejoined the band and rehearsed just enough to tour in Florida,' Irons continued. 'We toured a lot; we had a lot of work to do because the Red Hot Chili Peppers hadn't put out a record since 1985 and the next one wasn't coming until 1987.'

Kiedis described the outing that consumed the latter part of 1986 as 'one of those whore tours, being that we don't have a record out. We wanna rock the nation and make money at the same time.' And it was easier to tour than it was to write new material. Even the best gigs seemed to the band to disintegrate into one long blank, an hour or so of frenzied activity between late-night shenanigans. It was with considerably more conviction than he felt that Kiedis acknowledged that 'touring is like a time warp. It's mostly hotels and soundcheck, but we have some fun. You travel and meet people and play music, you see and experience all kinds of nutty, wild-ass experiences.

'On the other hand, there's no sleep and no good food and loneliness and despair. It's a fifty-fifty thing and there's not that much middle ground, at least not with my band. We're either completely ecstatic or completely miserable.'

The presence on the tour, which wound its way throughout the winter of 1986, of Thelonious Monster (fronted by Bob Forrest, the Red Hot Chili Peppers' sometime lighting technician) and veteran punks TSOL, more close friends from the LA club circuit, did not lighten the load. Rather, their presence accentuated the Red Hot Chili Peppers' own problems. Below par and bedraggled, the band literally lurched from show to slow death.

'The whole band was pretty much out of control by this point,' remembered Alain Johannes, 'and Jack could only do so much to stop the rot. He was the only solid centre in the group, the one that would pull everything together and make sure the next gig even happened.

On the occasions Kiedis or Hillel tried to dry out, Jack would be there for them as well. He had his hands full just keeping Hillel on track. Jack kept Hillel alive for years.'

For Flea, the guitarist's slow disintegration was harder to deal with. Like Johannes, he attempted distancing himself from Slovak's problems, realising only when it was too late that he was distancing himself from Slovak as well. He excused himself with a burgeoning diary of outside commitments. Together with Kiedis and Slovak, he had already played his own part in the creation of Thelonious Monster's debut album, *Baby, You're Bumming My Life Out in a Supreme Fashion*. Now he was looking even further afield. When Keith Levine, Public Image Limited's genius ex-guitarist, hit Los Angeles that summer of 1986, it did not take him long to link up with the bass player he once so nearly played alongside. 'Maybe we should make up for lost time?'

Flea leaped at the chance and, joined by Bob Forrest, he and Levine worked up two of the songs that would later appear on the Englishman's *Violent Opposition* EP, 'I'm Looking for Something' and 'Tang! Ting'. Then, when Levine announced his intention of recording a Jimi Hendrix song, Flea recommended he use the most Hendrix-like guitarist in the city.

Accompanied both to the session and on vinyl by Jack Irons, Slovak put all of his troubles behind him and laid down one of his finest performances ever, tearing up the rule book on 'If Six Was Nine' and, for a moment, Flea glimpsed the old Slovak. But it was gone the moment the recording was over.

Flea continued to broaden his orbit. Still taking tentative steps around the edges of the movie business, Flea landed small parts in Dean Stockwell's spoof mystery *Blue Iguana* and *Stranded*, a science-fiction movie in which he was rendered unrecognisable beneath layers of rubber makeup.

He achieved a personal ambition when he accompanied Thelonious Monster into the studio to produce one track ('Walking on Water') for inclusion on their *Next Saturday Afternoon* album.

And, finally, he proposed marriage to his girlfriend. Loesha, as Flea affectionately called her, was barely out of high school, eight years Flea's junior. But she was a rock of much-needed stability. As a sign of his devotion, Flea had her name tattooed around his left nipple, complementing the FLEA that was inked into his scalp.

EMI America had been more patient with the Red Hot Chili Peppers than perhaps they deserved. Although Irons exaggerated when he said, 'They knew they had a band who could go out and play 3,000-seater venues all over the country, even though we didn't really sell records' (actually the band's average crowd still numbered under one thousand), Flea agreed with him. 'I felt a lotta times that the only reason they [EMI] kept us was because they would go to [one of our] shows and see 3,000 kids going wild. They didn't understand it, they just thought of us as cash for them down the line.'

Nevertheless, it is true that there was never a clear relationship between the number of records the Red Hot Chili Peppers sold – an average of 75,000 for each of their previous two releases – and the number of people they played for live. And EMI were confused. Late in 1986, sensing that, with the right handling the Red Hot Chili Peppers could indeed challenge the Beastie Boys for the crown of white rap supremacy, EMI America relinquished its hold on the group and transferred them to the specialised EMI Manhattan.

'The [old] company's attitude was almost like "Do what you like, it's probably not going to sell anyway",' explained Kiedis. 'They didn't say very much to us when we'd have albums out, because they really weren't sure what to say, or how to approach radio stations.' Flea continued, 'the new [label] is much more competent and fun to deal with. They have a much more sincere appreciation of our music.' And they were no less demanding when it came to hearing that music.

By Christmas 1986, this latest 'whore tour' had been in progress for three physically and emotionally exhausting months. But, even when it finally shuddered to a halt, there was no respite. It was time to begin work on the group's third album; the only problem being, they had no idea what they were going to put on it.

'We had to focus on writing songs for the new album,' said Irons. 'Whatever problems were going on around us and within us, had to be put on one side; we just had to do it.' For a time, too, they seemed to have turned things around. The *Rocky Mountain News* reported that Kiedis had gone into drug rehabilitation, with Flea admitting that the band had a lot of problems, which they 'worked out . . . personally'. Two years later, Kiedis himself admitted that he'd 'found drugs had stopped being a good time and they were consuming too much of my time and becoming a negative influence instead of a mind-opening one'.

He pointed to the new album's opening cut, the frenzied 'Fight Like a Brave', as a portrait of that clash. The song, he explained, was 'a metaphor for trying to encourage someone who feels as though they don't really have a chance, [as though] they're grovelling in the gutter of life. It's an encouragement to tell them that no matter how low you've gone, there's always hope for a revival, whether it's spiritual or mental.'

These sentiments were to be sorely tested in the months to come. In the meantime, it was apparent only that Kiedis's lyrics, like his life, were changing, turning inward as if in absolute rejection of their creator's past and present. Flea described the change as a growing process, claiming that experience, both public and private, instilled into the Red Hot Chili Peppers a wisdom belied only by their penchant for 'still doing stupid things'.

He also knew, however, that this wisdom was a delicate flower, that it demanded careful nurturing. He only hoped that the group's next producer would have a firmer grip on the proceedings than his predecessors.

The Red Hot Chili Peppers were bombarded with suggestions of possible candidates and patiently they met with what Flea described as 'a bunch of different bozos'. Not one of them was suitable. Someone recommended the band meet with the Beastie Boys' mentor, the mercurial Rick Rubin. He didn't stay long, either. 'It was a very unhealthy feeling in the room [where I met the group],' Rubin said. 'Just bad news, negativity all around, lack of organisation between the members, lack of trust. Really not a good feeling.'

Malcolm McLaren, one-time manager of the Sex Pistols and Bow Wow Wow but, since then, a rising presence on the white hip-hop scene, also expressed an interest in working with the band, but talked himself out of contention when, as Flea explained, 'he started pontificating about how we would play simple Chuck Berry style rock'n'roll . . . Anthony would be the star, and the rest of the band would stay in the background playing music that was [30] years old . . . and dress[ed] up in his new "skate punk" fashion.' Flea's response was to pass out on the floor, although he recalled enough of the conversation for it to 'partly inspire' one new song, 'Backwoods'.

With Keith Levine still in town, the band ran through some demos under his supervision. It was, Flea recalled, 'an intense chemistry of people working together', but Levine was 'far from the babysitting type figure we might have needed at the time. Our working relationship did not last too long.'

Only one man, producer Michael Beinhorn, was able to see past all the difficulties. Established through his work with Nona Hendryx and Herbie Hancock, Michael Beinhorn was the 'coolest' of everybody the Red Hot Chili Peppers interviewed, Flea explained. He was also the strictest, as the Red Hot Chili Peppers learned when the time came to

start the album's pre-production process at EMI's rehearsal space on
Sunset Boulevard, in January 1987. The studio was familiar territory
for the band, and house engineer Jim 'JB' Bauerlein was already a
friend. Feeling relaxed and confident, then, the Red Hot Chili Peppers
brought just five completed songs to the session . . . and Beinhorn was
furious. It was about time, he reasoned, that someone took these
Peppers in hand.

'Working with George [Clinton],' Flea explained, 'we spent a lot of
time partying. He works by creating a real jovial atmosphere to record
in. Working with Michael Beinhorn, it was done very efficiently. We
worked. Sure, we joked around, but we [also] spent a lot of time in
the studio making it happen.'

To be closer to the project, Beinhorn temporarily relocated himself
to an apartment in the same Hollywood block as Kiedis and manager
Lindy Goetz. He dogged the group's footsteps, arranged meetings and
conferences at which he demanded updated progress reports. Yet still
the simple mechanics of getting the material into the studio was
tantamount to slavery. Even the five songs that were already complete
needed to be reworked, said Beinhorn, while 'everything else on the
record [was] created while we were in pre-production. It took a lot of
work and a lot of concentration.'

It was 4 May 1987 before Beinhorn and Bauerlein, his pre-
production engineer, were prepared to take the Red Hot Chili Peppers
into Capitol Studios, and much later before the producer was able to
tell journalist Steve Roeser that the band ranked among 'the most easy
to work with, open people I've ever dealt with. I think they are more
open to another individual coming in and messing with their creative
process in order to help take them further. In their own way, they're
extremely professional – much more so than a lot of other people I've
worked with, who had a really difficult time with the idea of someone
coming along and making very strong decisions of a creative nature
that affected them. These guys were not about that.'

The song that set the scene for the entire period of recording, which
impressed upon Beinhorn exactly what the Red Hot Chili Peppers
demanded from him, was the supreme autobiography of 'The Organic
Anti-Beat Box Band'. Reinventing themselves as the Fax City Four, the
song was steeped in irony; the organic anti-beat box band had already
suffered their flirtation with drum machines, back when Andy Gill
tried to hone their sound down to the common denominator
demanded by radio. But the song extended its reach much further
than that, towards a bashful, but justified, acknowledgement of the

undeniable influence the Red Hot Chili Peppers were having on their immediate musical surroundings.

Across their hometown, the Red Hot Chili Peppers were blazing a trail of young, committed funk bands, some (Thelonious Monster, Fishbone and fIREHOSE among them) themselves already riding the very same circuit the Peppers themselves roamed, others just beginning to awaken from the dormancy into which the periodic upheavals of the music industry had thrown their music.

When the Red Hot Chili Peppers invited Fishbone's Norwood Fisher and Angelo Moore along to help out on the new album, they weren't only acknowledging their friends. They were also acknowledging the ties that bound their bands together.

The Organic Anti-Beat Box Band was also gathering itself some new tricks. 'I used to be totally anti-drum machine,' Flea admitted. 'I felt that anything computerised was wrecking music by getting away from pure human emotion. But now I'm amazed by the artistic creativity of someone like [hip-hop producer] Hank Shocklee, who makes these amazing collages that sound so good and have so much emotional value.' The chorus of friends and, with Loesha Balzary among the participants, family who turn up on the recording offer a triumphant affirmation of the Red Hot Chili Peppers' new-found tolerance.

'Some people,' Flea continued, 'are so proud of the fact that they play these screaming macho lead guitars and they think it's terrible that someone would use a machine.' It was ironic, he noted, that the majority of those bands ('your Wingers, your Poisons') were 'playing such cynical, corporate, formula music', ensuring that American hard rock would remain 'one of the driest, stalest forms of music. Ninety per cent of pop music is shit. The mediocre are constantly rewarded for following trends; artists just follow their art and don't think about trends.' Or, as Bob Dylan once wrote, 'Don't follow leaders, watch the parking meters.'

It was Bob Forrest who first suggested that the Red Hot Chili Peppers tackle Bob Dylan's 'Subterranean Homesick Blues', and Kiedis promptly agreed with him. 'Funk comes in all shapes and sizes,' he enthused, 'and I'm sure that there is some brand of funk to be deciphered in [Bob Dylan's] music. Just because he was so great!'

Dylan's first-ever Top 40 hit, 'Subterranean Homesick Blues' was 22 years old when the Red Hot Chili Peppers took advantage of it, but it retained a potent message, particularly after the group so ruthlessly distorted its medium. The song was written, after all, in 1965, at the dawn of the hippy era, in the still-building heat of a peaceful revolution that would, its acolytes fervently believed, eventually tear the establishment apart. It was only later, with the 60s in their coffin and the dreams in pieces at the feet of the disillusioned multitude, that anyone realised that it was the revolution that was the aberration, not the 200 years of ever-greedier, ever more demanding American history that preceded it.

A decade later, Ronald Reagan ushered in another revolution and, for some – the economic suffragettes who revelled in the pejorative nickname of 'Yuppie' – the unlimited wealth he promised to all was as intoxicating as any heady brew of the past. But, as the 1980s progressed, the long hours and the hard work merely put lines on the face, not bread on the table. Among the millions of disenfranchised kids who saw in the faces of their own friends and families the true gulf between Reagan's haves and America's have-nots, a fury now boiled, a fury that was given its public face by the Raising Hell tour.

In the hands of the Red Hot Chili Peppers, 'Subterranean Homesick Blues' spoke as loudly to these kids as it had to Dylan's believers years before. With an archetypal Pepper rhythm, Dylan's ferocious denunciation of the culture he viewed around him was recast with blinding clarity; and, if some of his original imagery appeared wise long after the fact, elsewhere it was right on.

Michael Beinhorn instantly grasped the significance of the song. He also understood the significance of the Red Hot Chili Peppers. Anxious not to repeat the mistakes they made with George Clinton, he made certain that he familiarised himself with the group's live show. It was this familiarity that bred the studio perfectionism that the Red Hot Chili Peppers, at times, found difficult to comprehend. Only when it was over could they salve their wounds and admit that the suffering was worthwhile.

Even before the reviews came in and, without having heard the assurances of their fans, the band members were convinced that they had finally made the album they'd been threatening for so long, that which could only have been made by four people who had already lived through so much together. The Uplift Mofo Party Plan was more than a simple record; for each member of the Red Hot Chili Peppers, it was his personal tribute to his three dearest friends.

Not everything about the album went according to plan, however, even once the recording was over. Still pursuing the depraved depths of lyrical promiscuity that fired so much of Freaky Styley, living up to his own reputation as a no-holds-barred sex fiend from hell, Kiedis's proudest moment, in lyrical terms at least, was 'Party on Your Pussy', a song that hitherto might have provoked little more than a raised eyebrow among the EMI hierarchy. Even with a few audible 'fuck's and the gratuitous repetition of the title, the song offered little that the group had not sung before.

In 1987, however, two years into the bloody reign of the Parents' Music Resource Center (PMRC), nobody was taking any chances, On jacket, inner sleeve and label alike, 'Party on Your Pussy' was retitled 'Special Secret Song Inside'. The lyrics, which are scarcely audible in the recording (and were, in any case, scarcely more obscene than the uncensored 'Backwoods'), were omitted from the otherwise comprehensive song sheet and, as if to ensure there was no mistaking the content of the album, Gary Panter's characteristically chaotic sleeve design was slapped with the printed warning EXPLICIT LYRICS: PARENTAL ADVISORY.

The PMRC represented one of the periodic surges of righteous indignation that have stricken the American rock'n'roll music scene ever since television's *Ed Sullivan Show* in 1956 showed Elvis from the waist up only, in fear of the effect his pelvic gyrations might have on a nation of impressionable children and sensitive advertisers.

In 1963, Oregon garage band the Kingsmen came to the FBI's attention when it was rumoured that their hit single 'Louie Louie' was littered with obscene language. (Three decades later, it was finally revealed that it was!) In 1970, Richard Nixon's outspoken vice-president, Spiro Agnew, condemned rock'n'roll as 'blatant drug-culture propaganda' and pleaded with America to 'move hard and fast to bring it under control' before it completely sapped 'our national strength'. And, in as much as rock'n'roll was an integral part of the now rampant anti-war protests that devoured the government's domestic agenda as ferociously as the Vietnamese conflict engulfed its foreign affairs, he was correct.

The attacks continued. The FBI hounded John Lennon for three years, desperately seeking the evidence that American law, if not its own morality, required in order to deport him. In 1977, the imminent arrival of the Sex Pistols aroused such passions that only an appeal to President Carter ensured that the band's tour could go ahead. Other British punk bands, regarded in their own land as considerably less of a threat than the Pistols, were not so lucky. The mildest legal pretexts were invoked to bar Sham 69, Attila the Stockbroker and many others from performing in the Land of the Free.

Where the PMRC differed from these past guardians of morality was in the methods by which it approached its foe. The group was founded in May 1985 when three women – Pam Howar, Susan Baker and Mary Elizabeth 'Tipper' Gore – quite independently caught themselves listening to the lyrics of the songs which their children, their friends and, in Howar's case, their aerobics instructors were playing. Rude lyrics, shocking lyrics, coarse lyrics.

'We got together,' Mrs Gore explained, 'and said, "these things were happening to us in our homes".' Up to that point, the trio's reaction was the same as and, in some ways, considerably less extreme than that experienced by any parent upon learning that the music blasting from an offspring's bedroom contained material that outraged their own personal sensibilities. A letter the group mailed to a number of friends and associates, inviting them to a discussion at a Washington church the following month, admitted as much.

'Some rock groups,' the invitation declared, 'advocate satanic rituals . . . others sing of killing babies'. And others recommended 'open rebellion against parental . . . authority', as though rebellion were not one of the very pillars upon which rock'n'roll was built, even back in Mrs Baker's teenage years, when this self-described 'golden oldie' was happily listening to Fats Domino and Chuck Berry. What forced people to take notice of the so-called Washington Wives was their rank. Mary Elizabeth Gore was the wife of Tennessee senator (and future vice-president) Al; Susan Baker was married to President Reagan's treasury secretary, James; Pam Howar was wed to the owner of a major Washington construction company. The PMRC grew from there.

Lobbying the Recording Industry Association of America (RIAA), the umbrella organisation that represented the nation's major record labels, the PMRC demanded that all albums that could be considered 'objectionable' be prominently labelled according to the offence. An 'X' would indicate explicit sexual or violent content, an 'O' condemned occultist material, a 'DIA' warned of songs glorify drugs and alcohol – and so on until Frank Zappa, one of the PMRC's most vociferous critics, asked whether 'the next bunch' would include 'a large yellow J on material written or performed by Jews'.

Its confidence boosted by the apparent willingness of several RIAA members to go along with a modified version of those demands, and campaigning now for this initial victory to become an industry standard, the still predominantly female PMRC brought its battle into its fast-swelling membership's own backyard, the halls of government wherein many of their husbands worked. In mid-September 1985, the Senate Committee on Commerce, Science and Transportation sat to consider the PMRC's requests.

'That a Senate committee which normally presides over such esoteric issues as trade reciprocity should be interpreting the lyrics of Bitch's "Be My Slave" is not surprising,' reasoned *Rolling Stone* in its report on the proceedings. 'The wife of its chairman, Senator John Danforth, is affiliated with [the PMRC]. So, too, is the wife of Senator Hollings.' So, of course, was the wife of Senator Gore.

The PMRC's prime case, that a parent has a discretionary right over the music a child listens to and should be afforded some means of personally checking the record prior to purchase, was never seriously challenged. Albums, cassettes and CDs are unique in the mass media in that they are seldom offered for sale unsealed and, even if listening booths were reinstated in nationwide record stores (as Twisted Sister frontman Dee Snider suggested when he appeared before the committee), few parents would have either the patience or the willpower to listen to an entire album in search of a single reference to having smacked-out anal sex with the devil.

Although the Senate committee was granted no powers of legislation, by November, twenty RIAA member labels, the EMI group included, were agreeing to print warning labels to alert consumers to potentially controversial subject matter. Of that twenty, one, Fairfax graduate Herb Alpert's A&M, reversed its decision shortly afterwards. The remainder, however, stayed meekly in line.

The battle lines were now drawn. Until the warning labels became universal, the PMRC insisted, the music that Senator Ernest Hollings dubbed 'porn rock' could still assail 'the tender young ears of this nation'. The counter-argument was that, if stickering became universal, the effects on those same young ears could be equally harmful. For many children, music is an outlet for emotions that cannot otherwise be expressed, a means of living vicariously through another's words and deeds. With that avenue closed, who knew what might develop?

The pressure increased once the tabloid press, already enthralled by this latest attack on the twentieth century's naughtiest offspring, caught wind of several unrelated teenaged suicides, provoked, it was alleged, by rock'n'roll lyrics.

The deaths, it was supposed, were inspired by songs called 'Suicide Solution' and 'Shoot to Thrill', and it was a measure of just how seriously the matter was being taken that, not only did the bereaved parents take their accusations into the courtroom, albeit unsuccessfully, but during one of the ensuing trials the defendants (heavy metal band Judas Priest) were confronted by one WB Key, a witness for the prosecution who has made a career from discovering Satanic messages in .everything from song words to Ritz Crackers and even restaurant placemats.

Throughout the first year of the PMRC's existence, the group's prime target was heavy metal. Of the 'Filthy 15' artists that the Washington wives named-and-shamed in their debutante manifesto, no less than nine of the cited evil-doers were associated with that genre. Of the remainder, three more were members of Prince's characteristically explicit stable. That left soul novelty act the Mary Jane Girls, Madonna and, incredibly, Cyndi Lauper. According to Mrs Gore, all represented 'a sick new strain of rock music glorifying everything from forced sex to bondage to rape'.

Twelve months later, however, a new menace was brought into harsh focus. Within hours of the rioting at Long Beach Arena, Tipper Gore added rap to her list of musical menaces. 'Angry, disillusioned kids unite behind . . . rap music and the music said it's okay to beat people up.' She would be on the front lines again in 1989, as state authorities set about purging local communities of 2 Live Crew's As Nasty as They Wanna Be. Soon, as journalist Ira Robbins put it, it would be 'a crime to tell a dirty story with a beat'.

The arguments voiced by rap's defenders, the Red Hot Chili Peppers among them, held little water, either with Tipper or her increasingly rabid supporters. And, although they treated the entire affair as a joke, the Red Hot Chili Peppers' own compliance with EMI Manhattan's injunctions against 'Party on Your Pussy' dealt a considerable blow to their own personal credibility. How, it was asked, could a group hold itself up as champions of a liberated lifestyle when it was not even capable of standing on its own rights? 'It doesn't bother me at all,' Kiedis stated. 'Our lyrics are very explicit and, if they wanna inform the buying public, I have no problems with that.'

Four years later, however, when Kiedis took part in MTV's pre-election Rock the Vote campaign, demanding that viewers defend their right to free speech, the spectre of 'Special Secret Song Inside' still hung over him. It only furthered the irony that the party whose platform offered the most hope to free speech advocates, the Democratic Party, was running on a ticket that would give the vice-presidency to Tipper Gore's husband.

8. I THOUGHT IT WAS RATHER AMUSING

The Uplift Mofo Party Plan was released in September 1987 to reviews that, if not generally better than those that greeted *Freaky Styley*, were certainly more widespread. *Paper* described it as 'perhaps the hardest rock'n'rap record to date', adding that 'Fight Like a Brave' (released as both a single and a brilliant Dick Rude-directed video) 'is the perfect blend of Run DMC/Beastie Boys metal-rap and Parliament acid funk'n'roll. As the guitars wail,' reviewer Steve Blush continued, 'you realise that the Chili Peppers can pull it off live, which is more than can be said for their rap brethren. The Red Hot Chili Peppers are probably too hard for urban contemporary radio and too silly for the beat box crew, but boy, can they rock.'

As far as the Red Hot Chili Peppers themselves were concerned, such a response was certainly merited. 'When the Peppers formed,' Flea told *Paper* later in 1987, 'we had a very important secret plan. First was to make a great record. Second step was to make a great video. And the third step was to make a great tour. That was our secret plan. We figure we've done step one with *Uplift Mofo Party Plan*. As far as that record goes, I think it's the most complete record that we've ever made, in that I'm happy with every aspect of it. I think it's captured the live intensity of the band and it's captured different aspects of what we play musically.'

That said, he remained adamant that the Red Hot Chili Peppers' immediate goals did not include getting 'commercial airplay' or becoming 'big commercial pop stars'. The Peppers were secure in their underground niche and he knew that stardom could only drag the group's secrets out into the world.

But still it hurt that, upon release, *The Uplift Mofo Party Plan* scarcely performed any better than its predecessors. Suddenly, Flea admitted, the group felt 'trapped . . . cheated'. Artistically, he believed, *The Uplift Mofo Party Plan* was 'a cool record'. But 'it was getting no play at all'. Matters worsened when EMI declined to release a single of 'Behind the Sun', an ecologically aware lyric built around a positively gorgeous guitar line hatched by Slovak. The group was convinced that such a release would make all the difference and, five years later, when a reissue did become a hit, 'it was hard to resist shouting aloud, "I told you so!"' Lindy Goetz told *Billboard*, 'The band and I felt this could have been our first radio track.'

EMI Manhattan didn't agree, however, and it remained apparent that, if the Red Hot Chili Peppers were ever to get their message across, it would have to be from the stage. Immediately following the early autumn release of *The Uplift Mofo Party Plan*, the Red Hot Chili Peppers returned to the road, renting what, by past standards, was a luxurious mobile home for the occasion, and launching a tour that would again carry them through to the new year.

In hindsight, the bill for the first leg of the jaunt appears almost legendary. Opening for the Red Hot Chili Peppers were Faith No More, the San Francisco band that, a few years down the road, would be running the Red Hot Chili Peppers a close race as the hottest breakthrough band of the age. In 1987, however, with original vocalist Chuck Mosley still firmly in place (he would be replaced by the so-charismatic Mike Patton in spring 1988), Faith No More rated no more than the forty minutes or so allocated to them at the wrong end of the evening.

Rarely did the tour touch down at any venue capable of holding more than 700 people and, on the occasions that it did, only New York's Ritz and Atlanta's Metroplex served up a capacity crowd. At other halls, Trenton's City Gardens and Kidnappers in Charlotte, the stage offered depressingly unobstructed views of the far wall. The fact remained that, after four years of almost constant touring, the Red Hot Chili Peppers still fitted most comfortably into the minor league clubs.

Accepting this fact was not, however, painful. 'We do the best show we can, whether we're playing for ten people or a thousand,' Flea boasted, adding that some of the Red Hot Chili Peppers' most memorable performances came when their backs were, given the size of some venues, literally up against the wall.

Back in 1985, at the now-defunct Hugs in Louisville, Kentucky, the nightclub's operators were forced to summon the police to calm down the frenzied audience and prevent people from getting crushed against the stage and, when the Red Hot Chili Peppers returned to the city two years later, the manager of the Macauley Theater assured the local press that 'with the reputation that the band has, we want to prevent problems before they happen. I understand some fans tend to get excited, with a lot of action and movement, but we plan to have a handle on it.' She also promised, 'We'll have extra security people there with the power of arrest.'

New Orleans was even wilder, with the Red Hot Chili Peppers forced to leave the stage, in the vain hope of cooling down a crowd of kids who were trying to wrestle Slovak's guitar away from him. Soon, even Flea was acknowledging that the pressure was starting 'to wear a little on us'. Speaking with *Rocky Mountain News* reporter Justin Mitchell on the eve of a December performance in Boulder, Colorado, he mentioned the raging snowstorm that restricted the attendance at the band's Oklahoma show to just 100 people. The night before that, 'we played for 1,200 people in Dallas.'

The madness reached its peak on 20 January 1988, as the Red Hot Chili Peppers played North Hollywood's Palomino nightclub, a small club that was better known for staging country and western shows, and whose audiences seldom exceeded a few hundred. Tonight, several thousand people descended upon the venue and, as showtime approached, those who couldn't get in decided to take matters into their own hands and force their way inside. The police arrived just as the Red Hot Chili Peppers took the stage; Slovak had not even plugged in his guitar before the lawmen closed the show down.

The strain, Flea continued, 'manifests itself in different ways. Mainly with us being sick of each other, little things that get on our nerves being magnified about fifty billion times. It's like being stuck in the same mobile home with eight other people for days at a time. You wind up sticking the gerbil in the fish tank.' Then you sit down again and ride another few hundred miles and, before you know it, another few months of touring have passed and the crisis points are coming so hard and fast that it's only with hindsight that you even know they were there.

Even from ten rows back, Slovak looked haunted. His eyes, so laughingly alive earlier in the day, were clouded, although whether by grief or pain or something else entirely, it was impossible to ascertain. Later, someone remarked that they'd heard him and Kiedis hard at it backstage before the show. But someone else insisted Slovak hadn't even been around before the show; that he'd turned up just a few minutes before it got started and he wasn't even allowed time to change his clothes before being hustled onstage and handed his guitar.

Following the show, as St Louis's Mississippi Nights reluctantly emptied after an April evening of bone-crunching mayhem, the tension between the band members was still tangible. Though nobody wanted to speak, you could see the question in everyone's eyes. What happened out there?

Slovak sat off to one side, silent. He felt as though he'd been touring forever, the faces and places blending into one another in one long blur of memories that might not even have been worth remembering. The few people who did venture over to him quickly wandered away again. He had fucked up and even those visitors who didn't notice anything amiss, who hadn't heard the bum notes or registered the slackening timing (or who had, but thought it was all part of the show), knew that. The almost indecent haste with which the dressing room emptied, leaving only the band and one or two sturdy hangers-on, was proof enough of that.

Irons, as loyal to his friends today as he was back then, measured his words carefully as he recalled all that was tearing the group asunder. 'People had been dabbling in drugs all along. But, although you could say the dabbles were a problem, they didn't really become problems until maybe a year, maybe two or three years later, depending upon the person.' By the early spring of 1988, Slovak's problems were there for everyone to see. What burned his friends up was the fact that, at first, they didn't notice them.

To the people around the Red Hot Chili Peppers, it was Kiedis, not Slovak, who kept them awake at nights worrying. 'They were all afraid that I was going to die because I would just take too much too often for too long a period of time,' Kiedis confessed two years later. 'Hillel was much more subtle and much more cunning in his disguise. He had everyone believing that he had it under control.' Even today, people who knew Slovak still remember the utter disbelief with which they heard the news of his death. No one suspected how far he had gone.

The first time Slovak sampled heroin, it made him throw up. It was as though his body, behaving in much the same fashion as the antibodies within it, recognised the danger in which it was being placed and responded in the only way it could, by forcing the substance back out. But Slovak persevered, until the nausea turned to warmth, an indescribable glow that lit up his entire being. He learned to control the vomiting and, as his usage increased, his awareness of what the drug was doing to him diminished proportionately. Perhaps as early as 1984, but certainly long before the spring of 1988, Hillel Slovak became an addict.

It was willpower and Slovak's uncanny knack of finding a supplier in every new town that convinced his friends otherwise. Only if his sources let him down, or if the dose he purchased in some way disagreed with his body's own demands, did the mask slip. Then he would become irritable, unreliable and, to those who recognised the signs, troubled.

Heroin is not a recreational drug. Rather, it is a leech, clinging to body and soul, draining both of their reserves. It feeds upon itself and it dominates its host mercilessly. It has been claimed, both by the members of the medical profession and by some recovered junkies, that heroin withdrawal is not unlike suffering from a bad dose of flu. The symptoms that John Lennon reported in 'Cold Turkey', the song title itself a chilling euphemism for the appearance of a withdrawing addict's skin, are recognised by doctors and junkies alike. The temperature does rise until it explodes into fever, and the sheer weight of physical lethargy and mental hopelessness make even the slightest effort appear Herculean.

Involuntary muscle spasms, the source of the expression 'kicking the habit', diarrhoea and vomiting follow, as the body wrestles to purge itself of the poison. And, as the pain increases, so does the knowledge that it will take just one quick fix to end it. Without the will to see the battle through, the addict plunges into a circle not of pain and pleasure, but of pain and normality. For heroin is devious, convincing the user that it is the high that is the natural state of being, and that anything less than that is unpleasant. In St Louis, as on so many other occasions before and after, Slovak was feeling unpleasant.

There was more, however, to Slovak's addiction than simply the need to stave off the pangs of even a brief, involuntary withdrawal. Slovak 'was probably a little manic-depressive to begin with,' Alain Johannes conjectured, remembering the bouts of insecurity and jealousy to which the guitarist was so frequently prone. 'I think he was having problems dealing with reality in general. Hillel was very sensitive and he tried to mask it. He was always trying to play a role, which is one of the reasons people do drugs in the first place.'

The role Slovak was trying to play was that of the wild crazy man. Day after day on the tour bus, night after night in another strange town, he yearned to be home, to lock himself away with his guitar, his records and his paintings. Instead, he was crashing through a circus that he no longer understood, which had left town without him.

It was Kiedis who finally figured out what was going on, in St Louis, in Chicago, everywhere that Slovak had, for no apparent reason, spent the night firing blanks. But it wasn't Slovak's behaviour that clued him in. It was his own. Kiedis was already aware of his problems, aware that he was reaching a demoralising low, 'just kind of hanging out on the streets and doing my thing and not much else'. And, with this awareness, there came another, even more shattering, realisation. 'I became so familiar with the nature of addiction that I knew Hillel was in as deep as me. He was just more in denial. Hillel thought he had power over the dark side.'

The dark side. In modern times, it is an overused cliché, a self-conscious reference to the pseudo-mysticism of George Lucas's *Star Wars* adventures. But, in the private world through which Kiedis and Slovak now moved, it meant something deeper and far more sinister. It represented the subterranean landscapes of the mind, the ones through which heroin spread its insidious message: 'I'm all right, you're all right. It's everyone else who's got problems.' As he felt his friends draw away from him, as he withdrew further into his own little world, those words echoed ever louder through Slovak's haunted head.

'It was real hard for me to tell him to his face how much I loved him and how much I wanted to make music with him,' Kiedis later confessed. From deep within the black depths of his own addiction, the singer clung to the ray of light that was the Red Hot Chili Peppers, and tried desperately to make Slovak see them in the same way.

Addressing himself as though he were talking to Slovak, Kiedis knew, 'We've got to be clean. We've got the Red Hot Chili Peppers in common, we've got our friendship in common, we grew up together, we love each other. I want to spend my life with you making music.' But he never said those words out loud. Instead, he wrote Slovak letters. Letters that he never mailed.

On 20 April 1988, the world held its breath and awaited Iran's inevitable response to the massed American destruction of two Persian Gulf oil platforms. On the tarmac at Algiers airport, 37 people, including members of the Kuwaiti Royal Family, were contemplating their fate at the hands of the Shiite terrorists who had already proven their willingness to kill. Across the border in Tunis, Abu Iyad, deputy chief of the PLO, was shot and killed on the orders of the mercenary Abu Nidal. To each of the three men jousting for the Democratic Party's nomination in the forthcoming American elections, the Middle East was a flashpoint that simply would not go away.

For the first time since the Vietnam War, a US Presidential election was not going to be fought on domestic issues alone. The role of President of the United States was now a global one. And, when Flea cast a resigned eye over the Democratic ticket, just for a moment, he regretted his Australian citizenship. 'If I were an American citizen, I would have voted for Jesse Jackson.' Instead, it was Michael Dukakis who would be up against the inevitable Vice-President George Bush come November and, for the Red Hot Chili Peppers, like so many other young Americans, it was difficult to pinpoint any difference between the two.

Even as Jackson's campaign ran itself into the ground, the Red Hot Chili Peppers continued to sing his praises, delighting a near-capacity crowd at California State University in Northridge with a slow and deliciously detailed description of precisely which bodily part should be painfully removed from the other candidates' bodies. As the tour bus rolled into Pittsburgh, such imaginings did much to break the monotony.

Towards the back of the bus, away from the noise, if Slovak was aware of Angelo Moore watching him, he didn't show it. Touring in support of their second album, the screaming energies of *Truth and Soul*, Moore and his Fishbone fellows joined the tour in St Louis at the Red Hot Chili Peppers' request. The more friendly faces they could squeeze onto the bus, the better. Thelonious Monster was there as well and, between them, the three bands formed the biggest mutual appreciation circle in LA, that which Kiedis described as a group of bands 'that are considered "underground" in Los Angeles, but still have more to say than the entire Top 40 put together.'

Moore's concern for Slovak, though, was rooted in something deeper than mere appreciation. He felt as though he could see right through him and right through the response of the other Red Hot Chili Peppers as well. And he didn't like what he saw.

Slovak sat silently, his mind picking up the pieces of a future that he truly believed was just around the corner. He was convinced that his days as a Red Hot Chili Pepper were numbered; convinced, too, that the conspiracy against him stemmed not from his drug use, but from jealousy. It was he who turned the group on to Jimi Hendrix, but Flea who went out and got the guitarist's face emblazoned upon his shoulder. It was he whose guitar lines cut the swathes of sweeping melody through the garbled lyrics and thundering rhythms that were the Red Hot Chili Peppers' stock-in-trade, but everybody else who took the credit. And it was he whose groupies would be chasing the rest of the band on the nights – and there were so many of them just lately – when the last thing he wanted to do was stay up all night fucking. In unwelcome moments of brilliant, paranoid clarity, Slovak cursed everyone whose antipathy was stifling his musical and personal creativity. If there was ever a time when Slovak truly teetered on the brink of a total collapse, this was it.

But this was not the right time to be coming unhinged. After a slow start, *The Uplift Mofo Party Plan* finally broke into the *Billboard* album chart, coming to rest at No. 143 – small fry by most people's standards, but red hot for the Peppers. At long last, the purpose of the almost non-stop touring that had occupied the band since Jack Irons rejoined seemed about to pay off.

Even the record company was overjoyed. Midway through a contract that still had four more albums to run, the label, too, was finally seeing the past pay off. A return to the studio to commence work on an immediate follow-up to *The Uplift Mofo Party Plan* was scheduled for 28 June 1988. And before that, there was a European tour, the Red Hot Chili Peppers' first. Before any of that took place, however, there were questions still to be answered.

Slovak was not the only member of the group who spent the weary hours of travel wrapped in thought. For Kiedis, Flea and Irons, too, contemplation of the unthinkable was now an unwelcome part of their everyday lives. For too long the band had been carrying Slovak. Every night it was the same; as soon as he could, Slovak disappeared into the streets. His entire attitude appeared to be that of someone who couldn't wait to get the whole affair over with, so that he could return to the private world through which he really moved. And, though he only ever missed one show, the group had endured enough of his suffering. It was time, Kiedis cursed bluntly, for Slovak to either 'shape up or ship out'.

It was not a decision the Red Hot Chili Peppers took lightly. Even as they outlined the best way to break the news to their friend, their eyes registered their disgust. This was Hillel they were talking about, not some workaday axe man who never fitted in. For the first time, the Red Hot Chili Peppers were forced to admit that the dream, their dream, of four high-school friends who stuck together to stardom had gone seriously awry.

They knew what people were saying about Slovak, how the Hollywood grapevine was already buzzing with tales worthy of even Syd Barrett, the legendary genius who founded Pink Floyd before exploding into deafening obscurity. The stories were bullshit, but they circulated anyway. There was the night, the grapevine insisted, when Slovak spent an entire evening playing one song, blissfully unaware that the band was trying to play another. Or the one when he was said to have cranked his amplifier up so high that the rest of the band spent much of the show signalling their road crew to turn him down. In the end, the sound guy cut him out altogether.

He would supposedly disappear from the stage during performances and, more times than anybody could remember, he would still be telling the band he wasn't ready ten, sometimes twenty, minutes after the show was scheduled to start. It didn't even matter that most of the time the people who told such tales related them second-hand at best. If they weren't true, there were plenty of others that might be. 'Hillel definitely shut us out,' Kiedis lamented, and it wasn't only his bandmates who were distanced. Slovak's own brother, James, did not learn of the guitarist's addiction until one of the Red Hot Chili Peppers' roadies told him, shortly before this latest tour set out. He was shocked, but when he confronted Slovak the following day, he was reassured. Hillel told him that he'd already quit. Back out on the road, however, it was clear that he had not.

With three albums behind them, the Red Hot Chili Peppers were still better known for putting socks on cocks than records on the radio. They were not losers, by any means; *The Uplift Mofo Party Plan* proved that. But Kiedis, Irons and Flea were also well aware that, if they were to maintain even the mild celebrity they now possessed, there was no room for error. Just one weak link in the band's ranks could spell the end of everything. It needed only for the Red Hot Chili Peppers to miss a few gigs, or even miss a few beats onstage at a prestigious show and all that they had created around themselves might collapse.

Right now the group's reputation for abandoned partying, on- and off-stage, worked in their favour. But it also hinted at an irresponsibility the Red Hot Chili Peppers could not afford to let flourish. Promoters, not yet wary of booking the band, were wary of the legend nevertheless. And, as if that weren't enough, there was also the forthcoming European tour to contend with.

The Red Hot Chili Peppers' second visit to London was scheduled for less than a month away and, with the Beastie Boys having already fanned the flames in which Britain burns her rock'n'roll martyrs, there was no room whatsoever for error.

It is a time-honoured tradition in British rock history that police rush in where promoters fear to tread. It was no coincidence that, a decade before, the moment the Sex Pistols stopped making headlines in concert, Johnny Rotten started to make them on police reports instead. Ten years before that, it was the Rolling Stones who slipped directly from concert hall to courtroom, when Mick Jagger, Keith Richards and Brian Jones were confronted by a succession of trumped-up drug charges.

Such witch hunts were cyclical and the decade had come around again. The white heat of tabloid outrage into which the Beasties ran, the purported tales of hotel walls painted with excrement and cancer-stricken children being mocked by foul-mouthed rappers, was simply the warm-up. The Red Hot Chili Peppers had no intention of being the headline act.

Slovak had to go.

Slovak survived the show at Pittsburgh's Graffiti Showcase on autopilot. Afterwards, there was a party, but he couldn't even remember if he'd attended it. Rather, he sat half-listening while the rest of the group teased Kiedis about how he spent the evening, sitting on a bed with an under-age blonde, prattling on about how his father was dating the girl who posed for the Rolling Stones' infamous *Black and Blue* billboard poster. Kiedis didn't touch the girl; she wasn't even old enough to get into the show. No way was he going to fuck her. And was it just Slovak's imagination, or was there really a glint in Kiedis's eye? This band's got enough problems as it is.

Since the last bust-up between Kiedis and himself, last night or last week or whenever it was, Slovak concentrated on bridging the gulf that was growing between himself and the others. It was just that sometimes it didn't come out right, as though he and they used identical words but spoke completely different languages.

Only occasionally were the barriers lifted, when he and Irons drifted naturally into one of their spirited debates about music and art; when Kiedis flopped over and rapid-fired his scattershot jokes; or when Flea started talking about how the tour itinerary yawned ahead of the band, days spiralling into weeks which would spiral into months, which could even spiral into years if there wasn't a let-up soon. His wife was expecting the couple's first child and every day he was parted from her left its mark in the bass player's eyes.

'How's Loesha?'

Flea looked up awkwardly. 'Fine. She's coming along just fine.'

'It's going to be a girl, you know.' Slovak was convinced of that, had known it since the first time he caught sight of the teenage bride's slowly swelling stomach. More than anything in Flea's future, baby Clara was to remind him most of Slovak. 'It was one of the last things we got along about.'

On 22 April, the Red Hot Chili Peppers played the Ritz in New York, then took some days off to sink their teeth into every delight the Big Apple had to offer. But, somehow, no one was in the mood for partying too much. Every day brought them closer to the future they did not want to face.

It was to be another week before Kiedis, Irons and Flea finally made up their minds to bring everything out in the open. May Day found them at the Bayou in Washington, DC, a Prohibition-era club whose boards had hosted some of the biggest names in the business, back when they were among the smallest. U2, REM and Guns N' Roses all played the Bayou on the way up the ladder and, as the Red Hot Chili Peppers milled among the gaggle of fans who awaited their arrival outside, it was very easy to believe that they, too, would one day rank among such august company. Only when they were alone again, inside the darkened club, did the euphoria fall away. Tonight, they determined, was the night.

'Don't do this, man.' Angelo Moore was waiting for Kiedis as he walked across the darkened dance floor.

Kiedis looked at him, puzzled but bracing himself nevertheless for what he thought, or maybe knew, Moore was about to say. He allowed himself to be led to a seat.

'Anthony?' The horn player's voice carried no less weight than his eyes. Even before Moore completed his sentence, the enormity of the act that the Red Hot Chili Peppers were contemplating struck Kiedis like a thunderbolt. Moore saw it and pressed home his advantage.

He gestured at Flea and Irons, busying themselves around the stage, at the rest of Fishbone and the Monster, standing around in loose knots talking and drinking. 'Bands like us are on a sinking ship. If we're ever going to maintain a stronghold in this world of meaningless pop music, we've got to stick together.'

He ground a fist into his cupped palm for emphasis. 'No matter how tough the times get, we really do have to stick together, because we share a common bond of honesty and truth and soul.'

Kiedis waited silently, momentarily stricken not only by the force of Moore's remarks, but by the truth of them. 'They had a really profound effect on me,' he admitted later. 'It dawned on me that we did, in fact, have to stick together if we wanted to stay alive.' To have dismissed or even admonished Slovak would have been to throw away everything the Red Hot Chili Peppers represented. He did not need to be punished for his drug addiction, he needed to be helped.

Thanking Moore with his eyes as much as his words, Kiedis wandered back over to Flea and Irons. 'Forget it,' he told them. 'Hillel doesn't need us. We need him.' That night's show was one of the greatest the Red Hot Chili Peppers had played all tour long.

'The term drug addiction doesn't mean you're a bad guy,' Kiedis explained. 'It means you've got a problem, a sickness. It's a disease that can afflict anybody, just like heart disease.' Just as you would never abandon a friend who was suffering from that, so you could never abandon one who suffered from addiction.

The Red Hot Chili Peppers set off for Europe following their sold-out show at the Atlanta Metroplex on 7 May. The scheduled highlight was an appearance at the annual Pink Pop Festival in the Netherlands and, all the way over, the mood was light-hearted. Kiedis and Slovak were promising to stay clean and, this time, Flea, Irons and Lindy Goetz believed they meant it. Before leaving, Goetz talked late into the night about the kind of response the band might receive from the British, but it came down to simple common sense in the end. After the Beasties, the Brits expected trouble. Which meant that everything the group did, they would do with the tabloids already on their case.

'Think of it like Hendrix having to follow the Who at Monterey,' Goetz warned, 'because that's what they're all expecting. You've just got to make sure that when you burn your guitars, you don't catch light to your socks as well.'

Spirits were high. 'The kids are going nuts over there. There's nothing happening in England that you'd want to even pretend you enjoy.' Kiedis waved a copy of an English music paper above his head. 'Anyone want to see the competition?' As Flea took the bait, reaching towards the flapping pages, Kiedis snatched them away again. 'Well, you can't. Because there isn't any!' In a deep, sonorous voice, he began to read from the week's top singles: Teenybop icons Bros, shopping-mall songstress Tiffany, a remixed, rehashed rendition of New Order's 'Blue Monday' and a decidedly redundant Beatles cover performed by a band with the dramatically ominous name of Wet Wet Wet. If any country needed a taste of the Red Hot Chili Peppers' special blend of fun, funk and fucking, it was Britain.

Slovak and Irons, meanwhile, were locked into planning their own itinerary, wracking their brains to remember every last club associated with Jimi Hendrix's two-decade-old rise to fame: the Scotch of St James, where he played his first London showcase, and the Bag o' Nails, where his genius was demonstrated to his incredulous peers; Kingsway Studios, where the guitarist cut 'Hey Joe'; the Finsbury Park Astoria, where he torched his first guitar. Every so often the pair would fire a question into the air: 'Hey, any of you guys know where Jimi played in Manchester?'

Another must was the Royal Albert Hall, the vast, domelike concert hall that took one look at George Clinton and forbade him ever to darken its hallowed doorstep. Any place that uptight surely deserved a quick visit! And finally there was Abbey Road, the north London studio complex that will forever be associated with the Beatles.

Part museum, part shrine and with its real function as a recording studio buried beneath the Beatles graffiti that is painstakingly painted out every six months, Abbey Road overlooks the pedestrian crossing upon which the Beatles were photographed for the cover of their final album. A rectangular zebra stripe stretching across Abbey Road itself, for fifteen years the crossing has remained a popular tourist haunt. Look across at it any day and the visitors will be forming themselves into posses of four, then taking the same strides across those hallowed black and white lines.

There is not an album cover in the world that has inspired more imitation than the Beatles' *Abbey Road* and the Red Hot Chili Peppers were not going to lose their own opportunity to walk in the footsteps of pop's Fab Four. But the Red Hot Chili Peppers were no ordinary tourists. They were not content for one of their number simply to ape Paul McCartney and remove his shoes. Convening on a brisk May morning, before the city was even awake, the foursome stripped off all their clothing, affixed the inevitable tube socks, then strode out into the chilly air. Days later, the photographs were made available to the British press.

'Europe was crazy,' Jack Irons recalled. 'The sock thing had gotten completely out of hand, it really was demanding.' At many shows, the only thing the audiences knew was the crazy stunt with the socks and the Red Hot Chili Peppers were hard-pressed to retain even their traditional sense of humour as journalist after journalist queued up to query the routine's genesis. Their music didn't even enter into it.

Irons was adamant: 'The Red Hot Chili Peppers were doing things that a lot of people thought were funny and were jokes. But whenever we played the songs, we were very serious about playing. It was just the presentation which seemed goofy or loony, but it was a very serious goofiness. There was a method to the madness.'

Attempts to emphasise this, unfortunately, fell by the wayside. EMI never released the Red Hot Chili Peppers' first two albums in Britain, confining themselves instead to a meagre pair of singles, 'Hollywood' in August 1985 and 'Fight Like a Brave' two and a half years later. For a public whose acquaintance with the group, therefore, went no deeper than a brief contemplation of their influences and a series of hysterical photographs, the Red Hot Chili Peppers were little more than a wild novelty act. The band's club shows in London, Leicester and Manchester were less a musical event than they were an opportunity to see four men take their clothes off and hang footwear from their phalluses.

Caught in the sheer madness of such a reception, the Red Hot Chili Peppers did little to help themselves rise above their reputation. At a festival in Finland, the final show after seven months of ball-breaking touring, the group made an appearance onstage with the headlining Ramones, just as the group was launching into its opening 'Blitzkrieg Bop' – unscheduled, unwanted and, to the delight of the watching Finns, unclothed.

'We loved the Ramones and that's how we showed our appreciation for what they were doing,' Flea excused the band later. 'We were delirious, but they were furious! Johnny Ramone wouldn't even look at us and DeeDee was just shaking his head angrily.' Backstage, all was contrite as the Red Hot Chili Peppers, still clad in little more than their barely contained smirks, were given a righteous dressing-down by the Ramones' outraged manager, Gary Kurfirst.

'This is the most unprofessional thing I've ever seen in my life,' he roared. 'You'll never get away with this.' Standing, heads bowed, in a row before him, the Red Hot Chili Peppers were doing their best not to break out into further fits. But, as the tirade continued, it grew harder and harder. From the corner of one eye, they could see Johnny, DeeDee and Marky Ramone scowling furiously and that just made the whole affair even more hilarious. Like four vigorously shaken bottles of beer, the Red Hot Chili Peppers were on the point of explosion.

And then Joey Ramone, standing quietly off to one side, spoke up. 'Actually, I thought it was rather amusing.'

In Amsterdam, on either side of the Pink Pop Festival, the Red Hot Chili Peppers spent most of their time hanging out at Hank ('Henky Penky') Schiffmacher's Tattoo Museum, in the basement of a Hell's Angel coffeehouse. Henky Penky's made a convenient base for the group. A great bear of a man, described by his clients as the da Vinci of the tattooing world, Schiffmacher had decorated his parlour with countless photographs of, seemingly, every picture he ever etched indelibly into another person's flesh.

The Red Hot Chili Peppers took their places around the room and awaited Schiffmacher's pleasure. Since Flea set the ball rolling with his tattooed bust of Jimi Hendrix, Irons and Kiedis had joined the club, rolling into a roadhouse during *The Uplift Mofo Party Plan* tour to have their own first tattoos: a whale and a dolphin for Irons; for Kiedis, a stunning portrait of the Nez Perce Indian Chief Thunder Travelling over the Mountains (the Chief Joseph of history), who died in 1904. In later years, the Sioux warrior leader Sitting Bull would join him, one on each shoulder.

On that first trip to Holland, however, Kiedis was preparing to endure the first pricks of the enormous cubic Indian totem image that would eventually engulf his back. Schiffmacher told him it would be the work of many visits, each one very time-consuming (up to six hours at a time) and also very painful. Kiedis replied, jokingly, that given his own schedule, it would also take several years. As for the pain, it would be worth it in the end. Through Schiffmacher's magic, Kiedis's fascination with America's aboriginal heritage, later immortalised in the song 'Johnny, Kick a Hole in the Sky', would eventually carpet his entire body.

Henky Penky's was not Amsterdam's only attraction. There was also the Walletjes, the Dutch city's infamous red-light district, in whose windows and doorways sex is less an act of passion and more a test of endurance; where the hookers pride themselves on keeping their cool in the face of any demands whatsoever. Even Slovak, whose sexual appetite declined as his heroin intake increased, and then faded completely in the pain of cold turkey, emerged from the district with a smile on his face. It was the first time he'd really looked happy since the group left Los Angeles.

'He was really ill,' Kiedis remembered. For three weeks or so, Slovak remained true to his pledge to stay clean, but his respect for his friends' wishes did not make his withdrawal any easier. Rather, he obsessed on the subject, prolonging his pain beyond even the reach of heroin's grasp.

'He didn't seem to have compassion for his life, or consider that he wasn't beyond death or humiliation because of drugs,' mourns Kiedis. 'Here he was in the face of misery, but he still wasn't ready to concede that drugs were lessening his level of life and beauty.'

The group was still in Europe when EMI released *Abbey Road*, an extended-play single so named for its cover photograph, taken that infamous morning on the Beatles' zebra crossing. Bringing together four tracks from the band's last three albums, the EP then led off with Jimi Hendrix's 'Fire', recorded at breakneck pace during the *Uplift Mofo Party Plan* sessions, but omitted from the finished album.

Hendrix purists catching the Red Hot Chili Peppers in concert, drawn by a glimpse of Flea's tattoo, perhaps, or simply the group's acolytic reputation, recoiled at the sound of the group's rendition. With riff and solo garbled into one and Kiedis even reciting Hendrix's own ad-libs, the performances could best be described as a travesty, could easily be construed as an insult. Those onlookers could not have known, as the Red Hot Chili Peppers knew, that 'Fire' meant much the same to them as it had to Jimi. And for many of the same reasons.

As another audience howled at the sight of the socks, roaring louder than it had all night and the popping flashbulbs caused the auditorium to vanish into stroboscopic blindness, Kiedis would turn, still smiling, to Flea and ask with his eyes the one question he knew whose answer still hurt, the same question a bored, bemused Hendrix asked time and time again: what about the music, man?

Setting the song down on vinyl was the Red Hot Chili Peppers' way of putting the music back in the spotlight. 'Fire' was not the only Hendrix song in the group's repertoire; neither was it always the one they performed the best. But, behind the cocks-in-socks cover art, it was certainly the most appropriate.

The Red Hot Chili Peppers returned to Los Angeles in early June to find American sales of *Abbey Road* sustaining the breakthrough made by *The Uplift Mofo Party Plan*. There were still a couple of weeks to go before they needed to knuckle down to the new album, and they needed the time to unwind. Michael Beinhorn was going to handle the sessions again and the group wanted to be at their best to confront him. He was a great producer, Kiedis said with a laugh, 'even if he does seem to be very anal-retentive'.

Beinhorn himself could hardly wait for work to begin. Although he knew the sessions promised another long, hard-working haul and, although he was convinced that the Red Hot Chili Peppers would again present him with nothing more than a handful of sketchy song ideas, Beinhorn was fired up for the occasion. There was an abandoned majesty to the Red Hot Chili Peppers that he had never experienced in the studio before, a thrilling sense that, even under the tightest regimen, the proceedings were forever on the verge of spontaneous combustion.

He didn't know just how tragically imminent that moment of unforgettable fire was.

Kiedis and Slovak were both using again. From the moment their plane touched down at LAX, they were looking to score, abetting one another in their race towards self-destruction, but careless of one another, too. Even with no more than two weeks to go before they were due in the studio, their lives were once again on hold; as Rolling Stone Keith Richards once remarked, 'Junk takes the place of everything. You don't need a chick, you don't need music, you don't need nothing.'

Days that should have been spent at least talking about the next record were, instead, frittered away on long journeys across town in search of the next fix. Time that could have been spent cementing into their own psyches the weeks of studied abstinence from heroin that they had undergone in Europe was thrown away. And friends who might normally have been there to pull their heads from the dragon's teeth had concerns of their own to look after.

Flea was at home with Loesha, whose delivery date was now just around the corner. Irons, too, was preoccupied, trying to maintain his own mental equilibrium in the face of his friends' defiance. Not for the first time, he believed the resolve Kiedis and Slovak demonstrated in Europe was going to last. The knowledge that it hadn't, that perhaps it never would, caught him completely unawares.

A couple of times he looked over at the telephone and thought about calling Johannes and Schneider. What Is This broke up shortly after Irons quit and, having salvaged what they could from the aborted album sessions, the couple were now in England themselves, pursuing their new Walk the Moon project at a studio in the West Country city of Bath.

But Irons also knew things weren't going too well. The producer the duo was working with, David Lord, made his name at the forefront of the pop computer boom and was now so intent upon adding his cold electronics to Walk the Moon's organic energies that Johannes and Schneider were spending most of their time in the rest room playing darts. Lord had taken complete control of the sessions and the last thing Johannes and Schneider needed was to hear of Slovak's latest transgression. They'd learn all about it soon enough, when they came home in October. Irons dismissed them from his mind.

Kiedis, too, was feeling dismissive. It was a week since he last spoke with Slovak; almost as long since he, Irons and Flea last chewed the fat together. The studio deadline was hanging over him, but he blanked it from his mind. There were a couple of songs already set to go and the Red Hot Chili Peppers never felt awkward about writing new ones in the studio. As far as Kiedis was concerned, tomorrow could take care of itself. Hey, it always had, hadn't it?

He didn't know that tomorrow – 27 June 1988 – Hillel Slovak would be dead.

9. I'M WEIRD, BUT I NEVER FELT WEIRD

In July 1999, eleven years after his older brother's death, James Slovak published his own remembrance of his sibling, *Behind the Sun*, an oversized 'coffee-table' style book of Slovak's photographs, diaries and paintings. It was a beautiful tribute, although James – now working as a film editor – admitted that there were times when it seemed impossible to believe one was even required. He picked up his brother's paintings and diaries from his apartment soon after his death, but actually coming to terms with that death was a lot harder.

'I dreamt that Hillel was still alive for the first six months after his death,' James recalled. 'Then, suddenly, I had a dream where he told me he was dead, but he was all right. I still miss him, but I'm at peace about it.'

Published on James's own Slim Skinny Press, *Behind the Sun* featured reproductions from the guitarist's journals, not only detailing his life with the band, but also discussing his personal battles with the lifestyle that was to kill him. Kiedis and Flea, too, added their own thoughts to the book – for them, as much as James Slovak, it was a publication that they had waited a long time to endorse.

Death is Mother Nature's greatest contribution to rock'n'roll, the last-ditch gamble for a comfortable berth in the history books. Had Jim Morrison not died in 1971, would he live on in the tangled web of Christ-like imagery from which he today hangs suspended, a leather-drenched Lizard King forever bucking Daddy the Admiral's belligerent beliefs?

Had Kurt Cobain not committed suicide in 1994, would his genius have survived the continued incisions of a media that was only too proud of its ability to chisel away at his fragile psyche in the years before he decided that he'd had enough of their invasions? And, had Jimi Hendrix not passed away in 1970, would he, too, have eventually fallen into decline, first equalled, then eclipsed by the brilliant wave of new guitarists: Robin Trower, Ritchie Blackmore, Mick Ronson, who emerged during the early 1970s? In death, Hendrix led by example; in life, he could have been left for dead.

Hillel Slovak was neither Jimi Hendrix, Kurt Cobain nor Jim Morrison. He wasn't even Sid Vicious, Darby Crash or GG Allen, punk icons whose deaths epitomised the lifestyles they led, senseless, nihilistic and, as the only way of surpassing the legends woven in life, beautifully romantic. He was just Hillel, the 26-year-old guitar player for the Red Hot Chili Peppers.

News of his death was slow in circulating and brutal in its delivery. The first his brother James heard was when a couple of friends arrived at his apartment that evening, to take him back to Slovak's flat to identify the body for the waiting policemen. There was no room for mythmaking; none of the drama of Brian Jones's passing, the message being relayed to the rest of the Stones as they introduced his replacement to the album then in progress; nor of Brian Epstein's, breathlessly pursuing the Beatles to the Welsh retreat where the Maharishi was holding hip court. Like James Slovak, Kiedis, Flea and Irons were at home when they heard the news, and they mourned their loss in private.

Jewish custom demands that the dead be laid to rest as swiftly as possible. For many of Slovak's fans, the first they heard of his passing was the obituary that ran in the *LA Times* on the morning of his interment, three days later on 30 June. Those who were able to attend the service at Mount Sinai Memorial Park did so quietly and unobtrusively. Others were still staring uncomprehendingly at the newspaper, long after the service got under way.

An autopsy was performed on 29 June, the day before the service. The results, a coroner's spokesman informed the press, were 'inconclusive'. It was only within Los Angeles's underground that the real cause was spoken of aloud, although even beyond that subterranean grapevine, there was little doubting the truth of the matter.

The previous Saturday evening, Slovak returned to his apartment in the arms of the one friend he knew he could rely on. His friend was hungry, so he fed it. But, that night, its appetite was simply too powerful. The drug he purchased on the street just hours before, hit his system like an express train. Unconsciousness slipped into coma, which slipped in turn into death. Alone, he lay in his darkened apartment until a concerned friend dropped by to see him on Monday.

That evening, Irons made the call to Johannes and Schneider that he had been delaying for so long.

The problems in the English studio had reached ridiculous proportions. Johannes and Schneider were cooling their heels for ten hours a day, wondering if Lord would ever call them back into the control room. All through one of the wettest summers that England had seen in a long time, the pair played darts, read magazines and daydreamed of home. Every day was wetter than the one before; there was nothing to do and nowhere to go. The sessions stretched ahead of them like an eternity. 'And then Jack called from LA to say that Hillel had just died,' Johannes said. After the call, barely able to speak, Johannes walked to the window and stared out into the rain. The studio overlooked a cemetery.

Kiedis did not even give himself time to think about what he was doing. From the moment he returned the receiver to its cradle, throughout the three days that followed and, even as Slovak's body was laid to rest, he remained numb, unable to believe a single thing that was happening. Everywhere he looked, Slovak's laughing, slightly elfin face was peeking out at him, his full lips drawn back in laughter. Any moment now, Kiedis expected his phone to ring or the doorbell to sound and there would be Slovak, brushing the dirt off his clothes and roaring, 'I really got you going that time! I mean, I really got you going that time!' Los Faces had never taken death very seriously.

Numbness gave way to horror, which succumbed in turn to terror. Slovak's fate could so easily have been his own and he wondered why it hadn't been. They'd both been in as deep as one another, but death was random. Would he be next? The most haunting burden of all was the bitter self-recrimination. 'In hindsight I wish I could have helped Hillel,' Kiedis admitted later. It took him over a year to realise it was 'ridiculous' to dwell on the tragedy: 'You can't blame yourself.'

But still, in unguarded moments, the guilt would resurface. 'I could have saved him,' Kiedis blurted out during one interview. 'I know CPR really well and I've brought back a couple of friends who died from an OD.' If he had only been there that night in late June, he could have brought Slovak back as well.

Kiedis needed to get away, to some place where the past couldn't follow him; where the pain wouldn't leap from every single memory. The moment the memorial service was over, Kiedis threw a few clothes into an overnight bag and headed across the border for Mexico. Suddenly nothing mattered any longer: not the band, not his career, not his music and, most of all, not his drugs. He simply needed to escape.

He didn't know where he was bound. He simply drove, heading south and scarcely seeing the road ahead or the signs that flashed past alongside him. When the car did finally halt, it was at one of the tiny fishing villages that dot the country's Pacific coastline, a threadbare community that scarcely supports the hundred or so souls who make up its population. For Kiedis, the isolation was precisely what he required. Although he admitted to the *Phoenix Gazette* that 'I continued to use after he [Slovak] died', it was only for a short while.

For close to a month, Kiedis lived 'in this little hut out on the beach, basically drying out'. He walked, he fished, he did everything and anything he could that took his mind off his loss and away from the drugs that caused it. Only when he believed his body was finally acclimatised to sobriety did he return to Los Angeles, to begin the more complicated and even more painful process of piecing his life back together.

On 1 August 1988, precisely five weeks after Slovak's death and with the incentive of experience behind him, Kiedis came back from his seclusion. He has stayed clean, more or less, ever since. 'In that sense,' he later reflected, 'Hillel's death gave me a lot of strength to carry on living.' He added, 'I made a solemn vow when I got clean, to Hillel at his grave, that if I ever decided to go back to using drugs, that I would tell him first.'

'Anthony has always been the man of fucking steel,' Flea marvelled. 'The fact that he is as healthy as he is and weathered that shit that he has weathered is amazing.' Back in LA, Flea noted Kiedis's departure and envied his freedom. Loesha was into her final trimester, the baby was due in October and there was so much that needed to be done, so much he wanted to do, all of it, he vowed, for Slovak. Without Slovak's patience and dedication, Flea admitted to himself, he might never have learned to play bass guitar, might never have joined a rock'n'roll band. 'Knowing I'll never have the chance to share anything with him again,' he once acknowledged, breaking down, 'that's the worse thing.' Flea owed Slovak for his career; owed him, too, for the way he had behaved towards Slovak during the past year. He prayed Slovak understood; it wasn't him that Flea was trying to avoid, it was his habit.

'Hillel's death was the most awful thing that has ever happened to me,' Flea admitted. 'I knew he was doing drugs, but I didn't expect him to die. It's like one minute he's standing next to me onstage joking and playing and, the next minute, he's dead.' Yet, how could he battle and, more importantly, conquer the impotent fury of that realisation? By challenging the power of the very same kind of poisons that took Slovak away? Flea told the *New Musical Express* in 1994, 'I thought "[drugs] killed him, but they're not going to kill me. I'm just going to do them tonight." It was a mistake, but I made loads of mistakes.'

It was also a short-lived episode. With Kiedis still away, uncertain whether he would even return, Irons, Flea and Lindy Goetz knew that they had to try and keep the group going somehow, toying desultorily with the possibility of keeping the Red Hot Chili Peppers going with

a new guitarist and singer. Several people in LA today remember Irons
and Flea holding half-hearted discussions with various vocalists, 'but
they didn't know what they wanted; they didn't even know if they
wanted to keep the group going. Everything was up in the air right
then, and it took a lot of work to bring it back down again.'

A lot of emotions complicated the proceedings, but it wasn't the
apparent loss of Kiedis that held the pair back. It was Irons.
Devastated by his proximity to a lifestyle that could so cruelly, so
callously, snuff out his best friend's life, fearing that perhaps Slovak
would be only the first of his friends to go to so early a grave, Irons
could barely even bring himself to pick up the telephone when it rang,
in case it was somebody wanting to talk about the group.

When Flea called Irons, his messages went unanswered. Lindy
Goetz could not get through to him. Other friends, in or out of the
music industry, found Irons retreating behind a brick wall of absolute
wretchedness. He could sit for hours without speaking, or he could
be a dynamo of pointless energy. Either way, he was not the old Jack
Irons.

Knowing there was something terribly wrong with him, but not
caring what it was, Irons did not even resist when his family told him
they were planning to commit him to psychiatric care. It didn't matter.
Suddenly, nothing mattered. Wherever he was, the pain remained
equally intense, but somehow, if he just lay still, not moving or
thinking and barely even breathing, at least it was easier to simply stay
alive.

Irons withdrew completely. The sensation could be compared to an
elevator cable, pulled taut and twisted every which way until suddenly
it snapped and the elevator crashed to the basement floor. Irons's
entire being, his very reason for being, was aboard that elevator. For
weeks, he said, he lived literally from moment to moment. It wasn't
that he didn't want to think about the future, it was that he couldn't.
Contemplation of anything beyond the present left him feeling as
though someone had pulled the plug on his soul and his entire
existence was draining away. 'All of a sudden, all my feelings had been
taken away from me.'

Johannes and Schneider returned from Europe and went straight to
the hospital to visit Irons. He talked, recalled Johannes, of simply
abandoning everything and getting away to a little fishing village
somewhere. At other times, he considered throwing himself into one
of the marine-conservation groups that were so close to his heart. 'The
only thing I knew was that I wanted to get out of the music industry,'

Irons later admitted. 'In many ways, I think I blamed the business for what happened to Hillel.' His own musical career was certainly at an end. 'I just gave it up. I was just sitting in the mental ward feeling . . . nothing.'

'For a while,' recollected Johannes, 'it didn't look like he would ever snap out of it.'

Later, Kiedis and Flea were shocked at just how well they took the news of Irons's collapse and the only half-spoken realisation that he would never return to the group. They felt as though their emotions had gone on sabbatical. If anything struck them, it was the ridiculous irony of the situation, a sense that both their lives and their careers had finally come full circle and, once again, they were a pair of 21-year-olds with a record contract on the table in front of them, trying to explain why the rest of the group wouldn't be signing it. 'It looks like it's just us two again.' Kiedis smiled, wanly. And suddenly, looking at their loss from that perspective, somehow there appeared to be hope.

'The death of Hillel changed our entire attitude,' Kiedis explained a year later. 'Losing your best friend at the age of 26 is a mind- and soul-blower. But there was definitely an inspiration that came from Hillel dying, which helped sharpen the focus of the band. Flea and I were left with each other and we decided, 'Here's something we started a long time ago, that we haven't finished.'

They realised, he continued, that 'we had to bear down, change our lifestyles and look at what was important to us – things like friendship, love, making great music and not getting sidetracked by the more negative influences in life. We tried to use our loss as a bolstering, positive influence. If nothing else, to prove to the world what we were doing was worthy and legitimate. Hillel may be dead; we're not.'

When the proverbial and probably apocryphal 'source close to the band' described the duo's state of mind as something close to 'panic', Kiedis reacted angrily. 'I don't think "panic" is really the right word. What it was, all of a sudden our best friend had died and we were in total emotional dismay, and totally discouraged. Then Jack quit because he couldn't face the daily reminder of Hillel's death. We just all freaked out. It wasn't a panic because the most important thing wasn't "Well, we've got to get this record out by next year." It was "Let's look at our fucking lives and see what has to be done so we don't lose another person." '

Both Kiedis and Flea swore that less consideration was given to the idea of breaking up the band than to the positive consideration of continuing with it. 'I think we all needed time to gather our bearings. But there was never any question whether we wanted to continue with the band, because I think we knew in our hearts that we did and we always wanted to be playing in the Red Hot Chili Peppers.' Nevertheless, coming to grips with the harsh reality of Slovak's death was not easy. Neither was understanding the sudden impact with which unbidden feelings of inestimable loss could descend.

Just as they had five years earlier, Flea and Kiedis put the word out that they were looking for new musicians, although not necessarily for the Red Hot Chili Peppers. They simply wanted to play and, if anything developed out of that, so be it. Friends stopped by to jam and fans and strangers, too. With so much going on around them, for the first time since Slovak died, Kiedis and Flea were laughing again.

By the end of August 1988, the two were actively looking for the next generation of Red Hot Chili Peppers. 'We set out to find new guys.' Now it appeared that they had found them. Over the last few weeks, Kiedis felt as though a chord had been struck in his heart and, when Duane 'Blackbird' McKnight, one of George Clinton's axe-wielding lieutenants, and former Dead Kennedys drummer Darren 'DH' Peligro set up beside him, suddenly the Red Hot Chili Peppers were jumping again. Flea felt it as well and, after close to three months off the road, the worst three months of their lives, Lindy Goetz was talking tentatively of returning to live work.

They were not cured of their grief, of course. Two years later, the feeling of awful devastation was still there. One afternoon in 1990, Kiedis was climbing into his car when suddenly, as surely as if someone were holding a switchblade to his heart, his entire being was gripped by an indescribable terror and, in layers beneath it, unimaginable sadness and unbearable pain. Suddenly, he understood how Slovak felt, not only throughout that last year of increasing estrangement, but also as he lay that June night in his apartment, as the last spark of life was squeezed slowly from his body. He was absolutely alone.

Physically and emotionally, Kiedis had no one. Of course there was Flea, but he was back on top of his heart, raving about the band, daydreaming about the baby. Kiedis was Flea's friend, but that friendship was taken for granted. Kiedis tried to remember the last time he and Flea had suddenly, spontaneously, shown one another how much they loved each other.

His battle with heroin was over, but Kiedis had still to renew contact with the people he had left behind him – his parents, his friends, the entire life that he had once led. The only thing he could grasp was Los Angeles, the city in which he had lived for fifteen years. Sitting crying behind the wheel of his car, he remembered the jokes Alain Johannes used to make about the little angels that were forever looking over his shoulder and he saw them in the hills, the buildings and the bustle of strangers who went about their business around him. They were his angels and it was they who were looking out for him, 'more than any human being in the world'.

Without thinking, he turned the key in the ignition and started driving the few blocks towards his home. A song sprang unbidden to his lips, and he sang it to himself. 'Sometimes I feel like I don't have a partner . . .'

The mood remained with him all evening, but it was countered now by an awareness of all he did have to be grateful for. 'No matter how sad or lonely I got, things were a million times better than they were when I was using drugs all the time. There was no comparison.' He started scribbling lyrics – lyrics, because that was all he knew how to scribble. But it wasn't a pop song that he wrote. Instead his mind drifted back to the bridge where he used to score from the gang members and the things that went on beneath the bridge. It wasn't a song, it was an exorcism.

Out of pain came slow happiness. One afternoon shortly before Christmas 1988, Irons received a phone call from Joe Strummer. The former Clash vocalist was in Los Angeles, putting a new band together around the cream of local talent. Zander Schloss and Lonnie Marshall, two of the many brilliant young guitar players who filed through the ranks of Thelonious Monster, were already with Strummer, and Irons's name came up in conversation. Strummer's voice, BBC English gone to working-class pot, echoed down the line. 'I was wondering if you fancied coming down to play a little.'

Irons laughed aloud. 'You do know where I am, don't you? I'm in my pyjamas in a mental hospital. I haven't played drums in six months!'

But Strummer was adamant and, after he hung up the phone, Irons returned to his bed lost in thought. He had made a clean break. His drums were packed up in boxes somewhere and he didn't care where that was. But hey, this was Joe Strummer. Joe Strummer! 'And it struck me, there was no way I could turn this down!'

He made his way down to Strummer's rehearsal studio and, still shaking, trying to push everything out of his mind so that he could concentrate upon this moment alone, he started to play. 'An hour

later,' he said, 'we were cutting a track for Joe's solo album. Later, as
I was leaving, he told me to take my time, but whenever I was ready,
I should come back and we'd finish the record.' A matter of weeks
later, Irons was firmly installed in the Strummer band, bringing his
reborn magic to another six songs destined for Strummer's *Earthquake
Weather* album. He returned to the road as well, touring the United
States first with Strummer, then as a member of Hawthorne-based
snot-punk humorists Red Cross. A year after that, newly married and
with a child on the way, he was reunited with Alain Johannes and
Natasha Schneider in a new band called Eleven, as they set about
recording their debut album, the sophisticated *Awake in a Dream*. 'I
will never forget what Joe did for me,' Irons reflected.

Kiedis, too, felt himself emerging from the shadows. He met actress
Ione Skye at a party during the run-up to *The Uplift Mofo Party Plan*.
Sixteen years old and still a student at Hollywood High, Ione was the
daughter of 60s pop icon Donovan, but was better known from her
acting debut two years earlier, alongside her brother, Donovan Leitch
Jr, in the movie *River's Edge*. 'I was like, "Why did they put me in this
movie?"' she later recalled. She'd had no training as an actress; she
hadn't even wanted to become one. But *Rolling Stone* called her 'one
of the year's most promising actresses', and her career blossomed from
there. Kiedis merely described her as 'one of the most ultimate angelic
creatures on earth'.

Ione (the name means 'Purple Heart' in Greek) moved in with
Kiedis shortly after they met. Quizzed by *Seventeen* magazine over how
the couple occupied their hours, she confessed that they spent most
of their time at home with their dog Ashley, watching old movies . . .
'anything with Vivien Leigh and Bette Davis. They're geniuses.'

The most significant event in the months that followed Slovak's
death, however, was surely the birth of Flea and Loesha's daughter
Clara. For days afterwards, the proud father could not stop himself
from repeating, 'Hillel was right. Hillel knew it would be a girl.'
Somehow, Clara's birth reaffirmed something that the surviving Los
Faces believed all along, but had never quite spoken aloud: that Slovak
was still with them, watching over them. From here on, they believed,
the only way to go was up. With this attitude of rebirth, Kiedis said,
'Flea and I realised that the Red Hot Chili Peppers was life to us. It
was both an outlet and a lifeline. We needed to hold on to it.'

The group publicly resurfaced early in September 1988, when
MTV's weekly alternative music programme *120 Minutes* aired a short
film of the Red Hot Chili Peppers playing at the Alcohol Salad in LA.

McKnight and Peligro again filled the spaces between Kiedis and Flea, and you could see the relief in the two prime Peppers' eyes. Back on stage, back in control of their destiny, Kiedis and Flea worked like they had never worked before, twisting the patently under-rehearsed quartet into a hydra-headed monster whose veins pulsed with the lifeblood of funk.

Appearances, however, were deceptive. On paper, McKnight and Peligro were masterful recruitments; from the beginning, the Red Hot Chili Peppers made it their business to straddle the gulf between punk and funk and now, with two of the genres' masters in their ranks, they were putting their dilettantism into perfect practical usage. But nobody expected the line-up to be anything more than a passing fancy. The group played just four shows, including the Alcohol Salad showcase, before McKnight took his leave. A handful of semi-serious recording sessions at Flea's home were scrapped simultaneously.

The parting was mutually agreeable. According to Kiedis, 'the best thing for Blackbird was not to be in the Red Hot Chili Peppers, but writing his own music and choreographing his own dance steps. He is an incredible guitar player, one of the best wandering the globe.' He just wasn't right for the Chili Peppers.

Peligro was another matter entirely. Until the Dead Kennedys broke up in 1987, Peligro spent six years playing behind perhaps the most anarchic, certainly the most abhorred, of all California's punk sons. San Francisco's Dead Kennedys offended by their very existence. Their frontman, Jello Biafra, was a natural outrage; coupling his already finely abrasive personality with such songs as 'California Uber Alles' and 'Stars and Stripes of Corruption', he established the DKs among the most wanted men in California, on moral grounds, even if not criminal, and the last years of the band's career were spent battling against a legal system that seemed determined to deem them an obscenity. Peligro himself had all but retired his drumsticks when he received the Red Hot Chili Peppers' call, but he lost little time retrieving them.

Peligro knew that, as a musician, he possessed few of the attributes that the group themselves demanded. But when Kiedis said 'we wanted to work with him', that was enough. Three months after a blow that would have been sufficient to pole-axe many groups, the Red Hot Chili Peppers were not looking for musical compatibility, they were looking for friends. Only as the healing process continued, did Kiedis and Flea realise that Peligro was not working out any better than McKnight.

'At this point, I'd say we're rawer and funnier and a little bit sloppier than before,' Flea said before the group's 11 November show at the University Memorial Center in Boulder, Colorado. 'We played [together] for years and it wasn't until now that I realised how tight we'd gotten.' It was to re-create that tightness that Peligro was finally given his marching orders, a little more than a week later.

'It was tough,' agreed Kiedis, 'because we love DH as a person and he's a lovable guy and, like everyone else, he's got his problems. We wanted a guy who was a friend. That's why we hired him. But I think his drumming skills had deteriorated from the time he was at his peak with the Dead Kennedys. We really tried to work out the situation . . .' but it was a hopeless quest. Peligro specialised in the wild thrash drumming that drove the Dead Kennedys to such ferocious heights. The man who would follow in Jack Irons's footsteps, however, needed to be tighter, more precise. The thrill of seeing the Red Hot Chili Peppers back in action was tempered by the knowledge that more changes would be required before they were back firing on all cylinders.

John Frusciante was born in New York on 5 March 1971, but was raised in the San Fernando Valley. He was just the latest member of his family to have both profound musical ambitions, and the proficiency to back them up: his father was a concert pianist, his mother a singer, his grandfather a guitarist, his great-grandfather a mandolin virtuoso. 'I knew that I was gonna be a guitarist ever since I can remember,' Frusciante later reflected.. 'There were voices in my head that were telling me so.'

When his parents bought him his first guitar, it was as though a new best friend had walked into his life. Alone in his bedroom, Frusciante practised up to fifteen hours a day, playing along with old Frank Zappa and Jimi Hendrix records – 'every one I could get my hands on'. No less than Hillel Slovak, he saw in Hendrix the perpetual battle for perfection and balance, the bitterness of betrayal that only absolute expression could exorcise from the spirit.

His early years as a would-be guitarist were not pain-free. On at least one occasion, around the time he was seven, the sheer proficiency of the guitarists he was listening to, the Jimmy Pages and Eddie Van Halens of this world, 'seemed so far away' that he abandoned the instrument. A couple of years later, however, as the noises of the new wave began leeching into his subconscious, he began playing again – with his introduction to the Germs the key to the discovery that it ain't what you play, it's the way that you play it that matters the most. In his own words, then, Frusciante grew up 'masturbating a lot and practising guitar'. When he was nine, he had romantic dreams about bisexuality. 'The point is, I'm weird. But I never felt weird.'

At other times, Frusciante would speak nostalgically of one of his favourite childhood games. 'I had a friend and if one of us had to pass gas, we'd say 'Cuddle!' And the one guy would stick his nose against the other's arsehole. You got the purest smell of gas, undiluted by air molecules.'

He loved sports but dropped out because he believed he lacked the 'competitive edge' to succeed. Even at the lowest level, school sports in America are divided into leagues, 'taking all the fun out of simply playing'. During his final weeks on a baseball team, Frusciante spent his time haunting the right field, making up songs about how much he hated the pitcher. 'He was the stud, so handsome and everything. I thought he should die.'

Punk hit the young Frusciante like a tidal wave. 'It wasn't a competitive thing. It was your war against those fucking average white suburban bland idiots who were destroying the world. That rage connected so well with me.' Indeed, he would later date his own birth as a true guitarist to precisely that emotion. 'I was angry at two kids that I didn't like and didn't like me, so I went home and wrote thirty short punk songs in a row on my acoustic guitar. That was the first day that I really started playing.'

In fact, everything about the world pissed him off, but when he felt the strings with his fingers, they at least reassured him. He was an anchorite in the cave of his musical strivings and, downstairs, as his family listened until even a discerning ear could no longer distinguish between the records he played and the lines he repeated, they looked at one another and they, too, wondered, was he perhaps just a little bit strange?

'I had a big identity problem when I was younger,' Frusciante said. 'There was a time when I wanted to shave my eyebrows so I could look like Adrian Belew [the hauntingly youthful American guitarist who exploded to prominence in Robert Fripp's King Crimson].' When he awoke every morning, the first thing he did was play Captain Beefheart's *Trout Mask Replica* album. Listening to Zoot Horn Rollo's playing, he was convinced, assured him of a day of 'unbridled creativity'. Deprived of that early morning musical fix, he slouched through the day in a fit of utter despondency.

'He was a character out of a John Waters film without a John Waters film to be in,' Kiedis agreed, and Frusciante adored the compliment.

Indeed, Waters, called the 'Pope of Trash' by William Burroughs, remained part of Frusciante's pantheon of artistic geniuses until the movie director climbed aboard America's anti-smoking bandwagon in 1990.

'How could he quit smoking?' Frusciante demanded bitterly. 'How could he go over to the enemy?' In an age in which smokers found themselves the victims of the first waves of the petty-minded discrimination that today sees them ranked among society's greatest pariahs, Frusciante no longer regarded his omnipresent cigarettes as a relaxation. He saw them as a weapon in an increasingly one-sided class war and, every chance he got, he would defy the No Smoking signs that were popping up like mushrooms all over America. When he bought his first car, a Cadillac, he did so because it boasted the biggest ashtray. If people were so worried about second-hand smoke, he snapped, they should buy their own and stop using up everyone else's.

Frusciante discovered the Red Hot Chili Peppers when he saw them playing the Variety Arts Center in downtown LA. He was no more than fifteen at the time, but from that moment on, he said, 'their music meant everything to me'. He turned up at every show he could, thanking the merciful providence that dropped his family in Los Angeles. Anywhere else in the world, even in the state, and he may never have discovered the group. To be closer to the heart of the Red Hot Chili Peppers' world, he left home at sixteen and found an apartment in the city.

His dedication verged on fanaticism. Unable to persuade his friends to put out their own money for tickets to the band's shows, he would pay for them himself. 'I just thought that everybody should see the Red Hot Chili Peppers, because I thought they were the most fantastic thing to ever hit the earth.' He added that the first time he caught the band play, 'I thought, "Man, this is what I wanna do." ' Three years later, he would say, laughing, 'I still can't believe that I am actually doing it!'

Slovak was dead before Frusciante mustered the nerve to introduce himself to the band. He was just a kid, just a fan, but amid the confused comings and goings that were the hallmarks of the band's rehabilitation, when he mentioned he was a guitarist, Flea invited him along to jam. Frusciante neglected to say he had never worked with another musician in his life. 'It wasn't until I moved out of my parents' house when I was sixteen, that I realised that playing with other people was an aspect of my music that I needed to develop.' Two years later, it still needed work. 'All I really care about is playing like I've got a huge cock,' he said.

From the rehearsal room, Flea invited Frusciante back to his house. He had set up a small four-track studio in a back room and quickly discovered that demoing new material always worked better if there were other players around to bounce ideas off. Frusciante hit them back like a tennis pro. 'The things that I recorded with John sounded even better than what I recorded with Blackbird,' Flea raved when he next met Kiedis. The kid was strange, but he could sure play guitar.

Kiedis learned that for himself when Frusciante accompanied him along to a studio session with actress-turned-singer Kristen Vigard. A former understudy for the lead role in the Broadway version of *Annie*, and a reasonably successful TV actress thereafter, Vigard abandoned her acting career in 1986, as her own circle of friends became more musical than thespian. Now she was recording her debut album, and seemed intent on calling in as many of those friends as she could – with Kiedis, Angelo Moore and Norwood Fisher only the tip of the iceberg.

For Kiedis himself, the album's highlight had to be his dynamic duet with Vigard across a simmering version of Leon Russell's 'Out in the Woods'; Frusciante, meanwhile, was destined to shine on another number entirely, as he and Vigard both co-wrote and co-performed the melancholy beauty 'Slave to My Emotions'.

Despite the obvious talent with which Frusciante bristled, however, and even after Blackbird's departure, nobody entertained any thoughts of the teenager joining the Red Hot Chili Peppers. He was just a friend who played great guitar and he might have remained just that had Bob Forrest not phoned Kiedis one day to say that Thelonious Monster were also looking for a new guitar player. 'If you try out anyone who you think will fit, let me know. I'll do the same for you.'

Kiedis told Forrest he might as well stop looking immediately. He already knew who the Monster needed. 'He's a good kid. He's really talented and he's very knowledgeable musically. He knows all the shit I don't know. I basically know nothing about music theory and he's studied it to death inside out. He's a very disciplined musician. All he cares about is his guitar and his cigarettes. We call him Greenie because he's so young.' Kiedis laughed. 'But don't let that put you off.'

'Greenie' himself was less comfortable with the idea. Next to the Red Hot Chili Peppers, Thelonious Monster ranked among his all-time favourite bands. It wasn't false modesty that held him back; the boy was good and he knew it. For him to walk into Thelonious Monster and become their next guitarist would be like walking into the Vatican and becoming the new Pope. It just seemed like it couldn't be done. But Kiedis and Flea were adamant. 'Go for it!' To keep him company at the first audition he had ever attended, they even agreed to join him at the studio.

At eighteen, Frusciante was the youngest and, in terms of his track record, the most inexperienced guitarist in the room. When he mentioned he had never even played in a band before, Forrest almost told him to go off and form one first. Thelonious Monster were hardly big time, but they weren't Little League, either. The band certainly didn't have the time to be breaking in a greenhorn.

Then he started to play and Forrest knew that nothing else mattered. He glanced over to Dix Denney, the ex-Weirdo who was the Monster's other guitarist. He, too, was flabbergasted. Then he looked towards Flea and Kiedis, sitting silently on the sidelines watching. Forrest didn't understand how, but somehow he knew. They, too, had seen their future in the skinny, shaven-headed teen.

Forrest moved quickly. 'OK, you're in.'

Frusciante let out a silent cheer, while Kiedis and Forrest went into a quick huddle. He was still congratulating himself when Kiedis walked over and told him, 'In the Chili Peppers, that is.' John Frusciante's membership of Thelonious Monster lasted no more than five minutes. Now all he had to do was prove he was man enough for the Red Hot Chili Peppers. 'I had to strip when I joined the band. They insisted they see my erect penis.'

Frusciante made his debut with the group – brought up to full-strength for the occasion by Fishbone drummer Fish – during the Christmas holiday on local TV, on the show *2HIP4 TV*. But for many of the people watching, it was difficult to believe he had not been a Pepper forever. 'I knew all their guitar parts, solos, bass lines and lyrics,' Frusciante boasted later, giving birth to the future legend that he actually learned to play from listening to the Red Hot Chili Peppers. In truth, the greatest lesson he learned from the group was how to behave onstage.

'John was an absolute Hillel clone,' Alain Johannes declared of Frusciante's early days in the band. 'Not only did he play like him, he stood like him and moved like him as well.' As though his tender years had not yet given him the chance to find his own public persona, Frusciante stepped bodily into Slovak's shoes, until even Flea and Kiedis were wondering what was going on. But when they asked him to be himself, Frusciante misunderstood completely.

'When John first joined,' Flea commented later, 'he was not playing as much good stuff [as he would later], even though he was perfectly capable of it. He was worried about playing things that would please us, instead of just letting his natural playing flow.' There were other reservations, too. 'His head got a little swollen and he was running around being rude to girls and getting them pissed off. But,' he added indulgently, 'that's to be expected. When you're eighteen years old and you want to get laid really bad and, all of a sudden you're in a band, the girls all want to fuck. You're bound to go crazy!'

Frusciante agreed with Flea's summary. When he became a Red Hot Chili Pepper, he admitted, 'I wanted nothing more in life than to be a rock star. It was what I was working for and everything I wanted. So, for the first couple of years, I very superficially dedicated myself to that – getting drunk, getting together with girls, and not being true to myself.'

There were no doubts about Frusciante's ability to adjust, though, just as there were no reservations about Chad Smith, who finally replaced DH Peligro in the drumming seat in the new year. Some thirty drummers filed through the Red Hot Chili Peppers' audition room and most of them, Kiedis complained, 'were basically weakapotamuses. They just didn't have the emotional intensity or the physical talent to rock the Peppers.'

Twenty-nine such weaklings flailed at the waiting kit before Smith sat down to play and only one, Chris Warren, even threatened to fit into the band. Unfortunately, Flea later mused, 'he didn't know how to play the drums very well at all.' Something clicked, however – departing the audition, Warren forgot one of his cymbals and, when he called Flea to arrange its retrieval, the pair fell quickly into friendship. Soon, Warren came on board after all, as drum tech for the drummer who followed him into the auditions – a man-mountain whose very appearance filled the little Peppers with awe.

Denise Zoom, one of the band's friends from the LA scene, recommended him, saying simply, 'I know this guy from Detroit [who] eats drums for breakfast.' Chad Smith was a behemoth, taller and broader than any of the band. His hair exploded from his skull like a field of black corn, kept in place by a bandanna. A cut-off Metallica T-shirt struggled gallantly to hold his bear-like chest in place. At first the waiting Peppers thought he had wandered into the wrong room. 'He looks like he should be in some heavy metal band playing at the Troubadour,' Flea whispered across to Kiedis and Frusciante. 'He looks like a geek,' Kiedis hissed back. The group was within a breath of calling 'OK, next' when Smith started playing.

Kiedis's first thought was that the studio was being stormed by a herd of psychedelic gorillas. 'He was like a human Roman candle, spiralling out these intense musical spasms.' Screaming at the top of his lungs, smashing the drums like they were lifelong foes, Smith commenced laying down a barrage that the Red Hot Chili Peppers simply couldn't keep up with. They weren't even sure whether he was actually playing well or not. They were too busy laughing.

'All of a sudden,' Flea remembered, 'we thought, "This guy is playing his arse off" and everything else went by the wayside.'

Smith could see in their eyes that he'd made his point. The moment he walked into the audition, he'd seen that the Red Hot Chili Peppers 'needed someone to kick their arse'. As he played, he started yelling at Flea. 'Come on! Fuck! Piss! Doom! Come on!' Upon reflection, he added, 'Even they were like, "What the fuck?"'

Looking back, Detroit-born Smith agreed with his future band-mates' original reservations about his appearance. If the audition were a written test, he would have failed with flying colours. 'I'm from the Midwest. I have good morals. I was a fuckin' peanut butter and jelly guy, really involved in sports. More on the normal side.' If he was asked what he could introduce to the Chili Peppers, his answer would have been simply, 'Rock'n'roll'. As a teenager, his idea of heaven was the same as Irons and Slovak's . . . Kiss. As an adult, he had never even heard of the Red Hot Chili Peppers.

'You know the picture on the back of *Kiss Alive*, taken at Cobo Hall?' he said. 'I was there. In the twelfth row. The picture is of the sixteenth row. It was the coolest thing.'

After the audition, wiping away the sweat and cracking open a beer, Smith meandered over to where the others were sitting and outlined his musical pedigree. He was 26, the same age as Kiedis and Flea, a 1980 graduate of Bloomfield Hills' Lahser High School. With a guitar-playing brother and a pianist sister, he gravitated naturally towards drums and proudly described the first kit he ever owned, a pile of giant round ice-cream cartons that his father found behind the local Baskin-Robbins ice-cream parlour. Armed with a pair of Lincoln Logs for drumsticks, he said, 'I started pounding away . . . and, my parents were like, "Well he really likes those", so they got me a K-Mart [drum kit], real cheesy.'

In 1984, Smith joined singer Denny Backos, guitarist Tony Cutino and bassist Dennis Martz in the Detroit-based hard-rock band Toby Redd. ('I only play for bands with the name "red",' he growled.) When Flea and Kiedis recollected their own activities in Motor City,

mercilessly heckling local groups during breaks while recording
Freaky Styley, Smith had to think long and hard before carrying on
with his tale. 'I don't suppose you remember what any of them were
called, do you?'

Barely recalled even for the one album they released for an Epic
subsidiary in 1986, *In the Light*, Toby Redd broke up in 1988 (they
would reunite for a one-off show in November 2003), and Smith
decided it was finally time to scrape the Midwest off his heels. Loading
up his truck, he headed down to LA to attend the Musician Institute.
Less than six months later, he heard about the Red Hot Chili Peppers'
auditions. 'I just went in and rocked out!'

The Red Hot Chili Peppers were back on the road in March 1989.
Pre-production for their next album had got under way the month
before, but the group felt they needed a little more time together.
Leaving Michael Beinhorn back in LA at the Ocean Way Studios, they
set about breaking in their latest drummer in the same way they had
reintroduced Jack Irons to the pack three years earlier, with a short
tour of Florida.

Totally inappropriately, the outing ended at West Palm Beach's
Respectable Street Cafe. Even with only a handful of shows behind
them, this latest incarnation of the Red Hot Chili Peppers was
anything but respectable. When a pair of female fans asked Frusciante
for his autograph, he didn't even blush as he penned his offer to
'destroy your hymens'. But it was the following month, April 1989, at
the George Mason University Patriot Center in Fairfax, Virginia, that
the shit really hit the fan.

The group were backstage, changing their clothes after one of the
greatest shows they had played all year. As they prepared to leave, a
student who had volunteered earlier in the evening to drive them back
to their hotel arrived at the dressing-room door. Kiedis made some
light-hearted innuendos, then dropped his pants. While the student
covered her face demurely, he pulled them up again and thought
nothing more of the incident. Twenty-four hours later, Kiedis learned
that the girl had filed a complaint, charging him with misdemeanour
charges of indecent exposure and sexual battery.

Kiedis told Britain's *Kerrang!* magazine, 'We were all joking and
laughing together and, when she left, no one was under the
impression that she was perturbed by my nudity in the dressing room.'

He denied the accusation that he dangled his unsheathed manhood
in the girl's face and was incredulous at the subsequent reports that
he actually touched her face with it. 'I'm not that type of person,' he

insisted. Unfortunately, it was not the heavy metal magazine's readership he would need to convince on that score, but a Virginia courtroom, a full year later.

10. A JOURNEY INTO FUNKY THRASH

Once it started to dry, the blood didn't look quite so bad. The kid was standing upright again as well, muttering a string of curses as he half-kicked, half-flicked the puke off one sneaker. His left eye was closing up and he'd probably have one hell of a headache in the morning, but he'd live.

The crowd, cheated of its blood-lust, began moving away until there were no more than half a dozen onlookers left, standing in a loose semi-circle around the stage door. Pushing through them, one of the Palladium's hired security men asked again what had happened.

'I dunno. I was back there with my girlfriend and suddenly these guys started in on me.' He jerked a thumb towards the closed door behind him. A mousy brunette beside him, her face glowing red and streaked with tears, nodded. 'That's right, they just started. Then they threw him out here.'

'Were they with either of the bands?' someone asked. Before the kid could reply, somebody else spoke up. 'No. He never got that far.'

The security man wheeled. 'You saw it?'

'Yeah. Well, some of it. This jerk' – a teenage boy, his denim jacket framing a Fishbone T-shirt, looked incredulously at the kid – 'this jerk walked in and said he'd gotten some shit for the Peppers. These three guys told him not to waste his time and they just started arguing. I didn't see anything else . . .' His voice trailed off apologetically.

'Is this true?'

The kid nodded and the security man rolled his eyes. 'Shit man, I don't even like this band, but I'd know better than that.' As he went back inside, he laughed. 'Well, I guess you won't be pressing any charges!'

The Red Hot Chili Peppers returned to the road – albeit for just one show – on 11 July 1989, when they joined Fishbone, Thelonious Monster and the latest spasm to blitzkrieg out of the Los Angeles underground, Jane's Addiction, at the Hollywood Palladium. Indeed, of the four bands on the bill, it was Jane's Addiction who merited the most attention, from both the watching media and the moshing audience. While their compatriots had nothing more than broadening cult acceptance to boast about, Jane's Addiction's second album, *Nothing's Shocking*, was firmly on course for a quarter of a million sales – bearing with it Flea's own first shot at landing a best-selling album (the record would ultimately be certified platinum, for over a million copies sold).

Flea was thrilled when he was invited to add horns to one song, 'Idiots Rule', on what was to become *Nothing's Shocking*. He was already a confirmed Jane's Addiction fan – the first time he saw frontman Perry Farrell, he recalled, was at a local Jimi Hendrix tribute concert in 1986; the cream of the local underground played, but the only photograph anybody published was of Farrell, already a retina-searing blur of colour and activity, as he stepped out of his then-current band, the goth extravaganza of Psi Com, for the occasion. 'I saw the photo and I was "who is this guy?" ' Flea recalled.

He found out the following year. 'I saw Jane's play and I realised what an awesome band they were. Even though my band was coming from a totally opposite place, I could relate to their musical intensity. I knew I was a lucky son of a bitch when they asked me to play trumpet on "Idiots Rule". No question about it.' For the honour placed him firmly within the storm to watch, as so many would subsequently see, as the arty spark lit by Perry Farrell, Dave Navarro, Eric Avery and Stephen Perkins erupted into a conflagration that was destined to open the door through which all of the giants of the next five years, from REM to Nirvana, and onto the Red Hot Chili Peppers themselves, would eventually tumble.

Jane's Addiction debuted in LA in April 1987, opening for Gene Loves Jezebel at the Roxy. Further high-profile shows saw them gig alongside Peter Murphy, Nick Cave and Dream Syndicate, with a set that already included the incendiary burst of covers and originals that would characterise the band's national emergence a year later: 'Jane Said', 'Ocean Size', 'Whores', 'Sympathy For The Devil'. They became regulars at Scream alongside Human Drama, LA Guns and the infant Guns N' Roses, and contributed one track, 'Pigs In Zen', to 1987's *Scream: The Compilation* album. Suddenly, every label in LA wanted them and, while the band would sign to Warners as early as February 1987, still their first release, August's live *Jane's Addiction*, would be released through the band's management's own Triple X label.

With the local press now prostrate at Jane's altar, more prestigious shows followed, opening for X and the Psychedelic Furs in LA, before the group were introduced to the rest of America on tour with Love And Rockets through December 1987. By the time the band's second album, *Nothing's Shocking*, was ready for release, the whole country, it seemed, had opinions about Jane's Addiction – and they weren't all good.

Farrell made no secret of his desire to employ shock and outrage as readily as music, and the cover of *Nothing's Shocking* was designed to take that resolve to the limit. Musically, however, *Nothing's Shocking* addressed every accusation of talentless hype that had hitherto been levelled at the aural firestorm of the Jane's Addiction cacophony, and answered each in spellbinding form.

'Idiots Rule', with its staccato brigandage and honking belligerence, was simply one feast among many, but for fans of either the Red Hot Chili Peppers or Fishbone (Angelo Moore and Chris Dowd were also at the session), it offered a route into Farrell's assaultive world that might not otherwise have been so evident. Jane's Addiction guitarist Dave Navarro explained, 'I remember Perry telling [them] what to play. That's what was great about Perry. They had this horn section part worked out that took a Jane's Addiction song and, somehow, within one pass of tape, turned it into a Fishbone song.'

Flea received his first listen to the entire album in late June 1988, three months before it was released. 'Perry had just finished up recording, and we were on our way to a friend's house to watch the big Tyson–Spinks fight. On the way there, Perry was like, "Oh, this is my new record, listen to it." And then I realised what a great, great band they were. It was just a big, weird day. I heard *Nothing's Shocking* for the first time, Tyson knocked Spinks out in the first round, and then I came home and got the call that Hillel was dead.'

Since that time, Jane's Addiction had continued their rise, baiting their detractors with a stream of calculatedly controversial imagery and innuendo, even as they delighted an entire generation of would-be rebels for whom Guns N' Roses cut'n'paste bad boyisms were just a little too Hollywood to really cut the ice. Tours first with Iggy Pop and the Ramones, and then as headliners in their own right, kept Jane's Addiction constantly on the road, while further recognition rained down when they were nominated for the Grammys' newly founded Heavy Metal category, alongside AC/DC, Iggy Pop, Metallica and Jethro Tull – the eventual, if mystifying, victors.

Now they were back in Los Angeles and, if the evening's billing did not quite fit Jane's Addiction's own status – Fishbone headlined, Jane's Addiction followed, the Red Hot Chili Peppers and Thelonious Monster brought up the rear – their performance cemented their ascendancy regardless. Only the Red Hot Chili Peppers themselves were aware that their own lowliness on the bill absolutely belied the new resolution that was coursing through their veins; the belief . . . indeed, the instinctive knowledge . . . that they would not be propping up the Palladium bill for long.

They'd had their problems, they'd wrestled with their demons and they'd chased the dragon out of town. The sight of the three heavies kicking the shit out of a single punk on the street outside the venue served warning that from now on things were going to be very different around the band. As Flea himself affirmed later, 'Anyone coming to see us, unless they're really thick-headed and stupid, would have the sense not to offer drugs around. That's a really unpopular thing around the Red Hot Chili Peppers.'

Reformed addicts can rank among the most intolerant people one will ever meet. Few folk come down harder on smokers, for instance, than ex-smokers and few can preach more passionately on the perils of drugs than those who have travelled that long road themselves. That summer of 1989 there appeared to be a lot of weary travellers around.

When the then-First Lady, Nancy Reagan, launched her 'Just Say No to Drugs' campaign, she set in motion a chain of events that, a decade earlier, would have been regarded as unthinkable. The campaign was aimed squarely at what the media now called the 'MTV generation', the kids for whom rock'n'roll was the most sacred cow on earth and drugs the sacrament they consumed at its altar. Their lifestyle, painted in bold-lettered caricature by a media sated by high-profile drug busts, was one of unrelenting degeneracy and the icons they held dearest – the Jimi Hendrixes and Janis Joplins, the Johnny Thunders and Keith Richards – were the high priests of dope-crazed mayhem.

That, according to Flea, was 'the awful paradox of it all. There've been so many great musicians that have been junkies: Jimi Hendrix, Billie Holiday, Charlie Parker, Keith Richards, Iggy Pop. But all these people who do heroin think they're living this rock'n'roll fantasy. They don't realise that, if you read an interview with Charlie Parker, he'll say what wrecked his life was heroin.'

A little over a year before, Flea met up with jazz trumpet virtuoso Chet Baker, one of his long-time heroes. Sitting alongside the great man, listening to him play, then busking along with him for a few blissful hours, Flea was a shy little boy once again, standing proud but awkward while old Dizzy Gillespie clutched him to his side.

A few short weeks later, on 13 May 1988, Baker was dead, falling to his death from his hotel window while under the influence of drugs. And, while Flea agreed that 'it's a sad thing for anyone to die', he admonished his old idol regardless. 'If you choose that lifestyle, there is nothing you can do except kick it, go to jail, or die.' It was unusual, he said with a laugh, that he should find himself agreeing with Nancy Reagan. But this time she'd got something right. For the first time in history, drugs as a recreational or even a creative force in rock'n'roll were to lose their allure.

In late 1986, MTV, now the single most powerful institution in the music industry, launched its own Rock Against Drugs campaign. By the following January, members of Bon Jovi, Motley Crüe, Kiss, Dio and the Sex Pistols had filmed advisory clips that would be aired by the network, a battery of warnings that ranged from Crüe's Vince Neill stating 'I still party with the best of them, but now I do it clean' to Pistol Steve Jones's eloquent 'Drugs suck'. Aerosmith, whose Steve Tyler has made no secret of his former chemical intake, actually inserted a clause in their tour contract prohibiting drugs and alcohol backstage at their gigs. 'If I want to get high,' Tyler told his fans, 'I listen to music.' And top of his play list, he claimed, was *The Uplift Mofo Party Plan*.

To cynics, such earnest commentary reeked of hypocrisy. Rock'n' roll was founded on rebellion; in many ways, it *was* rebellion, a voice that cursed convention, defied responsibility and flaunted all the house rules. It was a weapon in youth's eternal war with its parents. Now, without warning or regard, it had become those parents, shaking a finger in concerned approbation. Drugs suck? Yeah, thanks, Mom.

But two years into Rock Against Drugs' crusade, the National Institute on Drug Abuse was able to report that, in almost every category, drug use among high school seniors had declined – in some cases, such as cocaine and certain tranquilliser use, quite markedly. Only one drug remained wholly unaffected, only one cause of death continued to climb: heroin.

Slovak's passing did more than alter Kiedis's and Flea's perspective on life and friendship. It also changed their perception of their own influence, as members of a rock'n'roll band, on their audience. In 1992, Kiedis would join forces with members of the Beastie Boys and Jane's Addiction for 'Trip on This', an anti-drug video produced for use in California high schools. But long before that, he and Flea crusaded hard, living and reliving the awful loss they had experienced firsthand. 'I'm very anti-cocaine and heroin,' Flea declared. 'I've just seen it destroy a lot of people that I love. I don't even like to pay attention to it, really, outside of telling everyone who's a junkie to fuck off and suck my arsehole.' He had discovered, through both personal and painful experience, a truth that escaped many other of the so-called counter-culture's other critics: the fact that the ethics of junkie chic *can* be separated from great rock'n'roll. And that the separation does not have to be painful.

In terms of rock'n'roll legend, image is often as important as music, a fact that MTV recognised even after it pumped out $3 million worth of Rock Against Drugs commercials. Rolling Stone Keith Richards has long since hauled himself from the brink of the abyss into which legend insisted he was plunging and, today, his glazed stumble could as easily be a by-product of old age as the result of another whirl on the chemical merry-go-round. But, even in health, Richards radiates a style – if no longer a lifestyle – in which fiction remains as immutable as fact. The MTV film crew that joined the Stones on tour in 1989 knew this as well as anyone. But, even in candid camera sobriety, the former World's Most Glamorous Junkie retained his title.

Iggy Pop, too, revelled in self-mythologising destruction throughout his darkest hours, the three-year period during which the self-styled world's forgotten boy remained bandless, contractless and, apparently, friendless. Two decades later, a cleaned-up Pop was complaining that his own audience still demanded that he be fucked up at 40-plus, that he carry into middle age the image he had worn through his teens. His rehabilitation, like Richards', is proof that you don't have to lie on an old self-made bed. You just have to look like you do.

Two years later, the Red Hot Chili Peppers would pay their own tribute to Iggy's longevity by recording his 'Search and Destroy'. For they, too, had that style. Their appearance, their behaviour, their sheer, untrammelled exuberance continued to exude the sense of abandon that created the hardcore, bone-crunching mayhem sex things from heaven all those years ago.

But, in so openly discussing and disavowing the fate that consumed Hillel Slovak, they were walking a tightrope from which, should they slip, their descent into schizophrenia would become apparent to the world. For now, suddenly and shockingly, the world's eyes were firmly focused on the Red Hot Chili Peppers.

Emotions ran high throughout the sessions for the much-delayed fourth album. Michael Beinhorn again accompanied the group into the studios, certain that he knew what was wrong with *The Uplift Mofo Party Plan*, certain that he knew how to rectify it. 'He was totally gung-ho,' Kiedis said with a laugh. The incident that sticks deepest in his mind is the last moment of pre-production. Beinhorn drew the band around him and, like a football coach priming his team for the game of their lives, he began to work on them.

'This is gonna be the greatest record ever made. This record is gonna be so damn great the world won't know what's hit it.' Over and over he bellowed and, with the band bellowing back at him, by the time the party was ready to hit the studio, they could have banged down the entire album in one take. But Beinhorn didn't work like that. He intended to push the group to its limits, drag them through the most laboriously painstaking sessions they could ever imagine. 'Don't think you're in here simply to make a record,' he told them. 'You're in here to fight a war.'

Studio takes became parade-ground drill but, though the group plotted rebellion, they never followed it through. Beinhorn knew exactly how far to push them and, just as they reached that point of no return, he'd gather them around to hear another finished song. 'We got some really good tracks out of it,' Kiedis was able to look back and say.

But anger was never far from the surface. Beyond those casual sessions with Flea and Peligro, and the no-pressure friendliness of Kristen Vigard's album, Frusciante had precious little experience in studio work. To him, Beinhorn's constant demands for perfection appeared foolish, as though the producer, rather than squeeze out the freshest music the young guitarist had in him, preferred to pound everything to the edge of sterility. The pair appeared unable to agree on anything. When Frusciante was satisfied, Beinhorn demanded more. When Beinhorn was happy, it was Frusciante who would demand another take, just one more opportunity to record a certain sequence in the hope of finally striking the chord that, to his mind, was missing.

Kiedis also found the process frustrating. The longer the sessions wore on, the more he and Beinhorn sniped at one another. It was this constant clashing of personalities that finally forced the sessions to close with less than thirty-eight minutes worth of usable material in the can. *Rocking Freakapotamus*, Kiedis's pet name for the project, would be brought up to full length with two older songs: the *Abbey Road* version of 'Fire' and 'Taste the Pain', recorded with Fishbone's Fish for the soundtrack of Ione Skye's latest movie, *Say Anything*, before Smith joined the group.

By the time of the Hollywood Palace show in July, *Rocking Freakapotamus* had been discarded as a title, in favour of *Mother's Milk*. The earlier name was instead donated to the band's Studio City-based fan club, *Rockin' Freakapotamus Peoplehood, Inc.*, leaving Kiedis to explain his reasons for the change. 'Mother's milk is a life-giving,

nurturing, intoxicating, good-natured, health-building, loving, com-
forting, warm, soothing substance. When you drink it, it makes you
feel good and makes you grow up strong and healthy. It wards off
infection and disease. And it's honest. It's pure and wholesome and
that's what we like to think our music represents.' Plus, Flea cackled,
'I've been drinking a lot of it from my wife's tit.'

Mother's Milk was previewed in early August 1989, during the
annual New Music Seminar in New York City. Invitations to the
album's launch party guided guests to the celebrated Tramps niterie,
then sent them across the street to Manhattan's only indoor miniature
golf course. Proof, *Billboard*'s Thom Duffy jested, that while 'you can
take the baby boomers out of the suburbs, you can't take the "burbs
out of the boomers"'.

The Red Hot Chili Peppers shared their big night with EMI
debutants Crazyhead, then made their way across the Atlantic for a
short European tour, highlighted by a massive free concert in
Amsterdam's Dam Square. At home, meanwhile, the charm offensive
got under way.

Kim White, the radio rep entrusted with the Red Hot Chili Peppers'
account, deluged the college circuit with the group's material. Trade
papers were whipped into a state of frenzy, not only by White's
enthusiasm, but also by the (untrue) rumour, emanating from the
trade journal *Hits*, that she was the topless model pictured on the
sleeve of the forthcoming album.

Within a week of its release, the first single from *Mother's Milk*,
'Knock Me Down', was at No. 24 in *Hits*' post-modern chart, compiled
from both sales and airplay in select key regions. Among the radio
stations sampled, 'Knock Me Down' was the most popular addition to
the alternative playlist and, seven days later, on 21 August, the
magazine reported the song was 'sweeping the airwaves'.

'Knock Me Down' was an old song by Kiedis's standards, partially
written even before *The Uplift Mofo Party Plan* sessions. Gentler than
much of the band's current fare, he 'had not thought too highly' of it
at the time and discarded it. It was only after Slovak's death that Kiedis
began re-examining the lyrics. 'I hadn't really thought about completing it until then,' he admitted. '[It] is about [Hillel] and myself; our
friendship together and the relationship between friends in general.'
Now its success took him by surprise, but 'I know Hillel would be
proud of it and that makes me feel really good. There's also the
possibility that wherever he is, he's heard this record and he gets off
on it.'

'Knock Me Down' eventually peaked at No. 4 as MTV slammed the video into breakout rotation and the song would undoubtedly have climbed even further but for one unforeseen hitch. On 28 August, EMI Manhattan released *Mother's Milk* itself, and everything else was forgotten.

The album slammed instantly to the top of what was, in those days, quaintly termed the New Music Chart and, in its wake, DJs began spinning a second song from the album, a firestorm raging around the charred skeleton of Stevie Wonder's 'Higher Ground'. It, too, stormed the 'post-modern' chart; the accompanying video, based by director Bill Stobaugh around some experimental psychedelic moving back-drops he'd made during his college days, became a seemingly permanent fixture on MTV – and remained so powerful a touchstone in the Red Hot Chili Peppers' own canon that, fourteen years later, directors Jonathan Dayton and Valerie Faris would revisit those same psychedelically tinged pastures for 2003's 'Zephyr Song' video.

Revelling in the luxury of having a real video budget for the first time in their careers, the films that the Red Hot Chili Peppers shot for 'Higher Ground' and, the day before, 'Knock Me Down', ignited the band's own fascination for, and swift mastery of, the video medium. And it is indicative of the sheer impact of the ensuing combination, the brain-charring juxtaposition of song, video and image, that the band's triumphs-so-far were suddenly revealed as simply the first stage of a far grander strategy. Long before the scheduled October release of 'Higher Ground' as the new Red Hot Chili Peppers' single, the national chart began beckoning the band.

Stevie Wonder himself took the song to No. 4 in 1973 and, as the Red Hot Chili Peppers' own version climbed towards similar heights, so Kiedis added Wonder's name to the pantheon of gods to whom the band was most indebted. 'To me [Stevie Wonder has] created some of the most beautiful and emotional music of the entire century. He has brought a great deal of happiness and sadness and bewonderment into my life. He's the kind of person that I would like to play my music for and feel proud of it.'

The response to *Mother's Milk* both staggered and gratified the Red Hot Chili Peppers. The album was cited in *Playboy* as 'the most dynamic punk funk connection you're likely to hear for a long time', and in the *Washington Times* as 'a journey into funky thrash, perfect for late night raw energy'. *Guitar Player*'s Joe Gore, describing the current edition of the Red Hot Chili Peppers as possibly 'the most intense yet', credited Frusciante with skills even Slovak could only have dreamed of having recognised. '[He] plays as if he grew up with one ear glued to a boombox and the other to a Marshall stack . . . a living archive of 70s metal and Funk riffs.' Bemused by such praise, Frusciante could only reply that without Slovak's guidance, spiritually if not personally, he might have still been practising his Zappa riffs in his bedroom.

But perhaps the greatest compliment of all came from the *Philadelphia Inquirer*. Analysing the Red Hot Chili Peppers' professed debt to George Clinton, journalist Tom Moon then proceeded to demolish Clinton's own newest album, *The Cinderella Theory*, at the same time pointing out that 'the game has been changed' – savagely rewritten by 'Clinton's students', a motley crew that included not only the Red Hot Chili Peppers, but also 'everyone from 24-7 Spyz to the Royal Crescent Mob to Fishbone to Thelonious Monster . . . who have radically expanded the P-Funk concept to include liberal helpings of heavy metal and hard rock and still more improvisatory dissonance. Though they excerpt a snippet of Fishbone and pay homage to Clinton with rubbery Funkadelic back-beats, the Chili Peppers are now developing an identity that doesn't depend on any one genre-specific posture.'

Among the people most gratified by the Red Hot Chili Peppers' burgeoning success was Dave Kendall, at that time host of MTV's alternative rock showcase *120 Minutes* and a long-time supporter of the band. '[*120 Minutes*] played the Chili Peppers throughout the lean years, when nobody else was,' he told *Alternative Press* journalist Jo-Ann Greene, 'and perhaps we helped keep them together.' But he plays down suggestions that MTV in some way 'made' the band. 'The Chili Peppers always had a very, very strong cult base of fans and it was the fans that really kept them going and kept them together.' Nevertheless, Kendall remains convinced that it was with 'Higher Ground' that the ball really started to roll. 'That song went into heavy rotation and, until that happens, a band isn't really going to make that much of an impact on MTV.'

'We poured our hearts and souls into this record,' Flea insisted. 'It's a really honest portrayal of our feelings.' Kiedis agreed. 'I don't know if our vision is more focused,' he speculated, 'but the thing about the Red Hot Chili Peppers is that we really mean what we say, and we say it in a way that no other band does.'

Now the group was being offered the opportunity to air those feelings across America, as EMI set about fortifying the media blitzkrieg that both defied and belied the anonymity in which the group laboured for so long. The catalyst on which that blitzkrieg would centre, of course, was the young man whose painting of a reclining nude graced the back of the *Mother's Milk* jacket: Hillel Slovak.

Suddenly the beast was uncaged and no less ferociously than when, in 1972, the New York Dolls' Billy Murcia OD'd in the tub from a veinful of smack. Before his death, no one would touch the Dolls with a ten-foot pole. Afterwards, everybody wanted a slice of a band whose members die as good as they look. Sex sells, but death obsesses and, though Rock Against Drugs had changed the message somewhat, the fascination remained the same.

John Blanco, music correspondent for the *Phoenix New Times*, wrote of Slovak 'jamming with his idol Jimi Hendrix in the celestial hang-out for rock'n'roll junkies'. The *Entertainment News* wire service headlined a syndicated interview with Kiedis, entitled DRUG DEATH A CATALYST FOR CHILI PEPPERS. Even in this new age of moral responsibility, old habits – and old equations – died hard. Sex and drugs still equalled rock'n'roll. As journalists delved deeper into the Red Hot Chili Peppers' past, the band represented a potent force in all three of those elements.

Were they, however, backing away from the edge? Success seldom comes without compromise of some sort and, to fans who had followed them in the past, the Red Hot Chili Peppers' very motivation somehow now seemed suspect, accusations that – though nobody would have believed it at the time – would still be hanging over the Red Hot Chili Peppers more than a decade later. In 2003, Flea was still defending the evolution of the group's music to CNN, when he snapped, 'it's easy to say, "Well, I quit doing drugs and my music changed." You know, everything is always changed. I don't think that my music's changed. The music that I composed, the music that we've composed together, has changed just as much during a time when we were high out of our minds . . . as it has changed during a time when we haven't been doing any drugs. It's just been a constantly evolving, changing thing. So I can't really just pin it to that, even though, obviously, that's a big change, you know?

'When you're high on something all the time, it's a lot different than when you're dealing with the pain that you're carrying around. I mean every human being has a giant, empty hole of pain and grief that they carry around with them. And everyone tries to fill it with something. So when you're dealing with it without being high and you're confronting that part of yourself, it's a lot different.'

In fact, it was not simply the band's perceived lifestyle that had altered. Their very attitude, too, seemed to have mellowed. Certainly the parental advisory stickers that decorated the *Mother's Milk* cover sounded a hollow warning after the Peppers' past excesses; few people could object to the majority of Kiedis's lyrics this time around, and many even found them laudable. In August 1990, after a citizen of Kiedis's own home state of Michigan commenced a letter-writing campaign to the *Battle Creek Enquirer* claiming that rock'n'roll, in promoting drug use, was undermining society, his opponents cited the Red Hot Chili Peppers as an argument against him: 'Cliff Day states that rock music promotes drug use,' wrote one correspondent to the newspaper, 'then asks the reader the last time he heard a secular rock song against drugs. I've listened to several over the last week, including . . . "Knock Me Down".'

Of course, the Red Hot Chili Peppers were conscious of their new-found responsibilities and they lost little time in demonstrating the fact. Recalling the maddening controversy that greeted Jane's Addiction's *Nothing's Shocking* in September 1988, the *Phoenix New Times* predicted that, whatever the fate of *Mother's Milk* itself, the front cover alone would 'raise as much of a stink' as *Nothing's Shocking* – at least among those souls who might take offence at the sight of a topless giantess cradling four miniaturised Red Hot Chili Peppers in her arms.

Kiedis's torso and a strategically placed rose camouflaged nipples the size of each band member's head but, when a national American chain store caught sight of the design immediately after placing an order for 50,000 copies – and promptly threatened to cancel that order – suddenly the *New Times*' warning took on new, dire financial considerations. EMI set about revamping the cover, enlarging the band members so that they might obscure even more of those breasts, and the Red Hot Chili Peppers happily abided by the decision.

'The art of the Red Hot Chili Peppers,' Kiedis commented firmly, 'is first and foremost that of our music, and we never change our music as a compromise for anybody's desires or tastes. That we should have to enlarge ourselves on the record [sleeve] is really not that big a deal. It's what's inside that counts.'

He might have added that like the socks, the anonymous model's breasts were simply a part of the packaging. If they detracted from the music, as in this case they certainly did, then the Red Hot Chili Peppers had no further use for them. Instead, he reminded readers of the British magazine *Kerrang!*, 'these things are so arbitrary anyway. Nobody kicked up any fuss over our T-shirts!'

Over the years, the Red Hot Chili Peppers both modelled and sold a variety of shirts, their designs ranging from a crude representation of their cocks in socks, to an even cruder portrait of Madonna masturbating to the Red Hot Chili Peppers. 'I don't think she's ever denied masturbating,' Kiedis said, excusing the shirt, 'or masturbating to the Red Hot Chili Peppers, for that matter.'

The ultimate response to accusations that the group had 'sold out', however, was to be found within *Mother's Milk* itself. 'Punk Rock Classic' was thought-provokingly ironic, a poke at the bands who had conformed to the norm, who would do anything for a whirl on MTV. Even as its own lyrics passed from dream to reality, 'Punk Rock Classic' was less a plea for success than it was a blueprint.

By April 1990, the Red Hot Chili Peppers had indeed landed the gold records they yearned for; two years later, they, too, had 'been on every cover, including *Rolling Stone*'. Life, it is said, frequently imitates art. Seldom does it imitate satire. It's a sign of just how high the band's stock soared, not only elevating *Mother's Milk*, but scooping up the group's back catalogue as well, that in 1992, Jack Irons guardedly admitted that his royalties from just one album and an EP pay many of his family's bills. Three years earlier, even as *Mother's Milk* debuted, he would have joined Flea in complaining he never received a penny from any of the records.

But the speed and the sudden impact of the Red Hot Chili Peppers' new-found popularity continued to exercise outsiders' suspicions and, in many of the interviews he undertook at the time, Kiedis constantly found himself on the defensive. Giving his critics more credence than they deserved, he reasoned, 'I think [what] we've created now is just as valid and potent as before. We like to expand our musical horizons with every record, whether it is to grow in a melodic direction, or just improve the arrangement of our songs. We're always trying to get better, to change and diversify, [and] I think we've managed that with this record.'

The arrival of John Frusciante, he continued, gave the group 'more melodic potential, so we explored that avenue and came up with songs like "Knock Me Down". That was something we didn't previously do, because it wasn't part of the talent in the band as it was before.' Besides, he could have continued, the Red Hot Chili Peppers remained in touch with their roots, as 'Good Time Boys', the opening cut from *Mother's Milk*, demonstrated.

Viewed in hindsight, with the Red Hot Chili Peppers' success confirmed, 'Good Time Boys' appears almost ironic in intent, a

dynamic tribute to the LA scene that could easily be seen as a farewell
of sorts. The lyrics not only trace the Red Hot Chili Peppers' own
career, travelling 'round the world gettin' naked on stage', but also
those of their contemporaries. While Jack Sherman, the band's
long-departed guitar player, was invited along to supply backing
vocals to both this song and 'Higher Ground', Thelonious Monster,
Fishbone, John Doe (late of X) and fIREHOSE all received name
checks in the lyrics. But not, as has been suggested, in the context of
bridesmaids trailing the Peppers up the chartbound aisle.

When 'Good Time Boys' was written, the Red Hot Chili Peppers
were still comparative unknowns. The song does not confirm some
star-struck estrangement so much as it cements the bond that holds
those bands together, demonstrating just how tightly knit a circle the
Red Hot Chili Peppers were moving in. (Mike Watt, bassist for
fIREHOSE, was remembered again two years later, when the *Blood
Sugar Sex Magik* album was dedicated to him, and would still be
touring alongside the Peppers in 2003.)

These friendships were in evidence throughout *Mother's Milk*.
Fishbone's Angelo Moore, the horn player who saved Slovak's job the
previous year in Washington, featured in the 'Knock Me Down' video;
Flea and Kiedis's old flatmate Keith Barry, now a self-confessed
journeyman musician whose credentials stretched as far as gigs with
Ray Charles and trumpeter Woody Shaw, contributed tenor sax. And,
together, insisted Kiedis, they represented 'the last of a dying breed.
There's a close brotherhood among [us], we're all good friends and we
spend a lot of time together, playing music and touring and just
basically sharing the same philosophy of life and music – ultimate
honesty in the expression of music.'

Now it was time to reap the rewards of that honesty. Tentative plans
for the Red Hot Chili Peppers to tour America with Aerosmith were
scrubbed. Instead, the group were lined up for a theatre tour of their
own, beginning at venues that held a thousand or so people but, as
the tour progressed, adding larger halls to the itinerary. The new year
would bring a return visit to Europe and, from there, the band would
be travelling to Japan.

Flea and Frusciante limbered up for the tour by flinging themselves
enthusiastically into an ad hoc punk group called Hate. But, even
there, their bandwagoning fame reached out to touch them, and they
were forced to withdraw after just a handful of shows when word got
around that the two Red Hot Chili Pepper lookalikes who were
turning up on the Hollywood circuit with refreshing regularity were

not lookalikes at all. Frusciante tried to maintain the deception, insisting that the whole thing was simply a crowd-pulling gimmick dreamed up by an unknown band, but he convinced no one. Wasn't it he, after all, who namechecked another member of Hate, Nicky Beat, midway through his personal acknowledgments on *Mother's Milk*? Bewildered by its own members' success, Hate ground to a premature halt shortly afterwards.

Unperturbed, Flea then joined Trulio Disgracias, a part-time floating anarchy in which he played trumpet alongside a pool of musicians from Fishbone and Thelonious Monster, but it was again a short-lived concern, destined to wind up just nights before the Red Hot Chili Peppers' own tour began.

Competition for ticket buyers' time and money was fierce that fall of 1989. The economic recession that would eventually cause the downfall of the first President Bush was already looming in certain parts of the country; people no longer had the cash to spend week after week on concert tickets. Instead, they chose carefully and they were granted an impressive roster to pick from.

Bon Jovi, the Cure, the Fine Young Cannibals, Love and Rockets, the Pogues and Simply Red were all on the road that September, and even they quaked in the shadow of the Rolling Stones, shuddering into live action for the first time since 1981. The music industry might be geared towards categorising its audience according to certain musical stereotypes, but any one of those acts was capable of detracting from another, attracting audiences that turned the strict pigeonholing of the record companies' sales pitch on its head. As the Red Hot Chili Peppers headed out, they could only hope that the success of *Mother's Milk* might cast them into a similarly borderless world.

Augmenting their own line-up with saxophonist Tree and two female back-up vocalists, and with the highly rated LA band Mary's Danish booked to support them, the *Mother's Milk* tour kicked off in Seattle on 9 September 1989.

11. TWO NAKED GIRLS AND A SPATULA ON A COUCH

Jimi Hendrix hated his birthplace with a passion. Even after fame took him by the hand, he returned to Seattle just three times: twice to perform and once to be buried. The city remained a Mecca for his fans, nonetheless. They came in droves to hover around his grave at Greenwood Memorial Park; to stare up at Garfield High School, where he whiled away his teenage years; and to gawk at the house on 26th and Washington, where the Hendrixes lived when Jimi was ten.

For the Red Hot Chili Peppers, there would be precious little time for sightseeing. In Seattle, as in almost every city, even their free time would be spent on promotional details: an in-store promotion at Peaches record store and recording station IDs for local radio. But they would be paying tribute to their idol regardless. When *Seattle Post-Intelligencer* reporter Gene Stout asked Flea if the group had anything special planned, the reply sounded spontaneous. 'We'll be playing some Hendrix. He's the all-time virtuoso of passion and emotion.' He didn't let on that the Red Hot Chili Peppers were now playing some Hendrix every night.

'Fire', 'Crosstown Traffic' and 'Castles Made of Sand' were all featured in the Red Hot Chili Peppers' thirty-song set, but it was not only Hendrix they remembered as they played those songs. Hillel Slovak, too, hung over the proceedings, so heavily that, in Atlanta later in the tour, Kiedis admitted his voice simply gave out on him midway through 'Castles'. 'I was looking up at the ceiling and it's painted with all those stars and clouds and stuff . . . and I couldn't get Hillel off my mind.'

From Seattle, the tour moved south to Portland, where the *Oregonian*'s John Foyston left readers in no doubt of the Red Hot Chili Peppers' appeal. 'This is the stuff that made them televise Elvis from the waist up, so we couldn't see these swivelling hips,' he declared and, afterwards on the street outside the Starry Night, a sense of absolute unreality remained. Foyston described one young man, in disarray after the concert, drenched with sweat. 'He'd lost his wallet sometime . . . as he leapt onto the stage and repeatedly dove off into the audience. He'd twice been wrestled down the stairs by burly blue-shirted security guards when they were able to catch up to him in the writhing crowd of 1,100. [But] he was ready to do it all over again. "I love dancing to a high energy band like these guys."

'That's a Red Hot Chili Peppers fan for you.'

But, if any conclusions were to be drawn from the tour, early though it was, San Francisco was the place to be. The Red Hot Chili Peppers had drifted in and out of the city many times in the past, but only to headline the clubs, sweaty dives like the I Beam and the Stone. This time, things were different. This time, they were playing the Fillmore, the legendary auditorium that once stood at the heart of the psychedelic explosion.

Ken Kesey held his first Bay Area Acid Test here and 3,000 souls lost themselves to the embryonic Grateful Dead. Otis Redding once headlined three nights, Jimi Hendrix kept going for six. Now the Red Hot Chili Peppers had made it and, for two nights, the old venue rocked like it hadn't rocked in years, and never would again. Little more than a month later, on 17 October 1989, a mighty earthquake rattled up Geary Street and the battered Fillmore closed its doors for the last time.

On 22 September, EMI made amends for what now seemed like a criminally low-key *Mother's Milk* launch party by hosting another, grander affair atop the Sunset Hyatt immediately after the Red Hot Chili Peppers' Hollywood Palladium show. Then the tour swung east through Arizona (for a Multiple Sclerosis Society benefit), New Mexico, Texas and on into the industrial North and Northeast.

There were some unscheduled stops, too. Mark Johnson, the Red Hot Chili Peppers' tour manager, remembered driving through the Canadian Rockies when suddenly 'the band decided to pull out the generators and amps and put on a show on the roadside. People were just pulling up and enjoying the music.'

Cruising on the adrenaline of their new-found success, the Red Hot Chili Peppers did not unleash the sock routine until the tour was almost two-thirds over. They scarcely needed it any longer; Flea's choice of stage garb drifted between his underpants and a disposable diaper and, if any of the band came on in a shirt, by the third or fourth number it would be flying into the audience. In Green Bay, Wisconsin, however, the crowd just deserved something special. It may or may not have been pure coincidence that *Spin* magazine's Dean Kuipers was also along for the ride.

'The crowd is fairly small, strangely restless, buzzing and hurting for relief from the sexual frustrations of a Midwestern farm town winter. Backstage, Mark Johnson produces a fresh pair of white tube socks. The Chilis rush from the cold dressing room into the friendly, swarming heat of the auditorium, wearing tennis shoes, hats and the socks stretched over their cocks. They rear back and launch into "Out in LA".'

The entire show rocketed past in a state of near-total undress. When Keith Barry's sock flew away, he didn't bother restoring it, but kept right on playing. Later, Frusciante's guitar roadie, Robbie Allen, emerged to whip around his willy like a rotary lawnmower. By the end of the evening, half the audience was almost naked as well. And, of course, there was hell to pay afterwards.

Nudity, as Kiedis has remarked on several baffled occasions, provokes a peculiar reaction from people. 'In a land where there is so much violence and corruption and racism and hatred,' he pondered, 'why should we think nudity is such a revolting thing? Nudity seems like a welcome relief from all [that] bullshit.' However, it was also an indictable offence, as the Red Hot Chili Peppers had come close to learning in the past.

In Vancouver one night, several years earlier, the band returned to their dressing room to discover the Mounties were waiting to bust them for indecent exposure. When Lindy Goetz protested that the band had not exposed anything even remotely indecent, the officers asked what would have happened if a sock had fallen away.

Gallantly lying through his teeth, Goetz launched into lengthy assurances of the true nature of the socks. 'The boys are all wearing G-strings beneath the socks and, to be extra certain, the socks themselves are held in place by wires. There is no danger whatsoever of them flying off.'

The Canadians bought the story but, in Green Bay, the venue's hired security knew the truth. Despite a tip-off from the show's overjoyed promoter, the band was not quick enough to escape the wrath of the morally shattered rent-a-cops, each one intent upon writing his name large in local lore. Not much ever happens in Green Bay in the winter and the posse didn't want this filthy pop group to change that. Kiedis was still denying he was even a member of the Red Hot Chili Peppers when he was thrown to the ground and busted for indecent exposure.

It took the good-humoured arrival of the real police to sort everything out. They might not have been too keen on nudity themselves, but the kids had fun and no one got hurt. Plus, reported Dean Kuipers, they recognised the band from MTV. Kiedis was released with no further ado.

The tour was into the home stretch. In Cleveland, two nights after the sock show, a mobile studio was set up to record the gig and provide some fresh meat for the B-side of the forthcoming 'Taste the Pain' single: Hendrix's 'Castles Made of Sand', 'Party on Your Pussy' and an uproarious adaptation of Thelonious Monk's 'Bemsha Swing', retitled 'FU'. In Atlanta, an up-and-coming new band called the Black Crowes was added to the bill. And, in San Diego on New Year's Eve, the Red Hot Chili Peppers found themselves in a similar position when they were invited along to open the recently revitalised B-52s' show at the Sports Arena.

The tour really climaxed, however, the night before, when the Red Hot Chili Peppers stepped out into the seething cauldron of the six-thousand capacity Long Beach Arena. More than three years had passed since the venue was the scene of rock'n'roll's worst-ever riot, when Raising Hell hit town, years during which both the police and the auditorium's own security had finally learned the lessons of the past. As showtime approached, the only fears concerned Kiedis.

Three nights earlier in San Francisco, the singer attempted a dramatic onstage pole vault with his microphone stand. He landed badly, tearing ligaments in his right ankle and, though this was not his first onstage injury (earlier in the tour he tore a rib muscle directly below his heart; in the past, ribs, knees, shoulders and ankles had all taken a beating), it was the most debilitating. As the arena show approached, there was the distinct possibility he wouldn't make the show. Even the quite unaccustomed thrill of riding a limo down Beverley Boulevard ('I normally ride my bike down here') was dulled for Flea by the spectre of Kiedis hobbling around on his cane.

The group huddled together for its pre-show ritual, slapping one another around the face and then kissing, close-mouthed, on the lips. 'If we don't do it,' Kiedis explained, 'we'll pay the consequences, like clearing out an 18,000-seat house.' Then he limped to a corner to complete his pre-show obeisance, a brief solo rendition of Paul McCartney's 'Live and Let Die': 'When you have a job to do, you gotta do it well . . .'

'The Chili Peppers hit the stage . . . and anyone who'd seen Kiedis that afternoon had to cringe every time he went high in the air, even if he did try to land on his good left ankle,' the LA Times' Richard Cromelin reported. Backstage after the show, reclining on the floor with an ice pack over his still-protesting foot, Kiedis was clearly in a lot of pain. But he had only one concern. 'Every time a visitor stopped by,' Cromelin wrote, 'Kiedis looked up and asked the ultimate Red Hot Chili Peppers' question: "did it rock?"'

In April 1988 the US trade paper *Billboard* ran a short news item describing how, after half a decade in recession, American record companies were once again beginning to pump money and muscle into their alternative promotion departments, and how they were already beginning to reap the rewards.

Nurtured by A&R staff who, it was stated, genuinely understood the college radio stations, championed by press officers who were on first-name terms with the staff of America's 'underground' press, talents as esoteric as Sinead O'Connor, Sonic Youth and Morrissey were finally beginning to emerge from brittle cult isolation. By the end of the year, Living Colour, the flagship of New York's Black Rock Coalition, had sold two million copies of their debut album, *Vivid*.

Like the Beastie Boys before them, Living Colour's greatest strength was their refusal to be bound by stereotypes. The Beasties were white, but played 'black' music, rap. The Living Colour members were black, but they played 'white' rock. Even though both groups had precedents aplenty, the very novelty of their position set them up for the future. A combination of luck, promotion and, presumably, talent did the rest.

To the Red Hot Chili Peppers, that success came as a mixed blessing. 'Living Colour to me sounds nothing like the Red Hot Chili Peppers,' Kiedis avowed. 'But on a daily basis I have to deal with "Wow, Living Colour's really biting your style. Y'ever see the guy [vocalist Corey Glover] onstage, he moves just like you."' While his own band still languished in relative obscurity, such comparisons hurt. A year later, however, that pain was forgotten. Now Kiedis welcomed Living Colour, 24-7 Spyz and all the other groups who had climbed high in the new climate.

'They kind of blew open the door we initially created ourselves. Whatever resemblance they may have to the Red Hot Chili Peppers, we take as a compliment. That we were able to influence somebody is one of the greatest compliments you can get.' Later, Axl Rose told John Frusciante that he wrote 'Rocket Queen' with the Red Hot Chili Peppers expressly in mind. Even Guns N' Roses had fallen under their spell.

But there was one comparison that really rankled. Even as the Red Hot Chili Peppers were squirting *Mother's Milk* throughout the nation, another Californian band, San Francisco's Faith No More, was reaping similar rewards with their latest release, *The Real Thing*.

In the two years since Faith No More ran a lowly second fiddle on the Red Hot Chili Peppers' autumn '87 tour, much had changed. Vocalist Chuck Mosley was gone, to be replaced by Mike Patton and, to the people to whom such things matter, if Patton was not consciously echoing Anthony's stage style, then human evolution had taken a strangely convoluted lurch in recent years – as Kiedis himself pointed out, 'I watched [their] "Epic" video, and I see him jumping up and down, rapping, and it looked like I was looking in the mirror.'

What hurt Kiedis the most, however, was the knowledge that, in many minds, it was he who was imitating Patton. 'It . . . really bothered me,' Kiedis confessed later. 'I thought, "What a drag if people get the idea that I'm actually ripping him off." ' Matters worsened when the Red Hot Chili Peppers reached Europe in August 1989. Faith No More had a considerable head start on them there and, if the Red Hot Chili Peppers' first visit was spent fielding questions about the socks, this one was taken up with defending themselves against Patton's thick-skinned supporters. Finally Kiedis snapped, accusing Patton outright of pirating his image. Patton fired back a broadside of his own and the feud, for that is how the media dubbed the dispute, went from there.

Kiedis laid out his side of the story. At a recent interview, 'the writer asked me, "Are you guys sick of people ripping you off?" I said, "Who are you referring to?" and he said, "Well, Mike Patton in Faith No More." So I told him . . . "yeah . . ." The thing is, I had no problem with him personally. I mean, I love *The Real Thing*, and I liked his vocals on that record. I mean, when I heard the record I noticed subtle similarities, but when I saw that video it was like, "Wait a second here, what the fuck?" '

Of course, the whole thing was foolish, as Kiedis eventually admitted. 'After it stewed in my stomach for a while, I just decided to accept it. He's just a kid. Besides, without his left foot he's going to have to change.' He laughingly revealed that Chad Smith was planning to grab Patton, 'shave his hair and saw off one of his feet. Just so he'll be forced to find a style of his own.'

But, though the feud was gone, it was not, it transpired, forgotten. And, a decade later, it would bubble up again in even more rancorous fashion.

The third single from *Mother's Milk*, 'Taste the Pain', hit the *Billboard* chart in February 1990 (it breached the British Top 30 in June). Over the claustrophobic pulsing of the Flea-and-Fishbone-fired rhythm section, and the jagged shards of guitar which duelled with guest cellist Dave Colman, Kiedis half-spoke, half-garbled the starkest lyric he ever wrote, an almost Doors-like farewell that slipped, on paper and in imagination, between Slovak's lonely death and, presciently, the near-simultaneous shattering of two of the band's closest relationships.

Throughout the recording of *Mother's Milk*, Flea was struggling to hold his marriage to Loesha together. Now, with him away from home for close to six long months and with no respite from this enforced separation in sight, the couple agreed to part. Baby Clara would remain living with her mother, but would visit Flea three days a week when he was at home. Although he seldom spoke of the parting, Flea was adamant that it was amicable. He and Loesha literally grew apart.

Ione Skye's departure from Kiedis's life was considerably less straightforward. The couple broke up at Christmas when Skye, whose career had grown proportionately with Kiedis's own, with roles in *Say Anything*, *Shock Wave* and River Phoenix's *A Night in the Life of Jimmy Reardon*, left him for the Beastie Boys' Adam Horowitz.

Skye had seen Kiedis through the most difficult period of his life; now that he was past it, she left and, though the rumour mill sought desperately for the little hint of scandal that would add fresh flavour to their widely publicised split, neither Kiedis nor Skye offered anything more than regret for the way things had ended. Kiedis responded simply, 'I'll probably miss her for the rest of my life.'

Still, controversy dogged the Red Hot Chili Peppers like Secret Servicemen. In London for the first night of a short British tour in February 1990, the group outraged the national music press by announcing that punk rock started in Hollywood, then launched into 'the proof' – a ghastly buzzing, *Melody Maker* insisted, 'that could have dropped out of a Yes boxed set. A high pitched jazz bore version of 'Anarchy in the UK', complete with hand-clapping singalong does little to further this theory.'

Another miniature storm erupted when the group insisted that they be allowed to perform 'Higher Ground' naked on British television's *Jonathan Ross Show*. Only when they were threatened with expulsion from the airwaves did the Red Hot Chili Peppers retract their demand, to content themselves instead with suspending Flea upside down by his feet for the entire broadcast.

Back in the States, meanwhile, an irate letter to the American skateboarding periodical *Thrasher* condemned Kiedis for a comment he made when discussing organised religion in an interview the previous November. 'My 15-year-old boy loves to skateboard,' the complainant pontificated. 'But tell me, what does [the following quote] have to do with skateboarding – "the word 'God' is kind of stupid"?'

Musician magazine followed in those identical, weary footsteps after it asked the Red Hot Chili Peppers to contribute an Agony Aunt-type column to its pages. According to Flea, the journalist requested that the band come up with the most outrageous answer they could think of, to the most innocuous questions they ever heard. But even he was probably not expecting Flea to insist that the only way to deal with a screaming baby was to 'tie up the brat and leave it in the closet'.

'I'm sorry if people took what we said the wrong way,' Flea apologised as a holocaust of readers' wrath descended upon his head. 'But I can't see how any thinking person would take it seriously.'

Being taken seriously, however, is one of the pitfalls of pop superstardom. When John Lennon opined that the Beatles were 'bigger than Jesus'; when Mick Jagger demanded that listeners 'please allow me to introduce myself' on the Rolling Stones' 'Sympathy for the Devil'; when David Bowie's publicist announced on California radio that 'everyone who works for him has slept with him as well'; these were remarks made in the heat of hype, comments that could only be taken in the context of the artist's work and career. But the Beatles saw their records burned, Jagger was pursued by Satanists and exorcists, and Bowie found anti-faggot, anti-odd-eyed-Englishmen-peddling-sicko-mindwarp-filth-in-America reactionaries picketing his shows. The Red Hot Chili Peppers were inching their own lives towards comparative respectability but, in the eyes of middle America, they were just one more perversion to add to rock's catalogue of outrage and gore. And fate was conspiring to ensure that they did not lose that reputation.

Shocked out of its middle-class rut not by the vitality of the Red Hot Chili Peppers so much as their sudden burst of success, MTV invited the band down to Daytona Beach, Florida, for the annual Spring Break television party on 16 March 1990. A beanfeast of self-indulgent pop chicanery, the Spring Break – in reality, the final recess in the college year before the examinations begin in earnest – had become a youth television institution, peopled by idiot grinning VJs and their clone-jock admirers, standing knee-deep in the surf to swill beer, crack jokes and, occasionally, tear themselves away from the camera to watch the odd band or two. The Red Hot Chili Peppers, whose frat-house popularity was now so well known that even their detractors were starting to mention it, were the ideal guests.

Even the restrictions of having to lip-synch 'Knock Me Down' were not going to cool the group's ardour. They point-blank refused to simply pretend to sing; instead, they would pretend to pretend and let everybody in on the joke. But the joke, it seems, went too far, although the incident began innocently enough. Flea was balancing precariously on Kiedis's shoulders when suddenly he toppled over. Reaching out to grab 'the first thing in front of me', Flea's momentum brought both him and his unwitting saviour, a twenty-year-old bikini-clad onlooker, crashing to the ground.

In full view of the cameras, Flea 'picked her up over my shoulder and, as far as I was concerned, she was as thrilled as hell'. What Flea didn't know was that Smith was now spanking his passenger's bottom.

Still spinning, Flea lost his balance once again. He and his load careened into Smith and crashed to the ground in an untidy heap. Then Flea, for reasons he still cannot recollect, stood over the prostrate girl's legs and suggested that they indulge in what Florida law calls 'an unnatural act' there and then.

Ignoring Flea's attempts to apologise – 'he sincerely did not realise that she was upset,' reflected one band associate – the girl tearfully made her complaints. Beach Rangers arrested Flea and Smith a couple of days later and it was with a body bag full of misdemeanour charges hanging over them that the twosome returned to LA, just as the state of Virginia handed down its opinion on Kiedis's year-old willy-waving episode. He was convicted of both indecent exposure and, somewhat surprisingly, sexual battery and was fined $1,000 on each count.

Even this was not to be the end of the affair, though. In October 1992, Kiedis was back in a Virginia courtroom, making further depositions after his alleged victim lodged a $4 million claim against the Red Hot Chili Peppers. She claimed the initial incident left her traumatised and, perhaps taking the incident somewhat more lightly than was appropriate, the industry magazine *Rock Pool* could not resist wondering 'how ugly a willy has to be before you're entitled to $4 million just for seeing it'. Fourteen months after that, in January 1994, Kiedis's part in a government-sponsored ad campaign promoting safe sex was withdrawn after the organisers learned of his convictions in Virginia.

Kiedis was reflecting upon the group's suddenly acquired Public Enemy status when he wrote, in *Details for Men*, 'Some time in the late 1980s, [we] reached a state of media popularity that caused some people to treat me with [a] type of distorted behaviour. People often thought that because they had seen me on television they knew who

I was. Journalists, fans and other miscellaneous knuckleheads have often accused me and my lyrics of being overly preoccupied with sex. But those who look and listen more closely will find that there are a multitude of topics addressed in the lyrics, music and attitude.'

But who was listening? Certainly not the authorities at the State University of New York in New Paltz. Within days of the Daytona incident, they ordered the cancellation of a planned free concert by the Red Hot Chili Peppers. And not the Daytona judicial system. On 6 August 1990, Judge Freddie Worthen sentenced Flea and Smith to each pay $1,000 in fines, plus $300 costs and to donate a further $5,000 to the Volusia County Rape Crisis Center in Daytona. They were also ordered to write letters of apology to their victim.

It has been suggested, with questionable justification, that both verdicts owed as much to the Red Hot Chili Peppers' new-found pop star status, and their prosecutors' desire to nail themselves a pop star, as to the perceived seriousness of their crimes. 'Until very recently,' exclaimed journalist Steve Dougherty as the Florida verdict was delivered, 'the group couldn't get arrested . . . and not for lack of trying.' Now, like the Rolling Stones in Britain a quarter of a century before, the Red Hot Chili Peppers were officially marked for death, a band whose very existence antagonised the system and whose sudden success rammed that antagonism down the establishment's throat.

'They totally tried to make an example of us,' Chad Smith accused after the Daytona trial. 'I'm not trying to blame anybody else, but the way it came out was that it was a real malicious thing, that we tried to beat this girl up.'

The ramifications of the Daytona Beach incident were not slow in making themselves felt, however, although readers of long-running *New York Daily News* columnist Jim Farber might have construed these Red Hot Chili Peppers to be a different kind of threat altogether.

In May 1990, EMI's video wing released the Red Hot Chili Peppers' first video collections, the *Positive Mental Octopus* compilation of past promotional films and the in-concert *Psychedelic Sex Funk Live from Heaven*, uncompromising souvenirs first of the stream of unsuccessful singles the band released in the years before 'Knock Me Down' raised them up, then of their riotous show at Long Beach the previous December.

Pricing both at a then-reasonable $15, the Red Hot Chili Peppers regarded the videos as a gesture of thanks to their fans, and were instantly rewarded when they were invited onto the first-ever edition of *Playboy's Hot Rocks*, a half-hour rock show introduced by the

pay-per-view television network *Playboy at Night*. Dedicated to bands
who had run into censorship difficulties with sexually oriented videos,
the Red Hot Chili Peppers aired the never-previously-broadcast
'Catholic School Girls Rule' video.

Jim Farber, however, was not so indulgent. 'Appearing shirtless
(and sometimes pantless) in all the clips, the Chili Peppers take more
lusty pleasure in their bodies than any group I have ever seen,' Farber
reported. '[They] frequently paw their bandmates, or at least pretend
to', pinpointing what could be construed as simulated masturbation in
the *Sex Funk* tapes and mock-kissing in 'True Men Don't Kill Coyotes'
and the live 'Sexy American Maid' as further fuel for his fury. 'With
good cause, this stuff p.o.'s my more politically correct friends no end.'
In their eyes, he concluded, such actions smacked of nothing less than
gay-baiting.

It was a peculiar interpretation of the Red Hot Chili Peppers,
suggesting emotions that the group members have never publicly (nor,
according to their friends, privately) subscribed to. Only Flea, discussing
a teenage bust for stealing wanton wrappers, had even suggested an
aversion to the company of homosexuals – thrown into a cell, he claimed
to have been 'hassled by gays'. But the lesson with which he returned to
freedom was not homophobic. It was a vow 'never to steal again'.

Farber's emphasis on the group's sexual attitudes (if not appetites)
was timely nevertheless, exquisitely timed to coincide with another, far
wider controversy, as the ongoing debate surrounding rap's overall
attitude towards sexuality exploded into nationwide prominence, not
through the auspices of the PMRC or some similar would-be regulator,
but from within its own community. Sexism was to be among the
topics under discussion at that year's New Music seminar and,
regardless of how people construed their stance, the Red Hot Chili
Peppers had no choice but to defend themselves.

Sensibly, they launched onto the offensive. 'There's such a wave of
redneck right-wing morality sweeping the country,' Flea complained.
'People have said we were sexist for singing "Party on Your Pussy", or
for Anthony making blatant sexual gestures. But, if sex is important to
someone, they should sing about it. I see nothing wrong with idolising
female genitalia, but just because we like it, it doesn't mean we're
homophobic. The relationship between music and sex is there to begin
with. And the relationship between sex and funk music is even more
[pronounced]. To deny that correlation is preposterous. We're young
men and sex is a very important part of our lives. It only makes sense
that we would express that in our music.'

Left: *Anthony Kiedis and John Frusciante*
(Matt Anker/Retna Ltd.)

Below: *The Evolution of Man*
(Robert Matheu/Retna Ltd.)

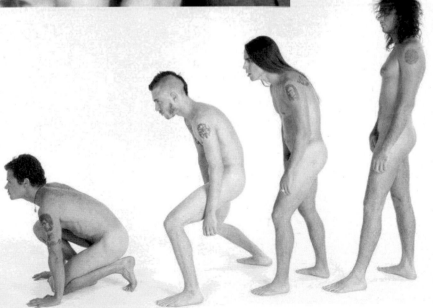

Right: *Anthony and Flea collect MTV's award for Best Breakthrough Video, September 1992 (Redferns)*

Left and below: *Anthony struts his stuff at the Brixton Academy in London in June 1990 (Sue Moore/Redferns)*

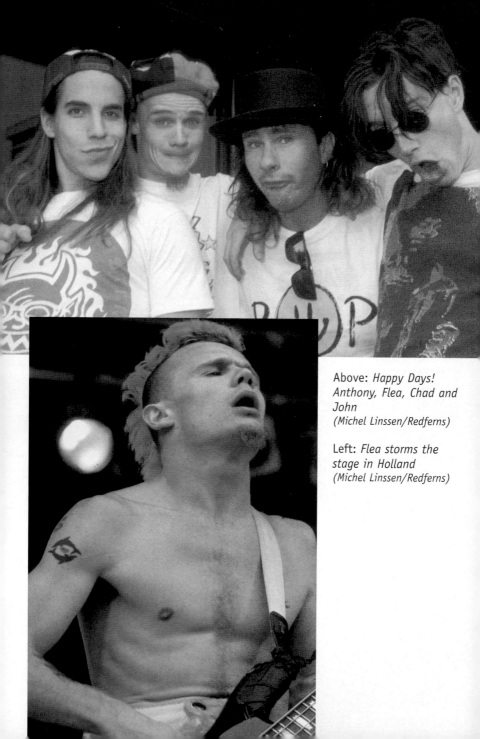

Above: *Happy Days!*
Anthony, Flea, Chad and
John
(Michel Linssen/Redferns)

Left: *Flea storms the*
stage in Holland
(Michel Linssen/Redferns)

Left: *Pearl Jam: Jack Irons introduced his basketball buddy Eddie Vedder to the band* (Michel Linssen/Redferns)

Left: *Joe Strummer: 'I'll never forget what Joe did for me' – Jack Irons* (Michel Linssen/Redferns)

Below: *L7: 'They're girls and they rock'* (Mick Hutson/Redferns)

Above: *The Peppers in 1993, with Arik Marshall, far left*
(Jay Blakesberg/Retna Ltd.)

Left: *'American Gothic' – Pepper style*
(Karen Miller/Retna Ltd.)

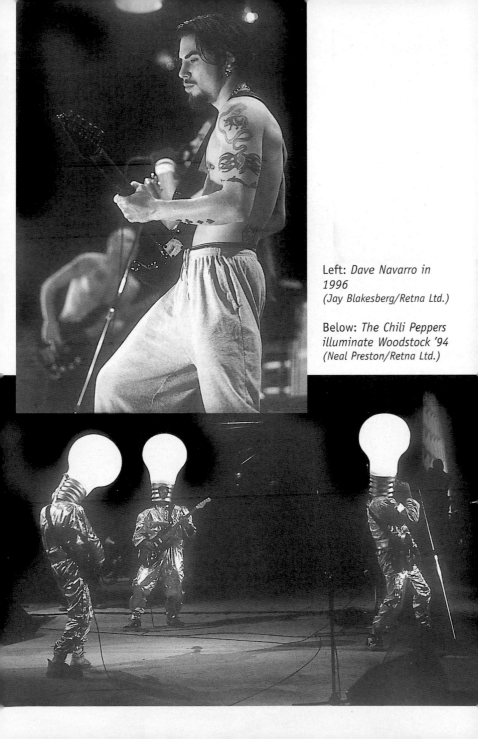

Left: *Dave Navarro in 1996*
(Jay Blakesberg/Retna Ltd.)

Below: *The Chili Peppers illuminate Woodstock '94*
(Neal Preston/Retna Ltd.)

Left: *Anthony on stage at V2001*
(Tim Auger/Retna Ltd.)

Below: *And the award for Best Status Quo impersonation goes to . . .*
(Elgin Edmonds/Retna Ltd.)

Plus, he claimed, 'We delve into spiritual love for the female gender as well as lustful sexual love.'

Neither could the Red Hot Chili Peppers rely upon the regular music press to clear their name. In a lengthy interview with the *Phoenix Gazette* in May 1990, Kiedis rebuked the journalists who trailed the group around the world, discussed 'every issue from ecology to . . . music to the culture of Native Americans', then turned in stories that revelled in sordid detail. *Spin* magazine's Dean Kuipers, for instance, 'spent six hours' talking with Kiedis, 'and within that article [published in *Spin*'s February 1990 edition], I open my mouth six times. There are six quotes from me, each of which is only about drugs. He makes me look like a very one-dimensional character.'

Rolling Stone sinned even more grievously. Jeffrey Resner accompanied the Red Hot Chili Peppers to Amsterdam, during the Dutch leg of the 1990 European tour and, according to Kiedis, 'the way he set up his article, he said Amsterdam is a town full of prostitution and there are drugs on every corner and people are smoking hash here and hash there, and it's Anthony's favourite town. He has to put those two things in the same paragraph, which is not fair.'

The Red Hot Chili Peppers hit Amsterdam with all the force of a tsunami. European MTV, taking a leaf out of its parent company's playlist, was airing 'Higher Ground' almost constantly; every radio was bleeding *Mother's Milk*. As the band warmed up for the long-since sold-out performance at the Paradiso, a converted church in the heart of the city, one travelling English fan's most fervent hope was that their set would comprise completely new songs. 'I don't think I could stand hearing 'Higher Ground' again tonight.' As if to test his bitter resolve, the radio blaring from a nearby shop kicked the song out one more time.

Henky Penky's Tattoo Museum was again commandeered as the group's unofficial base. It was their first visit since Slovak's death and neither Flea nor Kiedis was prepared for the sheer weight of memories that would assail them as they stepped into the well-lit parlour. Kiedis would also have plenty of time in which to contemplate his loss: Schiffmacher would be spending most of the afternoon drilling the singer's back full of ink as he continued working on the eighteen-month-old totem. While they waited, Flea, Smith and Frusciante passed the time with lesser tortures.

'The prostitute staring out of the basement window is giving the four wild boys a come-hither look that two of them can't resist,' *Rolling Stone* journalist Resner reported. 'One darts into her lair while his buddy waits patiently outside. About twenty minutes later, they trade places.' A part of Kiedis's anger at the story was due to *Rolling Stone* not spelling out which two members dipped into the city's pleasure pit and which two remained outside.

'I did some despicable acts,' Smith grinned later – so despicable, it transpired, that by the time the tour reached Hamburg, even he felt 'that I needed some disciplining'. While the rest of the Red Hot Chili Peppers amused themselves elsewhere, Smith headed down to the Reeperbahn, perhaps the most notorious mile of willing flesh in the world, and submitted himself 'to a bit of a spanking. I think my mother would be proud that I spent my money in such a good way.'

'Chad definitely has his bizarre behaviour patterns,' Kiedis joked. 'You might come home to a hotel in Baltimore to find him with two naked girls on a couch and a spatula in his hand. And that's just an inkling of it!'

The Red Hot Chili Peppers returned to the American stage at the end of April 1990, just as their contribution to the million-selling *Pretty Woman* soundtrack, 'Show Me Your Soul', was released as a single. Headlining the New York Ritz's Punky Funky Lovefest with a riotous performance that left band and audience alike wholly drained, the group eschewed their normal set and touched base instead with their greatest influences. To their traditional battery of covers they added songs by Parliament and NWA, Funkadelic's 'Cosmic Slop' and Sly Stone's 'Don't Call Me Nigger, Whitey'. *Mother's Milk* had just been certified gold (500,000 copies sold) and, as the band celebrated on the Ritz's hallowed boards, with EMI President Sal Licata the grinning guest of honour, the *New York Times* conveyed one more piece of respectability upon them. Their show, journalist Peter Watrous declared, was 'an invitation to partake in a new version of an old myth. Like the Beach Boys before them – and the Red Hot Chili Peppers are a 1980s version, in several ways, of the Beach Boys – they create an image of Southern California.

'But it is modern California, where everybody walks around in shorts, doesn't wear a shirt and has big tattoos and a great physique. And their music, hyperactive, reverential and loud, is meant for a party.'

It was the ultimate compliment, crowning the ultimate fairy tale. Suddenly, everything seemed worthwhile: the physical busts and the emotional bruises; the tears that sprang to Kiedis's and Flea's eyes whenever another journalist quizzed them about Slovak, the accusations that, in making a record that carried few blatant swear words, and fewer still promises, the band had sold out. The Red Hot Chili Peppers had made their pact with the Great Satan and they'd held on to their souls in the bargain.

'I think selling music is beautiful,' said Flea. 'Sure, art is a totally spiritual thing that you regurgitate just from living, thinking and breathing. But this is a business world. We make records and videos to promote our products, so we can drive around on tour buses, make money and then come home and swim in our pools.' He noted that 'the Red Hot Chili Peppers are so popular with kids. They buy our T-shirts, buttons, posters and hats', and prophesied that 'if we sold fuckin' little doodads to hang on their underwear, they'd buy them, too.' Two years later, the group's British fans proved him correct. Despite it retailing at around $100, they swiftly snapped up the limited edition *Chili Can*, a Christmas 1992 Red Hot Chili Peppers package that included a compact disc, a T-shirt, a pair of underpants and a long sock.

Only when it came to other people's work was Flea less than the model capitalist. Suddenly the Red Hot Chili Peppers found themselves the target of any number of earnest business moguls, anxious to have the group endorse some new piece of product. Despite the often lucrative deals they were offered, the band members refused. 'Maybe we should get the money while the going's good,' Flea mused. 'But, if you attach yourself to some big commercial product, how can anyone take anything else you're saying seriously?' The Red Hot Chili Peppers' music was sincere, he explained. But, 'if you say something from your heart and soul and the next thing you're saying is "I drink this drink", your soulful thoughts become as believable to the outside world as your drink comment.'

Around such deliberations, the Red Hot Chili Peppers maintained themselves in the only way they knew how. After seven years of constant touring, life on the road was a difficult habit to get out of and it was a sure sign of their new-found status that they made headlines wherever they touched down.

Their show in Baltimore was followed by a party at director John Waters' house and, within a week, the tabloid press was reporting a possible celluloid reunion. Waters remained tight-lipped. 'I look at my scripts as a disease. If I announce them too early, someone will invent the vaccine.' As far as the Red Hot Chili Peppers were concerned, Waters conceded only that he and they shared certain sensibilities. 'They're hip, young, rich and nude.'

The venues the Red Hot Chili Peppers were now comfortably filling were a far cry even from the oversized theatres they touched upon earlier in the year: Denver's spectacular Red Rocks, made so famous by the cavorting Bono and U2's *Under a Blood Red Sky* concert video, Salt Lake City's ParkWest and the Texan Riverfest festival. Appearing before audiences ten times the size of those that they once took for granted, for perhaps the first time the unassailable logic behind superstar stadium tours became apparent to the group. Once, the Red Hot Chili Peppers travelled to meet their fans. Now their fans travelled to see them.

12. A NERVY SLICE OF MELODRAMA

Everywhere they turned, the Red Hot Chili Peppers were in demand. Thelonious Monster split in 1989, victims of the drug-related disarray that would culminate a year later in the tragic death of guitarist Rob Graves. Bob Forrest promptly landed a solo deal with RCA and, as he began work on his own debut solo album, the Red Hot Chili Peppers were inevitable guests at the sessions. Unfortunately, even they could not salvage an album that Forrest later admitted 'came out sounding like a horrible piece of shit', and the tapes were all but abandoned, as Forrest instead set to work reforming Thelonious Monster around himself and a young Dutch bassist whom Flea had befriended, Martyn LeNoble. (One cut from the abortive album, a brief untitled instrumental, finally appeared on the Monster's *Beautiful Mess* album.)

Flea alone took time out to appear as guest bassist on rapper Young MC's *Busta Move*, while Kiedis reintroduced himself to Hollywood with a role as a howling Nazi surf punk in Patrick Swayze's crime thriller *Point Break*. And, in July, the group recorded three different versions of Bachman Turner Overdrive's mid-70s chest-beater 'Takin' Care of Business' for the soundtrack of the Jim Belushi/Charles Grodin movie of the same name, and made a dream come true for Lindy Goetz. Years before, he suggested that the band write a song that everybody could relate to, 'like "Taking Care of Business"'. The band complied. 'We came up with "I'm Going to Take a Shit",' Flea said with a laugh. 'It's something everyone does every day.'

Three months later, in October 1990, the Red Hot Chili Peppers were included among some 26 performers, ranging from Little Richard to MC Hammer, who would be guesting on *Raise the World*, a benefit album for the LIFE (Love Is Feeding Everyone) charity. The band remained tight-lipped about this ironical change of heart – 'Millionaires Against Hunger', the five-year-old *Freaky Styley* outtake that taunted the Band Aid generation, had just made its public debut on the B-side of the recent 'Taste the Pain' single. But the fact that LIFE operated among the homeless in the band's own home city certainly influenced their decision to participate.

If anything occupied the group's time during those months of unaccustomed ease, however, it was golf, as the *LA Times*' Maureen Sajbel discovered when she accompanied them to the Griffith Park course in Hollywood. 'Golf is an extremely suave sport,' Kiedis told her. 'When we're not playing music, we like to get suave on the course.' His tongue, despite the group's chosen attire of kilts and T-shirts, was not entirely in his cheek at the time and Sajbel gleefully agreed. 'Rock'n'roll and golf are not that unusual': Huey Lewis and the Doobie Brothers also played.

There were few such luxuries for Lindy Goetz. His own empire was expanding – when Thelonious Monster re-formed, Goetz's LGM Company assumed their management requirements. while he was also being linked with former Monkee Davy Jones, a long-time admirer of Goetz's technique. But it was the Red Hot Chili Peppers who continued to dominate his schedule, as the hunt for a new record deal got under way.

Little more than a year before, the Red Hot Chili Peppers were unknown, just another loser band eking out an existence in the underbelly of America's rock'n'roll underground, scratching its way through a long-term record contract that almost certainly would not be renewed when it expired in three albums' time. Now it was the Red Hot Chili Peppers who held the option of renewal, who were debating whether or not they even wanted to see their contract through to the end. No longer underground, scarcely even an alternative band, the Red Hot Chili Peppers had touched the pulse of the pop mainstream and, if they liked what they felt, the mainstream enjoyed their caress just as much. As 1990 passed by, Goetz was himself passing time searching for a new home for the band.

The Red Hot Chili Peppers' reasons for wanting to quit EMI were not difficult to deduce. Although the company remained faithful to them throughout their years in the commercial wilderness and never, as Kiedis remarked, 'made us do anything we didn't want to', there was also a sense that those years may have been fewer had the company only put some weight behind the band's releases.

EMI's refusal to release 'Behind the Sun' as a single in 1988 was one case in point, but there were plenty of others. Even the label's handling of Mother's Milk came in for criticism. It sold plenty, the band acknowledged, but if EMI had been more aggressive, it would have sold plenty more. They did not want to risk the same thing occurring again.

'Mother's Milk could have done more,' confirmed the watching Jack Irons. 'EMI just didn't have the vision to make it go further than it did.' Kiedis continued, 'We knew the record we were about to make was going to be the greatest piece of music we had ever compiled and EMI simply wasn't deserving of us. They had always sucked in the past, they were always dropping the ball, coming up short on a regular basis. There was no way we wanted to pour our lives into a record and give it to this inept company, so we decided to look for a company that was more competent, more musically connected.'

With only one gold album behind them (sales of *Mother's Milk* now exceeded 650,000), the Red Hot Chili Peppers' decision to quit EMI was nevertheless fraught with danger. The paths of rock'n'roll history are littered with the corpses of bands who got too big too soon, then crashed to ground the moment they were called upon to deliver something to top their last performance. But the Red Hot Chili Peppers were unshakeable in their belief in themselves, particularly after Goetz began quoting back the telephone-number-sized sums that they were suddenly being offered.

Mother's Milk was the fourth of seven albums the Red Hot Chili Peppers were scheduled to deliver to EMI. Extracting the band from that contract was a task that involved Eric Greenspan, the band's lawyer throughout their entire career-to-date, in some of the most satisfying legal work of his career-so-far. As the offers for the Red Hot Chili Peppers' signatures mounted up, he negotiated for the group to buy out the remainder of their EMI contract, but sweetened the pill by giving EMI the option to lift any single track of their choice from the band's own next album, for inclusion on some future Red Hot Chili Peppers compilation.

Then, with the past sorted out, it was time to take care of the future. Several labels bid seriously for the group, among them Virgin, MCA, Geffen and, perhaps surprisingly, Rick Rubin's Def American.

Much had changed since Rubin turned down the opportunity to produce the Red Hot Chili Peppers' third album, both for the group and for Rubin. By 1991, Def American was among the premier independent labels in the country, boasting a roster of artists that ranged from Scotland's Jesus and Mary Chain to Flipper and the Red Devils, all bound together by a successful distribution deal with the giant Time Warner empire. The label's autonomy, greater than that enjoyed by many other so-called alternative companies, appealed to the Red Hot Chili Peppers even as it turned them off. Def American would certainly be able to offer the personal touch that was distinctly missing from the band's relationship with EMI. But it was not a wealthy company, at least by comparison with the major-league players who were coming in to bat behind them. Regretfully, the band turned down Rubin's offer, much as the heavily bearded New Yorker expected them to. Instead, Rubin was handed the runner-up prize: a second chance to produce an album with the group. And, this time, he accepted.

In Kiedis's words, 'we schmoozed and we went to every label there is'. Most showed an interest, most made extravagant promises that might easily have turned more impressionable heads. But the Red Hot Chili Peppers had heard enough promises over the years. What they wanted was hard cash and, when Epic Records, a subsidiary of the multinational Sony Music, offered an estimated $5.7 million for three albums – 'more money,' an astonished Kiedis said, 'than we thought humanly possible' – the auction closed. While the lawyers gave the proposed contracts one final going-over, the band had their photographs taken with Tommy Motola, Sony Music's president.

That evening, Chad Smith was relaxing at home when the telephone rang.

'Hello, Chad? This is Mo Ostin, over at Warner Brothers' – Warners was one of the Red Hot Chili Peppers' many disappointed suitors and Ostin was its president. Smith returned the greeting, hoping his voice wouldn't give away how puzzled he felt and hoping, too, that this wasn't a last-minute bid to try to change the band's mind. As a matter of fact it was, but as Ostin talked, it really didn't come over like that at all. 'Hey, you didn't go with us, but good luck anyway.' When Ostin hung up, Smith was still staring at the receiver in amazement. 'The president, the fucking chairman of the board of Warner Brothers! To call a lowly fucking band guy and wish us good luck! A real class act.'

Meanwhile, Flea, Frusciante and Kiedis were receiving similar phone calls from Ostin and reacting in the same shocked way. Suddenly the Epic deal didn't appear quite so important after all. 'I was so touched by his humanness,' Kiedis explained. 'It really made me feel that maybe Warner Brothers was the place we would feel more at home. At the last minute, we had a pow-wow and decided to go with Warner Brothers.' While a stunned Epic howled at the altar, the Red Hot Chili Peppers eloped with Warner. The final cost of their signatures has been estimated at up to $10 million for three albums, plus options.

Had the Red Hot Chili Peppers but known Mo Ostin, they would have realised that his behaviour that evening was not at all out of character – even among his rivals, Ostin was regarded among the last true gentlemen left in the cut-throat world of record company hierarchies. An accountant by profession, Ostin was employed as one of Frank Sinatra's personal bodyguards when the singer decided to form his own record company, Reprise, in 1961. Staffing it with the men who had already served him well, Sinatra appointed Ostin to the position of president, a post he retained even after the label was sold to Warner in 1967.

Reprise was not a winner. Not Sinatra, nor Dean Martin, nor the Kinks, the label's biggest names, were selling many records anymore and, had Ostin not decided to follow his own nose rather than that which dictated the label's traditional middle-of-the-road direction, there was a very real danger that Reprise would simply disappear within the belly of its leviathan parent. Then, in May 1967, Ostin laid out $120,000 for an unknown black guitarist whose work, legend insisted, Ostin had neither seen nor heard. He signed him on reputation alone.

A month later, Ostin and his family stopped by the Monterey Fairgrounds to watch his investment's American debut. Afterwards he could barely speak for embarrassment. What Reprise had signed was a musician whom the British press was proclaiming a genius. What it got was a raunchy, thrusting demon who wore a pink feather boa and set fire to his instrument.

Jimi Hendrix was not Ostin's first rock signing, but he was certainly his first truly inspired one. Others quickly followed. Some, like Neil Young and Emmylou Harris, repaid his faith many times over; others, like Marc Bolan's T-Rex, arrived in America as ready-made superstars, only to discover that this time the United States wasn't so willing to let Britain dictate its tastes. Through thick and thin, Ostin remained the eternal gentleman.

Almost a quarter of a century had passed since then, years during which Ostin had risen to the top of arguably the most important major record company in America. Few people were surprised when they learned of his latest dramatic coup, snatching the Red Hot Chili Peppers away from a rival company at the eleventh hour. Ostin was a man who always knew what he wanted and he generally got it as well. And what he'd got this time was the hottest band in the land.

In 1991, Madonna invited the world to play Truth or Dare. Since their inception in 1983, the Red Hot Chili Peppers had insisted on living it. A blistering riot of mindfuck rhythm and tortured voice, the Peppers represented all that is unholy about rock'n'roll. They resisted the creeping Bono-isation of the MTV generation, they refused to don the post-Reagan, post-AIDS, post-Yuppie responsibilities that success in the early 1990s automatically conferred.

Satanic exorcists nailing chickens to the church, they became the archetype of rock rebellion: Elvis in '56, swinging those hips and curling his lips; the Stones in '63, long-haired loudmouths pissing up the wall; Alice in '72, dismembering dolls and school's out forever; Perry Farrell in '88, insisting nothing was shocking when everything was. If they hadn't existed, you'd have to invent them, but if you did that, no one would believe you. Every decade, it seems, rock'n'roll contracts near-terminal lethargy. As the new decade got into its stride, it was the Red Hot Chili Peppers who were supplying the cure.

For a long time, Kiedis doubted whether Rick Rubin really was the right person to handle the cauldron of frenzy that these Peppers unleashed. Unbidden, his mind kept sliding back over the producer's own track record: for every Beastie Boys he worked with, there was a thrash-happy Danzig; for every Public Enemy, there was a Slayer. As Rubin's name crept higher up the lexicon of great producers, so his powers of discrimination, it appeared, had declined.

Kiedis was still deliberating when Rubin paid a visit to the Hollywood house Kiedis had just moved into, paid for from the Warner Brothers' advance. Manoeuvring his way through the chaotic treasury of carefully mounted paintings and casual stacks of books, Rubin was on a fact-finding mission. If the normal process of preparing an album is called pre-production, this meeting was part of the *pre*-pre-production process, a chance for artist and producer to discuss their personal visions of the record and to see just how closely their ideas matched. It was never too late to back down.

Despite his initial reservations, Kiedis quickly warmed towards his visitor. Uncompromising both in appearance and in attitude, Rubin approached rock'n'roll as though it were Lady Chatterley and he the gamekeeper, coarsely suggestive, violently seductive. He did not merely want to possess it, he wanted to conquer it. His was a spirit Kiedis had been aching forever to meet.

'You get to know the guy and you see how cool he really is,' Kiedis marvelled afterwards. 'Rick has this real sense of identification with all of the red-necked white trash of America and he wants to be totally tapped into giving those kids something to work out their ya-yas with.' The Red Hot Chili Peppers, in Rubin's eyes, were the ultimate workout those ya-yas could receive.

The pair were running through some of the lyrics Kiedis had already completed when Rubin suddenly came across one song he had not been shown. It was called 'Under the Bridge'. Kiedis baulked. That was something he hadn't intended Rubin to see, 'this really sad thing, sort of sensitive'. It recalled the hours he had spent downtown with the gangs, looking to buy the drugs that would help him erase another day from his diary – and which did, in fact, start life as a diary. 'It was kind of an a cappella poem I would sing out of my notebook,' he recalled. 'It's about some hardcore self-destructive memories. But it's also about shedding the burden of those demons and knowing that there is always the possibility of emerging from that fucked-up space.' Bearing in mind Rubin's bullish reputation, in person and on record, Kiedis was convinced the New Yorker would hate it.

Rubin, however, was adamant that he should hear everything Kiedis had to offer. 'Sing it for me.'

Kiedis shook his head. 'I haven't even shown it to the band yet.'

'That's all right. Sing it for me and I'll tell you whether or not you should.'

Kiedis complied and Rubin was 'knocked out'. Later, when Kiedis took the song into rehearsal, the band, too, was 'floored by it. As a result, it ended up on the record.' And Rubin, having unwittingly passed a test which Kiedis himself was unaware had been set, ended up as producer.

Before even Kiedis acquainted himself with the concept, Rubin realised that the Red Hot Chili Peppers need not be bound by either reputation or tradition. The moment he heard the gentle, almost folky 'Under the Bridge', he knew that the album he intended recording with them would soar high above all such concerns.

'I think for a long time the Red Hot Chili Peppers felt neglected, or weren't taken as seriously as they should have been,' Rubin explained later. Recording the album 'was a really magical time for them; all at once it took them to the point where [they knew], "This is our big opportunity to make our favourite record and really have people listen to it seriously." I think they've really lived up to that.'

Rubin played down his own contribution to what became *Blood Sugar Sex Magik*, to the point of describing his own duties not as production but as structural, 'Having to do with turnarounds, getting in and out of choruses, putting in space – whatever it takes to make a song sound like it's not just parts strung together.' Pressed for further detail, he also admitted that it was his idea for the band to leave the entire world behind them and record the album in total isolation.

Driving through Laurel Canyon one day, Rubin chanced upon a decaying but still striking hacienda with a TO LET sign outside. It was perfect. For the same amount of money as it would cost to book a conventional studio, he told the band, 'we could rent this place for a few months, move in our own gear and record the album there. What do you say?' (Rubin would eventually wind up buying the place.)

The hacienda had no working telephone and Rubin insisted its address remain a closely guarded secret. Even after they agreed to the madness, therefore, the band members knew they were facing a gruelling sabbatical. The idea was that everybody – band, engineers, family and essential hangers-on alike – would live together for as long as it took. They would hire a cook and quickly procured the services of a former *Playboy* model who spent every day listening to a radical left-wing radio station.

They would employ a security service and found a guard who was not only prepared to move in with them, he even brought his own Nintendo system. Eventually the group would reluctantly be forced to fire him; he spent so much time saving Mario's butt that he would never have had the energy to save his employers. But the sense of togetherness was reinforced by the arrival of Flea's brother-in-law, Gavin Bowden, and his omnipresent video camera. Armed with a $60,000 budget and an endless supply of black and white film, he would be shooting the entire recording process for a full-length promotional 'video press kit'.

Jokes flew about the old seventies bands who disappeared into the country 'to get their heads together', or U2 camping out in an Irish castle to work with Brian Eno. Kiedis and Flea reminisced about George Clinton's isolated farmhouse studio, where they rehearsed the *Freaky Styley* material. In the end, only Smith refused to go along with the idea. He preferred the comforts of home. But he was drawn in, regardless.

'The best thing I did to prepare for this record,' Flea said after it was over, 'was to lose my phone book and break my foot, both of which happened right when we moved into the house. That helped me concentrate. I had no contact with anyone for a couple of months.'

Of everybody, John Frusciante appeared best prepared for the long haul. He regarded it not only as a chance to make a record, but also as an opportunity to sever the infinite tangle of umbilical cords that bound him to the outside world. 'There are missiles flying through the city every day,' he warned the handful of journalists who were invited to the hacienda as the recordings came to an end. 'And they're aimed at everybody creative, not just the Peppers. They could be coming out of clocks, or the television, or a garbage can and you've got to be aware of them all the time.'

Behind the walls of the hacienda, he felt secure. The missiles could not get through, the phones did not ring, the postman never knocked. He didn't have to shake hands he didn't feel like shaking.

Listening in, Flea tried to put a lighter face on Frusciante's bizarre reasoning. 'You can go into some bitchin' recording studio and, for all you know, Poison or some stupid shit was on the tape player before you were. Can you imagine going on a machine that had the vibe of Poison on it and trying to do something cool? That's sick, man.'

The hacienda was huge, so huge that it took the best part of a day simply to hook up the stereo system, its speaker wires trailing crazily into every room in the house. If someone wanted to tour the building and find the CD player, all they needed do was grab hold of one wire and follow it. Unless, of course, they followed a microphone cable instead, strung up and down stairs and snaking into the bedrooms where individual band members would record their personal show-cases.

The walls were left bare except for the graffiti that two-and-a-half-year-old Clara Balzary scrawled during the three days a week she spent with her father. The hardwood floors remained unpolished and were obscured only by a few throw rugs. Downstairs, the foyer was littered with trash cans and hubcaps, an industrial percussionist's dream come true. An enormous parlour was dominated by an aging piano that rumour and countless offended eardrums averred had not been tuned in close to fifty years. Another room was turned over to a ping-pong table.

Upstairs, the band members' bedrooms were even more Spartan: bare mattresses, heaps of dirty laundry and the odd guitar or two. A few of John Frusciante's paintings were propped up around his bed. To the unprepared visitor, drawn to peer through the windows by the sticker-bedecked black Mercedes that Flea parked outside, the once proud hacienda resembled a bizarre, high-tech flophouse.

Only the basement, packed with guitar and bass amplifiers, and the library told tales on the house's new tenants. There, Rubin installed his old Neve and Soundcraft consoles, creating his own personal vision of a 'real' 24-track recording studio in a booming cavern within which the last thing he found room for was the technical gimmickry so beloved by other producers. Too many modern records, Rubin growled, were ruined by their creators thinking that, just because they had the equipment around, they had no choice but to use it.

'If it's not here,' he announced as he led the band around his den, 'then you can't have it, because you don't need it. And don't be thinking that, if you make any mistakes, you can just go back and erase them later. We're recording the basic tracks live and we're not going to stop the tapes for anything.'

Afterwards, he would let individual members overdub any special frills he deemed essential, but Frusciante, at least, didn't even require that minor indulgence. Not only were most of his guitar solos first takes, several of them were cut along with the basic track. In a more expansive mood, talking with *Guitar Player*'s Joe Gore, Rubin explained, 'I like the organic sound of everyone playing in the same room together, facing each other. If you don't worry about the perfection of individual parts or perfection of sound, you get the best performance.'

But the shroud of secrecy that cloaked the sessions was not impenetrable; the Peppers did not have the hacienda all to themselves. Was it the truth, or merely the workings of the ever-alert publicity machine, that insisted to visiting journalists that, since it was built in 1917, the house had been home to Rudolph Valentino; that Prohibition-era tunnels connected it to a neighbouring property, once inhabited by the escapologist Harry Houdini; that, when Kiedis was fourteen, he had dated a girl who lived there; that the Beatles dropped acid there during one of their visits to Los Angeles; that even Jimi Hendrix had lived there? And that some people were living there still, unseen but not unheard as they went about their nightly business through the deserted, blacked-out hallways?

At first the sudden chills that cut through the warm California night air were put down to freak air pockets, the midnight cries to cats or kids. Only when those explanations started to pale, and people began becoming aware of the uninvited presence that shared the old house with them, did the band call in the ghostbusters.

'There are definitely ghosts in this house.' John Frusciante was adamant. 'But they are very friendly. We have nothing but warm vibes and happiness everywhere we go in this house. Flea's daughter Clara loves it and she knows better than anyone else.'

The two psychics who were called in didn't agree. Neither did the medium whom they insisted accompanied them on their mission. As though she were a Hollywood actress sliding effortlessly into a part for which she had rehearsed forever, the medium allowed one of the 'spirits' in the hacienda to enter her body. For a few moments, all was still. Like onlookers encircling a car crash, Rubin, Goetz and the Red Hot Chili Peppers drew closer.

They were curious, but restless; the performance was a complete non-starter. Then the girl screamed and they all jumped back a foot or more. The presence in the house was evil! It sought out creativity and stifled it, sacrificed it to its own innate loathing. The girl had done her homework; no one who lived in that house and practised art had emerged from its embrace unscathed. Hendrix was dead, John Lennon was dead, the 1920s gangsters who fought bloody gunfights on the stairs were dead, and all before their time. The Red Hot Chili Peppers were in mortal danger. The only way to ward off evil was to exorcise the house. And that, the psychics explained once the girl emerged from her chilling trance, was very expensive.

'We didn't know whether to believe it at first,' Frusciante cursed afterwards. 'But basically, they tried to scare us. These guys do their first couple of visits for free, acting like they're just nice people who are interested in this kind of thing. Then they scare everyone and charge money. If I see them again,' he ruminated, 'I think I will just hit them in the face.'

The psychics got just one thing right. One of the rooms, an alcove off the second floor, they proclaimed, had a very spiritually sexual vibe. As every eye turned to stare at Frusciante, the guitarist admitted, 'I hadn't masturbated the whole time that we'd been there, because I was so concentrated on my music. But then I slept in that room and I couldn't resist the temptation to masturbate.' As he did so, 'I actually heard a woman being fucked in there.'

The sessions were drawing to a close. Twenty-four songs were recorded in eight weeks, more than enough for three full albums. But Rick Rubin wanted to try one more thing. The group had expressed an interest in covering Robert Johnson's 'They're Red Hot', but the house, Rubin decided, wasn't the right place to do it. They should go outside, to the hill that rolled from the back of the house and set up their equipment there.

To the roaring accompaniment of the passing 2 a.m. traffic, the Red Hot Chili Peppers recorded the song that, even more than 'Out in LA', summed up what the group was all about: pure driven mania, a high-speed freeway collision between the ghosts of rock'n'roll past and the spirits of that still to come. Then, with the mixing process completed, all that remained was to figure out which songs could be fit onto the album.

The compact disc revolution that, even before the Red Hot Chili Peppers took their first dynamic steps into the marketplace, was already sweeping vinyl into oblivion, changed more than the way people listened to music. It also altered the way it was presented to them. Perhaps the greatest limitation of vinyl was the amount of music that could be realistically crammed into its grooves. For an artist at his creative peak, 45 minutes was little more than a glimpse inside his soul. Exceed that limit, however, and suddenly the marketing men would begin talking of product strewn with fresh paraphernalia: double albums presented in lavish gatefold sleeves, free twelve-inch singles of indispensable overflow, bonus cuts appended to cassette tapes alone.

CDs, however, seemed to stretch forever. For many musicians, the whole notion of having to cherry-pick a productive recording session fell by the wayside overnight. The very concept of a double album being served up as something special suddenly appeared ridiculous. Only true vinyl archaeologists could pick up a full-length CD and mourn the days when record companies would spend a few extra cents on cardboard and vinyl, then add a few extra dollars to the overall price.

But even crammed to within three seconds under the CD's then-perceived threshold of 74 minutes, *Blood Sugar Sex Magik* could hold less than two-thirds of the sessions' output, and so the laborious task of consigning material to the cutting floor began. The instrumental 'Fela's Cock' could go. So could 'Sikamikanico' and a couple of other, somehow substandard compositions. But was it perfectionist artistry or a more down-to-earth awareness of songwriting royalties that also demanded the omission of three songs that, in intent, at least, stand alongside even 'Higher Ground' and 'If You Want Me to Stay' in the band's catalogue of crucial covers: a studio version of 'Castles Made of Sand'; another Hendrix song, 'Little Miss Lover'; and Iggy and the Stooges' self-defining 'Search and Destroy'?

According to Frusciante, 'They were good, but not so exceptional as you'd want them on a record', and only fans picking up the 'Give It Away' twelve-inch single, or British vinyl pressings of the album where the Stooges song was present, were in a position to argue with part of his pronouncement. The Peppers' version of 'Search and Destroy' owed little to its creators' prototypical garage band sound, but it retained its spirit regardless, sputtering nihilism that only gradually descended into grinding discordance.

The song had little in common with the rest of *Blood Sugar Sex Magik* but, like 'They're Red Hot', it encapsulated the Red Hot Chili Peppers regardless. This was the first Red Hot Chili Peppers album to be written and recorded from a position of stardom; if anything could have dismissed the pre-release possibility that the group might rest content on its laurels, 'Search and Destroy' was it.

In the event, such fears were not allayed until long after the publicity machine previewed the song titles and hinted, in its own way, that *Blood Sugar Sex Magik* represented the greatest departure yet from the Red Hot Chili Peppers' norm, even as it remained true to two of the band's strongest traditions – sex and death. 'Funky Monks', with its warning that 'there are [none] in my band'; the innuendo-whipped 'Suck My Kiss'; and the epic eight-minute 'Sir Psycho Sexy' ('there's a devil in my dick') were as crudely suggestive as anything in the band's explicit heritage, justification in their own right for the parental advisory stickers with which Warner wallpapered the CD case.

Their corollary, however, was equally powerful and, were some independent watchdog to institute stickering albums for reasons other than obscenity and evil, equally deserving of attention. 'Under the Bridge', the atypical ballad that Rick Rubin thought reminded him of Neil Young, and 'My Lovely Man', both remembered Slovak with tender attention. Neither was the group limited to its own interpretation of its past. Both the title track and 'The Greeting Song' earned comparisons with Led Zeppelin, with 'Blood Sugar Sex Magik' itself adding a brand-new equation to the blackboard as Kiedis lowered his voice to a sultry growl straight out of a Beefheartian epic.

Elsewhere on the record, the majestic 'Breaking the Girl' revelled in a mature sensitivity that few observers ever dreamed of unearthing in the Red Hot Chili Peppers and, regardless of their personal opinion of *Blood Sugar Sex Magik*, few of its reviewers could deny that the Red Hot Chili Peppers, having been asked to pull a rabbit from their hat, extracted a behemoth instead.

'This record sounds like a band playing music,' Flea boasted, not a bunch of musicians putting the latest studio technologies over their listeners' ears. 'It's very minimal and it's very live. When I hear it, I get a picture of a hand hitting a guitar, a string vibrating.' Even its title, Kiedis told the *Observer* newspaper, 'is an eloquent but abstract description of how we feel. We live in a world packed with desensitising forces, that strip the world of magic. And music can help restore a sense of magic. The world is full of negativity, but we fight back with positivity. We're inspired by oceans, forests, animals, Marx Brothers films. We can't help but project uplifting vibrations, because we love each other so much and get off on playing together.'

Even Frusciante's revelation, a decade later, that the mood was often strained in the studio, could not dampen the enthusiasm with which the group attacked the material. He told *Total Guitar* magazine, 'Flea and I were smoking a lot of pot, especially me. Anthony wasn't and it disconnected. I thought it was having a good effect on my music, which in a way it was. But it's the energy of the four of us that makes

the music, not smoking pot or any other drug.' Nevertheless, watching
the footage that Gavin Bowden shot of the recording process from a
decade's distance, Frusciante sadly mused, 'it was the last happy time
for me before I left the group.'

Warner certainly knew how to market a band and the publicity
campaign that preceded the release of *Blood Sugar Sex Magik* was
executed to textbook perfection. Gavin Bowden's video recounting of
the album's creation was edited down to one hour and released to the
media under the title *Funky Monks*; further footage was clipped for the
'Suck My Kiss' video, and the five-figure production costs were
themselves quickly recouped, when *Funky Monks* was placed on
general sale.

This initial onslaught was followed by the Red Hot Chili Peppers'
new single. 'Give It Away' was a maniacal speed rap that, in stark
contrast to much of the album, was archetypal Red Hot Chili Peppers,
jarring and, once it reached the point of saturation at which radio and
MTV aired it, irritating as hell. In terms of the band's reputation,
however, it was both the ideal appetiser and the ultimate statement of
intent. Reassured by the frenzy of 'Give It Away', the Red Hot Chili
Peppers' traditional audience swarmed towards the album. And, a little
over a year later, in February 1993, the song earned the band a
Grammy as 1992's Best Hard Rock track. Alongside Eric Clapton and
k.d. lang on the winners' rostrum, the Red Hot Chili Peppers cut an
incongruous, if somewhat puzzled, shape. 'It's not even a hard rock
song,' a confused Flea protested, 'it's a funk song.' But, as he told
Variety, if the Grammy committee wanted to honour the Red Hot Chili
Peppers ('they probably just felt sorry for us'), they would receive a
warm reception. 'We'll take it.'

With the hardcore following now satisfied, it was time to break the
Red Hot Chili Peppers into the larger marketplace. 'Under the Bridge'
was every A&R man's dream and that despite Chad Smith gently
warning, 'It doesn't really have a hook.' REM had already proven that
catchy choruses are not the universal panacea that pop's Tin Pan Alley
heritage insisted upon, when the moody 'Losing My Religion' stormed
the bastions of crossover superstardom. But, according to *Rolling
Stone*'s David Fricke, 'Under the Bridge' went even further.

'Gently anchored by a lilting, skeletal guitar riff that faintly echoes
Jimi Hendrix's "Little Wing" [or, perhaps, "Angel"] the song is light on
radio-friendly pomp and direct in its confessional detail.' More
importantly, the song flouted 'the long standing school of thought on
the Red Hot Chili Peppers. [They] have finally scored commercially

with a nervy slice of melodrama that is streets away from mosh-ville [and] locker-room chuckles.' Even more than the lightning strikes of passionate introspection that illuminated *Mother's Milk*, Fricke proclaimed, 'Under the Bridge' was evidence that the Red Hot Chili Peppers had finally discovered maturity. He might as easily have said that maturity had discovered the Red Hot Chili Peppers.

Blood Sugar Sex Magik was released in late September 1991, slipping with arrogant ease into charts that were still dominated by country icon Garth Brooks, Metallica, Tesla and Guns N' Roses. Over a year later, it continued hovering around the US Top 10, working its way towards triple platinum status, while the Red Hot Chili Peppers continued to bathe in its spotlight.

At the MTV awards on 9 September 1992, Stephane Sednaouri's brilliant video for 'Give It Away', with its four silver-painted Peppers going wild in the desert, strolled away with the 'Best Breakthrough Video' award. And, while other bands posed and pretended on the ceremony's stage, the Red Hot Chili Peppers stole the show.

On a stage choked with dancers, the group ripped through their prize-winning single and, according to London's *Daily Mirror*, the following morning, '[the] zany rockers left MTV bosses fuming. Flea managed to upstage bad-boy rivals Guns N' Roses by stripping to his underpants; simulating sex as he performed; inviting scantily clad girls onstage.' Flea defended himself with a smirk. 'Award ceremonies are boring. We wanted to liven things up.'

Hoping to recapture the spirit of camaraderie that pervaded those earlier, club-based tours with Fishbone and Thelonious Monster on board, the Red Hot Chili Peppers intended that their latest jaunt, hot on the heels of *Blood Sugar Sex Magik*, should similarly showcase artists they believed in. Unfortunately, their good intentions seldom took into account their potential guests' own ambitions.

Ice Cube, a former member of the explosive NWA, ranked among the most volatile figures on the Los Angeles rap scene but, with his own platinum-selling album behind him (the ultra-controversial *AmeriKKKa's Most Wanted* sold a million in 1990), he was now 'too expensive' for the Red Hot Chili Peppers. So was Lenny Kravitz, the young psychedelic warlord who wrote songs for Madonna (she recorded his 'Justify My Love') and who also worshipped Jimi Hendrix – he covered 'If Six Were Nine' on an early B-side.

Other names were floated. Fast-rising Seattle grunge heroes Soundgarden were a possibility; so were the all-girl rockers L7. But finally, a concrete line-up was arrived at. Kiedis himself selected Chicago's

Smashing Pumpkins after catching them on *120 Minutes* and sensing 'this very different, beautiful musical aesthetic'; while Pearl Jam were another Seattle band, who owed their very existence to the Red Hot Chili Peppers' intervention.

San Diego native Eddie Vedder, 'Crazy Eddie', as Flea referred to him, was simply a kid whom Jack Irons befriended during his time with Joe Strummer, but who had since become a permanent fixture within the drummer's circle of friends. He was always around, cheering from the sidelines as Irons reconvened with Alain Johannes and Natasha Schneider, to begin scheming their new band, Eleven; he was among the first to offer his congratulations after Irons's wife discovered she was pregnant with the couple's first child. And, when Irons, Flea and a few other friends decided to head off to Yosemite National Park for a ten-day backpacking expedition, of course Crazy Eddie had to be included in the party – if only to bring some additional craziness to the outing.

They were driving home at the end of the trip when Irons popped a cassette into the player. He'd recently been contacted by a couple of Seattle-based musicians, Jeff Ament and Stone Gossard, with a view to forming a new band with them. Both were former members of Mother Lovebone, a hard rock outfit that flourished briefly and brightly towards the end of the 1980s, but who fell apart following the overdose death of frontman Andrew Wood. Now, as they attempted to piece together a new group with guitarist Mike McCready, Irons was one of the players they were trying to lure up to the Pacific Northwest to join them.

With so much else going on in his life at the time, the trio's instrumental cassette, the so-called *Stone Gossard Demos 91*, was never going to lure Irons away from LA. He turned the group's offer down but, when the duo asked if he knew any other drummers . . . or vocalists . . . that they ought to listen to, Crazy Eddie's was the first name off his tongue. Two months later, Vedder was on his way to Seattle – Pearl Jam was born; and now, as the Red Hot Chili Peppers prepared for their latest tour, Irons came through for the new group once again. Kiedis continued, 'Jack called Flea and said, "I'm friends with these guys, they just finished their first record, would you consider taking them?"'

Kiedis was instantly impressed by Pearl Jam. Unaware, at the time, of the long history that the individual musicians shared on the so-incestuous Seattle scene of the day, he was astonished to find 'they really have their shit together for [a] young, first-record band'. Indeed they did. 'The crowd on the [Peppers] tour was insane,' recalled Dave Abbruzzese, the eventual occupant of the Pearl Jam drum stool. 'I mean, they were still there to see the Peppers, but when we played, it was crazy. We'd play for like thirty minutes, and it was like the Smashing Pumpkins had to earn their forty-five minutes and the Peppers even had to earn theirs. By the end of that tour, it was almost like they were our audience in a lot of respects.'

The Red Hot Chili Peppers and Pearl Jam bonded further over their mutual love of basketball, and the friendship that developed was not a passing, on-the-road fancy. Paying back the good word that Irons dropped into Flea's ear, Vedder invited Irons and Eleven to tour with Pearl Jam when they headlined across the United States and Europe in 1992, while he and Kiedis shared their friendship with the world when they kissed, full on the lips, backstage at the MTV video awards.

Jack Irons's own involvement with Pearl Jam, meanwhile, was further consummated in late 1994, when he was recruited to replace the outward-bound Abbruzzese, first on tour and then in the studio. The ensuing *No Code* album was widely acclaimed as Pearl Jam's freshest since their debut *Ten*, and the band were happy to pass the credit onto Irons. 'Jack had toured with us,' Gossard mused, 'and we were desperate to get in and record some songs that had his original flavour.' Irons would remain a member of Pearl Jam for almost the next four years.

13. PEAS AND CHIPS, ECSTASY TRIPS

It was inevitable that the *Blood Sugar Sex Magik* tour should prove the most successful the Red Hot Chili Peppers had ever undertaken. Even audiences who had never heard the band beforehand knew the words to 'Under the Bridge', while the appearance of little Clare Balzary onstage at New York's Roseland brought a standing ovation even before she launched into a faltering performance of 'The Alphabet Song'.

Night after night was sold out long before the tour rolled into town and night after night, too, the Red Hot Chili Peppers would send their audience home grinning like loons, having invited them first to partake in seemingly the band's most private moments. At Boston's Walter Brown Arena on 1 November, Kiedis even demanded the crowd share in his 29th birthday celebrations, bringing members of Smashing Pumpkins and Pearl Jam onstage to join in the fun and roaring his approval as loudly as the crowd when Eddie Vedder emerged naked except for one long, pendulous sock. Memories of the outing proved pervasive, too – almost a decade later, when *Rolling Stone* magazine gathered up its own 'greatest concerts of the 90s', the Peppers/Pumpkins/Pearl bill was an effortless inclusion.

For Kiedis, however, if there was any one moment when he realised that, at last, the Red Hot Chili Peppers had finally risen into a whole new universe, it came in the distinctly down-to-earth surroundings of a men's room, at a party somewhere. Standing at the urinal, he suddenly became aware of the man next to him singing, in a most unusual key, 'Under the Bridge'. 'And I thought, "OK . . . some drunken guy singing one of our songs next to me at a urinal. We've definitely made it now." '

Yet, even as the group reaped the rewards of so many years spent chasing their tails around the American club circuit, everybody could feel the shadows lengthening over their own peace of mind. For John Frusciante, the past three years of his life could best be likened to building a house in the eye of a hurricane. Barely 21, his entire existence had been turned upside down. He felt as though he were on permanent public display and, as his natural love of solitude battled with his duty as a Red Hot Chili Pepper, he became moody. When old friends dropped by the dressing room to greet him after a show,

he lapsed into bouts of sullen silence, convinced that their attention
was a reflection not of his own personality, but of his fame. Pearl Jam's
Jeff Ament remembered, 'John was having a real hard time, and there
was a ton of pressure.' No matter how successful the shows themselves
were, Frusciante was collapsing inside.

The outlets he once enjoyed, jamming with friends in small clubs,
were suddenly out of bounds, as the fate of Hate, that ad hoc jam band
he formed with Flea, uncompromisingly demonstrated.

Even before the *Blood Sugar Sex Magik* tour left the starting blocks,
Frusciante was praying aloud that the Red Hot Chili Peppers could
steer clear of the larger auditoriums and halls that their popularity, of
course, now demanded. He wanted to recapture the eye-to-eye
attention of an audience, not become just another cavorting insect on
a platform half a mile from the back rows. Despite the assurances of
the rest of the group that the Red Hot Chili Peppers were powerful
enough to bridge even the soul-sapping void of the largest arena,
Frusciante's heart sank when the itinerary finally arrived. There was
scarcely one venue that held less than two thousand people, nor one
that promised to be anything more than an aircraft hangar.

Touring, however, was but one symptom of an even greater malaise.
The very nature of his career left Frusciante anguished and drained if
he allowed himself to contemplate it. But, as he withdrew into himself,
so he withdrew himself, too. During the weighty bout of interviews
that accompanied the release of *Blood Sugar Sex Magik*, Frusciante's
input decreased as the work load increased. 'I started to hate being a
rock star . . . I really hated interviews, photo sessions and fans asking
for autographs.'

Early visitors, journalists representing the musical (as opposed to
music) press, found the guitarist forthright and chatty, anxious to talk
about the recording process and to highlight both his own contributions and those of his bandmates. Only occasionally, if the conversation turned towards the immediate future, did his eyes cloud and his
effervescence subside. And, as that future drew ever closer, Frusciante's grip upon his feelings slackened.

The Red Hot Chili Peppers should have spotted the warning signs
then. But Frusciante was young, he was healthy, and they thought he
was clean. And that was all that mattered. Journalists put his manners
down to petulance or pretension. It was easier for everybody to simply
observe Frusciante as another piece of furniture, albeit one that would
blurt out an occasional growl whenever a question struck him as
unnecessary or foolish. He was a musician first, a performer second

and an acrobat – the role into which most outsiders wanted him to fall – last of all. In that light, his behaviour was almost understandable, as Frusciante himself explained.

'So many people miss the point with us. They copy the thumb slapping or the silly faces, but they miss the essence of what we really are.' Cradling his Stratocaster, even in the sanctity of a Thai restaurant, he resembled nothing so much as a terrified child warding off the devil with his lucky rabbit-foot talisman. 'Every time I read something about what we are, or what we're supposed to be, it completely misses the point. We're trying to tap into all the good vibes in the universe and yet all we ever see is "cocks in socks". It's ridiculous. People always have to bring things down to their lowest common denominator to understand it. They'll do that and I'll sit here and play the fucking guitar.'

It would be another year before Flea was finally able to place Frusciante's increasing belligerence in its true perspective. 'Part of it was the pressure of constant touring. Given all that goes on with the Red Hot Chili Peppers, it's easy to let the rest of your life fall apart, and I think John needed to take care of his life, his sanity and his peace of mind, because it was driving him batty. He needed his space.'

At the time, Flea counselled patience and worked diplomatically to shield Frusciante from the more asinine questions that were thrown in his face. But even he still wondered what could be made of a man who once publicly claimed, 'It's a wordless state I'm in, as if outer space were walking through a room outlined like a person.' Sometimes, as journalist Bob Mack noted, 'John takes this stuff too far.' Unfortunately, that wasn't all he took too far. Four years later, Frusciante finally acknowledged what only a few whispered asides dared suggest during his tenure with the band. He was using heroin.

Even before the Red Hot Chili Peppers immortalised him in a song on their *Mother's Milk* album, basketball player Earvin Johnson ranked high in their dreams. 'Just to hang out with him,' Flea speculated, 'to be his friend. That would be . . .' – for a moment, words failed him. 'That would be so cool.'

Standing six-foot-nine in his stocking feet, Lansing, Michigan-born Johnson has been called 'Magic' ever since a local basketball reporter wrote about the Everett High School junior as he scored 36 points, made 16 assists and snared 18 rebounds in one game. The name stuck and Johnson lived it with a vengeance. In 1980, he joined the Los Angeles Lakers and the team that had hitherto been beaten finalists in more championship play-offs than any other, suddenly soared to the top.

For the next nine years, the Lakers dominated basketball's Pacific Conference league like no team in history. Five times they won the national championship, the first in Johnson's debut season, twice more they finished runners-up, and as the team's honours mounted, so did Johnson's. He was voted the NBA's Most Valuable Player three times; three times more, the MVP in the play-offs. For any bunch of kids growing up within shouting distance of the Lakers' home, there was no questioning who the greatest basketball player of all time was and, when the Red Hot Chili Peppers recorded their own paean to Magic, it was plain that, at heart, they were still that bunch of kids.

'There is a beautiful relationship between basketball and music,' Kiedis explained. Johnson appealed because he played a similar kind of game to the Red Hot Chili Peppers, one that was based on 'assisting and supporting and helping the other guys on your team to do well, so that the team as a whole can excel'. At the close of the 1990–91 season, Johnson led in all-time most assists with 9,921, an astonishing average of 12.5 assists per game.

'None of us are out there soloing to attain egocentric, grandiose delusions of rock herodom, or anything like that,' Kiedis continued. 'It's all about playing a part to make the songs sound better and we really learned that lesson from Magic Johnson and the Lakers. Not to mention that when anybody can reach that level of superstardom and still be a humble, loving, compassionate human being at the same time, you know there's something to be learned!'

There was only one dissenter in the ranks: Detroit-born Chad Smith. In his eyes, Johnson was a traitor who turned his back on his native Michigan to play in sunny LA; for him, there was only one team worth talking about, and that was the Detroit Pistons. Among his most treasured possessions is a videotape of his drumming his way through the National Anthem immediately before a game with the Hawks in Detroit and, that summer of 1990, the Pistons proved his point beyond question when they trounced the Lakers by four games to nil in the championship play-offs. Kiedis wagered him $100 on the outcome of the games and Smith savoured every cent of his winnings.

The singer's revenge was sweet. 'I got Smith to record ['Magic Johnson'] before I told him what it was about.' Now, every time the Red Hot Chili Peppers performed the song in concert, the stage bathed in the Lakers' yellow and purple team colours, Smith would be reminded of his vocalist's perfidy. Only when a vociferous out-of-town audience launched into its own response to the song did his mood lighten and sometimes, as he played, Smith would begin chanting along with the crowd: 'LA sucks! LA sucks!' He also told visiting journalists that, if you played the song backwards, you could hear his subliminal chanting. 'It's just a shame compact discs won't do that,' he said with a smirk. 'You're missing a real treat.'

Unfortunately, Magic was not to remain long on his pedestal. On 8 November 1991, he announced to the world that he had tested HIV positive. He was retiring from professional basketball permanently. The Red Hot Chili Peppers were playing Philadelphia's Tower Theater that evening and the news impacted hard. Flea still managed to yell, 'I love Magic Johnson!' during the show, but the band's own ode to the sportsman was absent from the playlist. So, according to *Philadelphia Inquirer* critic Tom Moon, was a lot of the band's energy. The group hadn't quite turned on 'the rock-and-roll auto-pilot – [their] music requires too much muscle for that. But some of the will was missing.'

Johnson remained on the sidelines for less than six months. With the United States having finally gained clearance to field a professional basketball team in the forthcoming summer Olympics, Johnson renounced his vows and leaped back into the game. The Red Hot Chili Peppers celebrated with him by headlining an all-star AIDS benefit, at the Hollywood Palladium on 4 April 1992, arranged in part by the newly founded Magic Johnson Foundation.

The bill for the event was incredible, as impressive as any summertime festival – backed up behind the Red Hot Chili Peppers, Fishbone, the Rollins Band, Primus and the Beastie Boys were all scheduled to play, while the evening's place in rock history was cemented when Perry Farrell and the again-sundered Thelonious Monster's Martyn LeNoble announced the benefit as the debut performance for their own new band, Porno For Pyros. And they, insisted Flea afterwards, were 'beautiful, man. It was a great night for music.'

Johnson himself did not attend the show; the bands were introduced instead by LA Lakers past and present Michael Cooper and Vlade Divac. But Flea and Kiedis didn't mind. They had already met their idol by then, and the experience was not so sweet.

Flea was invited to play in an MTV-sponsored all-star basketball game at Loyola-Marymount and, as the event drew closer, he could not contain his excitement. 'One of my team-mates is Magic Johnson,' he enthused. 'For me to score a jump shot off a Magic feed . . . that would be the greatest thrill I've ever personally had.'

But according to *Alternative Press* journalist Jason Pettigrew, the moment of meeting went terribly awry. When Flea mentioned 'Magic Johnson' to Johnson himself, the sportsman 'just wasn't interested. A while later, Flea and Anthony told the story on MTV, and you could see they were really hurt by Johnson's rejection.' But what goes around, insisted Pettigrew, comes around. When *Mother's Milk* first came out, he was among the first journalists to interview the Red Hot Chili Peppers and, the next time the band played the magazine's Cleveland home, he headed backstage to reintroduce himself.

'Pleased to meet you,' Flea responded as Pettigrew stepped forward.

'Again,' Pettigrew responded.

'Oh, yeah . . .' replied Flea, his eyes belying even the unconvincing hint of recognition his voice tried to convey.

Pettigrew caught the expression. 'Now I know how you felt when you met Magic Johnson.'

Flea's bewilderment turned to anger. 'Ah, fuck you.'

'No, Flea – fuck you.'

Afterwards, Pettigrew explained that he wouldn't normally have expected someone to remember him after three years and who-knows-how-many interviews. 'But we spent a long time together for that interview and I felt Flea really opened up to me about Hillel. I didn't think those were the sort of emotions you could just turn on and off for every journalist who came through the door.'

The Smashing Pumpkins' stint on the tour ended in New Orleans on 6 December 1991. The last of the shows, scheduled to carry the Red Hot Chili Peppers into the early New Year, would see them topping what was now officially the hottest package of the year, as yet more denizens of the Pacific Northwest, Nirvana, joined Pearl Jam on the bill.

When Geffen Records picked up Nirvana from Seattle's Sub Pop independent label, the transaction passed by all but unnoticed. Figureheads of Seattle's indigenous grunge scene though they were, in terms of even local public understanding Nirvana trailed some way behind the real pacesetters, Mudhoney, the Melvins and Soundgarden.

Bleach, Nirvana's debut album, offered little more than the band's stubborn cult status demanded and Geffen's interest apparently owed more to the company's insatiable appetite for minor-league alternative bands than anything Nirvana had accomplished in the past. But, the September 1991 release of the group's second album, *Nevermind*, was to prove a defining moment, not only in Nirvana's own career, but also in that of countless other so-called alternative bands as well. If Living Colour, as Kiedis once remarked, blew open the door that the Red Hot Chili Peppers themselves initially created, Nirvana ripped it off its hinges.

Selling 70,000 copies a day, *Nevermind* did not simply cross the divide between alternative rock and the mainstream, it obliterated it. Backed by a video shot in the gymnasium of the Red Hot Chili Peppers' own alma mater, Fairfax rock'n'roll High School itself, Nirvana's single 'Smells Like Teen Spirit' dominated alternative and Top 40 radio alike. And, when it ran its course, 'Come as You Are' simply picked up where it left off.

'Nirvana have done what the Sex Pistols and the Clash never did,' said Robert Roth, one of the myriad musicians who passed unnoticed through the embryonic superstars' ranks and who now fronted his own band, Truly. 'They've taken punk rock to number one.' The very week Nirvana joined the Red Hot Chili Peppers' tour, *Nevermind* ousted Michael Jackson's *Dangerous* from the top position.

Buoyed on a sea of pure anticipation, the tour moved from the LA Sports Arena two days after Christmas, to Del Mar and Tempe, Arizona. But the crowning glory was a New Year's Eve show at the sacred Cow Palace in San Francisco. For two decades, 31 December on the Bay belonged to the Grateful Dead, still the city's hippest sons even as they turned into grandfathers. Taking over the Oakland Coliseum, the Dead proved that the twentieth century could advance as much as it wanted, but some things would remain the same forever. Even the serried ranks of Deadheads drifting blissfully towards their annual communion, however, were no match for the 15,000 or so kids converging on the Cow.

Few of the reviews that appeared afterwards truly captured the magic of the evening. They dwelled on temporal themes: Nirvana's painstakingly systematic auto-destructive set closer, during which they deliberately unscrewed every nut on their instruments to hasten their approaching destruction; Eddie Vedder's suicidal leaps from the stage and beyond, into the seething mass of dancers; and Flea's dramatic entrance at the start of the Red Hot Chili Peppers' set, suspended by his feet from a rope that lowered him slowly to the ground.

Those things happened, of course, and each one drew fresh roars of approval from the belly of the Cow. But it was more than a simple performance that took place that night; more, too, than a noisy way of seeing in 1992. Sometime between Pearl Jam's entrance and the Red Hot Chili Peppers' departure, rock'n'roll was reborn, not as a freakish sideshow on the fringe of mass entertainment, nor as the puerile discharge of a thousand Identikit sallow, shallow pop stars, but as a living, fire-breathing way of life.

Ever since the jagged shards of punk first scattered like buckshot across the hide of rock'n'roll, pop music, that most gloriously subversive of all twentieth-century art forms, had lain moribund, a blazing comet obscured by its own trail of dust. Where once it moved with the passion of lovers, now it dribbled to stagnation, a static shower of increasingly placid, intrinsically flaccid movements that promised social dissidence but delivered cultural dissonance, the first strivings of a corporate rock garden in which everything, even teen revolution, would be served up shrink-wrapped and sanitised.

Musically, the alternative rock scene that was bursting into the first years of the new decade offered little that could be separated from anything that had gone before. Precedents for everything rang like bells through the music, whether it was the Black Crowes reheating the Humble Pie of their youth, Michelle Shocked taking chances on a theme of Joni Mitchell, or even the Red Hot Chili Peppers themselves, mugging funk on their way to a dream date with the Ohio Players.

It was within its own heart that alternative music defined itself, in its belief that what it was doing was important, not because it sprang from the frantic flailing of another desperate A&R man fighting to protect his free lunches, but from a sense of deliberate purpose that actively enjoyed banging its head against the walls of media apathy.

'I see Alternative music as something which challenges the expected norm of the moment,' insisted Robert Cherry, then-managing editor of what was then the scene bible, *Alternative Press*. 'It doesn't matter whether or not it's been done before; the fact is, it's not being done at the time and it doesn't fit in with the programming requirements of mainstream radio or television.'

Only when success embraced so many alternative acts that they themselves defined new genres – as when the original punk bands splintered into their own musical pigeonholes of hardcore, industrial, technopop and funk – could the ground rules be set for rock'n'roll in the 1990s. Until then, the music could not be categorised.

Paraphrasing the lyrics of his own 'Punk Rock Classic' shortly before *Mother's Milk* was released, Kiedis complained that, as far as the record companies were concerned, the only places where music could be marketed fell under 'some rigid category, like black radio, white radio, CHR radio, AOR radio, Top 40 radio, adult contemporary radio'. The record company would listen to the Red Hot Chili Peppers, 'and they say to themselves, "It's not adult contemporary, it's not AOR, it's not Top 40 . . . what is it?" And they'd send it out to the colleges, because the college radio circuit was the only thing that existed then for music which didn't fit into any other bag.'

Now the distinctions had become blurred. Perhaps audiences have always been willing to mix and match their musical mores, have been restrained only by the industry's insistence on pigeonholing their tastes. Because even that New Year's Eve at the Cow Palace was not unique; even the ragged distorted dichotomy of the Red Hot Chili Peppers' funk-fired speed, Nirvana's punk-powered metal and Pearl Jam's dense hard-rock roar merely cemented into place rock'n'roll's newly discovered appetite for change. But it confirmed so many promises that it might as well have been and, when the Red Hot Chili Peppers stepped into Vancouver's PNE Forum on 3 February 1992, the world, they knew, was at their feet.

Vancouver was the final night of a four-month-long tour that played to almost 200,000 people, set box-office records across the United States, established each of the bands who played their part in that success – Pearl Jam, the Smashing Pumpkins, Nirvana and the Red Hot Chili Peppers themselves – as the standard bearers of the new age. All four entered 1992 on the very edge of superstardom: the Red Hot Chili Peppers themselves would cross that brink when they returned from Europe and the Far East in June, to headline Lollapalooza II.

No matter how spectacular the bill may have been for the Red Hot Chili Peppers' winter tour, throughout the summer of 1991, just six months earlier, an even more varied package had taken to the road, and as it did so, a new word entered the musical lexicon: 'Lollapalooza'.

Lollapalooza was originally conceived as little more than a bonus-packed goodbye to Jane's Addiction. Having toured the US during late winter 1990, Europe through spring 1991, and back to New York for a sold out Madison Square Garden show that April, the band was exhausted physically, mentally and creatively. Which was when Perry Farrell dropped his bombshell. The next tour would be the band's last. But it would also be their biggest, as he unveiled the concept that would dominate the American concert circuit for much of the next decade and consume much of Farrell's time as well.

The portents for Lollapalooza were not, initially, promising. The dire economic forecasts that blighted so many tours already that summer were slowly coming to pass. The rash of top-selling outings that highlighted the previous fall were no longer a sign of the music industry's stability; now they were regarded as the calm before the storm. As Farrell, drummer Stephen Perkins and Jane's Addiction manager Ted Gardner worked on piecing together their band's farewell tour, it was hard to say what was the most frustrating: the bands who turned down the chance to appear, or those who just laughed scornfully at the whole concept.

Because Lollapalooza was ambitious. Drawing its local precedents equally from the package revues of the 60s, the multi-artist festivals staged in California during the early 1980s and the Gathering of the Tribes events staged by the Cult's Ian Astbury in late 1989, Lollapalooza was as much an attempt to figure out whether it was even possible to tour any longer, as it was to prove that, in alternative circles, elitism was dead.

With the complicated negotiations finally settled, Farrell announced that Jane's Addiction would be joined by punk veterans Siouxsie & the Banshees, industrial mechanoids Nine Inch Nails, rapper Ice-T, Living Colour, the Butthole Surfers and the grinding extremities of Henry Rollins's eponymous new band. A political sideshow, in the form of a rainforest's worth of information booths, would be organised in the hope that fans that came for the show might depart with opinions. Other distractions and attractions would blossom as the opening day drew closer.

'This is a pioneer tour,' Ice-T averred. 'All the groups in their own way have pioneered a certain form of music. None of us get played on the radio; to be able to pack arenas shows that people want to hear [what we are saying]. It's also a very educational experience. Everybody's taking a pill they're not used to.'

Of course, it was always Jane's Addiction's show. The 26 concerts that stretched to the end of August 1991 were the last gigs Jane's Addiction would ever play. But that was not the reason Lollapalooza sold out wherever it landed, nor the reason it finished a very profitable 25th in *Performance* magazine's listing of the year's top tours. Lollapalooza worked because it defied common lore, both within and without the music industry. It worked because it assumed its audience was intelligent enough to know what it liked.

The question that now demanded an answer was would it work again?

Gardner thought it could. Lollapalooza II would kick off in San Francisco on 18 July 1992, then edge its way in a shower of publicity up and across the United States. The line-up, finalised early in the New Year, would include Ministry, Ice Cube, Soundgarden, Pearl Jam, the Jesus & Mary Chain and Lush. The Red Hot Chili Peppers would headline.

It was an uneasy alliance from the outset. Despite the Red Hot Chili Peppers' and Perry Farrell's long-standing friendship, the quartet were among the bands that turned down an invitation to appear on the first Lollapalooza. With *Mother's Milk* imminent, they wanted to conserve their energies for their own headlining tour. The band members watched the outing's progress with interest, however. 'If I didn't get off on it so heavily last year,' Kiedis confessed once the 1992 line-up was confirmed, 'I wouldn't have been so inclined to be part of it this year.'

Equally, however, he was not afraid to voice his own reservations over the show. The Red Hot Chili Peppers' objections to the event were . . . would always be . . . aesthetic. The 1992 package, Kiedis complained loudly, was 'way too male' and 'way too guitar-oriented'. When he tried to redress the balance and convince the organisers to include L7 on the bill, they laughed at him. 'They said, "They don't mean anything",' Kiedis repeated incredulously. 'What do you mean? They rock and they're girls.' But when he tried to call Perry Farrell direct, he couldn't even get the guy's phone number. Instead, he was told to fax Farrell care of the booking agency. 'It was kind of upsetting to me.' (It would be another two years before L7 finally made it onto a Lollapalooza bill, for the 1994 event.)

America's last glimpse of the Red Hot Chili Peppers before they jetted off to Europe came with their appearance on *Saturday Night Live* in February. The group had already been invited to contribute a song to the sound track of the forthcoming *Wayne's World* movie, directed by *Suburbia* creator Penelope Spheeris and starring *SNL* regulars Dana Carvey and Mike Myers; this, however, was their first appearance on the show and they made the most of it. Their riotous performance, readily overshadowing that of the evening's hosts, Roseanne Barr and Tom Arnold, could be topped by just one further accolade. When the Red Hot Chili Peppers joined the *SNL* cast for the final curtain call, one scene was to remain ingrained in everybody's memory: Kiedis standing arm-in-arm with Madonna, the Queen of Pop with her newly crowned King.

A lot had changed in Britain since the Red Hot Chili Peppers first visited these shores. The charts, of course, remained their usual eccentric ragbag of rent-a-disco crowd pleasers, soap operatic bal-ladeers and the occasional flash of genuine inspiration. But, beneath that tumultuous facade, the nation that gave the world the Beatles and the Sex Pistols, the Stones and Led Zeppelin, was locked in an interminable death dance with a derivative drug culture that even its own participants did not pretend to comprehend.

The 'Psychedelic Revival', spawned by easy access to a new drug called Ecstasy, but powered by revisionist folk memories of the late 1960s, was in full swing. Instead of surging power, however, the juices tapped by MDMA, the subtle anti-depressant that was now so in vogue, dreamed of the ultimate trance, a gently drifting energy vampire that sapped even the old songs it sampled of vitality and verve. In the past, the Red Hot Chili Peppers had never resisted the temptation to describe their own sound as psychedelic. In Britain, the word seldom passed their lips.

'The English music scene sucks,' Flea complained. 'Every time I go over there I'm appalled.' One night he went to a rave, the new generation's answer to the 'Happenings' that fired the subculture of the 60s, at which ear-splitting electronic hypnotics clashed with drug-spiked punch and a visit from the law at closing time. As he stood at the rear of the venue simply soaking up the noise, Flea was suddenly accosted by 'this guy going "peas and chips, peas and chips" '.

Flea was baffled. 'What are you on about, dude?' 'Peas and chips, Ecstasy trips.' The guy was a pusher, using the improvised rhyming slang of the era to distribute his wares. 'When I said no,' Flea continued, 'the guy told me to get the hell out of there. To me, that's what it's like there: if you don't fit in with the current trend, then you're out. I think that's really lame.'

The feeling, apparently, was reciprocal, particularly among Britain's rock literati. *The Times'* David Sinclair opened his review of the Red Hot Chili Peppers' show at the Brixton Academy with an undisguised condemnation of a 'band whose talent for oafish, self-promotional stunts has long been more readily apparent than its musical achievements'. Not even a brief glimpse of the 'troll-like' Flea's genitals brought a smile to Sinclair's pen, while 'a steady incidence of "mother-fusticating"-style lyrics' prompted him to deliver nothing more than a tired acknowledgment of 'some mildly delinquent behaviour'.

The Red Hot Chili Peppers flew into further flak when they were thrown off the bill for the 12 March edition of *Top of the Pops*. The dispute apparently centred on the band's refusal to lip-synch, a *Top of the Pops* tradition which had seldom been broken, but which the group nevertheless refused to countenance. Stalemate was inevitable, but of course the BBC had the final word. Either you mime or you miss it. Disappointed, but with their principles intact, the Red Hot Chili Peppers cast one last glance at the Edwardian women's clothing they had been intending to wear on stage, and left.

If Britain was cynical, however, elsewhere Europe accepted the Red Hot Chili Peppers as conquering heroes, and it was with a triumphant headlining return to the Dutch Pink Pop Festival under their collective belt that the group headed back to Los Angeles in early April to headline the Magic Johnson Foundation's ACT UP AIDS benefit. Even without Johnson's presence, it was a special evening: *Blood Sugar Sex Magik* had just been certified platinum for American sales of one million. Backed up by a striking video shot by Gus Van Sant, director of Flea's last movie role in *My Own Private Idaho*, 'Under the Bridge' was lodged in the Top Ten, climbing towards its peak of No. 2, and Warner Brothers were prophesying similar success for the scheduled next single, 'Breaking the Girl'. The Japanese leg of the tour was long since sold out and Australia was preparing to receive the band like royalty. Not since the Beatles, close to thirty years before, had that country been whipped into such a frenzy of anticipation.

The rest of the group teased Flea that it was all because of him; he had not seen his homeland in over two decades, but Australia had seen him and that was all it took. Caught in the middle, Flea looked from one bandmate to the other, and wondered what on earth he was taking home with him.

By 7 May, the group had played four of its six scheduled Japanese gigs and everybody was looking forward to moving on. Someone had long since coined the term 'Chilimania' and, if there was such a thing, Australia and, alongside it on the itinerary, New Zealand had it. Every spare moment for the band seemed to be spent speaking on the telephone to journalists from one country or the other and most of them wanted to talk to Flea. But it was Kiedis who was wrapping up an interview with a New Zealand-based reporter when suddenly the door of his Tokyo hotel room flew open and Flea walked in. He looked shell-shocked: 'puzzled, sad, surreal' is how Kiedis remembered his expression.

'John wants to quit the band and go home right now.'

Still holding the telephone, but no longer remembering why, Kiedis looked at him in amazement. It took a moment for Flea's words to sink home; a moment more for Kiedis to be able to phrase any kind of response, no matter how monosyllabic. 'What?'

Flea repeated his news. 'John wants to leave. He's packing right now and he's flying out tomorrow. He'll do the show tonight, and then he's out.'

It was a joke, Frusciante playing mind games with his friends. Or it was ego? Calling Smith and Lindy Goetz into the room, Kiedis and Flea tried to figure out what they could offer the young guitarist. A little more limelight? A few more solos? A little more time at the front to show what he could do? What did he want?

He wanted to go home. When Frusciante finally linked up with the rest of the band, one look at him told them that he'd really had enough. 'I can't stay in the band any longer.' Frusciante spoke with a steady, determined air, as though he knew the band would try to persuade him not to go, but was also aware that no power on earth could stop him. 'I've reached a state where I cannot do justice to what we've created. I can't give what it takes to be in this band anymore.' Later, he continued, 'I was very confused. It got into my head that stardom was something evil. If you were a rock star, you were trying to put people on.'

He told *Kerrang!*, 'I saw death in everything around me. And everything that was beautiful represented everything that was sad, lost and gone. I couldn't listen to music, read books or watch movies anymore; I couldn't do anything and I didn't want to think. Everything made me miserable and all I could do was lie on the couch and stare vacantly into space.' It would be several years more before he could finally admit, 'I don't see it that way anymore.'

'What will we tell people?' Goetz asked. Frusciante suggested he simply echo the whispered rumours that already circulated every time journalists met to exchange their own 'freaky Frusciante' fables. The weird things he'd say, the odd things he'd do. The way he would go out to eat, but never let go of his guitar, his shaven head chain-smoking through every one-handed mouthful. 'Just tell everybody I went crazy.' Twenty-four hours later, he was gone.

The remainder of the group, staring down their final night in Japan, made their way directly to Australia. A frantic call home had already catapulted Thelonious Monster's former guitarist, Zander Schloss, onto a plane to meet them, and they hoped desperately to salvage at least some of the shows.

But the rehearsals went slowly and finally ground to a halt. Schloss was good, but it just wasn't working. The magic was missing; the spontaneous spark of creativity that raised a great show above an ordinary performance wasn't there. 'And Australia,' Kiedis told the fans who encountered him during his stay there, 'deserves better than ordinary.' Reluctantly, the Red Hot Chili Peppers cancelled the rest of the tour, vowed they'd return in the fall and took the next flight home to Los Angeles.

To Kiedis and Flea, it felt as though every wound left by Hillel Slovak's death had been reopened and brutishly stirred. 'During the making of *Mother's Milk*, I got really close with John,' Kiedis lamented. 'We sort of became best friends.'

He tried desperately to put a brave face on his emotions, but failed. 'Even my explanation of what happened to John will be nothing but my opinion and feeble understanding,' he told *Rip* magazine. 'It's all kind of confusing. From what I can see, he's a talented, artistic, slightly quirky person, as so many great artists are. He was so young when he joined the band and things happened so fast and furious in the few years he was with us. It was probably a lot more than he bargained for.' But the singer was also so hurt that it would be almost five years before he again spoke to the guitarist.

As for the future, he insisted, 'we have to look at it like, we've got to get someone who is just happier and just wants to rock equally as hard. There are a couple of people in Hollywood that we revere and admire greatly. We'll get in touch with them and start playing. We're not going to do a massive audition process. We're just going to look at people we know, and try to find that chemistry again.'

Yet there was also a sense of weary resignation in the band's attempts to view this latest calamity as anything other than a calamity, an awareness, as Smith put it, that Frusciante's departure was somehow inevitable. 'We should have seen it coming,' he mused later. 'John was eighteen or nineteen at the time. He had no experience what it's like to play in a band, let alone a band like the Red Hot Chili Peppers. I'm a huge Zeppelin fan, and I think I would have freaked as well, if [I'd] been asked to join Led Zeppelin as a drummer. It was pretty obvious that it couldn't work out. We just didn't see it at the time.'

Throughout these upheavals, nevertheless, Kiedis and Flea retained the sense of self-prophesising hopefulness that had always stood them in good stead. It didn't matter how big they became, nor how hard fate intended kicking them in the teeth. They, in turn, would always be ready to jump back smiling broadly. And the harder they were punished, the broader their smiles.

'Basically, the whole world is doomed,' lamented Flea in a moment of horrifying clarity. 'If America could have a decent leader, maybe things could change a little bit, but I think that it's highly unlikely that a really righteous leader could get into office. So the way that I try to make it better, especially since we're talking about the Red Hot Chili Peppers, is by playing music that could be spiritually uplifting, that could put people in a positive state of mind, where they would have the energy to get up and do something, anything, that's positive.'

'We may as well make the best of the world while we're around, by creating this swirling cauldron of positive psychedelic energy,' Kiedis added. 'We're trying to at least prolong the doom. That's really all you can do anyway.' He looked over at Flea and the man of a thousand hairstyles roared with laughter. 'That's right. In fact, we're thinking of changing the name of our band. We're changing it to the Doom Prolongers.'

It was not only the Oceania dates that were slaughtered by Frusciante's impetuous departure. A major Belgian festival was also scheduled, pitching the Red Hot Chili Peppers into action alongside Lou Reed, Bryan Adams and, once again, the Smashing Pumpkins. And immediately after that came Lollapalooza II.

Dave Navarro was the first name on the band's list of possible replacement guitarists. Since the acrimonious demise of Jane's Addiction, Navarro had lain low, surfacing only to cut a somewhat desultory solo album, form a short-lived new band called Deconstruction and turn down Axl Rose's suggestion that he join Guns N' Roses.

Now he was rejecting the Red Hot Chili Peppers as well and not, Britain's *Melody Maker* presumed, for musical reasons alone. Relations 'reportedly' were 'frosty' between Navarro and his former frontman Perry Farrell. With Lollapalooza just a month away, Navarro apparently remained wary of accepting any job that would bring him into such close contact with Farrell. In fact, as the guitarist explained later, he was wary about any offer that would bring him back into the music industry. 'I thought I wanted to be done with the whole . . . thing,' he reflected.

The Red Hot Chili Peppers' shortlist was growing shorter. They had been convinced that Zander Schloss would work out; then they were certain that Navarro would bite. Now there was just one name left to try, a balding young man named Arik Marshall who was brought into Flea's Trulio Disgracias sideline by his own older brother, Thelonious Monster's Lonnie Marshall.

Half black, half Jewish ('Blewish!' Marshall said with a laugh. 'Like Slash and Lenny Kravitz'), Marshall became friends with Flea long before he ever dreamed of playing alongside him. 'We'd always see one another around different clubs,' Marshall recollected, 'and something of a friendship developed over the years. It was like a mutual admiration thing. Flea and Anthony would come and see my bands, and I'd go see theirs.'

'The first time I heard Arik Marshall play was in some little club somewhere,' Flea remembered. 'I said, "Okay, this guy's funky" – like he was good, but I wasn't that impressed. Next time I heard him play was in Trulio Disgracias and, I said, "Whoa!" Then I heard him play with his brother Lonnie in [their own band] Marshall Law, and it was phenomenal! Amazing! Incredible! Like this psychedelic, liquid, funky trip. I thought, "This guy is the greatest fucking guitar player." ' As he wrapped up Trulio Disgracias on the eve of the Red Hot Chili Peppers' *Mother's Milk* tour, Flea told Marshall how much he'd enjoyed playing with him, and hoped, he said, that their paths would cross onstage in the future.

Enquiries around the Los Angeles grapevine supported Flea's admiration. A few months earlier, the Marshall brothers had joined Jack Irons, Alain Johannes and Norwood Fishbone in Floppy Sidecrack, a one-shot band whose sole reason for existing was to play a well-to-do graduation party out in Beverly Hills. They played three solid hours of funk covers, yet Marshall was so convincing they could have been his own compositions. According to Johannes, the Red Hot Chili Peppers were lucky Marshall even looked their way. He should have been snapped up by someone else years ago.

Now it was they who did the snapping and, leaving his brother to rebrand their band Weapon Of Choice, Marshall leaped gratefully into their jaws. 'I kinda figured these guys were gonna check me out,' Marshall, already labouring under the band nickname of Freak, told *Rip* magazine in January 1993. For five hours a day, five days a week, the Red Hot Chili Peppers laid down a martial law of their own, pounding Marshall with their music, their philosophy, their entire way of life. And, three and a half weeks after he joined the group, Arik Marshall stepped out in front of 60,000 Belgian festival-goers to play the biggest gig of his life.

14. I THOUGHT I WAS SUPERMAN

As Arik Marshall plugged in his guitar, the most indescribable feelings rushed through him. The Red Hot Chili Peppers' luckless record with guitarists didn't bother him; nor, once his ears acclimatised themselves to the roar of the crowd, did the knowledge that he was standing before more people than he had ever seen in his life. Behind him, Smith set the storm in motion. On the far side of the stage, Flea stood motionless, awaiting the moment the electricity would leap from bass string to finger and start his entire body shaking, like a stooge in the employ of some medieval exorcist. Next to him, Kiedis looked out at the crowd with those giant cow-brown eyes and slowly twisted his mouth in mock grimace.

Of course there were elements of his new calling that alarmed Marshall – reflecting upon his first cock-in-sock show, he admitted, 'I had to muster up some courage to put on one of those.' He also acknowledged the size of the shoes he was stepping into. 'There are some things that I wouldn't do any other way than how John did it, like the introduction to "Give It Away". Because I think that's an important piece of his, one which people quickly identify with. But in other areas – like solos and fills and things – I just interject my own stuff. So it ends up being fifty-fifty: I try to do his stuff exactly as he did it, and I try to do my own thing.'

Elsewhere, however, the newcomer seemed one step removed from the Red Hot Chili Peppers' habitual world of wildness. Alan DiPerna, who interviewed him in New York, reflected, 'It's hard to imagine Marshall vomiting in mid-sentence on an interviewer's shoes, or asking a female reporter if her nipples get hard during intercourse.' Still, at the time, no one doubted that the gangling rubber-face with the deep eyes and the thinning hair would work out fine.

Lollapalooza arrived, kicking off on 18 July 1992 at Shoreline Amphitheatre, in Mountain View, California. Still wrapped in the Cocteaus-esque miasmics which were their pre-*Lovelife* calling card, the opening Lush came and went to muted approval. Now Pearl Jam, the first of two Seattle bands on the bill, were winding up their own 45-minute set. The mid-afternoon sun was still hanging high and, as the band walked off, the first grumbles of discontent could be heard. Pearl Jam had a Top 5 album; in terms of immediate ticket appeal, they were probably the hottest band on the bill. Yet there they were, trailing five spots behind the headliners.

Backstage, the bands awaited their turn to perform. Everyone had itchy feet, but the Red Hot Chili Peppers in particular had something to prove. Lollapalooza was Arik Marshall's American baptism of fire, a sentiment the rest of the group took so firmly to heart that they would be encoring each night wearing specially designed volcanic construction helmets. As they played, jets of flame shot from the top of the band members' heads.

In the meantime, a long afternoon stretched ahead of them, although no one appeared to mind that much. The show was still fresh, the crowds still amusing. When Soundgarden, later in the day, threw a few lines of Nirvana's 'Smells Like Teen Spirit' into one song, the audience erupted. Nirvana had just pulled out of a projected Lollapalooza of their own, the cynically titled Lots o' Losers tour, and this was the closest that the mud-drenched faithful were going to get to the real thing all summer.

Kiedis shared their enthusiasm. No one, he was adamant, could ever confuse Nirvana with the Red Hot Chili Peppers, but still both groups were cut from a similar mould, a furious dismissal of the past ten years of turgid rock'n'roll history. 'The world at large is just completely bored with mainstream bullshit. They want something that not only has a hardcore edge, but that is real music, written by real people who wake up and have the unignorable need to create music.

'America is so middle-of-the-road that of course the only bands that are going to become huge are middle-of-the-road bands.' He ticked them off on fingers that were surprisingly delicate on so huge a hand: 'Guns N' Roses, Van Halen, Bon Jovi, Bruce Springsteen. We always swim against the mainstream, so it's difficult for us to reach that type of audience. But I think people are destined to become fed up with mediocrity and eventually they're going to turn to bands that are full of life, like the Red Hot Chili Peppers, Thelonious Monster and bands that are just oozing with life.'

Second on the Lollapalooza billing, Ministry's Al Jourgensen echoed the sentiment. 'I think it's great that Faith No More and the Red Hot Chili Peppers have Top Ten hits. I'd much rather have people exposed to that than another fucking Warrant or Winger.' He reinforced his sentiment by undertaking a devastating 'Chicken Mix' remix of the Red Hot Chili Peppers' own 'Give It Away' – so named because he brought a chicken into the studio with him, and only worked the faders that the chicken shat on. Nevertheless, he cautioned, 'the problem is, are the bands who are making it now going to turn around and become new-boss-same-as-the-old-boss? That's the crux of the problem.'

'All we ever wanted to do,' Flea growled from behind flashing green eyes, 'is play music that comes from our hearts.' Like a Catholic priest reciting Mass, he half-breathed, half-chanted the things that meant the most to him. 'Miles Davis, Ornette Coleman, Defunkt, Funkadelic, the Meters, James Brown. The real shit. That's where we're coming from: from jamming, from playing a billion hours of shit that no one will hear, from getting cosmic in a darkened room and developing musical telepathy.'

The telepathy wasn't faultless, of course. A new member inevitably introduced new musical creases to even the tightest ship and Arik Marshall was still feeling his way into the band's sound. It would be some weeks deeper into the tour before Flea could admit, 'We still have to work hard to make it happen, but the sparks are really starting to fly.'

Back at Lollapalooza, the Red Hot Chili Peppers' set list had just been approved and distributed, proof that even four minds in perfect harmony needed to know what their fellows were thinking. Although the group tried to keep their performance fluid, rotating songs as the mood struck them, the air of chaotic improvisation they maintained on stage was, by necessity, studied. You cannot go out in front of 30,000 paying customers and not know what the rest of the group plans to play.

Slowly the sky was beginning to darken. Ministry, who started life as a synthipop duo and then reinvented themselves as a cauldron of napalm-tinted hardcore fury, were midway through their set. No longer young, they were still loud and snotty and, even with half of their show pre-recorded, they lashed up a set that was the nearest thing to revolution most of the Lollapalooza crowd was ever likely to witness. No one was surprised, later in the tour, when the Detroit venue was trashed immediately before and during Ministry's set. Over $100,000 worth of damage was done to the Pine Knob lawn alone.

As the sun set, the Red Hot Chili Peppers finally took the stage. Journalist Lisa Ridley positioned herself at the fringe of one of the biggest mosh pits in history and watched as the crowd, already a broiling mass, was transformed into a human sea of rolling, crashing waves, undulating as far as the eye could see. 'Creating the impression that this was just another night and not merely [one of the first] of their latest incarnation, they stroll out and launch into "Give It Away". The Red Hot Chili Peppers seem almost to be making the set up as they go along: Flea's impromptu poetry soliloquy [based around Elton John's ever-stomach-curdling 'Tiny Dancer'] certainly appeared to take Anthony by surprise.'

So, later in the evening, would the volcanic hats, as their wind-whipped flames seemed to reach their flickering fingers deliberately towards his flailing hair. 'But the Chili Peppers make their point with fire. Their assumed casualness is really only an act; they know who they are and what they are and they care about both things deeply.'

'The thing about playing music,' Kiedis explained before the show, 'particularly the music the Red Hot Chili Peppers play, is that you want people to get dirty, you want them to be splashing around and getting caked in filth. That way, when they leave, they'll know they've been somewhere. In three weeks time, when they're still trying to get the mud out of their ears, they'll remember.'

The show moved towards its climax. While Kiedis wandered offstage, Flea sang a tight rendition of Neil Young's 'The Needle and the Damage Done' – a song, he confessed, that was meant to sound 'poignant and soulful, drawing on my deep well of dynamic life experience', but usually emerged 'quirky and cute and out of tune'. Nevertheless, the moment rarely failed to still the crowd. A lot of the kids in the band's early 1990s audience probably didn't even know the Red Hot Chili Peppers' own history, Kiedis and Slovak's hands-on experience of the destruction wrought by heroin. But, for those who did, Young's own aching exorcism, his memorial to a close friend who OD'd, could easily have become ham-fisted pantomime, pounding the band's painful martyrdom into the crowd like a sledgehammer. Instead, it captured a moment of supreme triumph. In the words of another bard, Bob Dylan, the Red Hot Chili Peppers had 'taken the cure and just gotten through'. It took them four years, two guitarists and several rivers of tears, but at last they'd buried Hillel.

Yet, still it sometimes seemed as though their troubles were only just beginning. Looking back, in June the following year, over the twelve months since Lollapalooza, the Red Hot Chili Peppers were also looking forward to an indeterminate age of uncertainty. They had continued scaling heights – no sooner were they off the Lollapalooza road than EMI enacted the clause in their final agreement with the Red Hot Chili Peppers, and unleashed What Hits!?, a career-spanning compilation album that brought the story bang up to date. Released just as Blood Sugar Sex Magik completed a year in the album chart and 'Breaking the Girl' peaked as a single, What Hits!? proved a major hit

in its own right, and spun off another smash 45 . . . a full five years
after the Red Hot Chili Peppers suggested it.

'We wanted "Behind the Sun" out in 1987,' Kiedis reiterated, 'when
it came out on *The Uplift Mofo Party Plan*. But EMI wouldn't let it
happen.' Now the company's Vice President of Alternative Marketing
(who dreams up these titles?), Mike Mena, was describing the track as
'a nice hybrid of styles that a brand-new Chili Peppers fan would like,
as well as the diehard fan.' An accompanying video was being pieced
together as well, combining animation and outtake footage from the
'Higher Ground' shoot. Five years too late . . .

There were further glories to be gathered when the Red Hot Chili
Peppers were invited to make an animated appearance on TV's *The
Simpsons*, lining up alongside the voices of Elizabeth Taylor, Bette
Midler, Hugh Hefner and Johnny Carson in that most beloved of
instalments, *Krusty Gets Kancelled*.

Broadcast in the US on 13 May 1993, and subsequently described
by the American *TV Guide* magazine as one of the 'funniest moments'
and 'greatest episodes' in TV history, the Red Hot Chili Peppers were
among the army of celebrities – all dear friends of Krusty the Klown's,
of course – roped in by Bart to relaunch the old comedian's career in
the face of fresh competition from a rival TV channel, the ventril-
oquist's dummy Gabbo. The Red Hot Chili Peppers' own contributions
to the actual show proved fairly unmemorable, but artist Matt
Groenig's representations of them endure among fans of band and
family alike.

In June, a rambunctious new single, 'Soul to Squeeze', peeled off
the *Coneheads* movie soundtrack en route for an effortless Top 30
berth. 'Soul to Squeeze' itself was a relatively old song – the chord
sequence had been coined by Frusciante the previous year; and it
might have remained on the shelf had actor Dan Ackroyd not
personally approached the Red Hot Chili Peppers for a contribution
to the movie.

Hastily completing the recording, the band handed it over, then
hooked up with director Ken Kerslake – hot from his recent work with
Nirvana – to shoot an amazing video, a monochrome nightmare set
amid a circus freak show, that transformed Kiedis into a gorgon, and
shot a Conehead out of a cannon. But, even as one marvelled at one
of the most spellbinding videos the group would *ever* make, one could
not help but wonder . . . just how much of a group was there actually
left? Arik Marshall was nowhere to be seen and, at the end of June,
the Red Hot Chili Peppers told the world why.

Even as a summer of European festivals beckoned tantalisingly from over the ocean, Marshall – 'a terrific player who stepped in and rocked with us', as Flea put it – left the band. Like Jack Sherman, like Blackbyrd, like Zander Schloss, he was a great player and a good friend. But the emotional connection that his bandmates demanded simply wasn't there, and no amount of friendship was going to change that. Marshall moved on to play with Macy Gray among others (he joined John Frusciante among the guests on her 1999 album *The Id*); the Red Hot Chili Peppers returned to square one – and placed a 'Guitarist Wanted' ad in the *Los Angeles Weekly*.

The response overwhelmed them; more than that, it exhausted them. After taking over a thousand calls a day for three days, the band were forced to have the phone disconnected. They knew it would be crazy, but nobody ever imagined it being *this* crazy. It was as though every guitarist in the city had the band's number, from the Frusciante clones who had every last note of *Blood Sugar Sex Magik* on tap, to the most hapless, hopeless unknowns who thought penile dimensions were the only criteria that counted. But not one fitted the bill – not even Primus's anonymously masked Buckethead, who came down to audition at the same time as he confessed that he'd never heard any of the Red Hot Chili Peppers' music.

Still the audition went ahead, with Buckethead pulling out every one of his stylistic stops . . . so many that, at the end of the session, the entire room rose to applaud. Even he, however, would not be offered the gig. Although Flea was thrilled to find the star 'sweet and normal', he was also adamant upon the Red Hot Chili Peppers' requirements; someone '. . . who could also kick a groove'. And Buckethead, for all his brilliance, didn't do that.

After all the auditions, just one name emerged from the soup. Texas-born Jesse Tobias was a self-taught guitarist whose first band, Mother Tongue, had relocated to Los Angeles from Austin in 1991, after a year spent ploughing the local circuit. Originally an all-instrumental act, the group shifted its focus after bassist Davo began improvising spoken word passages over the music – an almost avant-garde act within the so-traditional confines of the Texan scene and one that, in a way, shared at least a little common ground with the Red Hot Chili Peppers' own origins. It was Davo, too, who initiated the group's relocation, when he booked them a couple of shows in LA in mid-1991. The gigs went so well that Mother Tongue abandoned Austin just a month later.

Since that time, the band had built up a hefty head of steam on the local circuit, attracting the friendship of the Cult's Ian Astbury, and beginning work on their debut album – those sessions were, in fact, still under way when the Red Hot Chili Peppers' call came, and Tobias found himself spiralling from the local club circuit to a summer show schedule that saw the Red Hot Chili Peppers headlining England's annual Glastonbury Fayre on 25 June, Dublin's Dalymount Park two days later and, thereafter, a string of continental festivals.

The new combination seemed to work well. Time and again, after all, the Red Hot Chili Peppers had proved they were at their best with their backs to the wall and, besides, they had now changed guitarists so often that this latest rotation was almost a fact of their life. But other forces were at work, that were destined to shatter this latest line-up, almost before it found its own feet.

First, Flea succumbed to a 'mystery illness', diagnosed by outsiders as chronic fatigue, but subsequently summed up by the bassist himself as a total breakdown. '[I] physically, spiritually, just kind of fell apart. Touring and a variety of personal things going on in my life, heartbreak, physical abuse to my body over the years because of drugs and lots of stuff.

'I thought I was Superman, but it all caught up with me, and I just fell apart. I felt so sick. I was in bed all the time, and it was completely traumatic because I was so used to playing basketball all day and partying all night and rocking out. And then all of a sudden I couldn't do anything. I was embarrassed that I felt so bad. It was the first time I was really forced to look inward.'

With Flea effectively flattened, there was no way that the band's festival schedule could proceed; and, with that blow there came the realisation that there was no way the Red Hot Chili Peppers could continue, either. Just one month after joining the band, Tobias completed the shortest residency yet in Red Hot Chili Peppers history and quietly departed. Again, his erstwhile bandmates blamed nothing more than a certain incompatibility for the severance, a failure to connect on the deep spiritual level that was the group's guiding force, and without which, they might as well not exist. (Tobias reappeared in Alanis Morrisette's live band in 1995, before forming a new band, Splendid, with wife Angie Hart.)

The Red Hot Chili Peppers ground to a halt but, even as Flea attempted to haul his life back on track, adhering to the doctors' recommendation that he rest for a full 12 months, the knock-out blows kept coming. On 30 October 1993, he headed down to the Viper Room to see John Frusciante playing one of his rare solo shows and found himself, instead, among the horrified crowd that watched as River Phoenix collapsed on the street outside the club.

Flea and the 23-year-old actor had been close friends since filming the movie *My Own Private Idaho* together in 1990; when the A&E television network researched Phoenix's story for an episode in their *Biography* series, previously unknown film footage of the pair jamming together on location ranked among the most memorable discoveries. The bassist was also prone to muck in with Aleka's Attic, the band Phoenix and his sister Rain had led since the late 1980s, joining them both onstage and in the studio, where a wealth of recordings included the two songs that would eventually appear on the animal welfare compilation albums, *Tame Yourself* and *In Defense of Animals Vol. 2*.

Now Flea rode in the ambulance that took the stricken star to the hospital, but nothing could be done. Phoenix – 'one of the kindest people I ever met in my life' – was pronounced dead at 1.51 a.m. 'When I think about River, I don't think about his death,' Flea said later. 'I don't get sad about it. I think about how incredibly fortunate I was to be friends with a person who looked inside me and saw things that no one else ever saw before.' The song 'Transcending', which would appear on the Red Hot Chili Peppers' next album, was written in the young actor's memory.

Work on that new album, of course, could not commence until the band replaced Tobias. Only this time, the chaos of auditions and rehearsals that scarred past processes was abandoned, as the band were finally able to unveil the guitarist they'd wanted all along. A full year after he turned down their initial advances, Dave Navarro was finally ready to step into the breach. 'I had nothing to lose, because I had nothing invested,' the guitarist confessed.

He had conditions, of course – no cocks in socks for a start ('Flea and Anthony have the personalities to pull that stuff off. I don't'); no daft gimmicks. They agreed, but still, Navarro's induction into the Red Hot Chili Peppers remained hard going. 'It was really rough. I didn't think it was right. I'd played with Flea before . . . but I'd never owned a Chili Peppers record. All I knew [was] that these were musicians I admired and wanted to play with.

'We rubbed each other [the wrong way] because I tried to play like I thought they wanted, and I think [Flea] was trying to play more like I was used to, and it didn't really work. I'd just joined the band, I didn't really know these guys . . . and immediately, we're writing music?'

Navarro told *Guitar World*, 'When I first joined the Chili Peppers, I felt like it was a whole other world [that] I had to listen to. I don't just want to call it funk, because the Chili Peppers are so much more than a funk band. But it was definitely heavily funk-influenced, which was an influence I never had. So that was something I had to look into.'

Kiedis was adamant that 'we never assumed anything about how Dave would play. I think in the first couple of weeks, we suggested he listen to a few different records, just to see how he thought about certain sounds and rhythms. [But] he didn't really need it or feel comfortable with it, and it just disappeared.'

Indeed, adapting to the Red Hot Chili Peppers' requirements was no more of a challenge than the one Navarro faced down twelve years before, when he was first introduced to Perry Farrell. He was a member of the metal band Disaster at the time, one of those doughty behemoths that the now-defunct American rock weekly *Creem* described as representing 'that generation of metal players that acknowledged little musical history beyond Led Zeppelin and . . . Eddie Van Halen.' Navarro adapted his style then; he would do it again now and, if there were any last, lingering doubts as to the suitability of the match, they were swiftly remedied in time-honoured Red Hot Chili Peppers style. Road trip!

Escaping not only the occasionally uptight mood that permeated the rehearsal room, but also the band members' own constantly conflicting images of LA, a city that seemingly grew darker, dirtier and more dangerous with every passing day, the entire group relocated to Hawaii for a time, simply to flush their hometown's toxins from their system. That, Flea said, 'was where the music started coming together'. The musicians played together, of course, but they also relaxed – exploring the awe-inspiring peaks of the islands' volcanoes, scuba diving in the clear blue Pacific, sightseeing. Reinventing themselves as La Sensatives motorcycle gang, they mounted their Harley Davidsons and rode for hours. 'We needed to get our bond going,' Smith explained, 'similar to when John and I joined before *Mother's Milk*. There's something to be said for touring and hanging out and getting to know one another personally and musically.'

Navarro agreed. 'Gradually, the more comfortable we became with each other, the more comfortable we became with just letting it come out.' But returning to LA to begin work on the basic tracks slammed them back to square one. 'We tracked, and nothing happened for a long time.' There were demons abroad, or perhaps old friends, and they needed to be exorcised before anything could proceed.

It was Kiedis who lay at the heart of the problem, as Smith told *Alternative Press*. 'We had a lot of music written before he came up with all of the melodies and lyrics . . . [he] really had to go through a lot' – 'a lot' that the grapevine lost little time in ascribing to the return of hard drugs to the singer's daily chemistry.

Kiedis himself would neither confirm nor deny the rumours. 'I had a lot of hardcore personal struggling to do with my own spirit. And one of the manifestations of that struggle was me taking more time than usual to write the words I wanted to write, and find the parts I wanted to sing.' More philosophically, he described the turmoil as 'a hardcore refresher course', telling MTV 'I needed something excruciating to kick my ass and let me know I needed to get back on the growth pole'. Whether that 'something excruciating' was in any way drug-related, however, was a private matter that the world at large had no business with. 'You're going to hear a lot of stuff and some of it might be true and some of it might not be true. And the only people who are going to know the truth are people that I'm intimate with.'

Neither did he regard any of the turmoil as problematic, stoically insisting that 'it was meant to take a lot longer, and it was meant for me to go through a lot more shit before I could have the clarity and the purity to express what I wanted to the whole time'.

Plans to begin work on the next Red Hot Chili Peppers album in autumn 1993 were shunted to one side; so, surprisingly, was the chance to appear at the Hollywood Palladium in January 1994, when the cream of the LA glitterati turned out in support of Fishbone frontman Norwood Fisher. The singer had been charged with kidnapping after he attempted to abduct a friend who was reportedly suffering from mental problems. Porno For Pyros, Primus, Tool and Alice In Chains all turned out to raise money for his defence (Fisher was eventually acquitted), but more than one observer noted the Red Hot Chili Peppers' absence.

In fact, the band itself was already deep into pre-production for their next album, and bristling excitedly at the ease with which the process seemed to be going. With Rick Rubin again overseeing the proceedings, the first song completed for the new album, 'Warped', was among the most frenetically hard rocking numbers the band had ever conceived, it quickly became apparent that Navarro was bringing more than a new face into the mix.

With his guitars firmly stalking the same textural landscapes that he staked out with Jane's Addiction, a mood that one writer later compared to 'U2 banging out an angry tribute to Queen', he was also introducing an entirely new direction, one that would lead the Red Hot Chili Peppers further from their traditional arena than they had ever strayed before – and which Flea seemed determined to embrace, as he continued shaking off the emotional residue of the near-total collapse he suffered at the end of the *Blood Sugar Sex Magik* tours.

Buoyed by sinister passages of murmured spoken-word, built around deep minor chords that rolled off maudlin pianos and acoustic guitars, the new music, the bassist acknowledged, was 'completely different from anything we've done. Dave's approach to the music is definitely a darker one. He's the total opposite of what John Frusciante or Hillel Slovak were. Dave was into taking his time and putting a lot of guitar shit on there, making a collage, whereas on the last record, John . . . didn't overdub anything.'

But even Navarro's impact, Flea mused, was secondary to his own. 'It's [going to be] a much darker, much sadder record, because we're definitely in a darker place. Everyone does their thing on it, but the skeleton for most of it was initiated by me, and I was in a dark, depressing, sad time for most of the recording.'

Navarro, for his part, summed up his contributions to the album by explaining, 'I think that everything that encompasses who I am, and who I've been in my life, has been brought to this band in an amicable way.' The scything guitars that dragged a shattered off-beat into the almost frighteningly introspective 'Deep Kick'; the almost nu-metallic thrusting of 'Coffee Shop' and 'One Big Mob', the heavyweight grandstanding of 'Walkabout', all offered brain-charring confirmation of Navarro's own insistence that 'I come from a slightly different place, musically speaking. These guys are percussive and sharp-edged, to use an expression that Flea has come up with, and I'm into melodic and ethereal sounds. And I think that the combination has really worked and given birth to something really new.'

Into the new year, a pair of reissues – 'Give It Away', in February, and 'Under the Bridge', in April – prefaced the band's return to action by meandering into the UK Top 20. It would be spring, however, before the new-look Red Hot Chili Peppers were truly ready for their great unveiling, as they were confirmed among the headline attractions at Woodstock 94.

Scheduled to celebrate the 25th anniversary of the original Woodstock festival, the event looked, at the time, like one of the most vomitous musical miscalculations of the decade, an attempt to restage the mythological epitome of peace, love and all that jazz, in the age of nihilism, hatred and corporate bloodsucking. Indeed, from the outset, Woodstock 94 seemed doomed, just as past efforts to rekindle that so-sanctified mood and moment had been doomed.

Staged on a farm in upstate New York at the height of the Vietnam War in 1969, the original Woodstock remained a palpable presence on the American psyche. It was the peak of the 60s experience; a decade born of trust had been betrayed times out of number, but still youth fought for the dream that had once been there for the taking. Woodstock, half a million people gathered for three days of peace and love and music, was the pinnacle of their achievement and, no matter how many years had passed since then, that achievement surely still meant something.

But the first attempt to reprise Woodstock, in 1970, was abandoned, while a Woodstock Reunion on the tenth anniversary of the original festival, was a sparsely attended, poorly promoted washout. 1989 brought a more concerted attempt at celebrating the festival, but passed by with little more than MTV screening unseen footage from the original weekend. And, as the 1994 event drew closer, nothing that the organisers announced seemed to dispel the pessimism that surrounded the looming event: not the 33-strong bill that made Lollapalooza look one-dimensional; not the decision to relocate the festival away from its original site, to the nearby town of Saugerties; not the news, from elsewhere, that a rival Woodstock was to be held *on* that original site, that same weekend.

Neither, once the crowds started arriving for the concert itself, were the early portents any improvement. The car parking lay anything up to thirty miles away from the actual festival site, and nothing more than a fleet of broken-looking school buses waited to shuttle ticket-holders towards the endless queues at the main gate. Rain was in the air, the mosquitoes were having a field day and, for the people watching it all unfold at home, courtesy of pay-per-view television, one comment from host Dave Kendall surely prompted them all to thank their lucky stars that they had not joined the exodus to Saugerties. Straining his eyes to see the row of portable toilets that hung on a distant horizon somewhere, and the crocodiles of people waiting (or, rather, not waiting) to use them, he shuddered, 'the stench is . . . spreading'. And it was.

But, despite all the hardships, all the horrors, and all the mudbaths of human waste, Woodstock 94 was an unqualified success; for the organisers, who were able to report the complete sell-out of tickets; for such bands as Green Day, the Cranberries and the Rollins Band, each of whom confirmed their promise of ascendancy with performances that remain memorable; and for any future cultural analysts who might care to inspect the event. Organiser Michael Lang told

Entertainment Weekly, 'the unique thing about this event is that, in '69, the generations couldn't have been further apart. Woodstock 69 was our generation proving itself. Woodstock 94 was a melding of the two generations. I think Generation X really came out of the closet.'

The Red Hot Chili Peppers shared, with Bob Dylan and Peter Gabriel, the pleasure of closing the show on the Sunday night, and illuminated the stage in literal fashion – they appeared clad in silver suits, their heads surmounted by massive glowing lightbulbs. Despite the up- heavals of the past year, and Dave Navarro's obvious nerves at making his live debut on such an immense stage, the band's set itself was a predictably crowd-pleasing mass of greatest hits – although, following on from an almost painfully soporific performance by the re-formed Traffic, even mundanity would have been a thrill for the waiting hordes.

'Playing Woodstock was a very exciting experience,' Flea acknowl- edged. Like so many others in attendance, he confessed, 'we went there really questioning the whole thing, questioning the fact that they were advertising peace and love and at the same time it seemed to be about corporate structures and merchandising. But, when we got to play, the energy of the whole thing really took over. There were zillions of people having a great time and it was our first show with Dave and we were really excited and we had a fun time.'

Two weeks on from Woodstock, the Red Hot Chili Peppers were at the Reading Festival, sharing the spotlight with Primal Scream, Soundgarden, Jeff Buckley and the cream of that year's Britpop fall-out, Radiohead, Tindersticks, Elastica and the inestimable Pulp. But, if there was any one event that struck a chord, it came in Pasadena, as the group was invited to open a couple of shows for the Rolling Stones on 19 and 22 October.

The billing itself was no great privilege – as the Stones ground around the USA, almost every city had been granted an opening slot from one alternative heavy-hitter or other. Besides, it merely rein- troduced Flea to Mick Jagger, upon whose Rick Rubin-produced *Wandering Spirit* solo album the bassist guested in 1993.

In terms of the Red Hot Chili Peppers' own mythology, however, the billing cemented a connection that had entertained fans for a few years now. The reasoning, excitedly spelled out to waiting micro- phones by a fan at Lollapalooza, was simply a matter of lining up the parallels between the two bands' careers. The weird thing was, there seemed to be a lot of them.

'The Stones had Geoff Marshall and the Peppers had Jack Sherman. Early days; doesn't count. Then there was Brian Jones who died and

Hillel Slovak who died as well. Then there was Mick Taylor who chickened out because he couldn't stand the pressure and John Frusciante did the same.' Pause in that narrative for the brief interregnum during which both bands tried out replacement guitarists and, finally, you arrive at the terrible twins, Ronnie Wood on the one hand, Dave Navarro on the other. 'See, it works whichever way you look at it. The Chili Peppers are the new Rolling Stones.'

There were other links, too. Both bands exist around one pivotal partnership and all but lifelong relationship – Mick Jagger and Keith Richard on the one hand, Kiedis and Flea on the other. Both, to many minds, personified a facet of society that society itself will seldom willingly confront. And both had had their run-ins with the law. Now both were on the same stage, the Stones touting their *Voodoo Lounge* extravaganza, and entertaining the watching media with the possibility that 'this might be the last time' (of course it wasn't); the Peppers with yet another rebirth, another resurrection, another frenzied assault upon the false glitter, the raucous greed and the plastic values of the mid-1990s world.

Coming off the road, the Red Hot Chili Peppers retreated to the same Van Nuys studio that Nirvana occupied during the recording of *Nevermind*. It was less than six months since Kurt Cobain, Nirvana's mercurial frontman, killed himself in his Seattle home, and the Red Hot Chili Peppers were almost worshipfully aware of the spirit, the vibe, that swept through the only 'big league' studio in which Cobain ever professed himself to be happy. That mood was only heightened, of course, by their insistence on lighting the studio only with candles – a technique that layered much onto the music that the band was recording, but played havoc on Gavin Bowden's attempts to follow up the *Funky Monks* video documentary with another, tracing the evolution of this next album.

While the Red Hot Chili Peppers worked towards their future, meantime, EMI took another opportunity of revisiting their past, as November 1994 brought the release of *Out in LA*, a well-selected collection of B-sides, outtakes and remixes, highlighted by a first-ever release for the group's debut demo tape, recorded with Rooster more than a decade earlier. It was a remarkable compilation, so much so that the Red Hot Chili Peppers themselves eventually took control of the project and supplied their own sleeve notes to the accompanying booklet. Prior to that decision being arrived at, a more distant associate (this author, in fact) was commissioned to document the collection.

Like your old grandmother used to say, 'if you can't shit, get off the pot'. Move along, get on with your job and, if you can't cut it, quit. As the 1980s wound along, the Red Hot Chili Peppers spent a lot of time on the pot – to very little avail.

It wasn't their fault, this commercial constipation. Between spring 1983, when they played their first ever live show as Tony Flow and the Miraculously Majestic Masters of Mayhem and, the fall of '89, when a fiery reappraisal of Stevie Wonder's 'Higher Ground' finally sent the Peppers spiralling skywards, Anthony Kiedis and Michael 'Flea' Balzary had already recorded three LPs, with three guitarists and three drummers. Their best friend, Hillel Slovak, was dead; another, Jack Irons, had checked himself into a mental hospital, unable to deal with the loss of Slovak. No, the Peppers weren't to blame for their commercial constipation, and this collection shows you why.

Anyone with even half an eye for the pre-fame Peppers will know the song titles here. 'Higher Ground' was the band's first hit single, 'Get Up and Dance' was their first single ever. 'Millionaires Against Hunger' was a Freaky Styley outtake, the Peppers' own response to Live Aid and 'We Are the World', 'Fight Like a Brave' was one of the highlights from the Red Hot Chili Peppers' third album and 'Behind the Sun' was the single that wasn't – the Peppers wanted it released in 1988, but really, what was the point? It wasn't like anyone would buy it.

Five years later, of course, 'Behind the Sun' became a big hit . . . but five years later, the Red Hot Chili Peppers could get away with a lot of things they once got condemned for, although it's still unlikely they'd have got very far with 'Party on Your Pussy' – which is why it was retitled 'Special Secret Song Inside', even before fame came knocking. No doubt the live version included here will raise just as many temperatures as the studio cut did back then.

You see, this is no random hits collection, no Best Of or whatever. Rather, it's a collection of some of the rarest Peppers recordings around, the rarest and the wildest – 12-inch club remix singles which sold minute quantities, non-album B-sides which deserved much better and a couple of songs which, like 'Special Secret Song Inside', were recorded in the one environment where the Red Hot Chili Peppers always had the world in their hands – in concert.

There they could forget that their record sales were barely enough to keep them alive; there they could forget that bands which had grown up behind them were suddenly streaking ahead. Onstage, the Peppers were untouchable and, if the groundwork for their eventual success was laid anywhere, it was in the clubs and dives of America, where the band learned their craft, paid their dues and built their reputation.

And what a reputation it was. The 'socks on cocks' routine may only have been turned on once every off-blue moon or so, but even so, when the Peppers played, anything could happen. Catch the version of Jimi Hendrix's 'Castles Made of Sand' and you can almost hear Flea's tattoo of the guitarist join in on the solo. Moments like that don't grow on trees, and when the Peppers did finally make it, all it proved was that the world finally realised that fact – and didn't want to miss out on any more. Today, the Chili Peppers are one of the hottest bands around. There's not really much to add to all that. Like I said, if you're a long time fan, you'll already know the songs, if not the mixes – nothing here's been on album before, although it's been crying out to be compiled for years.

But in some ways, you're better off if you're a newcomer to the Peppers' mighty mayhem, a recent convert or just a curious passer-by. Because you won't have a clue what to expect from these songs, except . . . except a roar of defiance and a scream of delight and, like they themselves occasionally remark, some hardcore, bone-crunching, mayhem sex-things from Heaven.

That kinda says it all, doesn't it?

15. TAKING YOUR CLOTHES OFF IS INTERESTING

The New Year opened, as so many seem to do, with reports of the Red Hot Chili Peppers' latest bout of studio activity vying with tales of a less salubrious nature, as word of Kiedis's struggle to get his private life back on track, and the wealth of speculation that flew around even his most guarded remarks on that subject, prompted *Alternative Press* magazine's Eric Gladstone to reveal 'rumours had been flying . . . that both Kiedis and . . . Dave Navarro were in drug rehabilitation programmes as recent as January of this year'.

Once again, however, journalists hoping to delve deeper into such legends were left to do so under their own steam. So far as the Red Hot Chili Peppers were concerned, there were so many other projects in the air, and that's what the musicians intended concentrating upon.

First, Flea and Navarro took time out to guest on Alanis Morrisette's *Jagged Little Pill* album (with wry serendipity, Jesse Tobias would find himself 'replacing' Navarro when Morrisette took that album onto the road later in the year). Flea and Smith's Thermidor side project, formed with Robbie King, David Allen and Pearl Jam's Stone Gossard, was also preparing to stir, laying down the finishing touches to their *Monkey on Rico* album. With neat circularity, the pair would also be granted their chance to work alongside Kristen Vigard, whose solo debut album, eight years earlier, had been graced by Kiedis and Frusciante – unseen in the movie *Grace of My Heart*, Vigard was nevertheless responsible for singing much of the film's original soundtrack material, and Flea and Smith were numbered among her backing musicians.

And the Red Hot Chili Peppers themselves were heading back onto the road, with a two-month US outing that wrapped up at the San Diego Sports Arena on 16 April 1995, just as American sales of *Blood Sugar Sex Magik* were certified quadruple platinum – four million copies sold.

May took the group to Australia and New Zealand, to finally fulfil the promises that the band made when Frusciante's departure forced them to cancel their first visit; then it was back to the States in June, for a headline berth at the Tibetan Freedom Concert in Golden Gate Park, San Francisco.

Schemed by Buddhist Beastie Boy Adam Yauch and underwritten by Milarepa, an organisation dedicated to non-violent social change, the festival was targeted at a generation who, as Bill Clinton's Presidency launched the United States into a new era of prosperity, had money in their pockets and were now looking for a cause to champion. However fleeting that confluence of social conscience and charitable affluence might turn out to be, the Tibetan appeal was one of several that met that requirement, although this particular afternoon did not go off completely as planned.

With a sold-out audience of close to 100,000 spread across the two-day festival (raising some $800,000 for the cause), the Tibetan Freedom Festival prided itself on its musical eclecticism – the Red Hot Chili Peppers were joined on the bill by the Smashing Pumpkins, the Beastie Boys, Biz Markie, the Foo Fighters and Pavement. Despite the good intentions of the event, however, it was to be a fractious occasion, as Smashing Pumpkins biographer Amy Hanson recalled: 'An odd afternoon . . . unfolded in stark opposition to the peaceable mood that permeated the theme itself.' The Chicago band found themselves the victims of a wholly unwarranted hail of cans and abuse, so much so that they abandoned their programmed set of hits and crowd-pleasers, and opted instead to throw a big 'fuck you' back at the crowd, and launch into a vicious near twenty-minute version of 'Silverfuck'.

The Red Hot Chili Peppers' set was less caustic, as they looked only to road test the new material, revelling in their reception, even as they registered the audience's reaction to the latest songs. And, as they left the stage, the general consensus seemed to be – so far, so good.

Not all of the group's activities were targeted towards the new album – Flea took time out to write and record a song for one of his personal heroes, boxer Mike Tyson, as the former champion was released from prison after serving half of a six-year sentence for rape; the song would never be issued, but Flea did, at least, mail a copy of it to Tyson.

The group's proximity to the controversial prize fighter was not, however, an omen that they could rely upon. *One Hot Minute* – the first all-new Red Hot Chili Peppers album in four years – was set for release in August, just as Tyson himself returned from the wilderness, by winning his comeback fight against Peter McNeeley in 89 seconds. The band's rewards, however, were not to be so obvious.

One Hot Minute did not sink like a stone, of course it didn't. Though it peaked no higher than No. 4 in the US, still its two million sales were almost double those of Nirvana's posthumous live *From the Muddy Banks of the Wishkah* – an album that *did* top the *Billboard* chart. But, whereas *Blood Sugar Sex Magik* had wrapped up the planet in the shiniest paper and bow it could find, *One Hot Minute* struck many listeners as something more akin to a few steaming seconds, and neither sales nor, once the band returned to the road, ticket sales seemed at all shy about making that point.

To take a positive spin on things, the comparatively poor sales of the album were less indicative of the record's quality as of a major change in the record-buying public itself. *One Hot Minute* was joined on the under-achieving shelves by new releases from any number of graduates from the Alternative Class of '91: Lenny Kravitz, the Spin Doctors, REM and Blind Melon, and that was only the Warner group's share of the market and, across the half-dozen 'major' labels that did business in the United States, the prophets of doom – surely the most over-employed figures in the entire industry – gnashed their teeth and worried about their pension plans, seeking out scapegoats in every arena they could find; and inventing them when they couldn't.

For the first time, the alleged indestructibility of CDs was haunting industry analysts. If you couldn't scratch a CD, then you'd never need to replace it, and that scratched a lot of sales. And then there was the market for second-hand CDs – again, if a disc's condition was unlikely to become an issue, then a few quid for a used copy was a lot more attractive a proposition than £13 or so for a new one. A few forward-thinking pessimists were even casting the first tremulous eye towards the Internet, and the slowly burgeoning penchant for downloading music from other users. It would be another five years or so before that particular spectre was finally seized upon as the greatest threat to the future of popular music since . . . ooh, since at least the last one . . . but, already, record companies were professing themselves to be 'hurting', and the bands that they represented were hurting alongside them.

But some groups did prove successful during 1996. The Smashing Pumpkins, rising hard and fast since the days when they toured America supporting the Red Hot Chili Peppers, sold close to five million copies of the double *Mellon Collie and the Infinite Sadness* (qualifying for no less than *nine* platinum discs), while Rage Against The Machine (triple platinum) Jack Irons's Pearl Jam debut *No Code* (double platinum), and the hot new talent of No Doubt (nine weeks at No. 1, and an incredible 10 million copies sold) all enjoyed phenomenal returns for their efforts, suggesting that, rather than look for outside causes for individual bands' sales dips, it might have been more productive to look at the bands themselves after all. And, when you did that, it suddenly became apparent just how lamentably *tired* a lot of them now appeared.

Rick Rubin hit the Red Hot Chili Peppers' malaise on the head when he mused, 'Taking your clothes off is interesting; putting your clothes back on is less interesting. It's less noteworthy. The [Red Hot Chili Peppers] are kind of still in the putting-their-clothes-back-on phase. . . . There's no question that the quality of the work just keeps getting better and better. But the general public does still seem to view them as a party band.'

Wise after the event, Flea agreed. 'When we first got together and went in the studio, I knew that there was no way we were gonna be as good as we would be after we'd made the record and toured and then made another record. It was the same thing with John Frusciante. When the Chili Peppers made *Mother's Milk*, I knew it wasn't going to be as good as after we toured and we made *Blood Sugar Sex Magik*. And I look for the next Chili Pepper record to be the greatest Chili Pepper record.' In the meantime, however, they had to live with the consequences of the one they had already made.

The first single from the new album, the delinquent slash'n'burn of 'Warped', tracked no higher than No. 31 in the UK in September 1995, its prospects further damaged when a flurry of old-style Red Hot controversy – but new-style prudish disdain – was levelled at the accompanying video. Wrapping Kiedis and Navarro in what appeared to be nothing less than a lingering kiss, the film raised eyebrows among even the band's most tolerant supporters, and drew widespread hubris from less understanding souls – fires that Kiedis promptly stoked when he lashed out at his critics with the insistence, 'We didn't grow up in a homophobic community, so we never worried about showing affection for one another, the "don't undress in front of me, I'm not like *that*" feeling.'

But even this fuss could not kickstart the old mania; rather it seemed to set the Red Hot Chili Peppers' own cause back even further, and the fear induced by this initial misstep proved contagious. Into the new year, 1996, the Anton Corbin-directed video for the group's next single, the introspective 'My Friends', was scrapped after Warner Brothers' marketing department announced they would prefer something a little less arty . . . Corbin placed the band in a dinghy, then set them adrift, creating a mood that was as lovely, and as isolated, as the song itself. But was that really the kind of imagery that would sell the song?

No! It would be far better, far happier, far more viewer-friendly, to scrap all the clever symbolism, and simply film the band in the studio, doing what they did. Gathering up Gavin Bowden's so-dramatically candlelit footage of the studio sessions, and restaging a few sequences of Kiedis's vocal performance alone, a new video was pieced together around the reality of a recording session and maybe it did the trick – 'My Friends' went on to top both the Modern Rock and Album Rock charts.

There were further eruptions around the 'Aeroplane' video, a beautifully choreographed modern interpretation of a 1930s Busby Berkeley extravaganza. With a women's water ballet team for the synchronised swimming displays, an army of gum-popping Mexican gang girls, cholas, well-disguised as Las Vegas showgirls, and Clara Balzary's pre-school class to sing and dance along with the end of the song, the video was a riot of colour, action and some genuinely amazing camera work.

But it could have been even more eye-catching, had the band's original vision for the video – with wall-to-wall nudity added to the mix – been permitted to take shape. But, with the lessons of 'Warped' still fresh in the mind, Warners put their foot down there as well, as though to say they were already having a hard enough time selling the band to the general public, without bringing the wrath of the PC police down on their heads as well.

Five years earlier, the Red Hot Chili Peppers had ridden unscathed through the flames of the various controversies they invoked, the accusations of sexist brainlessness and frat-boy misogyny that appeared to follow them every step of the way. But times had changed since then, and audiences had changed with them, abandoning the hedonism that once flew vibrantly across a landscape shaped by Guns N' Roses, Jane's Addiction and the Red Hot Chili Peppers themselves, in favour of a conservatism that was almost puritanical in its attitude towards 'mischief'.

Its precedents were not, ironically, too alien to any of those bands' own upbringings – a decade earlier, the hardcore scene had been ruthlessly sundered by the emergence of the so-called Straight-Edge movement, a brutally self-righteous creed that professed zero tolerance towards drugs, alcohol, even meat-eating and smoking. In only loosely acknowledged tandem with the Rock Against Drugs campaign, it was, in many ways, the ultimate in teen rebellion, the rejection of symbols that had lain at the core of 'mainstream' youth disobedience since the dawn of time, in favour of an attitude which even straight-laced prudes might have considered extreme. And that was what caused it to fade – where is the fun in not having any fun?

But it had never disappeared. Rather, the harsh moralities of Straight Edge simply absorbed themselves into the guilt-laden musings of grunge; the increasingly strident rhetoric of such pompous pontificators as Bono and Sting; and even the fast blurring horizons of the Christian Rock elite, as they strove to break out of their niche and into daylight. And now they were rebounding into the mainstream with a ferocity that was all the more frightening for appearing so benign.

In marketing terms, after all, this new climate meant only that, for better or worse, sensitivity sold – sensitivity for other people's feelings, for other people's moods, for other people's guilt. How far did that sensitivity need to travel, however, before it could be assuaged? And how extreme (as the album's own 'Shallow Be Thy Game' demanded to know) did the corresponding fundamentalism need to become before it crushed the very values that it was supposed to be espousing?

The band members themselves could (and frequently did) argue that much of their own sexual boisterousness was intended as affectionate tribute. But, not only does the public generally see only what it wants to see, it rarely actually thinks about any of it, and the brick wall of misguided morality that the Red Hot Chili Peppers had faced down so many times in the past again loomed before them. Only this time, the stakes were a lot higher; high enough, in fact, to invoke a fear that the group never even imagined in the past, that, perhaps, their time had come and gone; that they were as tired as those other acts that were dribbling to a commercial full stop around them.

Ultimately, the Red Hot Chili Peppers would sidestep the opprobrious oblivion that might have consumed them, the pure spirituality, honesty and openness of both their music and of their individual personalities eventually outweighing what even Flea contemptuously acknowledged as their reputation as 'nutty, zany guys . . . [who] want to party on your pussy'. But it would prove a long, difficult slog, and one that would come close to tearing the group to shreds before it could be resolved.

Around these obstacles, the band hit the road, kicking off their latest world tour at CoreStates Spectrum, Philadelphia, on 6 February 1996, before marching on for 64 shows in 21 different countries. Here, at least, they were on safe ground – although ticket sales were slow, most of the venues sold out, while the sense of insulation that the road naturally provides at least allowed the Red Hot Chili Peppers

to relax into their own chosen universe, of funk, fun and mischief . . .
it is unlikely, for instance, whether Daniel Johns, frontman with the
opening Silverchair, will ever forget the night when the Red Hot Chili
Peppers decided to take charge of his birthday celebrations, by hiring
a pair of strippers to appear onstage alongside him, and perform their
own routine while he tried to keep his mind on his own job.

Another highlight arrived when the band appeared alongside
comedian Ron Brackenridge ('my biggest fear was that I would be
heckled by Santa') at the Molson Ice Polar Beach Party, a webcast
festival staged aboard a Russian ice-breaker anchored in Resolute Bay,
700 miles north of the Arctic Circle. Neither had the so-called 'failure'
of *One Hot Minute* damaged their appeal in other arenas – when MTV
animation stars Beavis and Butthead were transformed to the big
screen, for the hit movie *Beavis and Butthead Do America*, the Red Hot
Chili Peppers were among the very first groups to be approached for
the accompanying soundtrack, and they responded with one of the
finest recordings that this incarnation of the band would ever make,
carving out a dramatic revision of the Ohio Players' 'Love Roller-
coaster'.

Neither was that the extent of their activities – for, if it had been,
its adherence to many of the qualities that had forever been associated
with the group's baser instincts (*Beavis and Butthead* was never the
most socially enlightened of television comedies) might well have
killed the group there and then. The quartet also turned their hands
to a fine version of John Lennon's first solo album-era 'I Found Out',
for inclusion on one of the most worthwhile compilations of the year,
a long-overdue tribute to John Lennon, that also drew attention to one
of the most overdue charitable organisations of the age.

Working Class Hero was the dreamchild of Lindy Goetz, as he threw
himself into Peace, an organisation dedicated to raising funds for, and
awareness of, the need to spay and neuter pets, to battle against the
ever-growing problems of wild and ferrule dogs and cats that now
roamed the environs of LA. The days when true men didn't kill
coyotes were long gone; now, even housewives baited traps for the
abandoned animals that struggled to survive in the cities and the
suburbs – a struggle that Peace believed should never have been
necessary in the first place.

With musical contributions coming in from as far afield as George
Clinton, Candlebox and sundry members of both REM and Pearl Jam,
and with a massive slice of Lennon's legacy being held up for
re-evaluation, *Working Class Hero* represented one of the most

enjoyable of all the myriad tribute albums that rained down during the mid-1990s. But still it was the Red Hot Chili Peppers who walked away with the critical honours, just as – or so their supporters said – they continued walking away with the same grip on a generation's consciousness as Lennon himself possessed.

'I Found Out' certainly emboldened a few listeners to predict that there might still be some life beyond the disappointments of *One Hot Minute*. Unfortunately, as 1996 drained out of the potato-masher, genuine signs of that life were becoming increasingly difficult to detect.

On 20 January 1997, taking a short break from the Red Hot Chili Peppers' own fast-filling schedule for the New Year, Flea and Jane's Addiction/Porno For Pyros drummer Stephen Perkins came together with Rage Against The Machine's Zack de la Rocha and Tom Morello for what they called *Radio Free LA*.

The event had been planned since November, and a Presidential election that was scarred by the lowest-ever voter turn-out in American history – proof, Morello and co. deduced, that mainstream politicking had completely lost touch with the issues that truly engaged the people. *Radio Free LA*, airing on the very night that the re-elected President Bill Clinton celebrated his inauguration with a backslapping beanfeast at the White House, was designed to provide that alternative.

Broadcasting to 60 radio stations across the US from the Sony Studios in LA, the two-hour *Radio Free LA* served up a dramatic fusion of music and confrontational politics, created with the stated intention to 'inform, educate, and organise listeners around socio-political issues while entertaining with music and humour'.

Interviews brought in figures from across the radical political spectrum: Michael Moore, Emily Hodgson, Leonard Peltier, Chuck D, Mumia Abu-Jamal, Noam Chomsky and Subcomandante Marcos of the Zapatistas were all featured. A live phone-in brought calls from death row inmates, while Beck and Cypress Hill both dropped by the studio to perform.

The Peppers/Porno/Rage quartet, meanwhile, took their own opportunity to intersperse the action with their often dramatically rearranged renditions of nine Rage Against The Machine classics. Flea himself never made any secret of his admiration for Morello's band, insisting, 'One time I saw them play – I think it was in Belgium – and there were probably about 30,000 people. I'd never seen anything like it. You could see the whole place moving like a big organism jumping up and down. It was the craziest, most intense thing I've ever seen. It was phenomenal.'

Radio Free LA was a brilliant, brutal performance; more than that, it ignited a partnership that would continue its vivacious sparking as the year continued to unfold. First, Flea and Morello united with Henry Rollins and the rap band Bone Thugs N Harmony, to record a version of the old Motown chestbeater 'War' for the *Small Soldiers* movie soundtrack; soon after, the pair were recruited by Joe Strummer to cut a song for the cult TV show *South Park*'s *Chef Aid* album.

Such activities were also a bright portent of how Flea would find himself spending the remainder of the year, embarking upon a musical journey that took him as far afield as the new album by electro-bluegrass stylist Michael Brook, a TV performance alongside Alaskan songstress Jewel and backing vocals for the rap band Livin' Illegal. For the Red Hot Chili Peppers themselves hadn't simply stalled. They had run into a wall of such colossal bad luck that it seemed they might never get back on a level footing again.

In January, the Red Hot Chili Peppers were announced among the headliners for the 1997 Tibetan Freedom Concert. Weeks later, however, they pulled out with the admission that they weren't sufficiently rehearsed to put on a show; fans were reassured with the knowledge that the band would concentrate instead on preparing for the next leg of their world outing, the summertime *Wild Tour* swing through the Far East. Shows were scheduled in Singapore, Japan, Taipei and Bangkok, before the group hit Hawaii and Alaska, the two non-continental US states that get the raw end of every touring itinerary – but which were favourite destinations for Kiedis and Flea when they fancied getting away from it all.

The sudden hiatus was no bad thing – at least it gave Smith more time to spend with his wife, Maria, following the birth of their daughter, Manon St John, on 3 March. However, even as the band's thoughts did turn again towards work, all their plans were shattered when Kiedis crashed his Harley Davidson motorcycle while out in LA on 13 July. He broke eleven bones in his wrist and, having endured five hours of surgery at Cedars-Mount Sinai Medical Centre, he was left with no alternative but to cancel the Asian shows altogether, and reschedule Honolulu and Anchorage for September.

Just one gig was salvaged from the original *Wild Tour* itinerary, as August saw the Red Hot Chili Peppers cross the Pacific to Japan, to appear at a festival staged on the slopes of Mount Fuji. But a bill that also included Green Day, Beck and the Foo Fighters was already being tossed in the teeth of a fast-brewing storm; with the still-convalescent Kiedis restricted to a stool in centre-stage, the Red Hot Chili Peppers were less than halfway through their set when Typhoon Rosie blew onto the festival site. She was not the most violent storm of the year, but there was no way the concert could continue – and no way back for the Red Hot Chili Peppers either.

Home again, the Red Hot Chili Peppers began planning again for those rescheduled shows in Hawaii and Alaska – at which point Smith came off his Harley Davidson while riding down Sunset Boulevard. He dislocated a shoulder and the gigs were cancelled once again, this time until December. Which is when the band's misfortunes turned full circle, as they confessed that they were again hopelessly under-rehearsed, and pulled out of the concerts altogether.

In twelve months of trying to work, the Red Hot Chili Peppers completed just one project, as Flea, Smith and Navarro, at least, combined to contribute one number, 'I Make My Own Rules', to the soundtrack to comedian Howard Stern's *Private Parts* movie. And even that wasn't exactly a great song.

Another nail was seemingly banged into the band's casket when Lindy Goetz announced his decision to step aside as the group's manager. Having already launched the Peace organisation, he and his wife, Cristine Allen Goetz, were also heavily involved with the non-profit LaGrange County Animal Welfare Association, and that was the direction in which Goetz now wished to turn his full attentions. Even before the group began the search for new management, the knowledge that they would never recapture the in-depth support and tolerance that hallmarked Goetz's service was as chilling as any of the other tests to which the Red Hot Chili Peppers would be put as 1997 passed by.

A lot of bands would have clocked this catalogue of disasters and put it down to bad luck. The Red Hot Chili Peppers, however, had been the butt of so many of Fate's little jokes that they believed they knew better. 'You never get sick for no reason,' Kiedis postulated and, were the group to step back and take a long, hard look at themselves, it might not be too difficult to determine precisely what lay at the root of their illness.

There would be no hasty declarations, no precipitous decision to split the band. But to try and predict any kind of future for the group required an optimism that even Flea was unable to muster. 'There's still a Chili Peppers,' he protested a few months into the hiatus. 'All those rumours about a break-up are bullshit, the kind of stuff that's made up by the press. We'll start writing again, but in our own time. Probably later this year. Maybe not. We'll see how things go.' But, even as Flea confirmed that the Red Hot Chili Peppers would live on, still it was not difficult to visualise an altogether opposite scenario. The group were asleep. And, if that sleep should slip into a coma, so be it.

In July, even as the year's catalogue of calamities began unfolding around him, Flea and another of the architects of *Radio Free LA*, Stephen Perkins, were reunited once again, as Perry Farrell declared the time was right to reacquaint himself with all the promises that Jane's Addiction left unfulfilled the first time around – and which his subsequent activities with Lollapalooza and Porno For Pyros pushed to the back of his mind.

Rumours of some kind of renewed Addiction had been rife for months, ever since Dave Navarro (accompanied by Flea) himself reunited with Farrell during the sessions for the second Porno For Pyros album. The two Peppers were onboard again when Porno cut one more number, 'Hard Charger', for the *Private Parts* movie soundtrack; even as the same team reconvened at the film's premiere, for a wild performance of both that song and the old Jane's chestnut 'Mountain Song', it was evident that something was afoot – and remained so, even after Jane's Addiction's original bassist, Eric Avery, unveiled his own new project, Polar Bear, to the media in April.

His often stormy relationship with Farrell, after all, was frequently cited among the principal reasons behind the group's original split, whereas Flea's friendship with the remaining members of the band had become very public indeed.

The Fourth of July weekend saw further action when Farrell, Perkins, Flea and Navarro performed acoustic versions of Jane's Addiction's 'My Time' and 'Ocean Size' at a Porno For Pyros show in LA, and Perkins admitted, 'after [we recorded] "Hard Charger", we started doing shows. Flea would show up and play with us, Dave would play with us. We couldn't think of a reason not to get together. We loved playing together, and the friendships were sprouting. It was *nice*.' However, even after the news broke in America later that same month, Farrell remained adamant that Jane's Addiction were not re-forming. If anything, they were re*laps*ing, and that became the official name for the tour that was set up for late autumn, the Relapse Tour. In any case, Flea's presence made it plain that this was no simple reunion – how could it be without Avery?

'I was disappointed that Eric didn't want to do this,' Navarro admitted. 'But I completely understand and respect his decision. Eric and I are still friends and we talk regularly, but I love playing with

Flea. There's no one I would rather have in the band if it wasn't Eric.'
His musical relationship with the bassist, he elaborated, was forever
expanding, '. . . constantly forging [ahead]. The way we play together
now, for me, is much more fluid and natural than the way we played
together on *One Hot Minute*.' 'We love Flea,' Perkins agreed. 'He's
taking us in directions we never thought possible.'

Flea was equally voracious in his praise for his new bandmates, but
singled Perkins out for especial praise. 'I'm so lucky to be able to play
with the guys I consider to be probably the two best rock drummers
in the world. There probably are other guys who are really great, but
I can't think of them.

'Stephen Perkins is more ornate and "precious" than Chad –
more involved in beautiful little things . . . I guess the difference is that
Stephen's a pot-head and Chad's a beer-drinking steak eater. Stephen's
playing is more like curlicues and ornate, pretty little things. Chad is
more John Bonham-style smashing. It's weird because Jane's Addiction, on first listening, seems like such a guitar band. A real vocals and
guitar, top-heavy band. But when I think of Jane's Addiction, I think
of it as a total bass-driven band. Like a reggae band or a funk band.'

As for the relapse itself, Navarro continued, 'Things just started to
evolve and fall into place. There are some feelings that have come up
during this project that I'd rather not face, but that's part of the reason
I'm doing this. It's an opportunity to redo some of the things from the
past and do them correctly or do them better. I mean, how many times
in your life do you get a chance to correct the past?'

He was adamant, however, that the project 'wasn't about trying to
put Jane's back together. We just wanted to figure out a way we could
all go on the road and play together again.' But of course it was more
than that. To an audience that, in the seven years since Jane's
Addiction sundered, had seen the group elevated to vast new plateaux
of shimmering legend and renown, there had never been a reunion
like this and, short of Kurt Cobain being miraculously regenerated,
there never could be. The 1990s, so far, had seen shockingly few true
giants arise from the musical swamps; and even fewer whose demise
could truly be said to have made as much of a difference to their fans
as their rise. Jane's Addiction were first among that few and, no sooner
were the tour's 23 scheduled dates announced to the public, than they
sold out, some in record time. Tickets for a two-night stand in New
York vanished within five minutes of going on sale.

After weeks of accelerating anticipation, Jane's Addiction made their
live debut on 24 October 1997 on MTV's *Live at the 10 Spot* concert

series. The following day, the tour kicked off in San Francisco, as Jane's Addiction made their way towards the release of *Kettle Whistle*, an anthology-cum-new album that featured four songs recorded by the latest band line-up. And, with Flea and Navarro apparently revelling in their new surroundings; and Navarro and Chad Smith continuing to sketch a side project of their own, a new band called Spread, the Red Hot Chili Peppers' future continued to be shrouded in doubt.

The string of cancellations and accidents that dogged the band all year long were only one symptom of the malaise that seemed to be sweeping through the ranks. Those allegations of renewed drug use would not lie down, growing so loud that, finally, Kiedis had little alternative but to acknowledge 'these spurts where I would go out and use. And everything would crumble. I'd slip back and forth.' Looking back from later in 1997, he confessed, 'over the last four years, the lion's share of my time has been clean. [But] all it takes is a short while of me using to really get dark and upset the balance.'

The popular grapevine was pointing similar fingers in Dave Navarro's direction as well but, even more alarmingly, supposedly 'informed' sources were delivering further mumblings about his very suitability for the group. No less than Arik Marshall and Jesse Tobias, it's all very well to be good friends and kindred spirits. But, unless that indefinable chemistry that can spark among the most unlikely bandmates is firing on all cylinders, then it doesn't matter how well you get on offstage. The moment you step on, you have to *be* on.

And the truth of the matter was, the Red Hot Chili Peppers were no longer *on*.

The rumours surrounding Dave Navarro grew stronger. So did a series of disquieting reports from the Jane's Addiction tour itself, as the guitarist's loathing for life on the road became more pronounced with every passing day. As 1997 finally faded into welcome oblivion and a New Year got under way, so did the whispering that surrounded his continued involvement in the Red Hot Chili Peppers and, on 3 April 1998, the announcement that everybody had been expecting for three months was finally delivered. Dave Navarro quit the band.

Back around the time of *One Hot Minute*, Smith told *Rolling Stone*, 'We were like *Spinal Tap*, but it was the guitar player that kept exploding.' And why should they break the habit of a lifetime? Adamantly scotching all the rumours that were inevitably flying, most notably, the increasingly threadbare accusation that drugs lay at the foot of the severance, Kiedis moved quickly to insist that Navarro's decision to leave was 'mutual', the result of that old rock'n'roll warhorse 'creative differences'.

Flea agreed, adding that he certainly hoped to work again with this 'epic and beautiful musician and human being. [It] just wasn't working out,' he continued. 'Not his fault, not our fault; it just wasn't working chemically. It wasn't a tangible thing where I can say we did this or he did that; it just wasn't working, and we parted ways with him.'

Navarro, too, placed a happy face on the split. 'The friendships we've established will remain forever eternal,' he said, before comparing his departure to the day he left home at the age of seventeen. The only real difference was that his father 'would have *never* suggested the light bulb costumes'.

Yet there was also a sense of accumulating thunder that overrode even the levity with which the musicians attempted to paint the parting, as Flea took to calling the past twelve months of the Red Hot Chili Peppers' life 'the year of nothing', and began talking aloud of cutting a solo album.

But even in despair, he remained desperate not to allow the Red Hot Chili Peppers to slip away; so desperate that, when he first called up Kiedis to discuss the band's next move, the singer was scarcely able to believe his ears.

'What do you think of playing with John again?'

Kiedis sighed resignedly. 'That would be a dream. But what are the odds that the chemistry would work for even a minute'.

Flea shrugged. 'A million to one.' But, deep down inside, he was willing to wager that the odds would prove much shorter than that.

16. A PERSON PEOPLE THOUGHT OF AS FINISHED

Since John Frusciante left the Red Hot Chili Peppers in 1992, the guitarist had cut a pair of less-than-well-publicised solo albums, 1995's sublimely titled *Niandra Lades and Usually Just a T-Shirt* and 1997's *Smile from the Streets You Hold*. Such activities did little, however, to camouflage the rumours that insisted the guitarist was homeless, penniless and collapsing beneath the burden of a death-defying drug habit. In a profile of Frusciante for Los Angeles' *New Times* in late 1996, writer Robert Wilonsky painted a grim picture of the guitarist as a gifted but tortured artist holed up in the Chateau Marmont Hotel in Hollywood, dangling precariously on the brink of a tragic overdose. His arms were a maze of track marks and abscesses and, bluntly, he admitted to shooting up for the first time immediately after the recording of *Blood Sugar Sex Magik*, and simply carried on from there.

His addiction, he confessed, cost him many of his friends. But the drugs served a purpose as well, helping Frusciante remain buoyant at a time when, with his memories of his tenure with the Red Hot Chili Peppers still fresh in his mind, he was otherwise destined to sink into depression. Now, he insisted, 'I don't care whether I live or die.'

In fact, by the time the story hit the newsstands, he had already decided which option he preferred, checking himself into a rehab clinic and moving rapidly not only towards recovery, but towards a return to playing as well.

It would not be an easy reintroduction. 'I had very little technical skill,' Frusciante conceded to *Kerrang!* in 2001. 'I'd hardly played guitar for five years; I'd mostly been painting. I was a person who people pretty much thought of as finished.' Flea, however, never abandoned him; even promised that, if Frusciante were ever able to clean himself up, they might play together once again. Now the bassist was ready to make good on that pledge.

In March 1997, Frusciante played the Whiskey in LA, alongside the latest reincarnation of Thelonious Monster. Flea was there as well, initially as a mere onlooker, but swiftly as a participant as well, leaping aboard the stage to jam alongside his old bandmate. It was a refreshing experience; soon, Flea was calling in Stephen Perkins to join Frusciante and himself in a new project, the Three Amoebas. The group was never going to amount to anything; in the three months that they spent jamming in Flea's garage, they never moved beyond tape-recording a few sessions. But the Three Amoebas proved that his years out of the spotlight had neither dented Frusciante's abilities, nor dampened his hunger to play. And hunger was the only thing that could ever bring the Red Hot Chili Peppers back together. That, and the friendship that bound the group together across their two greatest albums to date, *Mother's Milk* and *Blood Sugar Sex Magik*.

'I wouldn't be able to make music with the band if we weren't all friends,' Frusciante admitted. 'Being with each other and enjoying each other's presence is important for us to have a positive experience. We love each other, and that love comes out in the music.'

It was true. Even Kiedis, who admitted that he hardly dared accept Flea's endorsement as anything more than wishful thinking, understood that now. In the five years since Frusciante left the band, the singer had seen the guitarist just once, when he visited him in rehab following the Red Hot Chili Peppers' Mount Fuji debacle. And, even then, his visit had nothing to do with music. 'It was because I was happy that he was considering coming back to our world,' the singer reported. But once they did come face to face again, 'it felt amazing. Whatever happened before, it was all over with.'

A tentative jam session was arranged, just the four of them in Flea's garage – no pressure, no expectations, no sweat. And that was all it took. 'From the first time we got together to play,' Kiedis marvelled later, 'I felt completely levitated.'

Kiedis himself had undergone a form of spiritual renewal during the past year. The disappointments over the manner in which the Red Hot Chili Peppers' own career unfolded during 1997 were placed wholly into context when, finally despairing of achieving anything musical, the singer took himself off on a pilgrimage to India. Once there, he determined to make his own way by road, train and foot from the north of the country to the south, to absorb himself in the culture of the subcontinent, just as he had on a similar journey five years before, when he travelled to Indonesia and Borneo.

On that earlier adventure, Kiedis was mortified to discover that, no matter how far he travelled from home, home was always awaiting him when he arrived; horrified to visit marketplaces in the most out-of-the-way locations, to be confronted with the same T-shirts and CDs he left behind on the streets of LA.

'California had found a way to seep into these tiny nooks and crannies of the globe and affect people.' Now, however, he discovered a way in which to deal with the sensations of saturation that he knew he would encounter.

In between the wealth of adventures that he would experience as he travelled . . . the train derailment that almost crushed him between the wheels of two carriages, as he hung in between them to watch the landscape fly past; the long walk to visit a guru who was out of town when he got there . . . Kiedis cleared his mind by writing the song that would usher in not only the new age of the Red Hot Chili Peppers, but also a new sense of purpose within the group itself.

'Californication,' he explained, was 'about California and Hollywood having such a profound effect on the planet, of the good and the bad of that. Of how people dream of this weird, magical place that is really kind of the end of the world, the Western Hemisphere's last stop.' More than that, 'Californication' was a ruthless examination of the spread of American culture to cultures that should have had no need for it, the tale of the land that lies 'at the edge of the world', in the words of the band that was likewise positioned. It was also the very first song the band tried working on, following Frusciante's return to the fold.

Flea is adamant that it was 'a communal decision' to bring Frusciante back. But, he conceded, 'I've always been close to John and [I've] always done my best to be supportive of him no matter what he's doing. So it makes me happy just to see him doing well.'

'The way they took me back made me feel good about myself,' Frusciante continued. 'I had very little ability, but it didn't matter to them. It was just the spirit of what I was doing and the fact that it was me. It felt so good to have friends who really believed in me when nobody else did.'

The quartet continued to simply play together in Flea's garage, almost unwilling to disturb the magic of the moment by transferring their activities any place else. 'The chemistry was bombastic and beautiful,' Kiedis recalled, while Smith was similarly enthusiastic. 'It was really hot, and we just jammed. That's what we always did, and that's what was kind of lacking with Dave [Navarro]. Dave wasn't [into] a real jamming situation for our band. It's really important to just get in a room and make noise. A lot of times, a lot of our songs come out of that.'

Flea agreed, telling NYRock, 'we improvise a lot. We find a groove. We experiment and somehow it turns into music. With Dave, it wasn't possible to work like this. With him, it was more like a long thought process, endless discussions and it took a long time. We talked about what riff should be played and all that. With John it's completely different. We just play. I don't mean to dis Dave in any way. He is a great person and he's a great guitarist, but the way we work is just different. You never know why it happens with some people and not with others. It's pointless. It's like asking why you fall in love. There is no real reason, nothing that can be explained or that would make sense.'

But they were not going to push their luck. One of the reconvened band's first moves was, in true Red Hot Chili Pepper style, to put all thoughts of their career to one side and strike out for the wilderness. Smith was occupied elsewhere, but Kiedis, Frusciante and Flea piled into the bassist's truck, and headed out to Big Sur to surf. Not one of the trio was what you could call an experienced surfer but, as Kiedis put it, still it's hard to beat the thrill of 'getting up with the sunrise and paddling out'.

Of course they brought some guitars with them and, seated around the campfire they built on the beach, while Flea and Frusciante played, Kiedis wrote. Nobody was surprised when the first song out of his pen was one that captured that very moment forever, the fact that 'we were together after all this time, and doing something as pure as surfing and writing music.' 'Road Trippin'', as he titled the song, noted the presence of 'my two favourite allies' in its very first line; and, when it came time to shoot a video to accompany the song, it was the mood of that trip that the group strove to recapture, borrowing architect Harry Gessler's Malibu home, and surfing and singing their way through the shoot.

Frusciante's return was made official on 29 April 1998, just 26 days after Navarro's departure was reported and, even from the other end of an e-mail, one could sense the excitement with which the band's own associates viewed the reunion. Talking to *Rolling Stone*, David Katznelson, Warner Brothers' VP of A&R (and CEO of Birdman Records, which released Frusciante's *Smile from the Streets You Hold*) enthused, '[it's] a good thing for them. He's still a great guitar player, and I don't think people realise the significant part that John played in the Chili Peppers' sound. He wrote the music for "Under the Bridge" and "Breaking the Girl". It's great to get him in a room and hear him play the original version of "Breaking the Girl" . . . it's beautiful.'

As for the guitarist's now readily documented problems, he simply shrugged them away. 'He's in a good way right now. Flea wouldn't work with him if he wasn't clean.'

For the first time in a long time, the Red Hot Chili Peppers seemed complete. Around the same time as Frusciante's return was made public, the band unveiled their new management, the Q Prime company established by Peter Mensch and former Mercury records exec Cliff Burnstein. Smashing Pumpkins, Hole and Madonna had all passed through the company's books over the years; among the others whom the Red Hot Chili Peppers could now count as their stablemates, Metallica and Def Leppard were surely the most deafeningly prominent. It was all a long way from knocking around Lindy Goetz's office with their friends from Thelonious Monster but, the Red Hot Chili Peppers now understood, so were they.

The new line-up made its comeback with a special twelve-song performance and interview for KBLT radio on 5 June – the set, which stretched back to the first album's 'Police Helicopter' in search of material, closed with a fiery version of Black Flag's 'Nervous Breakdown' and any doubts that the band had placed past disappointments – *One Hot Minute* included – behind them were swept away an instant. 'It's definitely going to sound a lot more like what I did in the band than what Dave did,' Frusciante reflected on the roar that arced so gracefully out of LA radio that evening. 'As far as the funk, it should have a really heavy aspect of that. I don't really play that kind of heavy metal stuff.'

The following week, the Red Hot Chili Peppers took the stage at Washington, DC's, tiny 9.30 Club on 12 June 1998, the evening before they were scheduled to headline the latest Tibetan Freedom Concert at the same city's Robert F Kennedy Memorial Stadium. Deep within the sweaty confines of a venue they'd not visited since *Mother's Milk* was still fresh, it was a triumphant return, for the band in general and for Frusciante in particular, as the past six years of separation sloughed away as though they had never happened.

At the stadium the following day, however, all was chaos as a freak summer storm slammed into the crowd of 60,000 during Herbie Hancock and the Head-hunters' set. A lightning strike saw one fan raced to hospital, leaving the organisers, represented by Adam Yauch and REM's Michael Stipe, with no alternative but to announce that the rest of the show was cancelled.

Wherever possible, bands that had been scheduled to play on the Saturday were pushed over to the Sunday, but Red Hot Chili Peppers fans were to be left disappointed as it became apparent that there was no way to slide them into the revised running order. REM – playing their first-ever concert without drummer Bill Berry, the Beastie Boys and Pearl Jam closed the show but, as the crowd was pouring out of the gates, the Red Hot Chili Peppers appeared after all, leaping onto the stage for an absolutely impromptu fifteen-minute set. There was time for just three songs, 'Give It Away', 'Under the Bridge' and 'Power of Equality', and, as the first notes fed through the PA, 60,000 people did an about-turn and raced back into the arena. A lot of them were already kicking themselves for having missed the 9.30 Club show. They weren't going to make that same mistake again.

Days later, on 17 June, the revitalised Red Hot Chili Peppers were in New York, appearing at the Bowery Ballroom, just around the corner from the old punk hang-out CBGBs; then it was back to LA for the *Waiting for Iggy* benefit at Mogul's in Hollywood on 25 June. *Waiting for Iggy* itself was writer Susie McDonnell's well-regarded stage play about an all-girl punk band that opens for the legendary Pop on tour in the early 1980s, and the benefit, raising funds for McDonnell to rent a theatre in which to produce the play, attracted a wealth of local punk-celebrity benefactors, including Bob Forrest and the Circle Jerks' Keith Morris, all serving up their own interpretation of Iggy classics.

The Red Hot Chili Peppers themselves performed five. A solo Frusciante opened the show with acoustic renditions of 'Neighbourhood Threat' and 'China Girl', before the remainder of the band bounded on for brutal assaults on 'Loose' and '1970', from the Stooges' ever-seminal *Funhouse* album, and the inevitable 'Search and Destroy'.

To a world that was expecting nothing less than the total collapse of the Red Hot Chili Peppers, the band's return – and the rave reviews that accompanied their every step – was nothing short of Lazarus-like. Neither was their rebirth confined to domestic soil. Without the Red Hot Chili Peppers even setting foot on the continent, the band's European profile was soaring as high as their American status, thanks to a UK chart-topping cover of 'Under the Bridge,' by the all-girl singing group All Saints.

Behind the scenes, too, the mood was buoyant. Though he maintained a stoic silence on the subject, Flea had felt his own personal life unravelling, even as his professional life was getting back on track; there were moments, he subsequently confessed, when he simply found himself curled up 'in the foetal position, crying'. For the first time in a long time, however, he was able to balance his pain with the joy of seeing the Red Hot Chili Peppers firing on all cylinders once again. 'There were times when we were playing, I'd be thinking, "Man, I hurt so bad." I was saying these mantras to myself. "You really hurt right now. But play this music, because it's good." '

Kiedis, too, was adamant that the 'troubled times' were over, admitting that it was easy for him to forget that Frusciante had ever been out of the band. At the same time, however, 'I get reminded of it all the time. I'll run into Dave Navarro out in front of a restaurant, or some kooky kid will come up to me on the streets of San Francisco and say, "Oh, I love *One Hot Minute*. That was my favourite." And I'm like, "Really?" '

In fact, it swiftly became apparent that, so far as the Red Hot Chili Peppers were concerned, *One Hot Minute* could be all but expunged from their repertoire. Nothing from that album had entered into the group's (admittedly abbreviated) live shows so far, and, Flea's solo 'Pea' aside, it looked highly unlikely that anything would.

The quartet launched into prep work for a new Red Hot Chili Peppers album in July 1998, taking over what was once one of LA's most legendary studios, United Western – now renamed Ocean Way Recording – and, within three weeks, completing at least the instrumental tracks for a staggering 28 new songs. The only cloud on the horizon, they joked, was that Flea, Smith and Frusciante were so hot that Kiedis was genuinely struggling to keep up with them.

'A lot of the [new] songs started as jams,' Flea announced proudly. 'As soon as John came back into the band, we jammed in my garage all summer.' Kiedis, however, professed himself unimpressed. 'You guys might be able to bang out an instrumental a day,' he'd curse. 'It's not so easy coming up with lyrics to fit them!'

Once again, Rick Rubin was back at the controls, although it was a close-run thing. Having approached him early on in the process, and received a heartfelt yes, the band then had second thoughts and announced that they wanted to continue looking at other producers. Rubin, a little taken aback though he was, stepped back down – apparently, he even recommended a few other names that the group might want to investigate. But, even as the Red Hot Chili Peppers deliberated, one thought continued nagging at them. A glorious return to the days of the full *Blood Sugar Sex Magik* team was at their fingertips. They would be fools to turn their back on it – for who knew how long it would remain available?

More than that, Flea's own relationship with the heavily bearded producer had only grown stronger in the years since *Blood Sugar Sex Magik* first introduced them. Time and again, as Rubin set out on a new project, he would call Flea in to guest some bass onto the proceedings, be it Mick Jagger's first decent solo album, 1993's *Wandering Spirit*, or the latest in Rubin's unexpectedly productive partnership with Johnny Cash, 1996's *Unchained*. He was even able to find Flea and Chad Smith a berth alongside Queen, when he was invited to undertake some remix work as they prepared to unleash remastered versions of their back catalogue. Roger Taylor and John Deacon were no slouches when it came to laying down an earthquake rhythm. But even they were left aghast as the two Peppers rammed through an extended jam at the conclusion of the anthemic 'We Will Rock You'.

Receiving the band's recall, Rubin's own enthusiasm for the Red Hot Chili Peppers' latest project remained undiluted. 'They had been writing a lot,' he recalled. 'They hadn't made a record in a while, which was a positive thing. There was a lot of energy there; they were ready.' Neither was he willing to broach any comparisons with the first time he'd worked with the group. Back then, after all, 'they'd never really had any success. They hadn't broken through and dealt with all the bullshit that comes with being a big band. They're more grown-up now than they were then.'

It was Kiedis, however, who best summed up the state of affairs as the Red Hot Chili Peppers prepared to launch themselves back into the fray. 'If I've learned anything through the freaky tribulations of [the past year-or-so], it's that all of the setbacks, all of the losses and all of the gains, it's all for a reason. And things turned out just the way they were supposed to. I don't think we would have what we have right now, if all that messed-up stuff hadn't happened.'

Although the studio consumed much of their attention for the remainder of 1998, the Red Hot Chili Peppers continued to be visible. The weekend of 5/6 September found them in Las Vegas for a so-called *One Hot Weekend* that would allow them to give trial runs to a clutch of the new songs; 'I Like Dirt', 'Emit Remmus' and the gentle 'Scar Tissue' were all reeled out across the course of the weekend, together with the latest instalments in the band's ever-expanding canon of carefully chosen and ever-eccentric covers – the Jackson Five's 'I Want You Back', Fugazi's 'Long Division' and Elton John's 'Your Song'.

The group broke cover again in May 1999, this time in reaction to the Columbine High School shootings of the previous month, when two students marched into their Littleton, Colorado, school and opened fire on their classmates. By the time the bullets stopped flying, a dozen pupils, one teacher and both gunmen had died.

The fall-out from the shootings was as inevitable as it was tragic, with the usual array of right-wing commentators lining up to shoot fish in the barrel of blameworthy targets, and quickly settling (of course) not on a society that could breed such killers in the first place, but at the music which, allegedly, so warped their minds as to make massacres seem mundane. Gothic and Industrial, those electro-tinged half-breeds whose own preoccupations with aggression, violence and death readily painted a target on their own foreheads, were first before the firing squad but, across the music scene in general, the immediate guilt of *could we have changed things* rapidly gave way to the more realistic question, *can we change things*?

Within a month of the shootings, the Red Hot Chili Peppers announced a six-city *Teen Tolerance* tour, with high-school fans from each city along the route being asked to contribute their own solutions to the growing problem of school violence. Plans for such an outing had, in fact, been in the works for some time; the Peppers originally intended to stage a *High School Spirit* tour, in which their biggest fans in each city (as adjudged by radio competitions) would be awarded a private show at a club for his or her high school; Phil Manning, at Seattle's KNDD 'modern rock' radio station explained, 'we were already in conversations with the Red Hot Chili Peppers to do a free concert for high school students, but . . . the situation in Colorado forced us to rethink it, because we thought that wasn't the proper message, and we wanted to do something to raise positive awareness.'

Throughout the second half of May, the *Teen Tolerance* tour visited Portland, Seattle, Minneapolis, Pontiac and Philadelphia, while the Red Hot Chili Peppers also slid a handful of radio festivals into their itinerary – and swiftly discovered that the problems of violence were by no means exclusive to schools. In Chicago on 22 May 1999, for the New World Music Theater's Q101 Jamboree, a garbage-throwing near-riot by fans of the supporting Offspring saw the Red Hot Chili Peppers forced to execute an abbreviated set and, presumably, look forward to their next encounter with the SoCal punks, the following weekend at Baltimore radio WHFS's tenth annual HFStival, with considerably less enthusiasm than they might normally.

There, too, the Red Hot Chili Peppers were scheduled to appear immediately after the Offspring, and it was with considerable relief that the headliners were able to take the stage at the appointed time, without needing to wade hip-deep through tossed garbage first. Granted a police escort to the stadium, where 75,000 fans (plus Flea's mother and daughter) awaited them, the Red Hot Chili Peppers paraded an hour-long set that was already accommodating the best of their newest material, weeks before anybody would actually get a chance to hear it on CD. But only an hour's worth. Heedless of other acts' insistence upon dragging their live show out for two hours or more, the Red Hot Chili Peppers remained steadfast that an hour, an hour and a half tops, was the optimum length for the show and, though outsiders might have sniped at that insistence *before* they saw the band play, afterwards it was another matter entirely. No one would have had the energy to deal with anything more.

A battery of other shows at home and abroad carried the Red Hot Chili Peppers through the remainder of the spring and into summer, including a clutch of European festivals and, very pertinently, a benefit for the Musicians' Assistance Program, a charitable organisation dedicated to providing assistance for musicians requiring treatment for drug and alcohol addiction, regardless of their financial status.

The itinerary climaxed, however, on what was widely regarded as the biggest stage of them all, Woodstock 99 – the inevitable successor to the 1994 event; and the one that took every last dire prophecy of disaster to have been aired five years previous, and exploded them up to gargantuan proportions. Marking, this time, the thirtieth anniversary of the original event, planning for the occasion was under way even before the clean-up teams finished mopping up the 25th. 'Woodstock has become the Olympics of live music,' announced co-organiser Michael Long. 'Every five years we can step out of ourselves and celebrate diversity, great music and each other.'

But Woodstock 99 was a long way from Woodstock 94, let alone 69 – both physically (Rome, NY, is nowhere near Woodstock itself) and spiritually. Peace and love, the much-bandied watchwords of the Woodstock generation, have always come at a price of course, but $150 per ticket and $4 for a bottle of water at the height of a scorching late July was asking a lot of even the most committed pacifist, particularly at the end of a decade which had seen the very concept of a rock festival turned on its head.

No longer content to simply sit in a field (or, in this case, a former air-force base) and get off on the vibes (man), the Woodstock 99 generation wanted distraction, needed amusement, demanded excitement. And, if the festival organisers weren't going to provide those things, the audience was going to find them anyway. Moby hit one of the nails on the head when he told the BBC, 'you don't have a festival based on peace and love, and invite Kid Rock and Insane Clown Posse'. And so it transpired. Of all the flashpoints during the three-day event, the most serious occurred during appearances by bands whose very existence was founded on aggression. A rehabilitation counsellor,

David Schneider, later reported witnessing a gang rape while Korn were performing, while another rape was alleged during Limp Bizkit's set.

Later, it was pointed out that Woodstock was not the only legendary festival celebrating its thirtieth anniversary that year. On 6 December 1969, the Rolling Stones wound up their latest, greatest, tour of North America with a free concert at a disused speedway stadium in Livermore, CA. It was not their first choice of venue; originally scheduled for the better-appointed Sears Point Raceway, the organisers discovered just twenty hours before showtime that the site was no longer available. They moved to the only other feasible site and, in so doing, they presented the lexicon of rock'n'roll with a new word. That word was Altamont.

Nobody celebrated the thirtieth anniversary of Altamont, or the one murder, several rapes and countless beatings which occurred as the Stones' Hell's Angels security team kept the peace with pool cues and meaty fists; no misguided promoter sat up late at night on the telephone, inviting the cream of modern rock to come and re-create a night which has gone down in history as the darkest in the annals of rock'n'roll festivals.

But, as the fire tenders arrived to quench the thirteen conflagrations blazing across the Woodstock 99 festival grounds; as the police received the first reports of assault from still tearful young women; and the paramedics took away the last of the 120 hospital cases collected over the three-day weekend, including one man who was crushed beneath a toppled van, it was not too hard to imagine that someone, somewhere, got their anniversaries muddled up.

Arriving at the festival grounds just three hours before they were scheduled to play, the Red Hot Chili Peppers seemed to miss the majority of the problems that beset the event. Flea subsequently noted that he didn't know 'about all those fires and vandalism and shit, it all felt good to me . . . I feel like I can usually tell if the energy at a gig is dangerous or volatile, and it just did not feel that way to me.'

Other observers, however, noted how many of the fires were ignited while the Red Hot Chili Peppers themselves were on stage; were, in some cases, sparked by the band's own choice of closing number, Jimi Hendrix's 'Fire'. Indeed, as the band came out for the encore, recreating Jimi Hendrix's thirty-year-old showstopping mangling of 'Star Spangled Banner', Kiedis's own first words were 'Holy Shit, it looks like *Apocalypse Now* out there.'

But still Flea insisted that his only objections to the audience's behaviour were hatched as he watched the groping going on in the mosh-pit: 'I . . . didn't like [it] when guys would grab at the girls who had their tops off. Guys think . . . about girl tits all day and finally the girls are nice and free enough to let them flow and guys abuse the beauty of it all by groping without invitation . . . some nerve . . .' And, as for the performance itself, '[it] was a fucking gas. We rocked, had fun and got the fuck out of there before we knew what had happened.'

Repeating the schedule of five years previously, the Red Hot Chili Peppers followed their performance at America's most legendary festival with a slot in Britain, as they moved onto the Reading Festival – via a trip to Moscow where Flea, the eternal sightseer, paid a visit to the home of author Mikhail Bulgakov, once regarded among the Soviet Union's most dangerous dissidents (even posthumously, his books were banned), but since rehabilitated as one of Russia's greatest treasures, and a solid building block in the mythology of rock'n'roll as well. His best-known work, *The Master And Margarita*, was the inspiration behind the Rolling Stones' 'Sympathy for the Devil', and the tatty apartment building where he once lived is smeared in the graffiti of both that band's fans and his own.

The visit was documented among the very first 'Fleamails' that Flea (of course) contributed to the Red Hot Chili Peppers eponymous website, blueprinting what would soon develop into a wonderfully illuminating journey through the bassist's musical, literary and, occasionally, political beliefs for anybody who cared to follow. This stage of that quest, however, was perhaps tinged with just a little disappointment. Although visiting the house 'was a very touching experience', he would have preferred a shrine that was not littered with 'the puddles of urine left by all [Bulgakov's] literary fans'.

The 'Fleamails' were not the only innovation sparked by red-hotchilipeppers.com – which itself is partly operated by Kiedis's father, Blackie Dammett. With the recording and mixing finally at an end, the group's new album, *Californication,* itself would make history-of-sorts when the Red Hot Chili Peppers joined with fellow Q-Prime management clients, Def Leppard, to become the first bands of what industry analysts described as 'their calibre' to post entire albums online prior to their release.

Streaming through the website, *Californication* was premiered with three new songs a day for five days, a move that Q-Prime claimed was precipitated by their own realisation that fans no longer purchased new music based on hearing one single on the radio. Neither were there any fears of piracy – the music was coded in such a way that it could not be downloaded and Warner Bros' spokesman Bob Merlis admitted that, 'as with any Internet promotion, we were concerned about security. But we felt good about this. Getting airplay is getting airplay, you just have to define air.'

Heavily covered in the media as it was, the Internet promotion clearly helped the album's launch. *Californication* entered the US chart at No. 3, lining up alongside Smash Mouth's *Astro Mouth* as one of just two new releases to make that week's Top 10. Neither was the group's success to be limited to the album alone. Completely burying all memories of the sad performance of 'Warped', the first single from the new set, 'Scar Tissue', rose to No. 9 at home, No. 15 in the UK, and spent longer at the pinnacle of *Billboard*'s Modern Rock Tracks chart than any other song in history.

It rode in, too, on a magnificent video, a reunion with 'Give It Away' director Stephane Sednaouri, that put into pictures all that the band members experienced over the past five years. Beaten, bruised and bleeding, the quartet were filmed driving through the desert, their instruments broken and their bodies battered . . . but never slowing down, never giving up. The symbolism was heavy, but it was effective nevertheless, and the Red Hot Chili Peppers were rewarded with one of their most successful singles yet.

Further singles 'Around the World', 'Otherside' and the Europe-only 'Road Trippin'' were similar hits and, when the year's honours were totted up in early 2000, the Red Hot Chili Peppers found themselves nominated for no less than three Grammys, for Best Rock Album, Best Rock Song and Best Rock Performance. There was a more-or-less clean sweep at the dedicated rock'n'roll award ceremonies, too, with MTV further honouring the band by presenting them with the Video Vanguard Award, the music video industry's equivalent of the Oscars Lifetime Achievement token. There was even a gong for Blackie Dammett and his fellow web-weavers, as redhotchilipeppers.com won the first ever Best Artist Website award.

Everywhere one looked, *Californication* was a massive success, its impact amplified only the more when compared to the 'failure' of *One Hot Minute*, and Flea could not resist celebrating. '*Blood Sugar Sex Magik* was our fifth album; after that we were the "guys of the moment". Tattoos, cheeky comments, cool clothes or sometimes none at all, fat cars, all that stuff.'

By 1995–96, however, 'we weren't cool cats anymore, there were already Limp Bizkit and co. around. Therefore, we only had our music to offer and this is why we were so incredibly happy about our [current] success! A Britney Spears album is bought for two reasons:

The girls get fashion tips from the booklet, the boys use it for masturbating. I am very happy that our music is bought for different reasons, and I think it's better for business in general.'

Talking with *CDNow*, he hypothesised, 'if you eliminated *One Hot Minute* and made another record after *Blood Sugar Sex Magik*, it would be this record. This record picked up right where we left off with *Blood Sugar*, and I think we've grown a lot. It's a much more dynamic record. It's got a much more diverse array of sounds and feelings. It's just a very happy thing for us.'

Even the title, *Californication*, no longer bugged him as much as he'd originally thought. He was, he admitted, 'a little hesitant' that the implications contained within such a title would peg them once again as 'these California sex guys . . . Really, it's not about us guys being macho California studs at all. That's the last thing it's about.'

Rather, the song's condemnation of Hollywood's – and, by extension, American culture's – malign influence upon the rest of the world was more appropriately aligned with the Red Hot Chili Peppers' own burgeoning role as champions for an ever-widening litany of social causes, from their already well-documented support for the Tibetan struggle, through their long-standing championing of animal rights and ecological concerns, and onto their tireless presence in the world of local, LA-area, benefits and campaigns.

17. TIME TO SHOW A LITTLE LOVE BACK

Despite the massive reversal of the group's apparently plummeting commercial fortunes that was bound up in *Californication*'s reception and success, the following months nevertheless found the Red Hot Chili Peppers become involved in a series of bizarre situations and controversies.

The bizarre first – although it is not the incident that strikes one as peculiar, so much as the fact that it actually made the news. On 19 November 1999, *Rolling Stone* asked, 'How desperate are some people to get into the pants of their favourite rock star?' before reporting how a fan in Milan, Italy, sneaked into the Red Hot Chili Peppers' dressing room and stole Flea's favourite turquoise slacks. They were returned after Flea offered up a no-questions-asked reward of a permanent place on the band's guest list.

Confounding to some, too, was the group's continued failure (some said 'outright refusal') to include any material from *One Hot Minute* in their live repertoire, a decision that angered fans and apparently drew some withering commentary from a jilted Dave Navarro as well. The Red Hot Chili Peppers compensated fans for the omissions, however, with sets that delved in and out of the remainder of their back catalogue, looted their record collections for occasional surprises, and even acknowledged Frusciante's own solo activities with a performance of 'Usually Just a T-Shirt No. 3', from *Niandra Lades and Usually Just a T-Shirt*.

The greatest excitement, however – at least in the eyes of a media that had long since grown fat on the petty rivalries that occasionally bubble up between bands – came when Kiedis celebrated the tenth anniversary of his feud with Faith No More frontman Mike Patton . . . by reigniting it.

For Patton, much had changed in the past decade. Riding the success of *The Real Thing* through the summer of 1990, Faith No More were a featured attraction at festivals as far afield as Reading in England and Monsters Of Rock in Italy. A 37-city American tour with Billy Idol cemented their rise and, in January 1991, Faith No More played the massive Rock In Rio II festival in Brazil.

Loudly proclaimed one of the most eagerly awaited albums of the age, Faith No More's next album, *Angel Dust*, was released in June 1992, while the band toured with Guns N' Roses and Metallica. Their European success, too, was now immense, with Patton's personal star high enough to enable him to reactivate the band he used to play with, Mr Bungle, and launch them, too, as a commercially going concern. A suave cover of Lionel Ritchie and the Commodores' 'Easy' kept the Faith No More pot boiling, while there was also a hit collaboration with Boo Yaa Tribe, 'Another Body Murdered'.

However, sessions for Faith No More's next album were shaken by personnel changes and the ensuing *King for a Day, Fool for a Lifetime* album marked the beginning of the end for Faith No More. The group cut one final CD, *Album of the Year*, and toured through 1998. But they had split by the new year, returning Patton full time to Mr Bungle as they worked towards their own third album, *California*.

That in itself was to prove problematic. Having settled upon the album's title, Mr Bungle had already decided on a June 1999 release date when news came through that the Red Hot Chili Peppers' next album, with its decidedly similar title, was scheduled for issue on that same date. And no prizes, Mr Bungle's advisors mused, for guessing which one would be left behind in the nomenclatural confusion. *California* was delayed for six weeks, and the band got on with scheduling their next tour.

'We were looking at booking some Mr Bungle shows in Europe this past summer, some big festivals, which is something we'd never done before,' Patton told the Chicago listings magazine, *The Onion*. 'We figured it'd be a good thing. We'd get to play in front of a lot of people who wouldn't otherwise hear us. Our agent was in the process of booking these festivals, and it was becoming apparent that we'd landed some pretty good ones – one in France, another one in Holland, some big-name festivals.' And then, suddenly, they started to un-land them. Shows where Mr Bungle were destined to share the bill with the Red Hot Chili Peppers were now deciding that such a combination was no longer desirable.

Guitarist Trey Spruance continued, 'We were booked, months in advance, to do eleven festival dates in Europe. Come summer, we get a call from the three biggest of those festivals, all of them the same day, saying that we can't play, because the headlining band retains the right to hire and fire whomever they wish. We found out it was the Red Hot Chili Peppers, so our manager called their manager to find out what the hell was going on, and their manager was very apologetic, and said, "We're really sorry, we want you to know this doesn't reflect the management's position, or the band's for that matter, it's Anthony who wants this." '

Wearily, and thoroughly bemused, Patton sighed, 'there's nothing I can do about [any of] it. All I can really do is laugh. Or talk shit in the press, I suppose . . . which I guess is what I'm doing right now.' In fact, there was something the aggrieved Mr Bungle could do – and, that Halloween 1999 they did it, as they staged their own personal 'tribute' to the Red Hot Chili Peppers in Pontiac, Michigan, just down the road from Kiedis's hometown. Copping their rivals' most exaggerated stage moves, faking hardcore drug use and parroting back Kiedis's own past comments about Patton, band and audience alike had a wonderful time roasting the Peppers – but now the gloves were off.

Still denying that he had anything to do with Mr Bungle's earlier festival misfortunes, Kiedis was nevertheless incensed by reports of the Michigan show and, this time, he resolved to really do something about it. The two bands were scheduled to appear together at the Australian Big Day Out festival in the New Year, and Kiedis insisted, 'I would not have given two fucks if they played with us there. But after I heard about [the] Halloween show where they mocked us, and read another interview where Patton talked shit about us . . . I was like, you know what, fuck him and fuck the whole band.' Soon after, Mr Bungle heard the news. They were out of the Big Day Out.

For the Red Hot Chili Peppers, this first show of the new millennium was an absolute triumph, and the most intense warm-up imaginable for what was already shaping up to be a frenetic year of touring. Further gigs followed across Japan (headlining Tokyo's legendary Budokan), Australia and New Zealand, with the band determined to keep in touch with the folk back home by arranging to produce their own 'reality TV' show, a weekly ten-minute Internet broadcast that would combine exclusive live footage with behind-the-scenes action.

Masterminded by the z.com website, and set to continue on from the Oceania gigs, to the latter stages of the band's American tour, the series 'webisodes' eventually degenerated into little more than a succession of backstage visits from a succession of trendy guests: actor/comedian Chris Rock; actor/activist Woody Harrelson; environmental activist Julia 'Butterfly' Hill; spiritualist Caroline Myss; motivational author Dr Wayne Dyer; jazz musician John Lurie; and so on.

Little of the ensuing footage and conversation proved especially edifying; little justified Kiedis's pre-show promise that 'it's time to let the freaks into your house'. But still, at a time when most bands still saw the Internet as an as-yet untapped means of sucking further cash out of their most besotted fans, the Red Hot Chili Peppers were proving that communication can sometimes be as valuable as consumerism.

The Red Hot Chili Peppers returned to the US in February 2000, to begin preparing for the first stage of a marathon American tour, spread across half a dozen intense legs of concerts that would reach to the end of the year. Impressive, too, was their decision to share the limelight not with some up-and-coming band of unknowns, but with a group whose own public profile was almost as vast as their own, Dave Grohl's Foo Fighters.

The first 49 shows, running between late March and mid-May, and then through June and July, brought that bill to bear, a double-header package that raised further eyebrows when it swooped not into those cities that every tour itinerary stopped off at, but at the so-called 'b'-list of smaller cities around the country. Then, when the Foo Fighters dropped off the bill, the Red Hot Chili Peppers simply added Fishbone, the reformed Stone Temple Pilots (and, later, former Thelonious Monster frontman Bob Forrest's Bicycle Thief) to the bill, and marched on, breaking only to shoot a superb computer-game style video to accompany their latest single, 'Californication', with Jonathan Dayton and Valerie Ferris. There would be more filming as the tour played on – under the eye of director Wayne Isham, the Portland, Oregon, show was shot in its entirety for release the following year as the *Off The Map* DVD.

Neither did the end of the tour, in September 2000, spell any opportunity for rest, as the group edged instead into the battery of award ceremonies and one-off appearances that were now as integral a part of the year's-end calendar as regular concerts are throughout the other months. But, of course, there was room for eruptions within the smoothly flowing clockwork machine.

The routine commenced with the MTV Music Awards, the band's five nominations a cause for celebration that was instead transformed into a war of nerves as Flea argued first with Kiedis during the rehearsals, and then with his bass during the performance itself. The sound kept cutting out, was lost altogether during the final verse of the song, and Flea, resplendent in a newly coined 'Blow me I'm Famous' T-shirt, ended the number with a volley of shouted 'Fuck's.

His words were not broadcast and, as it transpired, the malfunction was only audible on stage. But still Flea's tantrums shook him sufficiently for him to confess all in a 'Fleamail' and conclude, 'maybe I need to have some good healthy sex' – an off-hand comment that provoked such a response that, in his next posting a few days later, the bemused bassist could only marvel at the absolute sea-change that had enveloped the band's universe. A decade previously, after all, such a confession would have provoked an avalanche of ribald sympathy. Now, it unleashed nothing but dismay and outrage, as that conservative army of fans whose tolerance seemed so essential to the band's very survival back around the time of *One Hot Minute* rose again to grumble at the Red Hot Chili Peppers' profligacy.

'The last time I wrote a Fleamail, I mentioned something about wanting to have sex,' Flea wrote. 'And people seemed to have responded to that in a strange way . . . I hear things here and there about my Fleamails, but that came back to me a lot, everyone mentioning it to me with some weird angle about why I would write that. People are so obsessed with sex, [but] it's only sex . . . what's the big deal? I just wrote down a feeling I was having, without thinking about it. Relax, it is fine.'

The end of October brought the group back into action as they lined up alongside the Foo Fighters, Tom Petty and the ever-tiresome Dave Matthews Band for the Fourteenth annual Bridge School Benefit concerts. There, the arena-style show that the Red Hot Chili Peppers had long since perfected was stripped back to smoky nightclub fashion, to amplify only the casual sensitivity and sensuousness that lay at the heart of the group's most personal work. Neither did the surprises end with the band's approach to their own material – a beautiful cover of Cat Stevens's 'Trouble' ended the Red Hot Chili Peppers' performance, and later in the evening, as a much-heralded Crosby, Stills, Nash and Young reunion rounded out the event, Flea was among the handful of special guests who joined them onstage for a closing rendition of Stills's 'Love the One You're With'.

The shows kept coming. On 4 November 2000 Kiedis was among the stars turning out to support a benefit for the Hollywood Sunset Free Clinic, the long-established (since 1968) facility that he himself had attended as a kid . . . 'the clinic helped me out, squared me away with a little illness I was experiencing at the time. It's time to show a little love back.' The following evening, the Red Hot Chili Peppers as a whole were back in more familiar surroundings, as they appeared as special guests at Pearl Jam's Seattle Key Arena homecoming shows over 5 and 6 November.

There would be further activity in December, as the Red Hot Chili Peppers went into the studio to cut three songs with trip-hop maven Tricky, as he worked towards his latest album, *Blowback*. It was a collaboration that the band themselves had been dreaming of since Tricky's initial emergence from Britain's trip-hop scene in the mid-1990s, but an exercise that was so audacious in its possibilities swiftly emerged a less than ecstatic experience for Tricky himself.

'[The] Chili Peppers [have] been wanting to work with me for seven years or longer,' he revealed, '[but when] I finally work with them . . . their manager is like, "Well, who is this guy Tricky? We sell 23 million albums or whatever. This guy, he's not on our Soundscan." '

The sessions themselves were successful. It was their aftermath that sent Tricky reeling, as even the ostensibly basic process of securing clearance to actually release the material turned into a Herculean marathon. Tricky continued, 'it was almost like I was begging them to clear it, so then my attitude is . . . "I don't want to work with your band. I don't even listen to your band, so just forget about it." But it was too late then. Little pop stars, they're just like little girls, man.'

Tricky's reservations notwithstanding, the Red Hot Chili Peppers remained in-demand guests, with Flea's workload, at least, springing one surprising reunion. In the years since he departed the Red Hot Chili Peppers, Cliff Martinez had established himself as a leading light in the world of movie soundtracks and, commissioned to score Steven Soderbergh's drug-trade epic *Traffic*, he recruited his old partner in rhythm to play on two tracks.

Flea, Martinez raved, was the 'master of the four-string electrical bassius-o-pheilius. What's always been fun about working with him is just the passion that he has for what he does. He plays every note like it's the last note he's ever gonna play. And that's a contagious kind of enthusiasm. You play with somebody like that and some of it rubs off on you, and you hope some of it rubs off on the CD. He's like one of the greatest bass players on planet earth.'

From one side of the cinema to the other. The veteran now of some 24 different movies, Flea signed up next to voice the character of Donnie in the animated feature *The Wild Thornberrys – The Movie*, in which America's *second* favourite cartoon family, the Thornberrys, travel to Africa's Serengeti to make nature documentaries – only to find themselves ensnared within a world of evil big-game poachers. Eliza Thornberry, of course, saves the day thanks to her secret ability to speak to animals to save them from poachers. Flea's role, on the other hand, portrayed him as what he described as 'a wild, free flowing maniac'.

While Flea busied himself there, Chad Smith was teaming up with Tom Morello and hip hop legends Wu Tang Clan, to re-record their own classic 'Wu Tang Clan Ain't Nuthing Ta Fuck With' for the *Loud Rocks* compilation, a CD compilation that focused upon hard rockers tangling with vintage rappers. He also spent time in England, linking up with Steve White, drummer with Paul Weller's band, for the sensibly titled Smith & White With Attitude Tour – a travelling drum clinic that attracted some of the largest audiences to such an event that the UK had ever seen.

He returned home on the eve of the Red Hot Chili Peppers' next live appearance, as they joined U2, Creed, Christina Aguilera and Bon Jovi among the performers at the inaugural *My VH1 Music Awards* in LA on 30 November. Continuing their domination of such polls over the last few years, the Red Hot Chili Peppers were finalists in five categories: Song of the Year ('Otherside'), Group of the Year, Best Live Act, Best Stage Spectacle and Video of the Year ('Otherside') and victors in two: Must Have Album (*Californication*) and Pushing the Envelope Video ('Californication').

The triumph placed the finishing touch on what Kiedis told *Rolling Stone* was one of the most 'amazing' years of the band's entire life. 'The best thing that happened to me was seeing my sister getting married,' he acknowledged. 'But also going to New Zealand and Australia to tour.' As for the future, meanwhile, his most pressing need was to move out of his rented apartment on Sunset Boulevard, and into a new house of his own – he'd sold his old one a couple of years before, and never found time to buy a new one; '[and then] start working on new material, because we're feeling it right now. In a few months we're going into John's garage or Flea's garage, just hang out and make music.'

Frusciante himself, meanwhile, was putting the finishing touches to his own new album, *To Record Only Water for 10 Days*. Set for release in February 2001, Frusciante enthusiastically described it as a solo album in every sense of the expression. 'I programmed the drums myself and played synthesisers and guitar and [sang].' Of course he also wrote all the songs, drawing his inspiration, he said, from all the songwriters he most admired in the past, from Lou Reed and David Bowie to Syd Barrett.

Instrumentally, however, Frusciante took his cue from a different direction entirely . . . one that his comrades in the Organic Anti-Beat Box Band of old might never have countenanced. 'Since I wanted to do it all myself, it's kind of inspired by Depeche Mode and New

Order,' he confessed – but even he dared not yet speak of the consequences of that discipline, as the Red Hot Chili Peppers themselves reconvened in the new year to begin plotting their own next album.

The band's immediate itinerary called for them to play their first live concerts of 2001 in South America, performing in front of 250,000 fans at the Rock In Rio III festival on 21 January and in Buenos Aires on 24 January – both Brazil and Argentina, the host countries, sent *Californication* soaring to platinum status. Frusciante, however, was more excited about the band's activities in the weeks before those concerts. 'We rehearsed for a few days before the South American shows . . . we were jamming and coming up with ideas for new songs.'

The music that was emerging, however, seemed strangely removed from anything the musicians themselves might have been expecting. 'The music we were doing reminded me of the early Public Image,' the guitarist said. 'I was playing a textural wall of sound and an influence of dub music in some of it. Really spacious.'

Neither did the mood change as the rehearsals and jams grew more involved. 'I'm so excited about the sound,' Frusciante remarked later. 'Everybody's approaching their instruments completely differently.' Frusciante, Flea and Bicycle Thief's Josh Klinghoffer had recently formed a Joy Division cover band so, while Flea busied himself learning Peter Hook's bass lines, Frusciante continued the musical re-education he'd begun during his solo album sessions, picking up synthesiser parts 'from different types of electronic music like Kraftwerk, Depeche Mode and techno music. I've been learning sequencer parts on the guitar as a technical challenge and to think of the guitar differently. I'm trying to get towards the purest representation of the feelings that I'm tuned into as I can.'

It was a process, he said, laughing, that quickly saw him 'trying to learn the technical high-end players of the new wave scene'. He was just entering his teens when the likes of Siouxsie and the Banshees, Magazine and XTC began pushing the limits of the British New Wave into whole new avenues of experimentation, and was now furiously delving back into that period. 'I learned all of John McGeoch's stuff in Magazine and Siouxsie & the Banshees, learned stuff by XTC. In the 80s, when I was a kid, everybody was impressed with your speed on the guitar. Everyone had forgotten about all those players that emerged in the late 70s and early 80s . . . I learned all The Smiths' songs – everything Johnny Marr did . . .'

It was an era, and a style, he reflected, that had too quickly fallen out of fashion for the musical directions of the day to be fully explored and exploited 'in the way that Jimi Hendrix did. That's why I want to include their approach and their style in my playing, and I think there's a lot more to be done.'

Neither did Frusciante restrict himself solely to the metal postcards of the New Wave. Another crash course saw him skewing even further afield, 'listening to English folk music like Steeleye Span and Fairport Convention, Bert Jansch, Richard Thompson' – artists who pursued traditional musical stylings, and converted them to thrusting modernity. 'I've been learning this completely new way of thinking about and using chords and rhythms.'

His education – and his bandmates' re-education, for Frusciante was never going to keep his new discoveries to himself – was necessarily placed on hold in February, as Frusciante alone flew to Europe to play a handful of solo shows in support of *To Record Only Water for 10 Days*. Further interruptions befell the process as the band as a whole stepped out for a handful more shows in their own right, including one that was especially dear to their own hearts.

Among the band's closest friends, Gloria Scott – a drug counsellor and 'resident Great Aunt' at the Hollywood drug rehab clinics Cry Help and Succaro – had few peers. She and Kiedis had known one another since the days of Anthym, and when she was diagnosed with the lung cancer that would eventually kill her, the Red Hot Chili Peppers were swift to link with the Musicians Assistance Program to organise a benefit to help her with the treatment; the Red Hot Chili Peppers themselves would also pay the rent on the ocean-view apartment where Scott remained until the end. (The song 'Universal Queen', on the next Red Hot Chili Peppers album, was written in Scott's memory.)

Tonight, however, there was still hope, and other bands swiftly rallied to the cause – the final line-up for the March benefit concert included Thelonious Monster, Neil Young and Crazy Horse, and DJ Paul Oakenfeld, and tickets – priced at $65 and $150 apiece – disappeared fast. Perhaps it was true, as more than one reviewer commented, that many of the audience seemed unaware of who Scott was – or even that the gig was a fundraiser to begin with. But the night itself was a spectacular success, both financially and musically.

The Red Hot Chili Peppers took the stage following a characteristically uncompromising performance from Young – in an hour-long set that was darkly reminiscent of his *Weld* experimentations of a decade before, he and Crazy Horse performed just half a dozen songs, drawing such classics as 'Like a Hurricane' and 'Cortez the Killer' out to impossibly protracted proportions, while the audience wondered whether they were witnessing a marvellous gig, or simply catching a long-winded rehearsal.

The Red Hot Chili Peppers' own set lay in stark contrast to that, a visual hit machine that saw every song greeted like a conquering hero, while teasing instrumental interludes left even experienced Pepper-watchers wondering whether the group was simply loosening up – or offering sneak previews of their latest material. It was no secret, after all, that the group was now deep into the pre-production stage of their next album and any clue as to its constitution would be seized upon with greedy alacrity.

In fact, the band members themselves were uncertain precisely what was going to emerge from their latest sessions, as Flea admitted. 'We always go on different projects . . . with no plan or anything like that . . . if we try to plan on something . . . it can never be as great as the spontaneity that happens, because that's really where the magic of music is at.' The only certainty was that Rick Rubin would again be producing, with Flea acknowledging that it would be 'unthinkable' to even attempt the project without Rubin at hand. 'He's actually been like an angel in my life. I love him.'

Indeed, Rubin was as anxious to mine new musical territory as the Red Hot Chili Peppers themselves. Having relocated from the garage to the recording studio, the group were working on the song 'Universally Speaking' when, according to Frusciante, 'Rick said . . . I should play glockenspiel on that song.' Fascinated by the suggestion, Frusciante returned to his New Wave collection and set to playing along with an old Fad Gadget record. Rubin, however, had something else in mind altogether . . . Sonny and Cher. 'It was Rick's idea to make that song sound as much like "I Got You Babe" as possible.' Unfortunately, 'the rest of the band didn't go for the odd arrangement' and the notion was scrapped.

Nevertheless, many of the more bizarre notions that surfaced during the sessions would be retained. 'We inspire each other constantly,' Kiedis told BBC DJ Steve Lamacq. 'It's not like we are left to our own devices. We have each other to introduce new ideas to. It's really about the four of us coming together. John is voracious with discovering new music. So I get turned on by music all the time, through his insatiable appetite.'

Flea, too, could not praise Frusciante's input highly enough. 'It's great to experiment with different instrumentation and to have different colours and layer different things over the core of what we are doing. In particular ... John ... was really learning about synthesisers and electronic music and was dead set on playing synthesisers on this record. He did a really beautiful job of it. As well as a lot of background harmonies.'

Yet Frusciante was not the only guiding spirit as the sessions went on. One of the key moments in the entire recording process, Flea told *Spin*, arrived one evening, as he himself was digging through some of his old records. 'I put on X's "Los Angeles" really loud, and I just had a total epiphany about why I wanted to play rock music in the first place. I started jumping around and threw my plate against the wall! I was smashing shit. My daughter was like, "Papa! What's the matter with you?" I threw myself on the ground. I was on the verge of tears, but also of ecstasy.'

Such revelations, like the innovations exploding around the group, bled effortlessly into the process, a period that was so productive that, when Perry Farrell contacted Flea to ask whether he'd be interested in joining this new year's planned Jane's Addiction reunion, the bassist declined. (Martyn Le Noble, bassist with Farrell's Porno For Pyros, replaced him.) In fact, the remainder of 2001 would allow the Red Hot Chili Peppers to stir only occasionally from the studio, although they were guaranteed a splash on the occasions that they did.

One quick break fell on 12 April, when they attended the ESPN television sports network's second annual Action Sports & Music Awards ceremony, to receive an Artist Contribution Award. Announcing the award, Ron Semiao, ESPN vice-president, explained, 'The Red Hot Chili Peppers have been an influential part of the skate culture for many years. Street skateboarders listened to them in the eighties when the action sports genre wasn't even developed. Today, athletes from all disciplines are listening to Chili Peppers CDs as they take their sports to new levels. We are thrilled to honour them as an influential band to the action sports movement.'

The band resurfaced again in August, when they linked once more with the Foo Fighters to headline that August's double-headed V2001 festival. Then it was back into the studio until, by December, only the vocals needed to be completed, leaving Smith, Frusciante and Flea free to indulge other ambitions – as Flea put it, 'since I'm a terrible singer there's not much for me to do at this point'.

For Frusciante, that freedom allowed him to link with Donovan Leitch Junior, son of the 60s singer-songwriter Donovan (and brother, of course, to Kiedis's old paramour Ione Skye), to perform the concert version of *Hedwig and the Angry Inch* at the final night of the three-day

Silver Lining Silver Lake Benefit show for the Hollywood Sunset Free Clinic. Leitch himself played Hedwig him/herself during the play's lengthy award-winning run, while the musical's songwriter, Stephen Trask and co-star Miriam Shor, were also taking part.

The Red Hot Chili Peppers themselves topped the bill on the festival's second night, following performances by Beck, the Jaguares and the Jurassic 5 (the opening evening brought sets from Elton John and Sting). A 45-minute performance allowed only a little space in which new material could be previewed, but 'Don't Forget', 'Universally Speaking' and 'Fortune Faded' all took a bow, while Kiedis was adamant, 'We're so happy with the songs we wrote that, eventually, our show will be full of them.'

Just a few blocks down the road from the festival site, meanwhile, Flea was also occupied with fulfilling an ambition he had nurtured for years, as he set about organising the Silverlake Conservatory For Music, a music school at which, he proudly declared, it was the *making* of music that mattered, not the technique and form with which it was done. No instrument was considered taboo, no musical discipline beyond the school's remit.

'It's sort of one of those things that can't really go wrong, the idea is so good' he boasted. 'As much as I wanted to create a place for people to learn music, I really wanted to create a place for teachers to work, too. I mean, to me, that's an equally valuable service.' His only regret was that his commitments elsewhere reduced his own involvement with the Conservatory to 'overseer and financial . . . guy'. He admitted to the *LA Times*, 'ideally I would love to teach'.

The idea for the Conservatory was first hatched when Flea returned to Fairfax High one afternoon in the late 1990s, to let them know, as he put it, that 'being a musician is a very valuable thing and as worth studying for as any other profession'. He was horrified, however, to discover that in the climate of educational cuts that were then (and still are) savaging school systems all across the United States, music had been all-but expunged from the curriculum. Fairfax once led the way in the arts, just as its graduates once led the way in the music industry. Now, Flea discovered, there was no school orchestra, no band, no suggestion whatsoever that music offered any kind of future for any of the students.

He was still reeling from this discovery a few months later, when he was asked again to step back into his past, and guest-conduct the Los Angeles Junior Philharmonic Orchestra at the Dorothy Chandler Pavilion. Of course he accepted – and, of course, he pulled the engagement off with style, executing a handstand and leading the young musicians through a rousing rendition of '76 Trombones' with his feet. But, afterwards, as he stood on the rostrum to accept the Orchestra's Golden Baton award, his frustration over the collapse of musical education in America came pouring out. 'I started talking about how public education needed to have music programs, and I got kind of hyped up about it. And that was another thing, like, "OK, I'm starting the school".'

In June 2001, Flea signed the lease on a former thrift store on Sunset Junction, and set to work transforming his dream into reality.

Accompanied in his endeavours by former Thelonious Monster drummer Pete Weiss and his old high-school friend, Keith 'Tree' Barry ('an amazing music teacher,' Flea raved, blessed with a 'gift . . . for making people listen'), the grandly titled Silverlake Conservatory swiftly gathered together a 25-strong faculty of teacher-musicians, specialising in everything from guitar and drums to sitar and accordion.

Unlike traditional music schools, however, the Silverlake Conservatory operated not according to some archaic system of accreditation and degrees, but simply upon individual pupils' willingness to learn. It was affordable: tuition fees were pegged at just a $20 'sign up' fee, followed by $20 per half-hour lesson. And it was utterly devoid of any kind of snobbery. Indeed, if any final shred of evidence was required to prove that Silverlake stood many miles from the traditional arena of musical education, a sign donated by one of the academy's first students spelled that out for all to see: 'NEWS FLASH: ALL THE TEACHERS WHO WORK HERE ROCK.'

18. WE HAD 50 BODIES ON A CHALKBOARD

Taking another break from the ongoing album sessions, Christmas 2001 saw Kiedis and Frusciante spin down to the Caribbean island of St Bartholomew for a holiday, to spend their time 'in this perfect blue water, just kind of bobbing in the swell'. The last few months, though ecstatic for the band members themselves, had taken a heavy toll on America – the 11 September attacks on New York and Washington, DC, plunged the country into a state of mourning unseen since the assassination of President Kennedy, almost forty years before. Now, more than three months after the event, television and the media were still wringing every last drop of doom and dire portent from the tragedy, as though willing the American people to simply slide deeper into despondency.

But to what end? At a time when the country should have been pulling together, to rebuild its shattered self-belief, to get on with its life, the economy was collapsing, paranoia was rife, fear was building. The Red Hot Chili Peppers themselves were not untouched by the tragedy – just two years before, on 26 October 1999, the group staged the *Around the World Trade Center Show* on one of the twin towers' observation decks, 1,300 feet above the street. They performed before 300 radio station competition winners, and it was chilling to realise that many of the people working elsewhere in the building that day might well have been among those who died on 9.11.

But should people dwell on that dreadful past? Or should they work, instead, towards building a better future? For Kiedis and Frusciante, as they frolicked in the surf of St Barts, the question had only one answer. 'All this talk about the world coming to an end and it's such a destructive time – that's bullshit,' Kiedis spat. 'There is more infinite beauty out there than there could ever be negativity. It's just like a growing pain for us – the September 11th thing. It's just the very nature of existence is there's this constant struggle between dark and light.'

The Red Hot Chili Peppers confirmed their own feelings for the damaged city when they turned out, the following 10 July, for a so-called New York Pep Rally at Ellis Island, in the shadow of the

Statue of Liberty. Conceived as part of the ongoing project to revitalise downtown Manhattan in the still-glowering aftermath of the attacks, a number of tickets for the event were exclusively reserved for local businesses and, via the Twin Towers Fund, for families of the victims of the 9.11 attacks. But the Red Hot Chili Peppers attended the event to celebrate New York's future, not to mourn its past, a declaration of faith that was already apparent in many of the lyrics that Kiedis was writing as his time in St Barts continued bouncing around his system.

Indeed, within weeks of the duo's return to LA, and the quartet's return to the studio, it was apparent that, once again, they had many more songs than they knew what to do with.

Songwriting flowed from the band. Kiedis told Steve Lamacq, 'We couldn't turn the faucet off. When we [went] into the rehearsal studio, we wrote too much. It was a bit unmanageable for me as a lyricist to be able to focus on. At one point we had fifty bodies of music on a chalkboard, and we're trying to figure out which of these fifty we should focus on.'

Rick Rubin encouraged such prolificness. Having started out recording at Sunset Strip Studios, Rubin then relocated operations to a seventh floor suite at Hollywood's Chateau Marmont Hotel, a building which housed a lot of memories, for the Red Hot Chili Peppers and for Hollywood itself. It was there that comedian John Belushi died; there that actor Montgomery Clift recuperated after shattering his face in a car crash and there that John Frusciante retreated when his post-Peppers life reached its lowest ebb. Like Columbia Pictures founder Harry Cohn is said to have once advised some young stars. 'If you must get into trouble, do it at the Chateau Marmont.'

The Red Hot Chili Peppers would not get into trouble. But they found much to inspire them anyway. Restriking memories of the time they spent at the hacienda in Laurel Canyon, recording *Blood Sugar Sex Magik*, the entire hotel room was wired for sound. There were microphones in the bedroom, a recording studio in the living room, the works. An ISDN line was installed, enabling Rubin to whack mixes back and forth across the Atlantic, after Frusciante was called to Europe for a few weeks mid-session. 'They'd send mixes through,' the guitarist marvelled, 'I'd give my comments and they'd change stuff and send the mix back.'

Despite such technological wonders, however, the 'studio' itself remained pleasingly intimate as the band set about redecorating the suite with Kiedis's beloved collection of old 40s and 50s-era movie posters . . . *Creature from the Black Lagoon* and *This Gun for Hire*; Andy

Warhol's portrait of Jean Cocteau; a Veronica Lake poster that Frusciante gave him for his birthday.

Concerns that the hotel's other guests might object to the goings-on, meanwhile, were deadened by the use of headphones for almost every operation, and Kiedis said, laughing, 'the loudest thing you can hear is me singing and screaming'. And still the only complaint he heard came as he boarded the lift one day, and found himself sharing it with 'this absolutely adorable and sexy girl from somewhere in the British Isles', a novelist who occupied the room next door, and turned out to be loving every minute of it. 'Even when it was antagonising me, I was enjoying it,' she told him. 'I'm in there writing next door to you. What you were doing kind of inspired me to get my writing going.'

Compared even to the grandiose launch of *Californication*, the July 2002 release of this new album, *By the Way*, saw the promo men pulling out all the stops, arranging a media blitz for the Red Hot Chili Peppers that culminated, in the week of the album's actual release, with a full seven days of band-shaped scheduling on MTV2 UK at the beginning of July.

Every hour on the hour, a Red Hot Chili Peppers video or live performance was slammed onto the airwaves. There was a one-hour documentary dating from the *Californication* era, *At Home with the Red Hot Chili Peppers*; a *Making the Video* special shot during the filming of the Jonathan Dayton and Valerie Ferris directed 'By the Way' promo; a 'reality'-style show in which a group of fans re-enacted the now-venerable 'Give It Away' video; a half-hour film from the band's 2000 performance in Moscow; and, rounding out the entire extravaganza, *A Night with the Red Hot Chili Peppers*, a two-hour special shot at the band's 4 June show in Paris, France.

Such a massive build-up for the album's release was no accident. From the moment its title track hit the airwaves as the Red Hot Chili Peppers' latest single, *By the Way* struck many listeners as the group's most unexpected, and certainly their most 'mature' album yet – one that might well take a bit of getting used to from fans who had long since decided what the Red Hot Chili Peppers 'should' sound like.

The shock would not prove terminal, of course; scrape past the initial unfamiliarity, and the band was certainly firing on every one of their best-loved cylinders. But still, *Rolling Stone* could not resist pointing out that there were enough harmonies to conjure visions of 'the Red Hot Mamas and the Papas', and Kiedis admitted that he relished the comparison.

'It just sounds better when you put harmony on there. We've done all varieties of vocals before and this is just a new and fun place to venture into. I do love the Mamas and the Papas and, maybe, subconsciously, I am inspired by them, especially Mama Cass. There have been times when I've been very down and out in my life and the sound of her voice has sort of given me a reason to want to carry on.'

Yet there was more to this new sound than a dose of sweet harmonies. Maybe it was maturity, maybe it was the need for a change, maybe it was even fear of reawakening the watchful puritans that gave Flea such a hard time over his 'I need sex' remark. Or maybe it was none of these things. But Kiedis's very approach to lyric writing had shifted somewhat, as he told *NYRock*. 'I put less sexual aggression into the songs and try to give them more soul. I don't feel like I have to hide behind an image anymore. I am who I am. I'm not a sex machine. I'm human, a spiritual being and there is nothing wrong with showing emotions. Now, I see being able to be emotional not as a weakness. I see it as strength. Even my lyrics are far more personal and, of course, due to that, more emotional.

'It doesn't mean that we've become softies or anything. The Funk is still there. It's still around, but he's a mean motherfucker. He's not in your face anymore shouting, "Here I am!" He approaches you quietly, lurks around and attacks you when you least expect it. Funk will always be our inspiration.'

Flea, too, relished the prevalent opinion that *By the Way* sounded nothing like any other Red Hot Chili Peppers album, that its mellow moods and melodic certainty might easily distract any listener searching for the funk of old. 'I have to advise them to listen to our old records, which are after all freely available. But this time it's definitely not a funk album – [and] I fuckin' love it! If this band wasn't able to reflect personal changes, if it was maybe only good for concealing these changes, then fuck, I wouldn't wanna be in this band anymore. There's nothing worse in this business than stealing people's time.'

Certainly, there was no let up in terms of intensity, a point that Frusciante was especially intent on pointing out. 'Friends who heard [the album] . . . used the term "laid-back". But I don't agree.' As he told the Dutch magazine *Oorgasm*, 'sometimes, a wild, aggressive song can be far less intense than the numbers we produced this time around'.

With all this in mind, of course, reviews of the album were generally cautious. Richard Cromelin, at the *LA Times*, cautioned his readers, '*By the Way* lacks the striking sparseness of *Californication*', warning that 'the ... rich ... arrangements' deployed orchestral strings, spacey effects and even acoustic stretches 'to vary the atmosphere. The band's sweet, suburban soulfulness gets sidetracked by lapses into generic forms, but when they head into the landscape of the eternal hangover, the Chili Peppers manage to provide comfort even as they search for it.'

But the changes that so many listeners confessed were the album's most immediate calling card could not dampen its spirit. One week after release, By the Way crashed into the UK chart at No. 1, dislodging the perennial Oasis from the top as it did so. Days later, the album found itself already being nominated for a Comet 2002 Award by the German music channels VIVA TV and ZDF.

Worldwide, By the Way went immediately into overdrive. Ireland, Holland, Finland, Norway, Belgium, Austria, Germany, Denmark, Sweden, Switzerland, Canada, New Zealand, Australia and Brazil joined the UK in sending it straight to the top immediately upon release; the US, Spain, Portugal and France drove it in at No. 2. The Red Hot Chili Peppers responded by embarking upon another round of globetrotting, with a sequence of festival appearances that took them as far afield as South Korea, where they shared the bill with Jane's Addiction; Japan, where George Clinton joined them on stage to perform a passionate 'Give It Away'; and Hawaii, before they headed down to South America for another round of massive stadium shows. Flea would celebrate his fortieth birthday in Buenos Aires.

The group were back in the Far East and Australia in November 2002, the itinerary this time including a paranoia-inducing appearance in Singapore where the band was warned, in no uncertain terms, that any display of public nudity whatsoever would result in their prompt arrest – which posed an equally immediate sartorial problem for Flea, who had recently taken to performing in nothing more than underpants, bright orange socks, shoes and hat. The outing then wrapped up at Bali's Garuda Wisnu Kencana on 14 December, when the Red Hot Chili Peppers played a hastily arranged benefit show for the families of the 200-plus people killed in a terrorist nightclub bombing two months earlier.

The New Year found the band in Las Vegas, for a celebration that Kiedis and girlfriend Heidi Klum kicked off in spectacular style when they joined the 300,000 or so revellers at Las Vegas's Strip ... and jumped the gun by chiming midnight a full ten seconds early. 'It's fucking New Year's, man. Happy New Year's!'

The couple had only recently been revealed as 'an item' by the Hollywood gossip columnists and would, within the year, hit the headlines again when they separated . . . on 23 November 2003, the *New York Post* reported that Ms Klum 'has dropped Red Hot Chili Peppers frontman Anthony Kiedis after quickly tiring of the rock-chick lifestyle'. For the time being, their partnership seemed capable of distracting any newsman from his other duties, as the Red Hot Chili Peppers themselves discovered this same time. The band were in the gambling capital of Nevada for a couple of holiday shows, but when the media summarised their activities, the concerts themselves scarcely got a look in. There were, however, further headlines after the quartet arrived late for dinner at the Nobu restaurant and were turned away. The fact that the restaurant itself was shut by the time they got there should have tipped the columnists off to the fact that nothing untoward had actually gone down, but then it wouldn't have been a story.

The Red Hot Chili Peppers' European tour kicked off in early February 2003, although it was not necessarily the most opportune time for the band to be on the road. Kiedis had been suffering from influenza since Christmas, and the rigours of touring were scarcely going to aid his speedy recovery. Indeed, by the time the band arrived in Stuttgart, Germany, for the final concert of this leg of the outing, the stricken singer simply couldn't continue. Having gamely battled through the dates so far, Kiedis finally decided, 'if I can't give one hundred per cent, I'd rather do it at a later time when I can give people my best'. He did make it onstage for a brief (three-minute) perform-ance at the Echo Awards, where the band were to receive a platinum plaque, but he missed the ceremony itself and, with his temperature soaring to a searing 103 degrees, the inevitable was finally accepted. The band cancelled that final concert and returned home, intent only on being back to full strength in time for the next leg of the tour, due to open in Glasgow on 5 March.

The beginning of May returned the Red Hot Chili Peppers to North America for a sensational performance at the Coachella festival. They were billed alongside the Beastie Boys and, 'like the Beasties', as VH1's review put it, 'the Chili Peppers focused their headlining slot on keeping the sun-drenched festival-goers on their feet. Though the band mellowed some on last year's *By the Way*, their hit-filled live show was as energetic as ever. Short of sporting only socks, the guys were their old selves, jumping around like caged animals, spouting random dialogue and giving it away now.'

The Reuters news agency was similarly enthralled. 'The Peppers aren't the wild and woolly outfit they used to be, but in the past decade, their addition of many wistful melodies to their heady brew of punk-funk has given the group greater musical depth along with commercial clout. The band delivered a hit set that ranged from the mid-tempo ballad "Scar Tissue", to their predictably crowd-pleasing anthem "Californication".'

The group's American tour got under way immediately after, getting off to a high-flying start, but crashing suddenly back to earth in late May. Joining Queens Of The Stone Age as the Red Hot Chili Peppers' support were Mars Volta, the highly regarded, self-ordained prog band formed in early 2001 from the wreckage of the kinetic punk act At The Drive In. That band's vocalist Cedric Zavala and guitarist Omar Rodriguez-Lopez were both to make the transition, to forge a new group that would, in the latter's words, exist 'free of boxes, free of conceptual limitations. We both knew that would mean a lot of sacrifice, a lot of broken hearts and a lot of change in our life. But we were both willing to accept that so that the music would not suffer.'

Completing the line-up with keyboardist Ikey Owens of The Long Beach Dub All-Stars and ex-Golden drummer Jon Theodore, Mars Volta also recruited De Facto's Jeremy Ward, to become the band's 'secret member', triggering samples and effects from offstage in much the same way as Brian Eno once worked with Roxy Music. His tenure with the group that Flea was already describing as 'the best band we've ever played with', however, was to be tragically brief.

Just weeks into the tour, on 25 May, Ward was found dead in his LA home, the victim of an apparent drug overdose. Mars Volta dropped out of the tour immediately, and Flea – for whom memories of Hillel Slovak's similarly lonely, similarly pointless, death came flooding back, was swift to mourn, 'I feel a deep melancholy about them not being with us [for the remainder of the tour]. God bless Jeremy.'

It would be some months before Mars Volta reconstituted themselves, and both Flea and Frusciante happily rallied to the band's cause, joining them at Rick Rubin's studio in Laurel Canyon to record their debut album, *De-Loused in the Comatori* – a concept album built around the life of Julio Venegas, an artist from El Paso who committed suicide in 1996. (The album was released in late 2003.)

But Ward's passing was not the only death to blight this leg of the tour. At the Verizon Wireless Amphitheatre in Charlotte, NC, on 6 June, during the intermission before the Red Hot Chili Peppers took the stage, 26-year-old student Ashley Farris was electrocuted as he walked barefoot in the rain on a lighted concrete and metal stairway.

A passer-by who tried to help him, Ryan Robards, was also electrocuted but survived.

The Red Hot Chili Peppers did not learn of the incident until the show was over. In a shocked 'Fleamail' the following day, Flea mourned, 'I don't know . . . what went wrong, but the guy went to have fun at a concert and never came home. Bless his heart. Whoever it is, he has been let in on the big secret. He is probably having a great time right now. My heart and my prayers go out to the person's loved ones.'

Placing the tragedies behind them, the Red Hot Chili Peppers returned to the road, across the US, and through Europe for a clutch of festivals, including Britain's V2003; there, on a stage illuminated by a dramatic firework display and a literally explosive lightshow, the Red Hot Chili Peppers inspired the *New Musical Express* to muse, 'Say what you like about the [band], but you definitely can't call them dull. They are, in fact, the anti-David Gray, twisting the minds of every dullard present tonight who couldn't quite escape from the main stage quick enough. It's awesome entertainment.' Group and audience were joined at the hip for the evening, locked into one another's lusty renditions of the group's biggest hits . . . 'an OD on nostalgia to the funk-rock of "Suck My Kiss", a singalong frenzy to "By the Way" . . . a heart-stopping moment of magic during "Under the Bridge" . . . and a bizarre desire to flirt with the intro to The Clash's "London Calling". Put it all together and you've got the craziest rock'n'roll circus in town.'

That circus remained on the road into October 2003, as the ringmasters returned to the United States to continue making a mockery of the twenty-year veteran status that the first history-hungry journalists were beginning to raise. 'It's hard to say exactly which day God created punk-stoked funk-metal grooves,' opined the *Boston Globe*. 'But He surely had the Red Hot Chili Peppers in mind. The band practically invented the genre-busting sound in the 80s – spawning plenty of imitators – and 20 years later they're still utterly intoxicating.'

Every place the band touched down, the reviews reminded them again and again that the crazy kids were now respected elder statesmen, with a career that had outlived not only all expectations, but a lot of rock's veteran hierarchy as well.

Two decades is a lifetime in rock'n'roll terms, after all – John Lennon's entire professional life, from playing the Cavern with the Silver Beatles, to his death outside the Dakota, barely scraped the twenty-year mark, Elvis Presley's only just surpassed it. It is how long the Rolling Stones took to journey from the untrammelled joy of 'Come On' to the desperate pits of 'She Was Hot'; it is almost as much time as Darby Crash spent on this planet. Yet the Red Hot Chili Peppers had not only hit the magic mark, they were showing no signs of ever slowing down.

'Their career has almost inexplicably – and certainly unpredictably – lasted 20 years,' marvelled the *Chicago Sun-Times*. 'They've sparked debates over musical integrity; they've guided the transition of their genre from funk-punk to rock-rap, and they've provided a gaggle of hits.'

And so on.

Not that such chronological nuances made any difference to the fans. As the *Seattle Post Intelligencer's* Bill White put it, the local Key Arena date was 'bursting with kids who weren't even born when the band began 20 years ago. But that didn't stop them from bouncing along with the animated quartet' for an exhausting 105-minute set that proved, 'even though their music has softened, they are still one of the most kinetically driven units in the business'.

Neither were the Red Hot Chili Peppers planning to change that billing. At a stage in their career when other bands would feel perfectly justified in grabbing every moment's rest they could get, a seven-week break in the late summer presented the group with nothing more than an opportunity to record a couple of new songs for the *Greatest Hits* album that Warners had scheduled for pre-Christmas release.

'Seven weeks of no gigs,' Flea marvelled on the band's website. 'We are gonna take two weeks off and then write and record two or three new songs . . .' Seven weeks later, he was back online to announce that they had, in fact, recorded fifteen. 'It was the fastest we have ever recorded so much material,' Flea continued. 'We gave it no thought, we just rocked and it worked well . . . [it] is among the most diverse and dynamic good-feeling shit we have ever done.'

Two of these songs, the two-year-old 'Fortune Faded' (itself selected as the band's latest single) and 'Save the Population' would be utilised on the compilation – with fourteen earlier hits also vying for space, plus a bonus DVD-full of videos, there was no room for more. And their decision was vindicated when MTV pounced upon 'Fortune Faded' and described it as a summary of the group's entire career, a combination of 'funky guitars, bobbing rhythms and vocals that range from percussive to smooth and tuneful, addressing everything the Chili Peppers have ever stood for – humour, sex and altered states of consciousness'.

But nostalgia was not – and has never been – the foremost thought on the Red Hot Chili Peppers' minds, even as so many around them insisted that they turn their attention towards it. Rather, the group remained a celebration not of some distant past or hoary archaeology, but of the Here and Now in all of its glorious modernity.

Reflecting upon his own departure from the band in 1992, Frusciante told the *Boston Herald*: 'I suppose at that time, as we were getting more and more popular, I didn't really believe it was because of our music. I felt like we had become this "cool thing" and that people were just finding out about it. I felt like it was a small percentage that were really there for the music. I guess I was wrong because, this many years later, people are still into us, and it is because of the music and that we stick out from other groups.'

Kiedis agreed. The times had changed, the musicians had aged. But, 'because of who we are, the way we live and what we do, we could be having dinner with the Queen of England and [we'd] still maintain our punk-rock relevance. We could drive in limos and private jets all day long, and we'd still be more punk rock than bands that call themselves punk rock today. All of our motivation is true and real, and that's more the essence of punk rock than people trying to sound like something that happened twenty years ago.

'This band means everything to me,' he continued. 'And I think I can speak for each one of us when I say that. There is a chemistry at work when the four of us go into a room that I've just never experienced with anyone else. We've learned from our mistakes and we've grown from our experiences, and I can only see this band getting better and better. I can only see this band sticking around for a long time to come.'

DISCOGRAPHY

SINGLES

08/84 Get Up and Dance (Dance Mix)/Baby Appeal (Club Mix) (EMI 7839) – US 12"

08/85 Hollywood (Africa)/Nevermind (EMI 7862) – US 7"

08/85 *Hollywood (Africa)* EP: Hollywood (Africa) extended dance mix/Hollywood (Africa) dub mix/Nevermind (EMI America 205) – UK 12"

10/85 Jungle Man/Nevermind/Stranded/Hollywood (Africa) (EMI 9466) – US 12"

10/87 Fight Like a Brave/Fire (EMI 56076) – US 7"

01/88 Fight Like a Brave/Fire (EMI America EA241) – UK 7"

01/88 *Fight Like a Brave* EP: Fight Like a Brave (Mofo Mix)/Fight Like a Brave (Knucklehead Mix)/Fire (EMI 12EA241) – UK 12"

05/88 *Abbey Road* EP: Backwoods/Hollywood (Africa)/True Men Don't Kill Coyotes (EMI Manhattan MT 41) – UK 7"

05/88 *Abbey Road* EP: Fire/Backwoods/Catholic School Girls Rule/Hollywood (Africa)/True Men Don't Kill Coyotes (EMI 12MT 41) – UK 12"

05/88 *Abbey Road* EP: Fire/Backwoods/Hollywood (Africa)/True Men Don't Kill Coyotes/Catholic Schoolgirls Rule (EMI 50285) – US 12"

–/89 *Unbridled Funk and Roll 4 Your Soul!* EP: Taste the Pain/Millionaires Against Hunger/Castles Made of Sand/Higher Ground (Daddy-O Mix) (EMI CD E2-50285) US promo CD

–/89 *Taste the Pain* EP: Taste the Pain/Castles Made of Sand/Special Secret Song Inside/F.U. (live) (EMI CD DPRO 04502) US promo CD

08/89 Knock Me Down/Punk Rock Classic (EMI MT70) – UK 7"

08/89 Knock Me Down/Punk Rock Classic/Pretty Little Ditty (EMI 12MTPD70) – UK 12"

08/89 Knock Me Down/Punk Rock Classic/Special Secret Song Inside/Magic Johnson (EMI 12MT70) – UK 12"

08/89 Knock Me Down/Punk Rock Classic/Jungle Man/Magic Johnson (EMI CDMT70) – UK CD

12/89 Higher Ground/Millionaires Against Hunger (EMI MT 75) – UK 7"

12/89 Higher Ground (Munchkin Mix)/Politician (Mini Rap)/Higher Ground (Dub Mix)/Mommy Where's Daddy (EMI 12MT 75) – UK 12"

12/89 Higher Ground/Higher Ground (Munchkin Mix)/Politician (Mini Rap)/Higher Ground (Dub Mix) (EMI 12MTX 75) – UK 12"

12/89 Higher Ground (Munchkin Mix)/Mommy Where's Daddy/Politician (mini rap) (EMI CDMT 75) – UK CD

06/90 Taste the Pain/Show Me Your Soul (EMI MT 85) – UK 7"

06/90 Taste the Pain/Show Me Your Soul/Castles Made of Sand (EMI 10MT 85) – UK 9" square

06/90 Taste the Pain/Show Me Your Soul/Castles Made of Sand (EMI 12MT 85) – UK 12"

06/90 Taste the Pain/Show Me Your Soul/If You Want Me to Stay/Never Mind (EMI 12MTX 85) – UK 12"

06/90 Taste the Pain/Show Me Your Soul/Castles Made of Sand (live)/Never Mind (EMI CDMT 85) – UK CD

06/90 Taste the Pain/Millionaires Against Hunger/Castles Made of Sand (live)/Higher Ground (Daddy-O Mix) (EMI 50285) – US 12"

08/90 Higher Ground/Fight Like a Brave (EMI MT 88) – UK 7"

08/90 Higher Ground/Higher Ground (Daddy-O Mix)/Fight Like a Brave (EMI 12MT 88) – UK 12"

09/91 Give It Away/Search and Destroy (WB 19147) – US 7"

09/91 Give It Away (single mix)/Give It Away (12-inch mix)/Search and Destroy/Give It Away (Rasta Mix)/Give It Away (album version) (WB 40261) – US 12"

12/91 Give It Away/Search and Destroy (WB 19147) – US CD

02/92 Under the Bridge/Sikamikanico/Give It Away (12-inch mix)/Give It Away (Rasta Mix) (WB 40358) – US 12"

03/92 Under the Bridge/Give It Away (WB 0084) – UK 7"

03/92 Under the Bridge/Give It Away/Search and Destroy/Soul to Squeeze/Sikamikanico (WB 0084T) – UK 12"

03/92 Under the Bridge/Give It Away/Search and Destroy/Soul to Squeeze/Sikamikanico (WB 0084CD) – UK CD

03/92 Under the Bridge/The Righteous and the Wicked (WB 18978) – US 7"

03/92 Under the Bridge/The Righteous and the Wicked (WB 18978) – US CD

04/92 Suck My Kiss/Search and Destroy/Fela's Cock (WB 40473) – US 12"

06/92 Breaking the Girl/Fela's Cock/Suck My Kiss (live)/I Could Have Lied (live) (WB 40521) – US 12"

08/92 Breaking the Girl/Fela's Cock (WB W0126) – UK 7"

08/92 Breaking the Girl/Fela's Cock/Suck My Kiss (live)/I Could Have Lied (live) (WB W0126T) – UK CD

08/92 Breaking the Girl/Fela's Cock/Suck My Kiss (live)/I Could Have Lied (live) (WB W0126CD) – UK CD

10/92 Behind the Sun/Fire (EMI 56949) – US 7"

2/93 Higher Ground/If You Want Me to Stay (EMI 57992) – US 7"

06/93 Give It Away/If You Have to Ask (WB W188C) – UK 7"

06/93 Give It Away (12-inch mix)/Give It Away (Rasta Mix)/If You Have to Ask (Friday Night Fever Blister Mix) (WB W188TP) – UK 12"

06/93 Give It Away (12-inch mix)/Give It Away (Rasta Mix)/If You Have to Ask (Friday Night Fever Blister Mix) (WB W188CD1) – UK CD

06/93 Give It Away/Give It Away (Disco Krisco Mix)/Give It Away (Scott & Garth Mix) (WB W188CD2) – UK CD

08/93 Soul to Squeeze/Nobody Weird Like Me (WB 18401) – US 7"

08/93 Soul to Squeeze/Nobody Weird Like Me (WB 18401) – US CD

01/94 Give It Away/Soul to Squeeze (WB 0225C) – UK 7"

01/94 Give It Away (12-inch mix)/Give It Away (Rasta Mix)/If You Have to Ask (Disco Krisco Mix) (WB 0225T) – UK 12"

01/94 Give It Away/Soul to Squeeze/Give It Away (12-inch mix)/Give It Away (Rasta Mix) (WB 0225CD1) – UK CD

01/94 Give It Away/Give It Away (Scott & Garth Mix)/If You Have to Ask (Friday Night Fever Blister Mix)/Nobody Weird Like Me (live) (WB 0225CD2) – UK CD

04/94 Under the Bridge/Suck My Kiss (live) (WB 0237) – UK 7"

04/94 Under the Bridge/Suck My Kiss (live)/Sikakikanico/Search and Destroy (live) (WB 0237CD) – UK CD

04/94 Under the Bridge/I Could Have Lied (live)/Fela's Cock/Give It Away (in progress: demo) (WB 0237CDX) – UK CD

08/95 Warped/Pea (WB W0316C) – UK cass

08/95 Warped/Pea/Melancholy Mechanics (WB W0316CD) – UK CD

10/95 My Friends/Let's Make It Evil (WB W0317C) – UK cass
10/95 My Friends/Let's Make It Evil/Coffee Shop/Stretch (WB W0317TX) – UK 12"
10/95 My Friends/Let's Make It Evil/Coffee Shop/Stretch (WB W0317CD) – UK CD

02/96 Aeroplane/Suffragette City (live) (WB 0331C) – UK cass
02/96 Aeroplane/Suffragette City (live)/Suck My Kiss (live) (WB 0331CD) – UK CD
02/96 Aeroplane/Backwoods (live)/Transcending (live)/Me and My Friends (live) (WB 0331CDX) – UK CD

06/97 Love Rollercoaster/track by Englebert Humperdinck (Geffen 22188) – UK 7"
06/97 Love Rollercoaster/track by Englebert Humperdinck (Geffen 22188CD)

05/99 Scar Tissue/Gong Li (WB W490C) – UK cass
05/99 Scar Tissue/Gong Li/Instrumental #1 (WB W490CD) – UK CD

08/99 Around the World/Yertle Trilogy (WB W500C) – UK cass
08/99 Around the World/Parallel Universe/Teatro Jam (WB W500CD1) – UK CD
08/99 Around the World/Yertle Trilogy/Me and My Friends (WB W500CD2) – UK CD

01/00 Otherside/How Strong/Road Trippin' (without strings)/Otherside CD-ROM (WB W510CD1) – UK CD
01/00 Otherside/My Lovely Man/Around the World (WB W510CD2) – UK CD

08/00 Californication/End of the Show (WB W534C) – UK cass
08/00 Californication/End of Show Brisbane/I Could Have Lied/End of Shoe State College (WB 30025) – Australia CD

01/01 Road Trippin'/Californication (live) (WB 546C) – UK cass
01/01 Road Trippin'/Californication/Blood Sugar Sex Magik (live)/Road Trippin' CD-ROM (WB 546CD1) – UK CD
01/01 Road Trippin'/Under the Bridge (live)/If You Have to Ask (live) (WB 546CD2) – UK CD

07/02 By the Way/Time/Teenager in Love (WB 42459) – UK CD
07/02 By the Way (video)/By the Way (live)/Making of the Video (WB 7599385772) – UK DVD single

278 RED HOT CHILI PEPPERS

10/02 The Zephyr Song/Body of Water/Someone (WB 424872) – UK CD

10/02 The Zephyr Song/Out of Range/Rivers of Avalon (WB 424882) – UK CD

02/03 Can't Stop/Christ Church Fireworks Music (live) (WB 5439 16672 2/7) – UK 7"

02/03 Can't Stop/If You Have to Ask (live)/Christ Church Fireworks Music (live) (WB (#9362 42607 2) – UK CD

02/03 Can't Stop/Right on Time (live)/Nothing to Lose (live) (9362 42608 2) – UK CD

05/03 Universally Speaking/By the Way (live acoustic) (WB 2/7-16653) – UK 7"

05/03 Universally Speaking/By the Way (live acoustic)/Don't Forget Me (live) (WB 2-42628) – UK CD

05/03 Universally Speaking/Slowly Deeply instrumental)/Universally Speaking video (WB 2-42629) – UK CD

11/03 Fortune Faded/Eskimo/Bunker Hill (WB 42680) – UK CD

11/03 Fortune Faded/Californication (remix by Ekkehard Ehelers)/ Tuesday Night in Berlin (WB 42684) – UK CD

ALBUMS

08/84 *Red Hot Chili Peppers*
True Men Don't Kill Coyotes/Baby Appeal/Buckle Down/Get Up and Jump/Why Don't You Love Me/Green Heaven/Mommy Where's Daddy/Out in LA/Police Helicopter/You Always Sing/Grand Pappy Du Plenty (EMI America 17128)

10/03 *reissue with bonus tracks:*
Get Up and Jump (demo)/Police Helicopter (demo)/Out in LA (demo)/Green Heaven (demo)/What It Is (aka Nina's Song) (demo) (Capitol 72435 40380-2)

09/85 *Freaky Styley*
Jungle Man/Hollywood/Amercian Ghost Dance/If You Want Me to Stay/Nevermind/Freaky Styley/Blackeyed Blonde/The Brothers Cup/ Battle Ship/Lovin' and Touchin'/Catholic School Girls Rule/Sex Rap/ Thirty Dirty Birds/Yertle the Turtle (EMI America 17168)

10/03 *reissue with bonus tracks:*
Nevermind (demo)/Sex Rap (demo)/Freaky Styley (original long version)/Millionaires Against Hunger (Capitol 72435 40377-2)

03/88 *The Uplift Mofo Party Plan*
Fight Like a Brave/Funky Crime/Me and My Friends/Backwoods/ Skinny Sweaty Man/Behind the Sun/Subterranean Homesick Blues/ Special Secret Song Inside/No Chump Love Sucker/Walkin' on Down the Road/Love Trilogy/Organic Anti-Beat Box Band (EMI Manhattan 3125 – UK)/(EMI Manhattan 48036 – US)

10/03 *reissue with bonus tracks*
Behind the Sun (instrumental demo)/Me and My Friends (instrumental demo) (Capitol 72435 40379-2)

08/89 *Mother's Milk*
Good Time Boys/Higher Ground/Subway to Venus/Magic Johnson/ Nobody Weird Like Me/Knock Me Down/Taste the Pain/Stone Cold Bush/Fire/Pretty Little Ditty/Punk Rock Classic/Sexy Mexican Maid/ Johnny, Kick a Hole in the Sky (EMI 3125 – UK)/(92152 – US)

10/03 *reissue with bonus tracks*
Song That Made Us What We Are Today (demo)/Sexy Mexican Maid (original long version)/Knock Me Down (original long version)/To Kareem (demo)/Castles Made Of Sand (live)/Crosstown Traffic (live) (Capitol 72435-40378-2)

09/91 *Blood Sugar Sex Magik*
The Power of Equality/If You Have to Ask/Breaking the Girl/Funky Monks/Suck My Kiss/I Could Have Lied/Mellowship Slinky in B Major/The Righteous and the Wicked/Give It Away/Blood Sugar Sex Magik/Under the Bridge/Naked in the Rain/Apache Rose Peacock/ The Greeting Song/My Lovely Man/Sir Psycho Sexy/They're Red Hot (WB 7599 26681-2 – UK/US)

09/95 *One Hot Minute*
Aeroplane/Stretch/My Friends/Warped/One Hot Minute/Coffee Shop/ Pea/One Big Mob/Deep Kick/Tearjerker/Walkabout/Shallow Be Thy Game/Falling into Grace/Blender (WB 9362 45733-2 – UK/US)

09/95 *One Hot Minute*
Aeroplane/Stretch/My Friends/Warped/One Hot Minute/Coffee Shop/ Pea/One Big Mob/Deep Kick/Tearjerker/Walkabout/Shallow Be Thy Game/Falling into Grace/Shallow Be Thy Name/Transcending/Melancholy Mechanics (WB 100213 – Japan)

06/99 *Californication*
Around the World/Parallel Universe/Scar Tissue/Otherside/Get on Top/ Californication/Easily/Porcelain/Emit Remmus/Velvet Glove/Savoir/

Purple Stain/Right on Time/Road Trippin' (WB 9362-47386-2 – UK/US)

06/99 *Californication*
Around the World/Parallel Universe/Scar Tissue/Otherside/Get on Top/Californication/Easily/Porcelain/Emit Remmus/Velvet Glove/Savoir/Purple Stain/Right on Time/Road Trippin'/I Like Dirt/(WB 10375 – Japan)

06/99 *Californication*
Around the World/Parallel Universe/Scar Tissue/Otherside/Get on Top/Californication/Easily/Porcelain/Emit Remmus/Velvet Glove/Savoir/Purple Stain/Right on Time/Road Trippin' + bonus VCD: Scar Tissue (multimedia)/Around the World (multimedia)/Otherside (multimedia)/Californication (multimedia) (WB 47868 – Euro)

08/02 *By the Way*
By the Way/Universally Speaking/This Is the Place/Dosed/Don't Forget Me/The Zephyr Song/Can't Stop/I Could Die for You/Midnight/Throw Away Your Television/Cabron/Tear/On Mercury/Minor Thing/Warm Tape/Venice Queen

COMPILATIONS & ARCHIVE COLLECTIONS
08/92 *Various States of Undress*
Higher Ground/Fight Like a Brave/Behind the Sun/Me and My Friends/Backwoods/True Men Don't Kill Coyotes/Fire/Get Up and Jump/Knock Me Down/Under the Bridge/Show Me Your Soul/If You Want Me to Stay/Hollywood/Jungle Man/The Brothers Cup/Taste the Pain/Special Secret Song Inside/Catholic School Girls Rule/Johnny, Kick a Hole in the Sky (EMI 4PRO 94762): promo cassette-only version of below, with extra track and alternate title

10/92 *What Hits!?*
Higher Ground/Fight Like a Brave/Behind the Sun/Me and My Friends/Backwoods/True Men Don't Kill Coyotes/Fire/Get Up and Jump/Knock Me Down/Under the Bridge/Show Me Your Soul/If You Want Me to Stay/Hollywood/Jungle Man/The Brothers Cup/Taste the Pain/Catholic School Girls Rule/Johnny, Kick a Hole in the Sky (EMI MTL 1071 – UK)/(EMI 94762 – US)

11/94 *Out in LA*
Higher Ground (12-inch Vocal Mix)/Hollywood (Africa) (Extended Dance Mix)/If You Want Me to Stay (Pink Mustang Mix)/Behind

the Sun (Ben Grosse Remix)/Castles Made of Sand (live)/Special Secret Song Inside (live)/F.U. (live)/Get Up and Jump (demo)/Out in LA (demo)/Green Heaven (demo)/Police Helicopter (demo)/ Nevermind (demo)/Sex Rap (demo)/Blues for Meister/You Always Sing the Same/Stranded/Flea Fly/What It Is/Deck the Halls (EMI MTL 1062)

–/94 *Greatest Hits*
Behind the Sun/Johnny, Kick a Hole in the Sky/Me and My Friends/Fire/True Men Don't Kill Coyotes/Higher Ground/Knock Me Down/Fight Like a Brave/Taste the Pain/If You Want Me to Stay (EMI 17719)

–/94 *RedLiveHotRareChiliRemixPeppersBox*
Give It Away (Live)/Nobody Weird Like Me (Live)/Suck My Kiss (Live)/I Could Have Lied (Live)/Soul to Squeeze/Fela's Cock/ Sikamikanico/Search and Destroy/Give It Away (12-inch mix)/Give It Away (Rasta Mix)/If You Have to Ask (The Disco Krisco Mix)/If You Have to Ask (Scott & Garth Mix)/If You Have to Ask (The Friday Night Fever Blister Mix) (WB 9362 45649-2)

–/94 *Plasma Shift*
The Power of Equality/If You Have to Ask/Breaking the Girl/Funky Monks/
Suck My Kiss/I Could Have Lied/Mellowship Slinky in B Major/The Righteous and The Wicked/Give It Away/Blood Sugar Sex Magik/ Under the Bridge/Naked in the Rain/A Pache Rose Peacock/The Greeting Song/My Lovely Man/Sir Psycho Sexy/They're Red Hot/ Give It Away [In Progress]/If You Have to Ask (Radio Mix)/Nobody Weird Like Me (live)/Sikamikanico/Breaking the Girl (Radio Edit)/ Fela's Cock/If You Have to Ask (Friday Night Fever Blister Mix)/Soul to Squeeze (WB 4490 – Euro)

04/98 *Under The Covers*
They're Red Hot/Fire/Subterranean Homesick Blues/Higher Ground/If You Want Me to Stay/Why Don't You Love Me?/Tiny Dancer (live)/Castles Made of Sand (live)/Dr Funkenstein (live)/Hollywood (Africa)/Search and Destroy/Higher Ground (Daddy-O Mix)/Hollywood (Africa) (Extended Dance Mix) (EMI 72434 94139-2 – US)

–/98 *The Best Of*
Behind the Sun/Johnny, Kick a Hole in the Sky/Me and My Friends/Fire/True Men Don't Kill Coyotes/Higher Ground/Knock

Me Down/Fight Like a Brave/Taste the Pain/If You Want Me to Stay (EMI 19706)

–/00 *The Best* Of
Behind the Sun/Johnny, Kick a Hole in the Sky/Me and My Friends/Fire/True Men Don't Kill Coyotes/Higher Ground/Knock Me Down/Fight Like a Brave/Taste the Pain/If You Want Me to Stay (Madacy 3123)

11/03 *Greatest Hits*
Under the Bridge/Give It Away/Californication/Scar Tissue/Soul to Squeeze/Otherside/Suck My Kiss/By the Way/Parallel Universe/ Breaking the Girl/My Friends/Higher Ground/Universally Speaking/ Road Trippin'/Fortune Faded/Save the Population (WB 48596-2 – UK/US): limited edition bonus DVD disc included, see below

MISCELLANEOUS RELEASES
–/90 *Pretty Woman* (soundtrack) inc. Show Me Your Soul (EMI 93492)
–/90 *Say Anything* (soundtrack) inc. Taste the Pain (WTG PK 41540)
–/92 *Wayne's World* (soundtrack) inc. Sikamikanico (Reprise 26805)
–/93 *Coneheads* (soundtrack) inc. Soul to Squeeze (WB 45345)
–/95 *Woodstock* (live) inc. Blood Sugar Sex Magik (A&M 540322)
–/95 *Revenge: A Tribute to Jimi Hendrix* inc. Fire (Gravity 682550)
–/95 *Working Class Hero: A Tribute to John Lennon* inc. I Found Out (Hollywood 162015)
–/96 *Twister* (soundtrack) inc. Melancholy Mechanics (WB 46254)
–/96 *Beavis and Butthead Do America* (soundtrack) inc. Love Roller-coaster (Geffen 25002)
–/97 *Christmas in Your Ear* inc. Deck the Halls (EMI 19553)
–/99 *Music for Our Mother Ocean Vol 3* inc. How Strong (Hollywood 162233)
–/99 *Woodstock 99* (live) inc. Fire (Sony 63958)
–/03 *We're a Happy Family: A Tribute to the Ramones* inc. Havana Affair (Columbia 86352)

VHS/DVDs
06/90 *Positive Mental Octopus*
Taste the Pain/Higher Ground/Knock Me Down/Fight Like a Brave/ Catholic Schoolgirls Rule (live)/Jungle Man/True Men Don't Kill Coyotes (EMI E5 1614)

06/90 *Psychedelic Sex Funk Live from Heaven* (Long Beach, CA)

Stone Cold Bush/Sexy Mexican Maid/Good Time Boys/Star Spangled Banner/Pretty Little Ditty/Knock Me Down/Nevermind/Magic Johnson/Subway to Venus (EMI E5 1627)

10/91 *Funky Monks* (the making of *Blood Sugar Sex Magik*) (WB 38281-3)

09/92 *What Hits!? The Best of the Red Hot Chili Peppers*
Behind the Sun/Under the Bridge/Show Me Your Soul/Taste the Pain/Higher Ground/Knock Me Down/Fight Like a Brave/Jungle Man/True Men Don't Kill Coyotes/Catholic Schoolgirls Rule/Fire (live)/Stone Cold Bush (live)/Special Secret Song Inside (live)/ Subway to Venus (live) (EMI E3 33155)

–/99 *Free Tibet 1998* (live compilation) inc. Give It Away (MVD 823)

–/01 *Rock Your Socks Off* (unauthorised documentary) (MVD 1532)

–/01 *Off the Map*
Around the World/Give It Away/Usually Just a T-Shirt #3/Scar Tissue/Suck My Kiss/If You Have to Ask/Subterranean Homesick Blues/Otherside/Blackeyed Blonde/Pea/Blood Sugar Sex Magik/Easily/What Is Soul?/Fire/Californication/Right on Time/Under the Bridge/Me and My Friends (WB 38530)

11/03 *Live at Slane*
By the Way/Scar Tissue/Around the World/Universally Speaking/ Parallel Universe/Zephyr Song/Throw Away Your Television/Havana Affair/Otherside/Purple Stain/Don't Forget Me/Right on Time/Can't Stop/Venice Queen/Give It Away/Californication/Under the Bridge/ Power of Equality (WB 48596-2 – UK/US)

11/03 *Greatest Hits* (bonus disc with CD *Greatest Hits* – see above)
Higher Ground/Suck My Kiss/Give It Away/Under the Bridge/Soul to Squeeze/Aeroplane/My Friends/Around the World/Scar Tissue/ Otherside/Californication/Road Trippin'/By the Way/The Zephyr Song/Can't Stop/Universally Speaking

SOLO RELEASES

FLEA
1995 Original Soundtrack: *Basketball Diaries*
inc. I've Been Down (Island 524093)

1996 Various Artists: *Small Circle of Friends* (Germs tribute) inc. Media Blitz (Grass 3038)

1997 Various Artists: *Lounge-a-Palooza*
inc. Love Will Tear Us Apart (with Jimmy Scott) (Hollywood 62072)

1997 Original Soundtrack: *Private Parts*
inc. I Make My Own Rules (with Chad Smith, Dave Navarro) (WB 46477)

1998 Original Soundtrack: *Small Soldiers*
inc. War (with Bone Thugs n' Harmony, Tom Morello, Henry Rollins) (Dreamworks 50051)

1998 Various Artists: *Chef Aid: The South Park Album*
inc. It's a Rockin' World (with Joe Strummer, Tom Morello) (Sony 69377)

1998 Various Artists: *Lost in Bass*
inc. Hangin' Around (with Andre Fox) (Aim 1101)

JOHN FRUSCIANTE
–/95 *Niandra Lades & Usually Just a T-Shirt*
Niandra Lades: As Can Be/My Smile Is a Rifle/Head (Beach Arab)/Big Takeover/Curtains/Running Away into You/Mascara/Been Insane/Skin Blues/Your Pussy's Glue/Blood on My Neck/Ten to Butter Blood Voodoo/Usually Just a T-Shirt #1–13 (WB 45757)

08/97 *Smile from the Streets You Hold*
Enter a Uh/The Other/Life's a Bath/A Fall Through the Ground/Poppy Man/I May Know Again John/I'm Always/Nigger Song/Femininity/Breathe/More/For Air/Height Down/Well I've Been/Smile from the Streets You Hold/I Can't See Until I See Your Eyes/Estress (Birdman 16)

02/01 *To Record Only Water for 10 Days*
Going Inside/Someone's/The First Season/Wind Up Space/Away and Anywhere/Remain/Fallout/Ramparts/With No One/Murderers/Invisible Movement/Representing/In Rime/Saturation/Moments Have You (WB 48045)

CHAD SMITH
1997 Original Soundtrack: *Private Parts*
inc. I Make My Own Rules (with Flea, Dave Navarro) (WB 46477)

2000 Various Artists: *Loud Rocks*

inc. Wu Tang Clan Ain't Nuthing Ta F With (with Wu Tang Clan, Tom Morello) (Sony 62201)

SESSIONS AND GUEST APPEARANCES

FLEA
1987 Warren Zevon: *Sentimental Hygiene* (Virgin 86012)
1988 Jane's Addiction: *Nothing's Shocking* (WB 25727)
1988 UK Subs: *Japan Today* (Enigma 72274)
1989 Keith Levene: *Keith Levene's Violent Opposition* (Taang 33)
1989 Young MC: *Stone Cold Rhymin'* (Delicious 12914)
1990 The Weirdos: *Condor* (Frontier 4623)
1991 Queen: We Will Rock You [CD single] (Hollywood 166576)
1991 Queen: We Will Rock You [single] (Elektra 66573)
1991 Various Artists (Aleka's Attic): *Tame Yourself* (Rhino 70772)
1993 Mick Jagger: *Wandering Spirit* (Atlantic 82436)
1993 Street Military: *Don't Give a Damn* (Capitol 89555)
1994 Jon Hassell: *Dressing for Pleasure* (WB 45523)
1994 Pigface: *Notes from the Underground* (Invisible 28)
1994 Sir Mix-A-Lot: *Chief Boot Knocka* (American 45540)
1995 Alanis Morrissete: *Jagged Little Pill* (Reprise 45901)
1995 Bam: *Rough Z'aggin Bible (Pray at Will)* (BAM 5000)
1995 Cheikha Remitti: *Sidi Mansour* (Absolute 2)
1995 Mike Watt: *Ball-Hog or Tugboat?* (Sony 67086)
1996 Cheikha Remitti: *Cheikha* (Absolute 5)
1996 Johnny Cash: *Unchained* (WB 43097)
1996 Original Soundtrack: *Grace of My Heart* (MCA 11554)
1996 Porno for Pyros: *Good God's Urge* (WB 46126)
1996 Various Artists (Aleka's Attic): *In Defense of Animals, Vol. 2* (Caroline 7536)
1997 Jane's Addiction: *Kettle Whistle* (WB 46752)
1997 Livin' Illegal: *Married to the Game* (Hollow Point 1966)
1997 Michael Brook: *Albino Alligator* (WB 46504)
1997 No Doze Funkmob: *Hooded Figures* (Game Related 7022)
1997 Various Artists (Jewel): *Live on Letterman: Music from the . . . Show* (WB 46827)
1998 G-Rap: Military Mindz (Beatbox 4139)
1998 Jewel: Spirit (Atlantic 82950)
1999 Banyan: *Anytime at All* (Virgin 46953)

1999 Various Artists (producer): *Best of Italo Dance, Vol. 2* (Disco Boom 130)
2000 UK Subs: *Europe Calling* (Released Emotion 012)
2001 Action Figure Party: *Action Figure Party* (Blue Thumb 543417)
2001 Gov't Mule: *Deep End, Vol. 1* (ATO 21502)
2001 Original Score: *Traffic* (TVT 6980)
2001 Rambient: *So Many Worlds* (Immergent 82006)
2001 Tricky: *BlowBack* (Hollywood 162285)
2001 UK Subs: *Mad Cow Fever* (Jungle 048)
2002 Alanis Morissette: *Under Rug Swept* (Maverick 47988)
2003 Mars Volta: *De-Loused in the Comatorium* (2003) (Universal 59302)
2003 Ziggy Marley: *Dragonfly* (Private Music 11636)

JOHN FRUSCIANTE

1988 Kristen Vigard: *Kristen Vigard* (Private Music 20644)
1997 No Doze Funkmob: *Hooded Figures* (Game Related 7022)
1999 Banyan: *Anytime at All* (Virgin 46953)
1999 Perry Farrell: *Rev* (WB 47544)
2001 Macy Gray: *The Id* (Sony 85200)
2001 The Bicycle Thief: *You Come & Go Like a Pop Song . . .* (Artemis 751070)
2001 Tricky: *BlowBack* (Hollywood 162285)
2002 Johnny Cash: *American IV: The Man Comes Around* (Universal 063339)
2003 Original Soundtrack (David Bowie): *Underworld* (Lakeshore 33781)
2003 The Mars Volta: *De-Loused in the Comatorium* (Universal 59302)
2003 Ziggy Marley: *Dragonfly* (Private Music 11636)

JACK IRONS

1984 What Is This: *Squeezed EP* (MCA SAR 36011)
1985 What Is This: *What Is This* (MCA 5598)
1985 What Is This: *3 Out of 5 Live* (MCA 39041)
1988 Walk the Moon: *Walk the Moon* (MCA 5791)
1989 Keith Levene: *Keith Levene's Violent Opposition* (Taang 33)
1989 Joe Strummer: *Earthquake Weather* (Epic EK 45372)
1991 Eleven: *Awake in a Dream* (Morgan Creek 20002)
1991 Michelle Shocked: *Arkansas Traveler* (Mercury 512101)
1993 Eleven: *Eleven* (Hollywood 161516)
1993 Sun-60: *Only* (Epic 53447)

1993 The Buck Pets: *To the Quick* (Virgin 46953)

1995 Eleven: *Thunk* (Hollywood 62012)

1995 Neil Young: *Mirror Ball* (WB 45934)

1996 Pearl Jam: *No Code* (Epic 67500)

1997 Various Artists (Pearl Jam): *Bridge School Concerts, Vol. 1* (WB 46824)

1998 Pearl Jam: *Yield* (Epic 68164)

2003 Eleven: *Howling Book* (Pollen)

2003 Pearl Jam: *Lost Dogs: Rarities and B Sides* (Epic 85738)

ANTHONY KIEDIS

1986 Thelonious Monster: *Baby, You're Bummin' My Life Out in a Supreme Fashion* (Epitaph TM 1)

1988 Kristen Vigard: *Kristen Vigard* (Private Music 2066)

1994 Dr John: *Television* (GRP 4024)

1997 No Doze Funkmob: *Hooded Figures* (Game related 7022)

2001 Tricky: *BlowBack* (Hollywood 162285)

HILLEL SLOVAK

1984 What Is This: *Squeezed EP* (MCA SAR 36011)

1985 What Is This: *What Is This* (MCA 5598)

1985 What Is This: *3 Out of 5 Live* (MCA 39041)

1988 Walk the Moon: *Walk the Moon* (MCA 5791)

1989 Keith Levene: *Keith Levene's Violent Opposition* (Taang 33)

CHAD SMITH

1986 Toby Redd: *In the Light* (Nemperor 4000-4)

1986 Twenty Mondays: *Twist Inside* (Spindletop 137)

1990 Second Self: *Mood Ring* (EMI 92121)

1991 Anacrusis: *Manic Impressions* (Metal Blade 26616)

1991 Queen: We Will Rock You [single] (Elektra 66573)

1994 Wild Colonials: *Fruit of Life* (Geffen 24625)

1996 Original Soundtrack: *Grace of My Heart* (MCA 1154)

1996 Thermadore: *Monkey on Rico* (Atlantic 82874)

1996 Wayne Kramer: *Dangerous Madness* (Epitaph 86458)

1997 John Fogerty: *Blue Moon Swamp* (WB 45426)

1997 Lili Haydn: *Lili* (Atlantic 83027)

1998 Leah Andreone: *Alchemy* (RCA 67696)

INDEX